D1180356

THE INDUSTRIAL HISTORY OF THE UNITED STATES

THE INDUSTRIAL HISTORY OF THE UNITED STATES

BY

WITT BOWDEN, PH.D.

Assistant Professor of History in the University of Pennsylvania

NEW YORK

ADELPHI COMPANY

PUBLISHERS

PRINTED IN THE UNITED STATES OF AMERICA
BY THE VAIL-BALLOU PRESS, INC., BINGHAMTON, N. Y.

PREFACE

In the writing of this industrial history of the United States, the author has ambitiously tried to combine a number of qualities not often joined together in a book of such extensive scope. He has tried to avoid pedantry and yet to incorporate a substantial body of knowledge, describing as clearly as possible the outstanding features of our economic landscape as they come into view along the main highway of our history. Without admitting to the narrative what is merely sensational, demanded as a stimulus by undisciplined and jaded appetites, he has not forgotten his own rebellion against the dry-as-dust compendiums sometimes masquerading as histories. He has been profoundly moved, in some degree contagiously, he hopes, by the living pageantry of continuing generations emerging from the old-world matrix, advancing across the ocean and the continent, and merging themselves on the one hand with the forces of natural environment and on the other hand with ancestral Europeans and all other peoples in a world economy.

What he has attempted is a meaningful synthesis intelligible to those without special historical training but with an intellectual curiosity concerning what industrial America has been. Perhaps a devotee of history may indulge the further hope that the gratifying of such a curiosity may in turn promote an understanding of what industrial America is, and a more intelligent part in determining what it is to become.

ACKNOWLEDGMENTS

As a former teacher of American industrial history and as a historian whose first interest has been industrial history, the author has garnered his data from many fields. Some of the books consulted are mentioned in the notes on books at the end of the volume. For numerous detailed suggestions growing out of the reading of part or all of the manuscript, the author is grateful to his colleagues, Professors St. George L. Sioussat and Roy F. Nichols; to Professor Joseph Mayer, of Tufts College; to an industrial executive, Mr. James A. Davies of the Westinghouse Electric and Manufacturing Company; to Mr. H. T. Warshow, editor of the recently published *Representative American Industries;* and chiefly to his wife.

CONTENTS

PART FIVE

CONFLICT

PART SIX

THE VICTORS AND THE SPOILS

PART SEVEN

CRUCIBLE OF INDUSTRY

PART EIGHT

THE NATION AND THE WORLD

PART NINE

INDUSTRY AND THE NEW SOCIAL CONSCIOUSNESS

PART I

OLD-WORLD EXODUS

THE INDUSTRIAL HISTORY OF THE UNITED STATES

CHAPTER I

EUROPEAN INDUSTRY IN THE AGE OF DISCOVERY

DISCOVERY OF EUROPE

Modern America in contrast with the America of the aborigines is a projection of Europeans and their institutions into the new-world environment. It was four hundred years ago that the horizon of our European ancestors expanded suddenly to include the new world. Many in reality and many more in imagination were pushing westward trying to learn the extent and nature of the *terra incognita* discovered by Christopher Columbus and named for Americus Vespucius.

Historians reverse the process and explore the Europe of four hundred years ago. The mariners fared forth in crude boats along uncharted sea ways, conquering space. It was on no mimic stage that they attained the heights of dangerous drama. Not dangerous and not dramatic perhaps but memorable to those who care for exploits of the mind is the quest of historians for the past. They have sailed in time as well as across the seas. One after one the islands and continents of history have come into view and taken their places on the charts of historical mariners. Their work has made possible not only the gratifying of a natural curiosity concerning our ancestors but an understanding of ourselves as well.

In earlier ages, when politics and war were the noble pursuits, the devotees of Clio, Muse of History, were disdainful of industry, which was for the base-born only. But in a democratic era they have learned, if not the economic interpretation of history, then at least the major rôle of industry in the affairs and the characters of men. The exodus of our ancestors from the old world and the genesis of new-world societies are not only traceable to economic influences—they are essentially in themselves economic phenomena.

The responses of the settlers to the raw and challenging environment of the new world were conditioned in the first place by their old-world origins and experiences. The first question that arises in a study of American industrial history is apparent: What was the nature of the European matrix out of which American industrial society emerged?

FARMING IN THE AGE OF DISCOVERY

If one could take an airplane trip over the Europe of the time of Columbus he would no doubt be impressed by the fact that towns were small and few and far between. But he would observe an ever-recurring clump of houses surrounded by fields, orchards, pasture and woodland. These clumps of houses were the agricultural villages in which a large part of the people lived.

Dominating the scene was the manor house of the landlord or his agent; and rivaling the manor house was the village church. The huts of the peasants might be of stone or adobe or timber: in any case they were wretched one-room affairs, with dirt floors covered by straw or rubbish, with thatched roofs, and with holes for chimneys and windows. Oftentimes this crude shelter was shared by pigs and poultry.

The peasants and their families, who lived in these huts, divided the fields by a curious arrangement into strips, each peasant having a number of long, narrow plots in different fields. Most of the work was done by hand, but the soil was turned by a crude wooden plow owned by the village and drawn by several oxen or occasionally by horses. Live stock were pastured together on the commons. Cattle, sheep, hogs, chickens, geese, and other poultry and live stock were very much smaller and cruder of type than at present. The yield of wheat, barley, and vegetables was much smaller, despite the two-field or three-field system by which a half or a third of the land lay idle for recuperating its fertility. Wheat was harvested by the hand sickle, threshed by the hand flail or by trampling, and winnowed by hand. Wool was not only sheared but washed, combed, spun, woven, fulled, dyed, and tailored by hand. If the peasant once in a great while had occasion to make a trip of a few miles, he was likely to find self-propulsion a better mode of locomotion than the two-wheeled ox-drawn cart, bumping over dry roads or miring to the hub in wet weather.

In a word, if a peasant of 1500 B. C. from Egypt or Babylonia or China could have visited a European agricultural village of 1500 A. D., he would have been pretty much at home. If a European peasant of 1500 A. D. could visit a present-day American farm, what would he think of tractors and automobiles, of harvesting and threshing machines, and sewing machines, to say nothing of the downright magic of electric lights, telephones and radios?

The peasant of 1500 A. D. had slight contacts with the rest

of the world. Stones for the village mill, metal or metal wares, salt, and a few other commodities commonly had to be imported, and there was in many regions a rapid increase of traffic, but in comparison with later times there was a remarkable degree of localism, isolation, and self-sufficiency.

EXPLOITATION OF PEASANTS

Workers on the land, though their labor is fundamental in the productive system of any age, have generally occupied a position of relative weakness in the distribution of income. Peculiar in form but perhaps not so different in effect were the various obligations owed by European peasants to other classes in the age of American colonization.

Custom decreed that the peasant could not be ousted from his holding (though the landlords of some regions, particularly England, were breaking down the custom and forcing the peasants off the land in order to enclose large tracts for sheep raising). Custom also decreed that the peasants in return for their holdings had to make payments and in most cases render services to the landlord. The best portions of the land were ordinarily reserved for the landlord and for the priest and these were tilled by the peasants in return for the right to till the rest of the land for themselves. And having done this, their obligations were by no means at an end. The landlord required them to patronize his mill, his baking oven, and his wine press, and took extensive dues or tolls. The peasants were expected to pay tithes and Peter's pence and fees for the various services performed by the priest. They were forbidden to kill game even to protect their crops, while they had no redress if their crops were destroyed by the reckless trampling of aristocratic sportsmen with dogs and horses. If they were unfortunate enough to be charged with offenses against law or custom or to have quarrels with each other or to incur the displeasure of the landlord, they must adjust matters in the landlord's court, paying him the fees and fines.

Innumerable other obligations and restrictions existed, varying from time to time and from place to place. These, in general, consumed the surplus product of peasant labor beyond what was necessary for his own crude maintenance, and reduced him to abject servility. English peasants, to be sure, had generally freed themselves from serfdom, with its obligation of personal services to the landlord, but with the enclosure of lands for sheep raising in the sixteenth century, there were many peasants who had cause to look back with longing to the good old days of serfdom. Ousted from the land entirely, they turned vagabonds, beggars, rogues, or sailors—and later swelled the ranks of emigrants to America.

BARONIES

The agricultural village, with its auxiliary manufacturing of the crude necessaries of the villagers, was the basic economic unit. The villagers produced what they themselves consumed and a sufficient surplus to maintain the other groups, sometimes described as the fighting and the praying classes. The former lived in the manor houses of the villages, and in the case of the wealthier and more powerful, in the castles and country mansions as centers of the baronies consisting of a varying number of villages. The bishops and the abbots were also landlords; the cathedrals and monasteries were comparable to the castles; and like the secular landlords, the churchmen commanded the allegiance of large numbers of peasants and appropriated the surplus product of peasant labor. In the case of the monasteries, the earlier monks themselves had engaged in productive labor, and in some cases they continued to do so, but in general, by the sixteenth century the members of monastic institutions lived largely on their age-old endowments and on the fruits of peasant labor exploited on the estates of the church as on secular estates.

TOWNS AND LOCAL TRADE

In the course of centuries, certain agricultural villages, castles, cathedrals, and monasteries that were favorably located had grown into towns. Their walls and towers, their houses with picturesque overhanging upper stories, and their narrow, winding streets conforming to the lay of the land, have survived in some instances with little change to the present. But now the spirit of those days is not in them.

For centuries after the fall of Rome, a large part of Europe was economically speaking virtually without cities. Borough and town and citadel are so many terms expressing the idea of protection or defense. But by the sixteenth century, the town population, though still numerically very small (London had perhaps 50,000 people), was a pushing, dynamic, assertive part of the population. With the townsmen was the future.

Economically, the first function of the townsmen had been to serve as middlemen between the villagers of adjacent communities. A village having a surplus of wool or hides and not enough grain, for example, found opportunity to exchange its surpluses for remedying its deficits at a market accessible to different villages. The men in charge of the market often found that they had time to spare, and instead of devoting it to farming, they frequently turned artisans and also set their families to work. The market gave them opportunities to get raw materials advantageously and at the same time to sell their cloth or shoes or implements. Among the craftsmen were "the butcher, the baker, the candlestick maker,'' and scores of others. But in comparison with the modern factory worker, the handicraftsman was a Jack of all trades. To run a machine for punching holes in leather for shoe laces is a simple operation; to take the crude leather from the tanner's hands and put it through the various processes, seeing it emerge literally from one's hands as a completed shoe ready to be worn, is quite a different problem. In order to be a full-fledged or master craftsman, initiated into the ''mystery'' or trade, one was expected to go through several years of study and practice, mostly practice, under the eye of a master craftsman in his own little shop. Having learned the trade as an apprentice, it was ordinarily necessary to serve for wages as a journeyman for a time.

The different types of craftsmen organized themselves into gilds, as had the merchants even earlier. The gilds were fraternal organizations giving their members an excuse for getting together for a good time, and serving as forerunners of insurance and mutual benefit associations. Their main functions, however, were to monopolize and to regulate the various trades. Monopoly of the shoe trade, for example, of a given town was regarded as natural and proper, partly because outsiders had no responsibilities in the town and therefore should have no privileges; and partly because the gild, being held by custom responsible for maintaining high standards and stable prices, must first monopolize the trade in order to regulate it. There was no sharp distinction between manufacturing and trade. A gildsman was buyer of raw materials and seller of his output. The gilds attempted to control quality and quantity of goods, to regulate the markets so as to give all gildsmen an equal chance, and to maintain prices and profits at a steady level.

INTER-REGIONAL TRADE

As long as trade was limited to the town and its tributary agricultural villages, or to unimportant items of exchange between towns, the monopolistic and restrictive gild system worked remarkably well. But by the sixteenth century trade had far transcended the limits of the gild system. How was it that people got about from town to town and from country to country and managed affairs beyond the simple limits of the craft gilds and the town markets?

Travel by water was simpler than travel by land, and Europe is peculiarly favored by nature with navigable waters. Examine a map of Europe and contrast it with other regions. It is readily seen that the indented shore lines, the seas and lakes and rivers gave access to other regions by water, especially in the small boats of those days, to a remarkably large part of the population. Furthermore, the small cost of boats made possible the independent shipping and trading activities of persons of small capital. On land, there were a few main highways kept in some semblance of repair, but in general the condition of the roads led to the carrying of goods by packhorses and packmen, sometimes traveling singly but more commonly in caravans. Individuals were subjected to such grave dangers, particularly from thieves, that it was customary to form temporary associations for mutual comfort and protection in going from one town or region to another.

In addition to temporary associations of the road, there were permanent gilds or companies of merchants. They were not partnerships or joint-stock corporations in the modern sense but were literally companies (*cum, panis,*—eating bread together) or associations of men with the same interests or activities. They made regulations to guide their members, but each member continued to carry on his business independently so far as capital invested and profits and losses were concerned. Among such associations were the Merchants of the Staple, for exporting English wool and other raw materials; and the Merchant Adventurers, a company of English merchants dealing in cloth and other commodities, particularly in Germany and the Low Countries.

In some of the maritime towns, particularly Venice, the town governments were organized for carrying on trade. Venice built fleets, manned and equipped the vessels, prescribed rules and regulations for sailing, and rented space in the ships to the merchants. There were also associations of towns, chief of which was the famous Hanseatic League of the Baltic region, consisting mainly of German towns, and serving in a sense as a government, the Germans having no effective central authority such as existed in France and England.

Now and then an individual merchant or mercantile house became exceedingly wealthy and powerful. There were the Medici of Florence, who rose to the heights of power and magnificence by means of mercantile and banking pursuits. There was Jacques Coeur of Bourges, whose wealth-laden Levantine galleys brought him the sudden favor of Charles VII and led to his equally sudden ruin at the hands of that fickle and covetous ruler. There were the Fuggers of Augsburg, so powerful as virtually to buy the imperial election for the Emperor Charles V. Such merchant princes often had large numbers of chapmen or petty traveling merchants in their employ, and often organized manufacturing enterprises by having large numbers of craftsmen employed to supply their needs, though the craftsmen, unlike the modern factory workers, were not under direct supervision. But ordinarily the larger merchants were primarily wholesalers and shippers, maintaining warehouses in different cities and depending largely on fairs for the sale of their goods.

THE MECHANISM OF TRADE

The processes by which commodities passed from producers to consumers were ordinarily very simple, the craftsman being buyer and seller as well as manufacturer. But in more distant trading, complexities arose.

The goods of commerce were produced in the agricultural villages, or in craftsmen's shops, or in the crude and small-scale mines. The first step was to send the goods to the local market, or perchance to sell them to pedlars or traveling merchants (chapmen). A large portion of such goods reached the consumer by the simple process of the consumer coming to the local market where the goods were first offered for sale. In other cases the chapmen who bought the goods at the local market sold them directly to the ultimate consumer.

Goods not thus disposed of were ordinarily bought at the local market by petty chapmen or by the agents of greater merchants or commercial houses and by them taken to a fair. A fair was in a sense a magnified market. It was ordinarily held annually or semi-annually. It was patronized to some extent by retail customers of the vicinity, purchasing goods as consumers. But it was mainly a place where merchants, large and small, met to sell the goods they had purchased in their own local markets and to buy the goods they hoped to sell in the same markets.

By an interchange of goods through local markets and regional fairs, Europe, northern Africa, and western Asia were knit together; and by means of overland caravans and sea routes, the system of markets and fairs in Europe was connected with a similar system of distribution in the Far East. Thus in the course of many months, or even years, western goods and particularly bullion found passage by the cumbersome machinery of markets and chapmen and fairs, over the tortuous trails of trade by land and by sea, to the mysterious eastern lands of luxury and the islands of the spices. By a reversal of the process, the exotics of the Orient and the precious products of age-old eastern art and skill found passage to the crude but vigorous Occident.

CHAPTER II

EAST IS WEST

EASTWARD EXPANSION

The first era of European expansion was directly eastward. The most advanced part of Europe in the production of luxury goods was Italy. Even Italian arts and crafts were in many ways inferior to those of the Levant and especially of the Orient. Western and northern Europeans therefore looked to Italy, and Italians fared eastward in quest of the treasures of trade with the Arabs of the Levant and through them with Orientals.

With the incentives of trade were mingled the powerful religious motives of the age of the crusades and the pilgrimages. The Moslem "infidels" (rather curiously thus described by the Christians; they displayed remarkable fidelity to their faith) were to be exterminated in the name of the cross. But many of the Christians who came to kill remained to trade.

SAILING WEST TO REACH THE EAST

In the fourteenth and fifteenth centuries, new waves of nomads (Ottoman Turks and Mongols) from the reservoirs of population on the Great Plain of northern Asia overflowed into western Asia and eastern Europe, forcing a recession of Europeans. Trade was not destroyed but was for a time disrupted, and the direct eastward advance of Europeans was checked.

About the same time came a series of events constituting one of the major movements of history—the maritime revolution. It was in this connection that Europeans executed a right-about-face from direct eastward to westward expansion as a method of tapping the treasures of trade in the Orient. In trying to enter Asia by the back door, they accidentally found themselves in the portals of the new world.

The possibility of reaching the east by sailing west had long been considered by students, on the basis of the view that the world is a sphere. It was thought to be much smaller than it actually proved to be. In geographic lore and in maritime experience the Italians excelled other Europeans. Because of this and of their favorable location, their city states had a virtual monopoly of the European distribution of Levantine and Far Eastern goods. If a western route should be opened up, they would not fare so well. Besides, their time was pretty well taken up, either with wars among themselves or with attempts to check the advance of the Turks. So, while individual Italians were prominent in the right-about-face of European expansionists westward, these individuals were in the employ of states along the Atlantic seaboard. Thus it came about that Italians were teachers of the Portuguese, that Columbus of Genoa and Americus Vespucius of Florence sailed under the flag of Spain, and that Henry VII of England sent John Cabot, by birth a Genoese and by adoption a Venetian, across the Atlantic and made in his account book the entry, "To hym that found the new Isle, £10."

The "new isle," so it was thought, was an outpost of India or Cathay—"the territory of the Grand Khan." Columbus, thinking he had attained his object of reaching India by sailing west, called the natives of the new world Indians, and in Cuba sent messengers in quest of the Great Khan.

After it was learned that a continent blocked the way to India, a large part of European endeavor was for a long time given to finding a southwest passage, a northwest passage, or a middle passage to the desired goal.

AMERICA BARS THE WAY

So America was an obstacle unfortunately encountered on the way to India! Its discovery was an extraneous episode that marred the plot of the play! The drama was the expansion of European economy. Several scenes had been played. Europeans had successfully expanded into western Asia, and had established connections, through the Arabs and others, with the producers of the coveted luxuries of the East. Enter the villain, or rather villains. Commentators once assigned the rôle of villain to the Turk alone, but it turns out that this is a misreading of the play. The Turk made trouble for Christian pilgrims in general and for Italian traders in particular, but to western Europeans the Italian himself was something of a villain in monopolizing the distribution of oriental goods in Europe. With Turk and Mongol athwart the routes of trade and forcing the Europeans backward in their tracks, and with Italians taking monopolistic tribute from their fellow Europeans, the drama of expansion had reached an *impasse*. Then comes the outwitting of the villains by a most surprising *coup de théâtre* —go west to reach the east! To find the sprawling, savage continents of the *terra incognita* athwart the western route must have been a disconcerting *denouement*.

EXPLORATION A BUSINESS VENTURE

In our present calm security and comprehensive knowledge of the world, it is easy to look back upon the age of discovery and think of it in terms of adventure and of drama. Adventurous and dramatic was the age, in many ways. But exploration and discovery were business enterprises. They were the culminating phases of one period of economic expansion and the initial stages of another period.

The Portuguese exploration of Africa lagged until skill was acquired in capturing the natives; and then, the slave trade becoming profitable, exploration of the "Land of Wealth" was carried forward speedily.

Columbus was not a scientist, nor was he a mere adventurer; he was primarily a business man, convinced that a western voyage would prove to be a profitable venture. His commission and supplementary orders provided that in return for his heading the expedition he was to be allowed one-tenth of the precious metals acquired; and since he was to furnish one-eighth of the capital, he was to be entitled to an eighth of the net profits accruing from trade. To facilitate the opening up of trade, he took with him letters from the Spanish rulers to the sovereigns of the Orient, whom he attempted to locate in Cuba. He promoted the slave trade, returning in 1498 with six hundred slaves. The tragedy of his later years was in large degree the failure of his dreams of wealth and power evoked by his mistaken view of having opened up a new route to the riches of the East.

The Portuguese, after making a profitable business out of the slave trade and the exploitation of some of the western islands, allowed their exploring zeal to lag. When Columbus returned with the announcement of a newly discovered route to India, anticipations of business profits by means of a rival route around Africa stirred them into action once more. The result was Da Gama's marvelous feat of seamanship in reaching India around the Cape in 1498. Remarkable, too, was his feat of merchandizing. It is said that he returned with a cargo worth sixty times the cost of the expedition!

SEARCHING FOR THE SOUTH SEA

When Europeans ventured westward in search of the East, they naturally were prepared to encounter unknown lands. Indeed, the commission of Columbus and the letter patent granted to Cabot both contemplated the possibility of discovering and acquiring lands. There was a natural disappointment at finding that these lands barred the way to their main objective, the Far East, and for a time the principal connection of Europeans with the new world was their effort to break through it or to go around it.

Just as the first voyage of Columbus incited the Portuguese to proceed with their quest of a route around Africa, so in turn the voyage of Da Gama stirred the Spaniards to redoubled efforts to find the eastern marts. The accidental discovery of the eastern coast of South America by Cabral of Portugal in 1500 led the Portuguese to take a hand in the quest for a direct westward route. Balboa's dramatic discovery of the Pacific Ocean in 1513 led to renewed efforts to find a strait in the region of Central America.

The finding of the way to the east by sailing west was at length accomplished by a disgruntled Portuguese captain in the service of Spain. With five ships that had seen their best days, with mediocre supplies and equipment, and with conglomerate crews, Magellan set out in the fall of 1519 upon the most remarkable voyage of history. He hoped to open up a direct westward route to the Spice Islands, and to establish the claims of Spain to a portion of these. Stern and bold as he was, had he known the length and difficulty of the voyage, it is hardly conceivable that he would have undertaken it. More than a year was expended in going from Spain to the Cape of Eleven Thousand Virgins at the straits. Passing the straits he pushed boldly into the world's greatest expanse of water. As the voyage lengthened beyond the direst forebodings of the crew, starvation was evaded by eating rats and gnawing at the leather used about the masts. Of the five vessels only one, after a three-years' voyage, returned to Spain, and the surviving captain was not Magellan but Elcano.

This costly and conclusive demonstration of the remoteness of the Indies from Europe by way of the west was far from sufficient to put an end to searchings for a serviceable passage. By 1525 explorers under the Spanish flag had traversed the shore lines of both continents from the extreme south to Nova Scotia in a futile quest for a practicable westward route of trade. There was of course no knowledge of the distance between America and Asia along more northerly latitudes, and so it was not unnatural for continued attempts to be made.

Henry VII had early patronized the Italian Cabots but it was almost a century later when the English displayed real interest either in the exploitation of America or in finding a passage through it to the Orient. Beginning in 1574, and continuing long after Drake's return in 1580 from his voyage around the world, several attempts to find a northwest passage were made by Frobisher, Gilbert, Davis, Hudson, and others; and it was not till the futility of these attempts became apparent that colonization was seriously undertaken. Indeed, even when the Virginia Company sent out the first successful colony, hope of finding the passage seems to have outweighed anticipation of new-world settlement. The rapid development after 1600, by the East India Company, of trade by way of the Cape of Good Hope, the beginnings of permanent colonization, and a gradual recognition of the futility of further search, combined to divert the English as well as others entirely from efforts to surmount the new world as an obstacle into efforts to appropriate, exploit, and colonize the Americas.

CHAPTER III

EUROPEANS ON THE SEVEN SEAS

QUEST OF TREASURE

The immigration of Europeans into the new world must be viewed as a phase of their general expansion, first eastward, then westward, and at length world-embracing in scope. Why did they leave home? If we ask the biologist he will probably reply by asking why bees tend to swarm into new colonies; why the English sparrow spread over America in a few decades; why the winged seeds of dandelion, milkweed and maple scatter far and wide. Europeans of modern times appear to have had, of all peoples, the lustiest of wings; and their flight seems to have been most aided by favoring winds.

Expansion was of course promoted by attractive conditions, real or fancied, outside of Europe. It was believed that there was treasure for the asking (or taking). Marco Polo in his *Travels*, published in 1477, though written much earlier, said that to the capital of Cathay all things most valuable in all parts of the world found their way; that Japan had inexhaustible supplies of gold and magnificent jewels; that various islands near the mainland were the sources of the pepper, nutmegs, spikenard, galengal, cubebs, cloves, and other spices and drugs and dyes distributed throughout the world, together with gold, rubies, sapphires, topazes, amethysts, garnets and other costly stones, in quantities exceeding calculation and belief. He related what had been told to him of how the royal palace of Japan had a roof and windows of gold and floors covered with bars of gold the thickness of his two fingers.

When Columbus returned, he fancied he had seen and made sure claim to the wealth of the Indies. "In thirty-three days I have passed over to the Indies," he writes. "It is a land to be desired and never to be relinquished," and he promises that it will yield to their Highnesses, the sovereigns of Spain, as much gold as they shall need, with spices and aloe-wood and cotton and slaves. And the men he has left will discover a thousand other things of value. As exploration of the new world progressed, stories of gold and other treasure caused a succession of "rushes," as when Fray Marcos was supposed to have discovered large cities with walls and guarded gates, with men and women alike wearing massive ornaments of gold, with silversmiths and iron forges and untold wealth of precious jewels.

The wealth of the Spanish dominions was grossly exaggerated, but there was much gold, and the natives had advanced in the arts enough to amass great riches in various forms. Farther north, the people were too crude to accumulate such treasure. But Europeans were lured from home to regions north as well as south by stories even more mendacious than those attributed to Fray Marcos. Thus it was said that in Virginia native offenders were shackled with chains of gold.

FREE LAND AND SLAVE LABOR

Large numbers were long attracted from Europe by gold and silver and jewels and prized exotics, but these treasures were gradually pushed into the background by free land and slave labor.

Title to the land was claimed by the sovereigns in the charters and letters patent issued to explorers. The explorers in turn were usually careful to claim everything possible for their rulers, as when Balboa in 1513, seeing for the first time the shores of the Pacific, claimed its waters, its islands, and its bordering lands in the name of the King of Spain, and twice repeated the claim, once when he reached the Gulf of San Miguel and again when with sword and banner he waded into the open waters of the Pacific. Subgrants could be had from the sovereigns, by companies and by influential individuals, and these in turn offered inducements to settlers. Thus Brazil was divided into "captaincies" or fiefs held by favorites of the court. Similar grants were extensively made by the Spanish government, especially to court favorites and to the church.

The Dutch government granted charters to trading companies, with landed rights included, and one of these, the West India Company, established the colony of New Netherlands. In order to promote settlement, large estates were granted to persons called patroons who would establish thereon as many as fifty settlers above fifteen years of age within four years. The rights of the patroons were similar to those of the feudal lords of Europe.

The English crown, as is well known, granted subtitle to its "plantations" either to companies or to proprietors. James I in 1609, for example, granted to the Virginia Company "all those lands, countries, and territories, situate, lying, and being, in that part of America called Virginia, from the point of land called Cape or Point Comfort, all along the seacoast, to the northward two hundred miles, and from the said Point of Cape Comfort all along the seacoast, to the southward two hundred miles, and all that space and circuit of land, lying from the seacoast of the precinct aforesaid, up into the land, and throughout from sea to sea, west and northwest; and also all the islands, lying within one hundred miles, along the coast of both seas of the precinct aforesaid." The name of Pennsylvania indicates the proprietary nature of its origin. Charles II in 1681 granted to his "trusty and well-beloved subject, William Penn, Esquire," and his heirs, as "true and absolute proprietaries," the extensive lands west of the Delaware River, to be called "Pensilvania" or Penn's forest.

The French were less inclined at first to stable settlement, the three thousand Frenchmen in America by the middle of the seventeenth century being dispersed in fur trading, exploration, and adventure, over an area fifteen hundred miles in length, from Acadia to central Wisconsin. The paternalistic and aristocratic government of France attempted to reproduce in this crude environment the agrarian arrangements and the social distinctions of the age-old and urbane civilization of France. Seigniorial rights were granted, particularly to army officers belonging to the lesser nobility. These rights were in imitation of the French landed system, with the various obligations of the peasants to the landlord. The seigniories were in most cases on a lakefront or a streamside. In some cases they were prosperous, but the system was too artificial to prove generally successful.

Thus the choice lands of the new world came under the control of Portuguese "captains," Spanish and French seigniors, Dutch patroons and companies, and English companies and proprietors. These various agencies attempted to promote the settlement of their lands, and offered inducements which attracted many colonists. But to the ordinary settlers the land was hardly free unless they were able to evade the obligations imposed by the owners. This they often succeeded in doing by turning frontiersmen and "squatters" beyond effective reach of the overlords. In any case the obligations and restrictions were slight as compared with those in Europe, and so the lure of free land or of cheap land attracted increasing numbers.

The overlords, however, were far from dependent on European settlers and laborers. With the advantages of free land were combined the prospects of slave labor to exploit the land. Portuguese exploration of the west African coast was for a long time chiefly connected economically with the slave trade. Columbus himself instituted slavery and the slave trade in America. He asked permission to sell slaves in 1494, took back a cargo of 600 in 1498, and introduced in the new world the system of compulsory labor already adopted by the Spaniards in their dealings with the conquered Moors of Spain. Enslavement of the Indians by the Spaniards was prominently connected with mining and was one of the principal causes of the rapid decline of the native population, which, in the Spanish West Indies, was indeed soon virtually extinct. The Indians living farther north were even less inclined to docility and servitude. In consequence they had become almost extinct when a reversal of policy served in recent times to enable them to maintain a precarious hot-house existence as wards of the government.

The resistance of the Indians to enslavement and to any of the substitutes for slavery involving compulsory labor led to the development of the African slave trade for supplying the overlords of new-world mines and plantations with labor. Europeans had long been acquainted with the slave trade, and the Portuguese in particular had bought African slaves from the Moors. The African adventures of the Portuguese were largely motivated, in the first place, by a desire to conquer from the Moors the Land of Wealth in the valley of the Senegal—wealth mainly in the form of slaves. With the opening up of the new-world mines and plantations, Africa vied with the new world and with India and Cathay as a land of wealth, because of the inexhaustible demand for slave labor.

TRADE

Europeans were attracted to other lands in the first place by the hope of finding gold and other treasures; and secondly by the anticipation of free land to be exploited by slave labor. A third and most obvious attraction was the lure of trade—including the slave trade.

Formerly the expectation of commercial profits was limited to a few because of the restricted market for imported goods. The spices, the jewels, the fine fabrics were for kings and lords and bishops, with the merchant princes themselves occasionally indulging their tastes in imitation of their royal and noble customers. With the cheapening of transportation and the general increase of wealth, these luxuries found a vastly wider market. With the introduction of tobacco, tea, sugar, cotton, rice, and other commodities used extensively by the middle classes and even by the proletariat, the percentage of profits was smaller but the quantity of goods was vastly increased. This meant, in turn, an increased number of Europeans attracted to other parts of the world to engage in commerce and in the production of the commodities of trade.

EXPULSIVE FORCES AT HOME

If conditions outside of Europe seemed attractive, conditions in Europe were expulsive.

Peasants were crowded together in agricultural villages, prevented by custom from improving their methods, and exploited by their landlords to such an extent that any surplus product beyond a subsistence was almost invariably taken from them. Particularly in England were they subjected to more than the expropriation of the surplus. They were being ousted bodily in large numbers from their age-old customary holdings in the agricultural villages in order that these might be turned together and enclosed for sheep walks. At the same time, the increase of gold and silver and the inflation of the currency enriched the landlords and wealthy merchants at the expense of peasants and craftsmen.

The nobles themselves were becoming increasingly restless and at the same time increasingly wealthy. The younger sons by primogeniture were barred from inheriting land or title, and were finding it increasingly difficult to secure positions in the government or the church sufficiently honorable and lucrative to satisfy them. To them the lure of adventure and the prospect of gain overseas operated in a peculiar sense, at a time when feudal warfare, obsolescent, was affording little opportunity for honor and adventure, not to speak of gain.

The bourgeoisie—merchants, bankers, middlemen—were of the vigorous, ambitious, pushing types, made doubly alert and active by the stirring events of the age of discovery.

The clash of creeds during the Protestant Revolt accompanying the age of discovery was a factor easily exaggerated but important. The religious conflict was more than a clash of creeds—it was a struggle between the partisans of the old order and those of the new for the control of clerical functions and church property. Clerical functions had their economic aspects, involving as they did extensive revenues and immense power. Church property included far more than the churches and auxiliary buildings. The church owned most of the educational and charitable institutions with their vested interests. It maintained important courts with profitable court fees. It owned innumerable franchises and special rights in connection with many of the markets and fairs, bridges and highways. It had the right of collecting tithes and various other revenues. It owned and administered a large part of the landed estates of all Christendom.

Before the dissolution of the English monasteries in the sixteenth century, they owned at least a tenth of the country's wealth. It can readily be seen that the bitter conflicts raging ostensibly around the question of authority for controlling men's beliefs entailed far more than creeds, and that the religious motives connected with emigration from Europe were not without an economic aspect.

These various attractive and expulsive forces, active during the age of exploration and discovery, awakened the imagination and stirred the ambitions and aroused the hopes of men to an unparalleled degree. In the projection of the old world into the new, economic motives undoubtedly were predominant. But other influences had their part, and not the least of these were love of novelty and lust of adventure, influential then with new-world pioneers as now with aviators who span the oceans, encircle the world, and conquer the polar wastes.

WHAT EUROPEANS TOOK WITH THEM

Europeans in their exodus took with them what their limited resources could secure and their small boats could carry—crude clothing, scant food, and a few tools. The miner's pick, the woodsman's ax and saw, the farmer's hoe, and for everyone a musket—these in symbol were the essential weapons for the conquest of nature and of man. With these were a few books and scientific instruments. Articles of trade included cloth "violet blew or red," "small hooks and fishing lines, Morris bels, Jewes-harps, Combes," and "fire-water" for the so-called Indians of the new world; while trade with the real Indians, the people of India, more commonly required gold and silver in exchange for their exotics and their finely fabricated goods. More important than the material equipment which Europeans stowed away in their crude sailboats was their social heritage. The transit of civilization was largely in the form of the ideas, customs, and bent of mind of those who left Europe.

WHAT THEY FOUND

As they expanded into various parts of the world, the peoples of Europe found varied conditions demanding radically different adaptations of their social heritage. After their expansion eastward had been checked, their first adventures beyond Europe were on the western shores of Africa. Africa in general long continued to be a *terra incognita.* The unlocking of its doors awaited the recent fashioning of keys to fit—railways, telegraphs, tropical hygiene, automobiles demanding rubber—in a word, pertinent scientific technology. Two things the early European expansionists found along the shores of Africa—an inexhaustible source of wealth in the traffic in slaves; and way stations or "refreshing points" while "climbing the seas" to India.

In the Far East, which they now entered directly through the back door of southern Africa, they found dense populations. They found a civilization old and urbane and in many ways far superior to their own, but weakened, as was Roman civilization more than a thousand years earlier, by barbarian invasion and internal decay. They found little chance for colonization but almost unlimited opportunities for trade and plunder.

To the southward in the new world of the Americas they found populous and wealthy regions, with many of the peoples well advanced in civilization, particularly the Incas of Peru, the Mayas of Central America, and the Aztecs of Mexico. Being unskilled in the arts of war with fire arms, warships, and steel weapons, but at the same time having an abundance of precious metals and other coveted goods, they and their country fell a prey to plunder, trade, and colonization, in the order named.

Northward, there was a thinly populated expanse of wilderness. There was little chance for plundering the natives, save by taking the land itself. There was little opportunity for trade of value, except by the gradual development of the fur trade. There was incalculable room for colonization and permanent empire building. In the midst of such an environment there was need for stern and primitive adaptations—as witness Braddock's disaster on the way to Fort Duquesne when he tried to use European tactics in the wilderness.

RIVALRIES

The most coveted prize, control of oriental trade, fell first to the Portuguese. Their empire rose quickly and as quickly fell. During the sixteenth century the Spanish dominions included a large part of the new world. In the seventeenth century the Dutch, especially in trade and finance, outrivaled even the Spanish. Portugal, Spain and Holland retired in turn to the background of the imperial stage and left the leading rôles to France and England.

Both of these countries were backward alike in exploration, in trade, and in colonization. Both carried on various unsuccessful ventures during the sixteenth century and both succeeded in establishing their first permanent colonies in the early seventeenth century. The outstanding form of business organization for promoting trade and colonization was the same in both countries—the chartered company.

The evolution of the company in England carried it through a number of stages. The earlier companies were not for colonization but exclusively for trade. They were merely associations of merchants with monopolistic rights in a region specified by the charter, and with regulations concerning the methods of carrying on trade. The later companies had monopolistic rights and regulations but unlike the earlier ones they frequently were organized for colonizing as well as trading; and instead of being mere regulated associations, they had a joint stock, the members consisting simply of stockholders as in a modern corporation.

The French companies failed to develop in the direction of modern business corporations to the same extent as did the English, and one cause of their failure seems to have been the more rigorous control of trade and colonization by the French government. Its paternalism is illustrated by the case of the Company of the Hundred Associates, based on the idea of reproducing the French seigniorial system in the wilds of French North America.[1] The English government was inclined to pursue a policy of allowing the companies to work out their own problems, and in consequence they evolved into powerful, semi-independent institutions, as the East India Company and the Hudson Bay Company.

The long-drawn-out conflict between the French and the English was fought in various parts of the world for more than a century, with all available weapons, military, naval, diplomatic, economic. In this conflict the continental colonies did not always occupy the center of the stage. The French, like the English, had gained a footing in the West Indies at the expense of the Spanish, and in the Far East at the expense of the Dutch; and world-wide commercial interests were at stake.

Historical perspective reveals the fact that the discovery of America was an incident in the larger movement of European economic expansion having as its immediate objective a more economical trade route to the Far East. English expansion was merely a phase—a belated but increasingly important phase—of this general expansionist movement. In this belated English expansion the Thirteen Colonies were regarded by Englishmen as relatively unimportant parts of

[1] See above, p. 23.

their new-world empire. The outstanding, overshadowing nation in world economy today, the United States of America, emerged out of a remote and incidental phase of old-world expansion.

PART II

NEW-WORLD GENESIS

CHAPTER IV

HOW COLONIZATION WAS FINANCED

ILLUSIONS OF EARLY PROMOTERS

"All the natives constantly affirm that in these parts there are nutmegs, mace, and cinnamon, besides pitch, Brazil wood, cochineal, and ambergris. . . . Besides, they positively assure me that there is a certain sea in the opposite, or western part of this province, distant not more than seven days' journey from our fort of St. George in Sagadahoc; a sea large and wide and deep, of the boundaries of which they are wholly ignorant, which cannot be any other than the Southern Sea, reaching to the regions of China, which unquestionably cannot be far from these parts." Thus wrote George Popham, one of the promoters of the Virginia Company, as late as 1607, from as far north as the mouth of the Kennebec.

Had it not been for such illusions it is doubtful if Englishmen could have been induced to venture their money and hazard their lives in the early exploration and settlement of America. To organize and plant a colony, or even to undertake an exploring expedition, entailed heavy expenses and extreme risk. The amount of money and resources and energy consumed and the number of lives lost in such enterprises before the establishment of Jamestown, the first permanent colony, are incalculable.

SOURCES OF WEALTH FOR NEW VENTURES

(1) *Enclosures*

England had been a relatively poor country. There was little surplus capital. Her kings and noblemen had gone to foreigners (to Jews, Lombards, Flemings, Hansards) for loans and for the financing of larger trading enterprises. But on account of her relative freedom from invasion and destructive wars, a surplus had gradually been accumulating, before the sixteenth century. During that century several new sources of wealth were tapped by men who were inclined toward business ventures such as colonization and trade.

One of these was the system of enclosures. The land of England, according to the system briefly described above,[1] had been divided into agricultural villages, or manors. In these the peasants held small tracts, and also by custom they had the right to pasture their live stock and fowls on the village commons. In the fifteenth and sixteenth centuries the demand for wool increased and made sheep-raising exceptionally profitable. Now sheep-raising meant that village agriculture must be given up, the villages thrown together and enclosed as sheepwalks, and the peasants ousted. Large areas of England were thus enclosed. One result was a great increase in the rents of landlords and in the profits of leaseholders. Another result was that by the ousting of the peasants there was created an abundant supply of cheap and dependent labor for employment in manufacturing and trade, as well as of unemployed laborers willing to hazard their lives for a living in the new world. Thus at the cost of intense and long continued suffering on the part of the peasants, enclosures increased the wealth of business men

[1] See above, pp. 4–6.

as well as of landlords, many of whom were willing to invest their surplus income in risky ventures.

(2) *Confiscations*

Another source of wealth among those inclined toward trade and colonization was the confiscation of ecclesiastical properties during the Protestant Revolt. The monasteries owned, at a conservative estimate, about a tenth of the wealth of England. Men of wealth often endowed priests with chapels for the chanting of masses for their souls or the souls of others. These chantry priests controlled large revenues and often engaged in charitable and educational work in addition to their chantry work in the narrow sense. Religious gilds owned resources roughly analogous to those of modern fraternal orders. Monasteries, chantries and gilds, with their independent endowments, were failing to keep pace with contemporary changes. The confiscation of their properties greatly enriched the government. But instead of being retained by the government, these properties were in large part rapidly alienated, especially during the reign of the boy King Edward VI, from 1547 to 1553, and were seized by greedy favorites and courtiers. The pious and sickly Edward was given to *praying;* his ministers and their friends spent much of their time in *preying.* From a third to a half of the confiscated properties seem to have been diverted into private hands without return either to the original owners or to the government.

All this was at basis not a creation of wealth but merely a transfer of wealth. But the income from the confiscated properties now assumed a much more fluid form. The new owners, in comparison with the ultra-conservative monks and chantry priests, were much more likely to invest the income in hazardous maritime and colonial undertakings. Particularly was this true when it became apparent that such enterprises could be profitably turned against the arch-champions of Catholicism, the Spaniards.

(3) *The Slave Trade*

Enclosures and confiscations in England were paralleled by slavery and expropriation of native wealth in Africa and the new world. The earliest way in which Englishmen shared appreciably in these new sources of wealth was by the slave trade. Englishmen were not the first to traffic in Africans for supplying new-world mines and plantations with labor, but their connection with the business was ultimately more extensive and profitable than that of any other people. A pioneer among Englishmen was William Hawkins, who as early as 1530 carried slaves from the Guinea Coast to Brazil. His more famous (or as some would have it, infamous) son, Sir John, was one of many who developed the trade with the Spaniards, defying Spanish laws which forbade the participation of foreigners in the trade of the Spanish dominions. The trade thus forced upon the Spanish authorities finally developed into a monopoly recognized by treaty. Thus the English made large profits by the sale of slaves. The slaves in turn were used by the Spanish in the new world to aid in producing that unparalleled flow of wealth which flooded Spain in the sixteenth century.

(4) *Tapping the Stream of Spanish Gold*

When the early explorers failed to find the spices and other prizes of oriental trade, they turned their energies largely into a quest for the precious metals. The Portuguese, the Dutch, the English, and the French were seldom successful. But the Spanish found almost inexhaustible supplies. In consequence the quantity of precious metals in western Europe trebled in the sixteenth century. In agricultural and industrial skill, the Christian Spaniards had been far excelled by the Moors and the Jews. Among the Christians, the heretics were most advanced industrially. With the expulsion from Spain of these elements of the population, and with the coincident inflow of gold and silver from the new world, Spaniards became increasingly dependent on foreign producers. English products either directly or indirectly found their way into the hands of Spanish consumers, while Spanish gold and silver passed into the hands of English producers.

But the English were not limited to this indirect method of tapping the stream of Spanish wealth. When Elizabeth turned her back on Philip II and the English church again forsook the faith of which Philip was the arch-champion, the two countries drifted rapidly into conflict. Officially they long remained at peace. But many Englishmen, with conglomerate motives of religion, patriotism, adventure, and profit, turned into buccaneers and roved the seas in quest of Spanish treasure ships. The "sea hawks" were far from confining their attention to Spanish vessels, but these were their choicer morsels. The classic instance is the voyage of Francis Drake around the world at a cost of about five thousand pounds, his lone surviving vessel, the *Pelican*, returning to Plymouth in 1580 with booty valued at more than half a million pounds.

Drake's exploits were in time of nominal peace, but open war was not long delayed. As long as a state of war existed, the surplus energy of Englishmen was used in fighting Spaniards and in preying on their merchantmen and treasure ships. Gentlemen of Elizabeth's day thought of the maintenance of at least one "sea hawk" as being virtually a part of the maintenance of their prestige as gentlemen. Public officials and the queen herself sought profit in such ventures.

THE RISE OF COLONIZING COMPANIES

Peace with Spain in 1604 left large numbers of sea captains and crews without employment. James I, though desirous of maintaining the peace, was willing to risk the wrath of the Spaniards by denying their claims to the unsettled parts of North America. These circumstances, combined with the lapse of the unfortunate Elizabethan grant of monopoly to Sir Walter Raleigh, account for the first successful colonizing venture. Raleigh, Gilbert, and others had made various unsuccessful efforts. The cost and the hazards indicated the need for some form of group enterprise. Companies had already been formed for trading in various parts of the world. For the Baltic Sea region there was the Eastlands Company; for Russia, the Muscovy Company; for the eastern Mediterranean, the Levant Company; for oriental trade, the East India Company. It was quite natural, therefore, that upon the expiration of Raleigh's monopolistic patent, a company should be formed for exploiting the North American territories claimed by England as a result of the voyages of the Cabots.

JAMESTOWN

As in the case of the other companies, a group of "adventurers," or persons willing to venture their money in the enterprise, petitioned the king for a charter. A group of men about London, and another group at Plymouth and Bristol, styling themselves "Knights, gentlemen, merchants, and other adventurers," that is, men willing to venture their money, secured in 1606 the first "Virginia" charter. The second group, familiarly known as the Plymouth Company, made an earlier start, but it was the first group, the London Company, that established Jamestown, the first permanent colony.

In 1609 the connection between the London and Plymouth groups was severed, and the London Company secured a new charter. The widespread popular interest is shown by the fact that more than fifty of the historic gilds of London subscribed to the funds of the new company, and that there were 659 individual subscribers, including peers, knights, esquires, gentlemen, clergymen, doctors, ship captains, and various other classes, besides merchants. Those who went in person were called "planters"; those who only subscribed their "monies, goods, or chattels" were called "adventurers." Shares of stock cost the "adventurers" £12 10s. each. Each "planter" was allowed a share on account of his venturing his life. Money was raised also by means of lotteries. At the end of seven years the total assets were to be divided among shareholders. It is estimated that by means of subscriptions and lotteries between 1609 and 1624 the company secured what was then the very large sum of £200,000.

The grant of lands made in 1606 was renewed with modifications in 1609. The control of the company and the colony was vested legally in a council, resident at London. Vacancies in the council were to be filled by majority vote of the members of the company. The immediate supervision of the colony was in the hands of a governor or his deputy, appointed by the council and resident in Virginia.

Men with money to invest were attracted by liberal tax exemptions to be enjoyed by the company in Virginia. The charter naturally had little to say concerning anticipations of profit from trade and precious metals such as the Portuguese and Spanish enjoyed, but it is well known that such anticipations were prominent in the minds alike of the "adventurers" and of the "planters." It was only by dint of hard experience and disappointment that the company came at length to depend on the slow processes of agriculture and ordinary trade. In the meantime the "adventurers" felt that they were having to send good money after bad.

PLYMOUTH

The Plymouth Company of 1606, after its unsuccessful attempt at colonization on the Kennebec, found difficulty in financing further ventures. In 1620 the leading members secured a new charter. Under this charter the company was known as the Council for New England. While the company was dallying unsuccessfully with the problem of colonization on a purely commercial basis, religion and chance came to the rescue of trade. A group of Separatists who, because of persecution by the Church of England, had found refuge in Holland, decided to look for toleration and better economic opportunities in the new world. They secured a patent from the London Company, permitting them to make a settlement in Virginia. Chance intervened to land them north of the London Company's territory, in the region subject to the Council for New England. A new patent was then secured, subjecting them to the jurisdiction of the Council for New England.

The Pilgrims had not been noted for wealth in England. Their sojourn in Holland had hardly added to their worldly fortunes. In order to finance their removal to America, they entered into "Articles of Agreement." Each "planter" or colonist was to have one share, and if he provided £10, either in money or in provisions, to equip himself for the enterprise, he was to have an additional share. Taking one's family or servants and provisioning them entitled a "planter" to still further shares. "Adventurers" or mere investors as distinguished from "the persons transported" paid £10 a share. The total number of shares formed a common stock. There were to be no dividends in the modern sense, but at the end of seven years there was to be a "division" of both profits and capital, including "houses, lands, goods, and chattels," among "adventurers" and "planters" in proportion to shares held. This agreement was later broken by the pilgrims on the ground that a "common stock" retarded initiative and industry.

THE MASSACHUSETTS BAY COMPANY

Early in 1628 the Council for New England issued a patent of great historic importance. Apparently unable to carry on successful colonization, it made a grant of land, in characteristically uncertain terms—the territory between the source of the Charles River and the head waters of the Merrimac, and extending from sea to sea. This grant was made as a business transaction to John Endicott and five others. This was the beginning of the famous organization known as the Governor and Company of Massachusetts Bay. Profits were anticipated by Endicott and his associates from ocean fisheries and fur trading, combined with agriculture on an aristocratic plantation basis. The undertaking was at first purely a business venture.

In 1629 Charles I began his "personal government," dispensing with parliament and to a large extent with the common-law courts, and carrying out through Archbishop Laud a more rigorous policy of enforcing uniformity in religion. In the same year Endicott's company with its extensive lands in America came under control of nonconformists. It was utilized by them not merely as a business enterprise but as an agency for promoting their escape from unsatisfactory conditions at home. The result was "the great migration." By 1642, when civil war began at home, the population had grown to sixteen thousand. Among the settlers of Massachusetts were many men of wealth and social position, who, ostrasized at home, were willing to hazard both life and fortune in promoting colonization in the new world. In consequence, the financing of "the great migration" was relatively a simple problem.

COLONIZATION BY PROPRIETORS: MARYLAND

One other illustration of the manner in which English capital found its way into new-world colonization must suffice. Maryland was founded not by a company but by an individual proprietor. Sir George Calvert (Lord Baltimore) was connected with the London Company and with the Council for New England. By 1625 he had become an avowed Catholic, but he maintained his personal standing with Charles I.

He became interested in colonizing Newfoundland, but a visit there convinced him he should look farther south. In 1629 he applied to Charles for a grant of land in the general region then known as Virginia. Controversies with Virginia delayed the grant till 1632. In the meantime he died and the charter was issued to his son Cecil. The extent of the grant was indicated so vaguely that boundary controversies long raged. In general the heart of the new plantation of Maryland was the region of the Chesapeake Bay, southward to the Potomac River and northward to the fortieth parallel.

This choice region was granted to Lord Baltimore on condition that one-fifth of the gold and silver ore discovered in the province be reserved for the crown, and that two Indian arrows of the region be delivered each year to the sovereign at Windsor Castle.

To the proprietor was granted "patronages and advowsons of the churches," by which he controlled the founding of churches and the appointment of clergymen. He was given extensive powers of government, including the collecting of taxes. As proprietor or owner of the land, he could grant sub-titles to portions of the land. The special right of creating manors was conceded. Lord Baltimore was to be overlord, with lords of manors under him, these in turn having peasants and laborers under them, holding manor courts, and in a word reproducing the aristocratic agricultural system of England.

With such remarkably favorable conditions, it is not difficult to see why Lord Baltimore was willing to venture his fortune in the development of his new-world "plantation." Nor is it surprising that he was able to induce men of wealth to accept grants of land from him on condition that they attempt with him the work of colonization. Religion here, as in New England, was a factor, but there is no reason to suppose that ordinary business considerations were subordinate.

LATER COLONIES

Pioneering in the colonization of the Hudson and Delaware river valleys was carried on by the Dutch and the Swedes. Financial arrangements were by means of joint-stock companies and proprietary grants somewhat as in the English colonies. English settlements in New York, New Jersey, Pennsylvania and Delaware, while promoted by proprietors, were a natural consequence of the acquisition of the New Netherlands from Holland and the expansion of the other English colonies.

The Carolinas were granted to eight proprietors, who spent considerable sums in financing colonization. But their attempt to introduce a feudal regime seems to have hindered more than helped the settlement of the region. Discontented elements from other colonies, particularly from aristocratic Virginia, were a more important source of population than the settlers brought in by the proprietors.

The one remaining colony of the original thirteen, Georgia, also owed its settlement partly to immigration from other colonies. But James Oglethorpe, who was influenced by a combination of ardent philanthropy and shrewd business sense, gained extensive financial backing in England for the colonizing of debtors and discharged prisoners, and also of German Protestants from the Archbishopric of Salzburg.

After the establishment of Virginia, Massachusetts, and Maryland, the main new element in supplying capital for colonization was the initiative of individual colonists. With definitely established centers of Anglicans, Puritans, and Catholics, in regions affording a wide range of economic activity, colonists with small resources and without the support of companies or proprietors came over in constantly increasing numbers. Adding not only their stock of goods and money but chiefly their labor, they rapidly enlarged the resources available for further expansion and development.

As a direct aid to colonization, the laborer's productivity was capitalized in a peculiar way. There were three types of labor in the colonies: slave, free, and indentured. Workers who were unable to pay for their passage sold their labor for periods ranging from four to ten years, entering into a formal contract or indenture. In some cases they were called "redemptioners," since by their labor they redeemed themselves from servitude. Ship captains frequently brought them over with the expectation of disposing of them by indenture to colonial employers, and thus received not only the passage money but often also a handsome profit as an employment agent. Nor was the business confined to workers who came voluntarily. Many were induced to come under false pretenses. The system also came to be used extensively by public authorities, who paid the passage money for various classes considered undesirable at home—not only criminals but "sturdy beggars," vagrants, and paupers as well.

CHAPTER V

FARMING AND FISHERIES

ILLUSION AND DISILLUSION

The early settlers had a boundless faith in get-rich-quick opportunities. The odor of spices faded and the glint of gold grew dim, but there was still the hope of finding a passage to the Indies. In the meantime innumerable futile experiments were made in the production of goods which Europeans had been securing from the Far East, and in the development of trade for the immediate profit of investors in colonizing enterprises.

There was one successful early experiment of this kind—the production of tobacco in Virginia. But before the adoption of tobacco as the staple for export, many fruitless undertakings exhausted the investments of the "adventurers" and the energies of the "planters." The second group of Virginia settlers, arriving in 1608, included Poles and Germans to supervise the making of pitch, potash and pearl ash. By dint of strenuous efforts a return cargo of iron ore and tar and pitch was assembled, much to the disgust of John Smith, who wrote the company that it would be better "to give £500 a ton for pitch, tar, and the like in the settled countries of Russia, Sweden, and Denmark than send for them hither till more necessary things be provided."

The "starving time" of the early Virginians and the hardships of other settlers soon made obvious the necessity of subordinating the profits of the "adventurers" to the survival of the "planters." Early illusions were dispelled by the struggle for existence. Out of that struggle emerged the basic industries of colonial America.

FARMING: THE SCRAMBLE FOR LAND

When it became apparent to the settlers that in the sweat of their faces they must eat bread, there followed a scramble for the lands that would entail the least amount of sweat.

Land policies varied widely. In Virginia, on the "division" of the company's joint stock in 1616, it was directed that every settler should have fifty acres. Colonists entering after 1616 at their own expense were also granted fifty acres. But the right to fifty acres, the "head right," came to be interpreted in such manner as to facilitate the ready transfer of such claims to the larger planters. Grants came increasingly to be made at the discretion of the governor and council, and as tobacco culture by slave labor gained ascendancy, large grants came to be made. The earlier small holdings along the streams were consolidated into plantations, and only along the ridges and in the back country were small independent holdings commonly found.

A similar system prevailed in Maryland, in the Carolinas, especially South Carolina, and even in Georgia, where the trustees created by the charter were at length forced to modify their regulations in such way as to permit consolidation of holdings, slavery, and in general, the plantation system.

The patroon system introduced by the Dutch in the Hudson valley led to the building up of some of the largest private estates in the colonies. With the acquisition of New Netherlands by England, the Dutch overlords were allowed to retain possession of their estates. In imitation of the Dutch, certain Englishmen also acquired large holdings. Relatively large estates were formed in the vicinity of Narragansett Bay. Slave labor was there used more extensively than elsewhere in New England.

In New England generally, and in Pennsylvania and New York with the exception of the choicer portions of the Hudson valley, small farms prevailed. The land held by the Governor and Company of Massachusetts Bay was under the jurisdiction of the General Court of the Company. Land was assigned by the General Court to the various towns or settlements, and the town governments had the duty of "dividing of lands to the several persons in each town." The amount and quality of land assigned was to be determined by the size of the family; by the number of beasts "by which the man is fit to occupy the land assigned to him, and subdue it"; and by a man's social position. "Men of eminent quality and descent" were to have "more large and honorable accommodations."

Another factor qualified the general rule of small and relatively equal holdings even in New England. After the home lots and the lots for public buildings and the town commons had been assigned, there remained "the common and undivided lands." Some of the later settlers were admitted to citizenship without sharing ownership of these lands. The original grantees or their heirs were "town proprietors," and the handling of the increasingly valuable lands not originally needed for actual use gave them a tremendous economic advantage.

In Pennsylvania, the land was owned by the proprietor but the policy of sub-grants was consistently liberal. Penn's *Body of Conditions and Concessions* of 1681 contained plans for the granting of lands to those who were unable to buy. The extensive German and Scotch-Irish movements into Pennsylvania were largely due to opportunities to secure cheap and fertile farms.

The Duke of York as proprietor of New York and Carteret and Berkeley as proprietors of New Jersey under grant from the Duke of York, were particularly desirous of attracting English settlers, and liberal terms were offered. New Jersey was settled to a large extent by New Englanders, who followed in large measure the precedents of the New England settlements. There were quarrels over quit rents—small fees in recognition of the proprietor's rights—but the colonists yielded and recognized the proprietary authority. New Englanders were prominent also in the settlement of New York and in the extension to New York of small holdings in agricultural communities.

TYPES OF AGRICULTURAL ECONOMY

In colonial days there early developed the three main types of agricultural economy long characteristic of rural life in America. If the historian may venture to use the somewhat arbitrary, short-cut terminology of the economist, these may be described as slave plantation economy, free village economy, and individualistic farmstead economy. These were natural adaptations of the colonists to the three main types of environment.

Settlers in the south found an extensive and fertile coastal plain. The main streams run from the Appalachian watershed into the Atlantic. The secondary streams run from the secondary watersheds in parallel valleys into the main streams. Most of the settlers who pushed their way along these rivers and larger creeks were in quest of land for tobacco. As early as 1612 John Rolfe, later the husband of Pocahontas, began the planting of tobacco, and in 1617 tobacco was grown in the streets and market place of Jamestown. When clergymen sought a charter for a college to aid them in saving souls, the attorney-general exclaimed, "Souls! Damn your souls; grow tobacco."

For growing tobacco the most readily obtainable laborers

first were indentured servants;[1] and later, negro slaves. Regimentation in relatively large groups was most economical. But a planter and his family and his servants could not live on tobacco, despite the report of Sir John Hawkins that the Indians by smoking it satisfied their hunger and lived four or five days without meat or drink. Plantations were likely to be far apart on the streams; and communication across the ridges with plantations on other streams was difficult. To bring in the necessaries of life by boat would be absurdly expensive. The result was that except for luxuries enjoyed by the planter's family, and for certain implements and supplies which could not be produced locally, the plantation was self-sufficing, like its medieval European prototype. Various crops besides tobacco were grown, particularly corn, wheat, and apples; and in the woods and the natural meadows, livestock flourished. Crude craftsmanship supplied a large proportion of the needs for fabricated goods.

But tobacco, or some other money crop, as rice or indigo in South Carolina, was the main concern of the typical planter. The small ships of the period found it possible to push their way up stream and touch at the planter's private wharf, taking on his tobacco and leaving him in return the luxuries of European marts.

Just as the slave plantation of the south was an outgrowth of southern conditions, so the free village of the north was a natural adaptation of the civilized European to the northern environment. As one advances northward the coastal plain becomes narrower, the Appalachian watershed swinging outward to meet the sea. In ages remote and from causes little known as yet, vast glacial masses moved southward as far as New Jersey, the southern limit extending thence northwestward through Pennsylvania. The crushing impact

[1] See above, p. 46.

of the ice left the surface rugged and rocky, with varied strata exposed, in contrast with the sedimentary or alluvial soil in the valleys of the coastal plain.

The plantation system demands large tracts of relatively uniform soil. In the north the surface was broken up into small diversified areas. The nature of the labor supply in the north also tended to prevent the establishment of large estates. The climate was not suited to negro slaves, and slaves were not adapted to the labor and skill necessary to bring the stubborn, rocky, and diversified soils under subjection. Dependent white labor could not be secured for plantations because of the abundance of frontier opportunity. The plantation was economically a business enterprise for the making of profits rather than for producing a mere subsistence. Profit making necessitated the production of surplus commodities for the market, as tobacco. In New England and in some other parts of the north, soil and climate were not adapted to the production of staples which could be sold extensively abroad; and in the absence of large towns and of urban industries, there was little demand for northern farm products at home. For profit, other occupations were in general pursued. Because of such conditions as these, large plantations in the north were generally impracticable.

Subsistence farming, particularly in New England, took the form of what may be termed free village economy.

Most of the New England "towns" were primarily agricultural communities. In any case, they were at first "communities" quite literally. It is true that the early communism in consumption goods such as existed at Plymouth was soon abandoned. Even titles to a large part of the communal lands were surrendered to individuals. But the New England town, as well as the free village or community copied from it elsewhere, like the slave plantation and in contrast with the individualistic farmstead, long retained a unified group economy.

The General Court of the Massachusetts Bay Company undertook to locate and fix the general boundaries of new settlements, in tracts of about thirty-six square miles. The settlers themselves, in town meeting or by means of selectmen, decided upon the essential features of community economy. The town common and the church on it or near it constituted the central part of the plan. Plots of land for the use of the several families of the group included space for the dwellings, barns, etc., and for gardens, orchards and small fields. Larger meadows and woods were reserved for pasture, the livestock as well as the pasture lands often being owned by the community. There were also common fields for tillage.

The first settlers reserved to themselves certain privileges, especially in the use of the common fields and pastures, and maintained in authority those of their own religious faith. With increasing need of manufactures, and with little opportunity for the export of staples, craftsmanship was encouraged, and some of the newcomers found in these opportunities a partial compensation for unequal privileges as to ownership of land.

Thus the adaptation of "the great migration" to the new-world environment was by means of a modified form of the old-world agricultural village. Continued immigration, combined with the natural increase of the population, led early to the "swarming" process, by which the village idea was ultimately carried not only throughout New England but to various other sections of the country. The tendency was accelerated by quarrels, especially by religious disputes, among the colonists.

The plantation of Virginia and Maryland and the free village of New England were natural adaptations of the old-world manor, township or parish. The plantation spread southward to the Spanish frontier and northward as far as natural conditions permitted, while in the Hudson valley nature made possible a similar but separately derived manorial system of overlords and tenant farmers introduced by the Dutch. The New England village spread northward toward the French frontier, and southward to the frontier of plantation economy.

Village economy was particularly important in the formative stages of colonial society, when a foothold and a subsistence wrested from stubborn nature and hostile natives were the main considerations. As New Englanders turned increasingly from village agriculture to fisheries and trade and the crafts, the village relatively declined, particularly in its communal aspects. As conditions became more stable and settlers found individual initiative and self-reliance increasingly sufficient, New England farming, and particularly farming in the middle colonies, became more individualistic, assuming the form of farmstead economy. The tendency was accelerated by the inequality of status accorded newcomers in the villages.

Individual small farms were not unknown in the south. Along the ridges between the valleys, and occasionally in the valleys themselves beside the plantations, were small farms tilled by the owners. White settlers who were unable to establish plantations were unwilling to become servile plantation workers. Indentured servants were commonly promised land by their indentures (though they were apparently often defrauded of it by their masters), and instead of continuing as plantation workers after their term of service, they preferred the precarious independence of small subsistence farming. There was a steady exodus of poor whites to the ridges and backwoods, and to the frontier colonies, and although some of them became trappers or adventurers and a few established plantations, most of them were free-lance farmers, isolated and largely self-sufficing. In North Carolina farmstead economy was particularly prominent.

Tobacco was extremely hard on the soil, and there was a tendency to abandon a plantation after a few years in favor of virgin soil—a tendency promoted by the prevalent view that fertilization of the soil spoiled the flavor of the tobacco. The lands thus abandoned by the planters were sometimes utilized by small-scale farmers. Thus farmsteads rather than plantations were here and there maintained even in the relatively favorable streamside locations of the tobacco country.

In the middle colonies, particularly in the areas not affected by the New England "swarming" process by which the New England village economy was extended, several factors promoted farmstead economy. These colonies were settled by Englishmen at a relatively late period, after the pioneering work had been done by Dutch and Swedes. Natural conditions were not suited to the plantation system, and on the other hand the relative security from Indians and from natural hardships made compact and cooperative village life less essential to survival.

In the older settlements of the middle colonies, farmstead economy was not so largely a self-sufficing, subsistence economy as in New England and in the south and on the frontiers. In Pennsylvania, New York, New Jersey and Delaware the soil was good, there were natural transportation facilities by water, and the growth of towns and trade gave opportunity for the sale of surplus products. In this respect they resembled the planters with their staple products.

SUPPLEMENTARY PURSUITS OF FARMERS

Planters who grew tobacco and other exportable staples, and farmers who commanded the markets for farm produce in the towns, had money for buying the things beyond the limits of their land or skill. Remoter farmers generally turned to industries other than agriculture for making money to pay for goods they were unable to produce.

One way in which most of the early settlers could earn money was by trapping fur-bearing animals. Particularly important was this source of income to the individualistic subsistence farmers of the lone frontier farmsteads, in giving them an opportunity to buy weapons and tools and occasionally other goods beyond their capacity to produce. At the same time the quest for furs was a most important factor in the extension of the frontier. Vast quantities of beaver, fox, otter and other furs were secured from the Indians by the fur traders, but for such additional furs as the farmer and ordinary frontiersman could bring to market there was usually a good demand. So important and stable in value were beaver furs that they were extensively used as a medium of exchange.

Another industry particularly important in affording supplementary income to farmers was lumbering. The forests of England, long inadequate, were further depleted by the increasing demands of tanners for bark, and of charcoal burners in connection with smelting before the introduction of coke-burning furnaces. For shipbuilding the forest resources of England were extremely inadequate. To meet both foreign and colonial demands, crude shingles, clapboards, laths, and staves could be made and ordinarily marketed during intervals of release from farm labor. Some farmers attained sufficient skill to produce marketable ship timbers, tar, and other products.

Fishing, mining, and the principal forms of manufacturing, so far as marketable products were concerned, were more commonly specialized and separated from farming. Mining, in spite of the frenzied early quest for gold and silver, was not important during the colonial period. The main development was in iron smelting, and may more fittingly be discussed in connection with manufacturing. Marketable manufactures, except of the cruder types such as those mentioned in connection with lumbering, were insignificant until late in the colonial period. The industries so far considered developed early and had a vital connection not only with the production of subsistence goods necessary for the survival of the colonists, but also with the creation of a surplus for the channels of trade. There was one other industry of great importance throughout the colonial period alike in furnishing food and in supplying articles of trade —the fisheries. Before passing to trade and exchange, this interesting occupation must not be overlooked.

THE FISHERIES

"And they affirm that that sea is covered with fishes, which are caught not only with the net but with baskets, a stone being tied to the baskets in order that they may sink in the water. And this I heard the said Master John [Cabot] relate. And the . . . Englishmen, his comrades, say that they will bring so much fish that this kingdom will no longer have need of Iceland, from which country there comes a very great store of fish." Thus wrote an Italian in England at the time of John Cabot's return. Soon thereafter began the exploitation of the inexhaustible resources of the northeastern American fisheries. Temporary fishing stations were in use long before either the English or the French had established colonies in America. Fifty years before the settlement of New England, the English sent each year a fleet of more than two score vessels to Newfoundland, and they were far behind the French and the Spanish and even the Portuguese. The New England fisheries were being exploited before the founding of Plymouth, as when John Smith returned in 1614 with a shipload of fish and furs. After the establishment of colonies, the industry developed rapidly, and became the principal source of profit alike to "adventurers" and to "planters"—in this case fishermen.

"Would you believe that a sandy spot, of about twenty-three thousand acres, affording neither stones nor timber, meadows nor arable, yet can boast of an handsome town, consisting of more than 500 houses, should possess above 200 sail of vessels, constantly employ upwards of 2,000 seamen, feed more than 15,000 sheep, 500 cows, 200 horses; and has several citizens worth £20,000 sterling! . . . This island . . . [Nantucket] contains 5,000 hardy people, who boldly derive their riches from the element which surrounds them." Thus wrote the author of *Letters from an American Farmer* concerning Nantucket, noted particularly as a whaling center.

Fishing for cod and mackerel along the coast required vessels of no great size or cost. In the early days whaling also was carried on near the coast. Sentinels were posted, and when a whale was observed, the whaleboat, a row boat with six men, was launched, and by means of harpoons the prey was often landed. When the whales and the cod forsook the Massachusetts coast, larger vessels were used, owned in some cases by groups of fishermen and in others by capitalists, and whale and cod alike were pursued to distant regions.

Toward the end of the colonial period, brigs as large as 150 tons were commonly used for whaling. Such a brig was manned by a crew of thirteen. There were two whale boats, each requiring a crew of six,—four oarsmen, a helmsman, and a man to wield the harpoon. One of the whale boats was held in reserve for rescuing the crew in case the boat in use should be destroyed by the whale. Such dangerous and skillful work required a body lithe and strong and a mind alert, and the finest coordination of the several members of the crew. Whalers rarely pursued the calling beyond the age of forty. The crew ordinarily worked not for wages but for a share of the profits in partnership with the owner of the vessel. Indians frequently were members of the crews.

The whaling and fishing industries provided a staple food for a large part of the colonial population. They furnished the leading staples of New England commerce, the exports of these industries after 1763, for example, amounting to more than half the total recorded exports. They afforded incentives for the building of ships, for the training of mariners, and for the extension of commerce in distant regions.

In the spring, New Englanders followed the codfish northward; in the winter, they pursued their calling in milder latitudes. They visited (wrote the author of *Letters from an American Farmer*) "the banks of Cape Breton, the Isle of Sable; and all the other fishing places, with which this coast of America abounds. By degrees they went a-whaling to Newfoundland, to the Gulf of St. Lawrence, to the Straits of Belleisle, the coast of Labrador, Davis's Straits, even to Cape Desolation, in 70° of latitude. . . . In process of time they visited the western islands, the latitude of 34° famous for that fish, the Brazils, the coast of Guinea. Would you believe that they have already gone to the Falkland Islands, and that I have heard several of them talk of going to the South Sea! . . . I was there [at Nantucket] when Mr. —— had missed one of his vessels; she had been given over for lost by everybody, but happily arrived before I came away, after an absence of thirteen months. She had met with a variety of disappointments on the station she was ordered to, and rather than return empty, the people steered for the coast of Guinea, where they fortunately fell in with several whales, and brought home upward of 600 barrels of oil, beside bone."

CHAPTER VI

TRADE AND FINANCE

THE FUR TRADE

Farming and fisheries, supplemented by lumbering and trapping, were the principal sources not only of subsistence but of surpluses for trade. While the colonists were blazing trails in the wilderness, they were able to make the wilderness pay a part of the costs. The abundance of fur-bearing animals in all of the colonies during their early history gave opportunities to the colonists themselves to engage in trapping as a supplementary occupation. Securing furs from the Indians in return for coarse blankets and showy and inexpensive goods was the one exception to the disappointment of Europeans in their expectations of lucrative trade by sailing west. It was carried on largely by land and by inland waterways, whereas other branches of colonial trade, even between one colony and another, were largely by sea.

Canoes penetrated the smaller streams, and between streams portages were established along the Indian trails. To the southwest, along the frontier beyond Virginia, the trade was so extensive as to justify caravans of pack horses. The trade in the south was dominated in turn by Virginians, Carolinians, and Georgians. The kinds of furs mentioned as coming from North Carolina shortly before the Revolution are typical. They included beaver, raccoon, otter, fox, minx and wild cat. From northern latitudes came finer and more varied furs. To the export of skins for furs were added hides for tanning. From North Carolina, in 1753, 30,000 deer skins were exported. On account of the poor shipping facilities of North Carolina there was a tendency for its products to gravitate to the harbors of South Carolina or of Virginia. About the same time it was reported that Pennsylvania's exports of "deer and sundry other sorts of skins" amounted to £50,000 out of a total of £705,500. But already the fur trade of the colonies below Canada had seen its best days. The effect of the English conquest of Canada was to shift fur-trading activities to this more northerly region, and the Revolution virtually completed the ruin of the seaboard fur trade. Its revival in what is now the United States awaited the opening up of the Mississippi valley and of the far west.

MEANS OF COMMUNICATION

The most extensive inland transportation was connected with the fur trade. But facilities were mainly those afforded by nature. On the small streams the canoe supplanted the sailboat; and between streams, Indian trails became portages, with more attention paid to forts than to the expansion of the trails into roads. Along these portages were built the later highways and railroads.

In the south, the streams were used almost exclusively. In the middle colonies the larger towns, New York and Philadelphia, were connected by roads which, before the Revolution, permitted the passage of the postal courier in thirty-six hours, and of the stage coach in three days. The New England towns were more likely to be connected by roads, but here as elsewhere, road improvement was limited to the removal of obstructions, a slight leveling process, and the building of an occasional crude bridge.

Roads were little used except for travel. Transportation of goods was mainly by water. The small size of the vessels, and the larger, more constant flow of water in the streams before the drainage system was transformed by deforestation, gave water transport facilities to a vastly larger area than at present. Ocean-going vessels ascended the Hudson, for instance, as far as Albany. There was a remarkable adaptability in making boats for the diverse conditions of navigation—an adaptability which gave Americans an unrivalled place on the water until they turned their attention more largely to land transportation.

SURPLUSES AND DEFICITS

The production of surpluses and the existence of corresponding deficits in accessible markets—these are obvious conditions of trade. At first glance the situation appears to have been simple enough. Nature adapted the colonies to certain types of production, as the Cape Cod region to fisheries and Virginia to tobacco. But manufacturing for markets was disallowed or discouraged; manufactured goods must be imported from England. The colonists were confronted not merely with the question of adapting their energies to natural conditions, but as well with the problem of obeying (or evading) regulations designed primarily to direct their energies into channels dug by English interests. The crown desired revenue. The proprietors and companies wanted large and early returns on their investments. English producers insisted that English and colonial markets be reserved, in case of rivalry, for their own output.[1] English producers were at that time able to supply the demand in England for foodstuffs and raw materials, with the exception of certain exotics, as well as the demand for most manufactured goods.

[1] For a discussion of mercantilistic regulations, see below, ch. 8.

Thus the opportunities for the sale of colonial surpluses were limited by public policies as well as by natural conditions. The actual production of surpluses followed substantially the lines indicated in the discussion of farming and fisheries. There was a persistent quest for "staples"—for goods which could be successfully produced in the colonies, and for which there would be a "staple" market or dependable demand.

DISTINCTIVE REGIONAL CONTRIBUTIONS TO TRADE

(1) The "Tobacco" Colonies

The colonies most successful in the quest for a staple were the "tobacco" colonies, Virginia and Maryland. Tobacco was the most important single item of export from the colonies. Other items of importance were wheat and corn, lumber and naval stores (ship timbers, turpentine, tar, hemp). With the exception of wheat, there was no major product in competition with English goods; and England by the end of the colonial period was rapidly losing self-sufficiency in the production of wheat. The people of the tobacco plantations engaged very slightly in manufacturing, shipbuilding, and shipping. English merchants brought English manufactures in English ships to the leading plantations as well as to the port towns, and transported the tobacco and other staples to the markets of England and the world. From the point of view of Englishmen (unless they believed with James I that the tobacco "custom" was "loathsome" and "nearest resembling the horrible Stygian smoke of the pit that is bottomless"), Virginia and Maryland were ideal colonies.

(2) *New England*

The main staples peculiar to New England were cod, mackerel, and whale products. But to Englishmen these were not "true" staples, because England also produced them. Complaint was made that fish, whale bone, and oil were "commodities which some of the colonies have run away with from England, by rivaling her in her fishery." The exports of the fisheries amounted in 1763 to more than half the total recorded exports. Of the remainder, masts, lumber, ships, potash, livestock and provisions made up the major items. It must be remembered, however, in considering statistics of colonial trade, that there was a large and lucrative trade not entered in the records.

Not only products of the fisheries but other characteristic New England goods were viewed by Englishmen as competitive rather than supplementary. New Englanders, therefore, were unable to profit extensively by English markets. They sought out markets in the other colonies, particularly in the West Indies, and exchanged provisions and lumber for molasses, which they made into rum, and from the sale of rum helped to pay for English manufactures. The better grades of fish were sold in the Mediterranean countries; "the refuse sort to the West Indies as food for the negroes." In the Mediterranean markets they frequently disposed of ship as well as cargo. One reason for this practice, no doubt, was the fact that the colonists were forbidden by law to import most foreign goods except by way of England.

Much of the income of New Englanders was derived from the carrying trade. "The people of this country [New England] are in a manner the carriers for all the colonies of North America and the West Indies, and even for some parts of Europe. They may be considered in this respect as the Dutch of America."

In connection with the carrying trade and with the extensive markets entered by them for the sale of their goods, New Englanders found many opportunities to buy at a profit for importation. The naval stores of North Carolina were imported partly for reexport and partly for use in the shipbuilding industry. West Indian molasses was imported for making rum, which was sold extensively in the colonies and abroad. In this connection New Englanders, particularly those of Rhode Island, engaged extensively in the slave trade. By means of their own products, particularly of the fisheries; by means of the carrying trade and the slave trade; and by means of profits on such imports as naval stores and molasses, New Englanders were able to import considerable quantities of the finer grades of English manufactures. But old England was never very well pleased with New England, because its tendency was to compete with rather than to supplement the economic life of the home country.

(3) *Georgia and the Carolinas*

The quest for staples, particularly in the southern-most colonies, led to many experiments. It was believed that if in their own dominions Englishmen could secure the luxuries they craved, the money otherwise expended abroad would be particularly efficacious in enriching the nation. Repeated efforts, therefore, were made to grow not only tobacco but nutmegs and spices, wine grapes and silk, indigo and rice, and other highly prized exotics.

Toward the end of the seventeenth century rice was introduced in South Carolina, and rapidly became the principal staple. The abundance of moisture in the soil due to the semi-marshy nature of much of the country, and the cheap slave labor readily available from the West Indies, were among the influences which made rice culture profitable, not only in South Carolina but in some portions of North Carolina and Georgia. In 1766 the governor of Georgia placed rice first in the list of Georgia's industries, and among the recorded exports its value was twice that of any other item. The export of rice was restricted for a time in the early eighteenth century to England, but ordinarily it was sent to various countries, particularly Holland, Germany, and the countries of the Mediterranean. Indigo never attained the prominence of rice, but its introduction, shortly before the middle of the eighteenth century, was followed by a rapid development, the exports from South Carolina increasing from 200,000 pounds in 1754 to a million pounds before the Revolution.

Until rice gave South Carolina a staple demanded in England, its commercial relations were largely with the West Indies on the one hand, and with the Indians on the other. Provisions, lumber, pitch and tar were sent to the West Indies, and sugar, molasses, rum, and slaves were imported. Charleston was the center of the trade with the West Indies, and to the same town came the traders with the Indians, who ranged westward for perhaps a thousand miles in quest of furs. To England were sent the furs, and also forest products, particularly naval stores; and from England came manufactured goods. With the rapid eighteenth-century expansion of rice culture, the earlier diversified agricultural and commercial activities declined, and South Carolina approximated the status of the tobacco colonies. Charleston, however, was a far more important commercial center than were any of the towns of Maryland or Virginia. So important were the merchants that in political power they rivaled the planters. The Carolinas had no such facilities for river navigation as existed in the tobacco colonies, and planters had to depend more largely on local merchants than did the tobacco planters, whose plantations were accessible in many cases to ocean-going vessels.

North Carolina had no such distinctive staple as tobacco or rice or fish, nor was it as important commercially as most of the other colonies. On account of the shallow waters and shifting sand banks along its shore line, it depended on small coastwise vessels or on overland transportation to the ports of neighboring colonies. The outstanding commodities contributed by North Carolina to colonial trade were forest products. These included lumber, staves, and shingles, and the several articles known as naval stores, such as tar, pitch, rosin, and timbers for bowsprits, yards and masts. In the production of naval stores, North Carolina became so successful that New England came to depend increasingly on supplies produced there.

North Carolina was described by unneighborly South Carolina critics as the "receptacle of all the vagabouns & runaways of the main land of America," and was denounced for "entertaining pirates." Many of the settlers were "poor whites" from other colonies, unable to establish themselves as planters, unwilling to submit to a servile status in plantation society, and desirous of establishing themselves independently in a new country. That they were willfully more inclined toward illegal trading than were the planters and the merchants of other colonies is extremely doubtful. But the nature of the country promoted piracy and smuggling. The shallow approaches, barring larger vessels, and the numerous indentations of bays, inlets, and streams made supervision by English officials as difficult as it rendered illegal operations by small boats easy. Both exports and imports were handled in large part by New Englanders as a part of their extensive carrying trade.

It seems, therefore, that the residents of the colony profited more largely as patrons and protectors of illicit traders than as actual participants in smuggling and piracy.

(4) *The Middle Colonies*

New York, New Jersey, Pennsylvania and Delaware were four of a kind in having a diversified list of articles of trade with no distinctive staple of their own. But they did enjoy a certain preeminence in what were commonly called provisions. They were particularly successful in the export of grains, notably wheat, of livestock, and of the food products derived from grains and livestock. As early as 1700 complaint was made that Pennsylvanians had made "bread, flower and Beer a drugg in all the Markets in the West Indies."

Provisions were supplemented by forest products common to all the colonies, ships "built for sale," copper ore, iron in pigs and bars, and, notably in New York, skins and furs. Most of the products exported from the middle colonies were sent to the West Indies, to other colonies, and to countries of Europe other than England. With the New Englanders they shared the coastwise trade. Among the goods sent to England were skins and furs, iron (late in the colonial period), and flax seed (to Ireland). Some of the goods secured in trade with other countries were taken to England, as logwood, mahogany, sugar, and rum. But in payment for their imports from England, consisting mostly of manufactures, they had to pay, as did the New Englanders, for the most part in cash.

MONEY AND EXCHANGE

How to obtain enough cash to pay for imports of English manufactures was one of the pressing problems of colonial trade. Commerce depends in the first place on the existence of surpluses and deficits in respect to the commodities of trade. It depends, in the second place, on a method of effecting a reciprocal transfer of surpluses to remedy corresponding deficits or needs. The simplest method is barter. *A* has a horse to spare and needs a cow. *B* has a cow to spare and needs a horse. *A* "swaps" a horse for one of *B's* cows. Perhaps the horse is worth more than the cow, so *B* gives *A* a pig or two to boot. By individual "swapping" and neighborhood bartering an immense amount of trade, extremely significant in the aggregate, was undoubtedly carried on. But when the surplus and the deficit occur at a distance, or when there is a series of surpluses and deficits, involving not merely *A* and *B*, but *A, B, C, D,* and others, then barter breaks down. Whenever for any reason a middleman is needed, barter is unsatisfactory if not impossible.

For the conduct of business on any but the simplest plan, a medium of exchange is of course essential. Colonial monetary arrangements were inadequate for several reasons. The colonists brought very little money with them. The glittering ores they laboriously unearthed and exultantly sent to England turned out to be pyrites or "fool's gold." The home government persistently attempted to prevent the flow of gold or of silver to the colonies, and as persistently tried to drain away from the colonies as much gold and silver as possible.[1] Added to these difficulties was the variety of coins in the colonies. Some money was coined in the colonies, but the main dependence was on English and foreign coins. Since the colonists traded extensively with the Spanish portions of the new world and with Spain, and since the Spanish empire was abundantly provided with precious metals, Spanish coins, particularly piastres, or "pieces of eight," were most prominent. The piastre, it is

[1] For a discussion of mercantilism, see ch. 8.

interesting to recall, was the ancestor of the American dollar. Coins of various countries, and with countless variations in the ratio of intrinsic value to face value, were in circulation. The different colonies had their own monetary regulations and standards (or lack of standards); and the absence of a coordinating authority made confusion worse confounded.

An intermediate stage between barter and money was the standardizing of commodities by assigning certain exchange values to them. At one time or another most of the colonial products at all stable in value were used in this way. Thus wildcat skins, in one instance, were assigned by public authority the exchange value of a shilling each; beaver, otter, and dressed deer skins, two shillings a pound; tar, per barrel, ten shillings; pitch, per barrel, one pound; and wheat, three shillings a bushel. Taxes and other obligations were often legally payable in commodities. Informal trading relations and private contracts would naturally take into account the fluctuations in values. The chief complaints seem to have been in connection with public revenues. In the payment of revenues and of other fixed obligations, commodities of least value and poorest quality would ordinarily be used. Thus we have a primitive illustration of Gresham's law to the effect that bad money drives good money out of circulation.

Instead of the commodity actually changing hands, paper representations often circulated. There were several forms of these. An ordinary due bill or receipt might serve. Orders calling for commodities in payment of taxes often passed for currency. The outstanding instance, however, was the tobacco warehouse certificate of Virginia. Public warehouses were maintained, with public inspectors, and for tobacco deposited therein certificates were issued for a given quantity of tobacco. The certificates changed hands indefinitely and constituted a fairly stable and satisfactory medium of exchange except for the smaller transactions.

Most of the colonies were less fortunate in having a staple equally satisfactory as a basis for paper currency, and in consequence most of them (and ultimately even Virginia) resorted to the issuing of bills or fiat money.

Massachusetts led off in 1690, to meet a debt incurred by a military venture against the French in Canada. By the same device the soldiers were paid, but depreciation of this paper (and corresponding increase in prices) soon began, and the soldiers lost nearly half their wages. Succeeding issues experimented with various devices, as fixing a definite date for redemption in silver. Different issues were given different values in public esteem, and grave confusion and uncertainty were added to the previous ills. To take care of the various outstanding issues, "new tenor" bills were printed, but these, instead of clarifying the situation, also began to depreciate and to add a new element of uncertainty. In 1739, efforts were made to curb the inflation of currency by the government. Contraction of the volume of money in circulation promoted the formation of banks with power to issue bank notes. Thus to the uncertain government notes were added the still more uncertain private bank notes. Soon thereafter the tangled financial web woven by Massachusetts was partially unraveled by parliamentary action. A grant of £175,000 was made by parliament, and the provincial government was induced to redeem outstanding notes at the ratio of seven and a half to one. In 1751 an act of parliament restricted and regulated the issuing of paper money in New England, and in 1764 in the rest of the colonies.

By the time the Gordian knot of inflation and depreciation in Massachusetts was being cut by official repudiation (or its equivalent in redemption at the ratio of seven and a half to one), most of the other colonies were also deeply involved. In Pennsylvania, where paper money was exceptionally high in value, the ratio of notes to standard coin was 18 to 10. In some other colonies the ratio was 11 to 1, but it was generally confused and variable.

Circumstances not familiar to the descendants of the colonists made their financial problem particularly acute. In the first place, they lived in a period of money economy, when credit instruments were imperfectly developed. The subsequent perfection of local, national, and international banks, with the pooling of resources in banks as reservoirs, made possible the almost universal use of checks, bills of exchange, and related instruments of exchange. Colonial merchants regularly bought bills on London, to be sure, but in general there was a much greater dependence than at present on actual money or else on barter. In the second place, the colonists did very little manufacturing, and depended on England largely for manufactured goods. At the same time, they were unable to pay Englishmen for manufactures by means of colonial products, because these products, with certain exceptions, notably tobacco, competed with English industries. Paper money, wrote Franklin, became "absolutely necessary to their internal commerce, from the constant remittance of their gold and silver to Britain." Colonial methods of increasing the medium of exchange, however unfortunate, are at least understandable; and the chief business of the student of history is to understand. Furthermore, the World War gave ample recent demonstration that such devices have by no means been restricted to colonial experimentation or need or to the inexperience of pioneering in modern finance.

CHAPTER VII

CRAFTSMANSHIP

EVERY MAN A CRAFTSMAN

Manufacturing in the colonies for markets was opposed by Englishmen. But to attribute the relative lack of specialized manufacturing solely or even mainly to their opposition would be absurd. Except for the more primitive arts carried on in subordination to agriculture or other basic subsistence industries, manufacturing in any age or society is a relatively late and specialized aspect of economic evolution. The ordinary colonist possessed a rough-and-ready skill in many crafts, but he exercised it mainly in making goods which he was unable to buy from the English.

Naturally, the colonists turned first to the subsistence industries. Almost everywhere, agriculture was for a time predominant. If not agriculture, then other basic industries connected with primary access to natural resources (as lumbering, fisheries, trapping) most profitably consumed the energies of the settlers. As soon as marketable surpluses in the basic industries were produced, colonial energy not required in these industries was naturally directed first toward commerce and the problems of exchange rather than toward specialized manufacturing. From the cities of the old world into the wilderness of the new, skilled artisans were not easily attracted. If they came, they were likely to be discouraged by lack of facilities for following their trades, or to be induced to abandon their callings as craftsmen by the attractions of cheap land, or of commerce, or of pioneering. It was not till toward the end of the colonial period that conditions were such as to attract any considerable number of craftsmen or any large amount of capital into specialized manufacturing pursuits.

Craftsmanship was none the less important from the beginning. Let each "planter" bring "fit implements for the work or trade he intends"—thus ran an early exhortation to settlers. But it was discovered that the successful colonist must have skill in wielding the implements of many trades, and even in making the tools.

The would-be farmer must first turn carpenter and mason and build his house. He must learn to repair and in part even make his plows and other tools. He must learn the art of tanning hides and shaping them into shoes and harness. He must content himself and his family with hickory chairs and split-log tables. In bad weather, slack seasons, and long winter evenings, he and his family must carry on such varied arts as milling, soap-making, preserving of foods, spinning, weaving, and garment-making. A little surplus wool or flax could be made into cloth for local sale or barter. A few staves or clapboards or "planks of walnut trees for tables or cupboards, cedar and cypress for chests and cabinets," might be salvaged from clearing the land for tillage and hauled to market. If such aids could be had for the purchase of essential tools or goods beyond their skill or their command of raw materials, they counted themselves fortunate.

As population and wealth increased and towns grew up, such primitive conditions slowly disappeared. But throughout the colonial period, the principal form of manufacturing was the domestic industry of essentially self-sufficing households and communities.

SPECIALIZATION

(1) *Forest Products*

It is not surprising that specialization first occurred extensively along the rather vague boundary line between manufacturing and lumbering. The abundance and variety of woodland resources embarrassed the settlers. The forests interfered with agriculture, with expansion, and with defense from the Indians. In clearing the land for tillage, most of the timbers were destroyed. Older men even of the present generation in many parts of the country delight to tell of the "log rollings" of their younger days, when incomparable giants of the forest were felled and chopped into sections, rolled into heaps by lusty farmers using poles as levers, and burned to ashes without a thought save "good riddance."

A decisive factor in salvaging something from the ravages of axe and fire was transportation. In the absence of roads, such heavy and bulky commodities obviously could not be transported from far beyond the fall line of the coastal streams or from regions east of the fall line if remote from navigable streams.

The demand for forest products was extremely varied. Englishmen had hopes of finding the exotic oriental woods, such as sandal wood, brazil wood, and mahogany, used for their fragrance, or dyes, or beauty of grain and finish. Cedar, cypress, walnut and wild cherry were poor but acceptable substitutes. England was virtually unpossessed of trees for furnishing masts and tar and turpentine and related products. Even ordinary lumber must be imported in large quantities.

The resources of the colonies that were particularly suited to exploitation because of transportation facilities and of prevailing demands included the white pine, cedar and spruce of New England; the fir of New York; the yellow pine and the live oak of the southern colonies; and the red and white oaks of various regions.

In the production of lumber, the ancient process of splitting or riving the timbers was extensively used. If necessary the riven timbers were hewn into requisite smoothness. Blocks of white oak, for example, could be riven into shingles, timbers for casks, and varied other forms, with astonishing skill and speed. Riven timbers were less uniform and smooth but were stronger and more elastic than sawn timbers. Saw mills were set up in the colonies earlier than in England. Their first use, naturally, was in the soft woods, the hard woods continuing for some time to be riven or sawed by hand.

The pines throughout the colonies, but especially the white pines of New England and the yellow pines of the south, gave rise to a series of related industries—the manufacture of tar, pitch, rosin, and turpentine. The making of tar was a simple process. Ordinary tar was made from dead pines. The hard, protruding knots of rotting pine logs were collected and heaped together on a slanting, hard clay floor; they were covered with dirt, and burned somewhat as in making charcoal. The tar ran down the inclined floor through a trough, and into a barrel. The making of pitch, the refinement of crude resins, and the extraction of turpentine were also conducted on a commercial basis, though less extensively than the tar industry.

In the hardwood areas, the making of potash held a place comparable to the tar and rosin industries in the resinous forests. The soluble portions of wood ashes were leached out by draining water through the ashes in barrels or other containers, and the potash was secured by boiling the water out of the lye resulting from leaching. Farmers used lye for making soap and sometimes made potash for the markets. Probably most of the commercial potash was made in small potash works in the towns, the ashes being collected from the neighboring farmers. The amount of potash exported annually from New England, the principal scene of its manufacture, was estimated shortly before the Revolution at 14,000 barrels, valued at £2 10s. per barrel. Pearl ash, or potassium carbonate, required in certain English industries, was made by exposure of potash to furnace heat.

(2) *Shipbuilding*

"They fell,—those lordly pines!" But from the wreck of God's first temples were salvaged the principal materials for one of the finest of man's creations:

> "Stanch and strong, a goodly vessel,
> That shall laugh at all disaster,
> And with wave and whirlwind wrestle."

When the *Mary and John* and the *Gift of God* cast anchors in the tide waters of the Kennebec River in August of 1607, the artisans on board proceeded to build the first English ocean-going vessel in America—the pinnace *Virginia.* By 1641, Plymouth colony adopted for its shipwrights the system of inspection and regulation in vogue in England. New England's initial lead in shipbuilding was maintained throughout the colonial period. Nearly all of the port towns built vessels, large or small, and ships of goodly size were early built in half a score of towns from Gloucester (Cape Ann) on the north to New Haven in the waters of the Sound. The increasing commerce of the middle colonies, and the discovery of the superior qualities of southern live oak for ship timbers, enabled the industry to prosper in some of the colonies south of New England, not only at Philadelphia and New York, but at some of the southern ports. Alike in cheapness and in quality, colonial ships often excelled the output of English craftsmen. In this respect shipbuilding was in rather striking contrast with most other crafts, which had much difficulty in competing with the English. There were no regulations against the building of ships in the colonies, whereas most manufactures were discouraged if not legally restricted. Shipbuilding materials had never abounded in England, and had been exhausted in other parts of Europe in the vicinity of suitably located shipyards, whereas colonial builders had readily accessible supplies of the best quality.

The English had to import a large proportion of ship timbers and other naval stores, either from the colonies or from the countries of northern Europe, and this led to an extensive transfer of English shipbuilding capital and skill to the colonies. Orders were frequently placed in the colonies with advance payments to the builders. Young and venturesome Englishmen with capital often financed the shipment of a cargo of English goods to the colonies, sold the goods, built a ship for a return cargo of colonial products, sold cargo and ship at home or in the Mediterranean markets, and repeated the process. Long before the end of the seventeenth century, more than a score of English orders were frequently received in a year by New England masters. New Englanders had few goods in demand in England with which to pay for the manufactures they regularly bought from Englishmen. English merchants, instead of insisting on payment in money, often accepted colonial ships in return for English goods.

Not only English agents in the colonies but Americans as well frequently built ships, took cargoes to the West

Indies or to Europe, particularly the Mediterranean countries, and sold ship as well as cargo.

Before the Revolution there was a decline in shipbuilding in New England, but the importance of the industry is indicated by the fact that in the New England colonies the number of ships built for sale after the Peace of Paris of 1763 averaged about seventy per year. This number was not much exceeded by the total number built for sale by Pennsylvania, New York, Virginia, and Maryland. It has been estimated that by the Revolution almost a third of the tonnage of the British empire had been built in the thirteen colonies. Ships built for sale brought a considerable direct income to the builders, but more important was the construction of the ships used in colonial trade and fisheries. These afforded not only an income to the builders but a continuing source of wealth to the users.

(3) *Textiles*

In the various forms of business so far considered (agriculture, the fisheries, trade, forest industries, shipbuilding) colonials in spite of certain handicaps had predominating advantages. In the manufacture of textiles, except of homespun for household use and neighborhood exchange, they labored under such difficulties as to prevent any considerable development.

The production of wool was difficult because of beasts of prey, particularly wolves, and because of the tendency of the English breeds to revert to more primitive types in the sterner new-world environment. Notwithstanding the difficulties, the colonial clip by the beginning of the eighteenth century was practically equal to the demand for wool. The supply thereafter continued fairly adequate, but very little wool was exported, and the quality was generally inferior to that of the European clip.

Wool was the most important fabric in colonial manufactures, but its use was confined almost exclusively to the widespread household and plantation manufactures in subordination to agriculture and other dominant pursuits. The status of textile manufacturing in Pennsylvania was described by Sir William Keith in 1728; and by substituting for "grain" the local staples of the different regions, his account is generally applicable: "Grain being the chief product by which they are enabled to purchase clothing and other European goods, those settlements which are back in the woods and far distant from navigation have not an opportunity of a market for grain, which will not bear the charge of a great land carriage, wherefore they raise no more corn in such places than what they consume themselves, by which means they can spare more time to work up as much wool and flax into cloth as they want for their own use."

Next in importance to woollens in household industry, and even more important in manufacturing for the market, were the products of flax and hemp. Flax was grown in large quantities. There is no evidence of any considerable export of flax or linens, but toward the end of the colonial period the shipment of flax seed, mainly to Ireland, assumed remarkable proportions. There were several ports of lading, but from Philadelphia and New York alone the exports shortly before the Revolution in some years amounted to nearly a quarter of a million bushels.

Nor was flax raised merely for the seed. The finer Irish linens required the harvesting of the flax before complete maturity of the seeds, while colonial linens, mostly homespun, were perhaps more durable but less elegant when made from flax from which the seed had been garnered. There is much information, casual and fugitive for the most part, of the manufacture of linens for the market, as for instance the account published in New York in 1754 of a vessel foundered on the way to New York from New Brunswick, with linens valued at £10,000 to £12,000, "manufactured in the Jersies and bringing hither for sale."

But the outstanding commercial articles produced from flax and hemp were duck and cordage. Hemp was grown extensively in the colonies, and was occasionally exported. Virginia and Maryland, about 1763, exported a thousand tons of hemp but retained for their own use four thousand tons. Although bounties were offered for its export, little was sent to England, and indeed there was frequent importation to meet colonial needs, especially of the New England cordage makers. Cordage and duck were used for various purposes, but the principal market demands (as distinguished from household needs supplied mainly by homespun) were for rope and sailcloth in connection with shipbuilding, shipping, and the fisheries.

Almost a symbol of the frontier was the homemade coonskin cap. Raccoon fur, as well as beaver fur, was used in the manufacture of hats and caps for the market. The finer hats were made of beaver fur, and were at first imported, but colonial craftsmen, having advantages of abundant raw materials, interfered seriously with English manufacturers. This provoked the enactment of the restrictive law of 1732, but most of the colonial demand for hats seems to have been filled by colonial manufacturers despite the law. For ordinary hats, raccoon fur and wool, especially the latter, were generally used in place of beaver.

The "King" Cotton of later history was not in the colonial era even heir apparent to the throne. To be sure some cotton was grown, and a great deal more was imported, but it was almost entirely absorbed by the domestic manufactures to supplement the supplies of wool and flax, and had therefore almost no place in the history of specialized, commercial manufacturing till after the colonial period.

(4) *Iron and Ironwares*

An augury of the importance of iron in American history was the shipment of ore to England from Virginia in 1608. The ore when smelted produced seventeen tons of iron, which the East India Company bought at £4 a ton.

The early history of the iron industry had little connection with the later familiar geography of iron and coal. Fuel for smelting was not coke but charcoal; and the ores were derived from secondary deposits long since for the most part abandoned. The ore used in New England and to some extent in other colonies was bog iron. This is iron deposited in lakes and bogs due to a chemical process connected with decomposing vegetation. This process dissolves the scattered iron salts in rocks and soils and precipitates them in sedimentary crusts or pocket-like deposits in bogs or other areas where they cannot be drained off in solution. In Pennsylvania and northern New Jersey, ore commonly known as rock iron was mined from veins, either by surface pits, or by tunnels, or by shafts. The ore was raised by hand windlass in buckets. To clear the shafts of water, hand pumps were used. By a chimney fire and a flue connected with the shaft, a draft was maintained for freeing the mine of gases. In connection with the larger mines, the ore was commonly washed by a water wheel turning a lateral shaft with spiral teeth by which the broken ore was forced through a water trough.

For the charcoal fuel, hardwoods were used, as hickory, ash or oak. The charcoal pit was a circular open hearth perhaps forty feet across. The wood was stacked in a crude cone, with a central opening or flue. The wood, perhaps forty cords, was covered with a layer of leaves and dirt two or three inches in thickness. The central flue, filled with kindling and fuel, was lighted at the top, and was fed by a draft through small openings at the bottom. By careful and sleepless attention the fire was kept going and at the same time prevented from bursting into flame. The charring process required a number of days, sometimes a week.

Here and there one can still see an eighteenth-century furnace, built into the side of a hill; a square, tapering stack perhaps thirty feet high, with egg-shaped interior; a lower reservoir for tapping slag and molten metal; and an opening near the bottom of the stack for the blast. One can imagine such a furnace in operation, with loads of ore, charcoal, and flux (limestone or oyster shells) being hauled to the hilltop and dumped in alternate layers into the stack at the top, keeping it filled; the bellows near the bottom, forcing air through the burning mass by means of a water wheel; and the flames and gaseous impurities escaping at the top. With the increasing heat, fusion began. The flux had the peculiar property of separating the dross from the iron and forming slag. As the mass melted, the liquid portions of course found their way downward through the stack, the lighter slag being drawn off at the higher level and the molten iron at the lower. The blast was kept going continuously for four or five months, and an output of twenty-five tons a week was ordinarily expected.

The iron was ordinarily run off into a sand mold or trench (the "sow") and from thence into lateral trenches (the "pigs"), and later refined into bar iron in forges. But instead of being run off into "sows" and "pigs," the iron might be run or "cast" directly from the furnace into a large variety of cast-iron goods, usually called hollow ware, as kettles, pots, and pans, firebacks and stoves, and even ornamental pieces.

Cast iron was neither ductile nor malleable, nor could it

be cast into small or intricate patterns. Wrought iron was sometimes obtained by a primitive "bloomery" process of fusing richer ores into a semi-molten state and refining them and improving the texture by repeated heatings and hammerings. Ordinary blacksmiths were able in this way to carry on the whole of the processes of reducing the ore to rough but effective wrought-iron tools and vessels.

But most of the basic raw material for the innumerable arts and crafts of the iron and steel workers consisted of cast-iron "sows" and "pigs." The cast iron was refined by several processes, till in some cases the result was a fairly good grade of steel. The most important of the refining processes in colonial days was the forging of bar iron out of cast iron by heating and hammering somewhat as in the primitive bloomery method. There were also in the colonies a few plating forges for hammering iron into sheets or plates (later done by rolling); and a few slitting mills for cutting and rolling iron into slits or strips. Slit iron was largely used for making nails.

Pig iron and bar iron were shipped to England in small quantities, but were used more largely to supply the needs of colonial blacksmiths, shipbuilders and other craftsmen having need of iron. Types of ironwares most successfully made in the colonies were described by an Englishman as those requiring "little expense and art and where, from the bulk or weight of the foreign manufacture, the expense which may attend the carriage is great. . . . Under the description . . . may be comprehended nails and coarse manufactures of iron, tools which relate to husbandry, to architecture, and which are used by most handicraftsmen; . . . anvils, forge hammers, anchors and cast irons of various kinds for mills, carriages, and other purposes."

In at least one field requiring special skill, colonial craftsmen were close rivals of Europeans. In the making of firearms, combining wood working and metal working, the craftsmen of Pennsylvania evolved a well-nigh perfect instrument—the so-called Kentucky rifle. But in general, importation supplied alike the finer wrought iron and steel and the better grades of secondary iron manufactures.

(5) *Rum*

Before the whiskey of the Scotch-Irish immigrants became popular, rum was almost without a rival as a beverage among the colonists. Beer, to be sure, was brewed, especially at home for home use; and among the wealthy various imported liquors were popular. But rum was for a time almost on a par with the necessaries of life such as flour. Its manufacture was by a simple process of fermentation and slight distillation of molasses, including inferior and soured molasses and the scummings from the sugar pans—"the very dregs and feculencies of the plant." A gallon of molasses made approximately a gallon of rum, and the price was rarely more than fifty cents a gallon.

The rum industry had many ramifications. It was the only important manufacture based on imported raw material, the molasses coming from the plantations of the West Indies. The British West Indies sent a great deal of rum as well as molasses to New England. Rhode Islanders claimed in 1764 that the colony imported about 14,000 hogsheads of molasses a year, of which not more than 2,500 hogsheads came from the British West Indies. Rum was used extensively in the African slave trade, the slaves in turn being sold largely to the sugar planters. Thus a sort of cycle was established—rum for slaves; slaves to the planters to produce molasses; molasses to New England for rum. One is reminded of the farmer whose ambition was to grow more corn with which to raise more hogs so that he could buy more land—to grow more corn to raise more hogs to buy more land, *ad infinitum.* New Englanders found a ready market for fish (even for the "refuse sort" as food for the negroes) and for various other products of the continental colonies in exchange for molasses, which thus became the basis of one of the important branches of colonial trade.

To an Englishman shortly before the Revolution, the amount of rum produced by New Englanders from West Indian molasses was "as surprising as the cheap rate at which they vend it, which is under two shillings a gallon. With this they supply almost all the consumption of our colonies in North America, the Indian trade there, the vast demands of their own and the Newfoundland fishery and in great measure those of the African trade." He adds that they are "more famous for the quantity and cheapness than for the excellency of their rum."

Another indication of the importance of the rum industry is the fact that it was one of the principal sources of money used by New England in balancing its unequal account with England. But the English government was more inclined to favor the islands than the northern mainland because they were economically supplementary rather than competitive, and because West India plantation owners often lived in England. In 1733 the Molasses Act decreed virtually prohibitive duties on molasses other than from the British West Indies. The act was evaded and the industry continued to thrive.

THE ORGANIZATION OF MANUFACTURES

Travellers in Pennsylvania about the middle of the eighteenth century were impressed by Germantown, then a village near Philadelphia, as being inhabited almost entirely by craftsmen, who "make almost everything in such quantity and perfection that in a short time this province will want very little from England." Among the manufactures mentioned were "thread stockings" ("above 60,000 dozen pair"), linens ("the Irish settlers make very good linens"), woolens ("but not, I believe, to any amount"), and "several other manufactures, viz. beaver hats, which are superior in goodness to any in Europe, cordage, linseed oil, starch, myrtle wax, spermaceti candles, soap, earthen ware, and other commodities."

Similar references frequently recur, and indicate extremely varied manufactures in many parts of the colonies. But rarely did they attain any but local significance. The manufactures chosen for separate discussion (those connected with the forests, shipbuilding, textiles, iron and ironwares, and rum) were of outstanding importance. In the first place they furnish illustrations of the transition of manufacturing as a phase of household economy to a specialized and independent status. In the second place, they entered significantly into the economic relations of the colonies with each other and with other countries, as in the rum industry. In the third place, they illustrate the main types of method and of business organization in manufacturing.

The equipment, the processes, and the control of manufacturing centered either in the household, or in the handicraftsman's shop, or in some type or other of mill and furnace.[1]

The prevalence of the simpler forms of manufacturing in connection with the agricultural villages, plantations, and farmsteads has already been noted. The classical illustration is homespun. There are survivals, as in the case of food preservation, on the most up-to-date farmsteads; and it is said that since the adoption of a recent amendment to

[1] For a more detailed discussion of this classification, see Clark's excellent *History of Manufactures in the United States*, ch. VIII.

the constitution, there have been revivals of manufacturing in the home for home use.

Wherever population becomes dense and interchange of goods becomes practicable, specialization is the natural result. As long as manufacturing is by hand rather than by power, the tools are inexpensive; and small, independent shops are practicable.

In the colonies, crafts arose following the same general course of development as in Europe. But the more scattered population, the frontier conditions, and the predominance of agriculture, with economical access to European manufactures, checked their development. The specialization or subdivision of industries into distinct crafts fell far short of the European system. The same colonial craftsman might make various kinds of shoes, and other leather goods, as harness, and even tan his own leather, nor was the demand for a particular article, as shoes, sufficient in most places to engage enough shoemakers for a gild. Labor turnover due to frontier opportunity also checked the rise of gilds. Craft gilds, therefore, while not unknown, were far from prevalent among shop craftsmen.

Household industry and handicraft shops alike involved to some extent the use of mills and furnaces, forges, kilns, etc. Plantations and even the smaller farmsteads were likely to have a small forge and anvil. It was a poor plantation that had no grist mill; and a tar pit or a tanning vat could be maintained by a farmer to supply his own needs and to supplement his income. A blacksmith, though using a forge, was essentially a handicraftsman.

But the use of a mill, a forge, a vat or a kiln did not necessarily create an industry. It was only when production was specialized and centered around such instruments, instead of merely using them in an incidental or supplementary way, that industries distinctively organized resulted. It was with these industries that the principal concentrations of capital and the larger groups of workers were connected.

A brickmaking establishment of 1664 was valued at $25,000 or $30,000. A New Jersey brewery, more or less typical, advertised for sale in 1748, was 48 by 70 feet. The establishment included a malt cellar, a horse-power malt mill, a copper of twenty-three barrels capacity, a storehouse, slaves, live-stock and houses for workers. Some breweries were much larger. A New England tannery as early as 1653 showed an inventory of 772 hides worth nearly $3000. "A representative colonial tannery, situated at Trenton, had 64 vats, 5 lines, 2 water pools, a bark house holding 300 cords, a currying shop and a skin dresser's shop, and facilities for making leather breeches." The owner of a Pennsylvania glass factory claimed an annual income of more than $13,000.[1] But the outstanding instances of the relatively large capital invested and number of workers engaged in mill and furnace industries are to be found in the smelting and working of iron.

The larger iron "plantations" or "manors" where the basic mining and smelting processes were carried on resembled in many ways the tobacco plantations of the south. The iron master owned an extensive area and was a baron, a lord of the manor. The "Big House" was the center not only of the mining and smelting enterprises but of the innumerable subordinate activities of a virtually self-sufficing community. A plantation in the literal sense was maintained. In Pennsylvania, for instance, the crops adapted to that region were grown, as wheat and buckwheat, apples, hay, oats, and rye. The master owned also a grist mill and

[1] These and various other illustrations of mill and furnace industries are mentioned in Clark's *History of Manufactures in the United States*, ch. VIII.

commonly a saw mill, and he maintained a supply of staple goods for sale to his dependents. The families of the wood-cutters, charcoal burners, furnace and forge workers, and others connected with the iron industry did most of the farm work, as well as the spinning and weaving and work of other crafts not connected with iron.

As a social and economic unit the ironmaster's estate closely resembled the plantation. In the latter, manufacturing was subordinate to agriculture; in the former, agriculture was subordinate to manufacturing.

PART III

SEVERANCE OF OLD AND NEW

CHAPTER VIII

SUBORDINATION

"HIS MAJESTY'S PLANTATIONS"

When today the King of England addresses parliament and speaks of "my ministers" and "my navy" and "my empire," it is understood that his phrases have only a ceremonial significance. In early colonial days, "his majesty's plantations" was a phrase of literal meaning. Under the king, the owners were chartered companies or proprietors with royal grants. The crown, the companies, and the proprietors found it necessary to make concessions to the settlers from time to time, but the proprietary idea prevailed. According to law and custom, one can do with his property whatever his interest as owner seems to dictate, subject, to be sure, to certain limitations imposed by his relations to others, particularly to other property owners.

The colonies were the property of the king, and under the king, of certain Englishmen. When sub-titles lapsed, the direct title reverted to the king, or in later theory to the crown. But whether the king, or an individual Englishman, or a group of Englishmen, or the crown on behalf of the country, was regarded as the owner, the concomitant idea of control in the interest of the owner was never abandoned. Unless Englishmen "keep their external provinces and colonies in a subjection unto and a dependency upon their mother kingdom," others "will carry away the greatest of advantage by the plantations, . . . leaving us . . . only the trouble of breeding men, and sending them abroad to cultivate the ground and have bread for their industry.''

Cheap labor was viewed as the great source of national wealth. Even convicts, if sent to the colonies, might enrich the home country, first, by relieving the country of their maintenance, and secondly, by finding productive work to do in the colonies. Thus colonial subordination was evidenced (said an Englishman opposed to the transportation of criminals) by ''the most cruel insult that perhaps was ever offered by one people to another, that of emptying our gaols into their settlements.''

Much was said about ''national'' wealth and the interests of the ''mother country.'' But whenever the general idea of the subordination of the colonies to the welfare of England was embodied in action, the welfare of the nation usually turned out to be the economic advantage of particular Englishmen. Americans, wrote Franklin, were willing to bear burdens and restrain their sense of grievance because of their respect and love for England. But when they realized that petty group interests were passing for national interests, they began to revolve their grievances afresh in their minds. ''It is of no importance to the common welfare of the empire,'' he observes by way of illustration, ''whether a subject of the King's obtains his living by making hats on this or that side of the water. Yet the hatters of England have prevailed to obtain an act in their own favor restraining that manufacture in America; in order to oblige the Americans to send their beaver to England to be manufactured, and purchase back their hats, loaded with the charges of a double transportation.''

CONTROL FOR TRADE'S INCREASE

''For the increase of Shiping and incouragement of the Navigation of this Nation, wherein under the good providence and protection of God the Wealth Safety and Strength of this Kingdome is soe much concerned''—thus characteristically begins the famous act of trade of 1660, with candid omission of concern for effects on the colonies.

The English navigation system is known to every schoolboy as one of the causes of the American Revolution and of the War of 1812. Various acts intended to encourage the use of English vessels had been passed during the fourteenth, fifteenth, and sixteenth centuries. But the first legal formulation of a comprehensive system of control was in 1651 by the Cromwellian government, which had been supported against the king by the merchants of London. This act was accepted, with modifications, by the Restoration government in 1660. By the end of the century a number of supplementary acts had been passed, and the administrative machinery had been improved. The Dutch were the acknowledged superiors of the English in manufacturing, finance, the building of ships, and the carrying trade (trade carried on between two countries or regions in the ships of another country). The acts of trade were therefore intended in the first instance mainly as weapons against the Dutch.

The main regulations affecting the colonies may be briefly summarized. Exports from the colonies must be in ships built, owned, and manned by Englishmen or colonials. Exports desired by England were put on an ''enumerated'' list, requiring shipment to England, and varying from time to time. But sugar, tobacco, rice, indigo, dye woods, tar, pitch, hemp, ship timbers, pot and pearl ashes, and hides were prominently included, and a decade before the Revolution all goods exported from the colonies were to be taken to England for use or for reexport unless their destination was south of Cape Finisterre (northwestern Spain). Many important colonial products were barred from English markets, as salt provisions and grains other than rice. Imports from European countries into the colonies must also be in English or colonial ships, and with a few minor exceptions must come by way of England. If colonials desired, for instance, to wear Italian silks, these could be had only by importation from England, with the various additional costs. The Molasses Act of 1733 was a modified expression of the same principle. It levied prohibitory duties on rum, sugar and molasses from non-British plantations.

CONTROL FOR MONOPOLY OF MANUFACTURES

The description of colonial industries has indicated that conditions in the colonies were not favorable for specialized manufactures. The colonists came mainly for adventure and quick wealth or for land. In the south, agricultural staples were more profitable than manufactures, and easy transportation by river facilitated the marketing of staples and the importation of manufactures. In the central colonies provisions constituted an agricultural staple. In New England agriculture was less profitable but trade and fisheries afforded greater profit than manufacturing. Throughout the colonies, frontier opportunities beckoned.

But in New England and to a less extent in the central colonies, conditions at length made manufacturing more profitable. These colonies engaged in the production of foodstuffs resembling England's agricultural products. English corn laws and other regulations, as well as economic competition, interfered with marketing their products in England. The Molasses Act of 1733 interfered with their West Indian markets. It was increasingly difficult to find specie to meet the constantly unfavorable balance of trade. Should they resort to smuggling? Or should they supply their needs by manufactures? They engaged in both. English restrictions on colonial trade increased the unfavorable balance of trade and stimulated manufacturing. The English in opposing colonial manufacturing unwittingly promoted illicit colonial trade.

Restriction of manufacturing was not so largely embodied in statutes as was the regulation of trade, more dependence being placed on administrative action. The commission of the Board of Trade, issued in 1697, emphasized the duty of the Board to throttle manufacturing in the colonies. Its various inquiries and reports were constantly concerned with the problem. Its instructions to royal governors, as in 1761, emphasized the restriction of manufacturing as one of the duties of governors. In some cases at least the governors took their instructions seriously. Particularly was colonial legislation favoring manufacturing discouraged. The privy council, for example, issued an order in 1724 commanding the colonies to refrain from imposing tariffs on English goods.

Parliamentary action against manufacturing first found expression in the textile industries. Competition with Englishmen in goods made of flax and hemp was not serious. But the woollen industry was the darling child of English mercantilism and must be carefully shielded from every adverse wind. As early as 1699 a law was therefore passed forbidding the making for the market of any articles whatsoever consisting in whole or in part of wool. Any ship or vessel, horse, cart, or other carriage laden with such goods for transportation to market was subject to confiscation, together with the manufactures; and in addition there was a fine of £500. The law was renewed in 1732. It was obviously impossible to prevent household spinning and weaving, and concerning homespun the law was discreetly silent. In 1732 a similar enactment forbade the making of hats for the market.

Another important industry to come under legislative

control was the iron and steel industry. On account of the declining supply of charcoal, England imported increasing quantities of pig and bar iron. In 1729, 19,000 tons came from Stockholm and Gottenburg alone. The annual cost of imports was running from £200,000 to £240,000. In consequence the makers of ironwares were desirous of allowing the colonies to smelt iron but of prohibiting the making of ironwares. The ironmasters and related interests, on the other hand, opposed the smelting of iron in the colonies, but were not averse to selling pig iron and bar iron to colonial manufacturers.

For several decades the controversy was now and then renewed. Action was in one way or another prevented until 1750. On account of serious problems of maintaining uninterrupted access to Swedish markets, from which about three-fourths of English imports came, it was resolved that "the duties on pig and bar iron made in and imported from his majesty's plantations in America ought to be removed." The parliamentary committee in charge of the matter was ordered to include in a draft of a bill for removing duties on pig and bar iron "a clause or clauses to prevent the making of steel, and setting up slitting mills and rolling mills."

The bill as finally passed removed the duties from pig iron and allowed bar iron free entry into London (later changed to give unlimited free entry). As to steel and ironwares, the law decreed that "no mill or other engine for slitting or rolling of iron or any plating forge to work with a tilt-hammer, or any furnace for making steel, shall be erected, or after such erection, continued, in any of his majesty's colonies in America." Such places were to be adjudged common nuisances.

An incidental method of discouraging manufacturing in the colonies was by passing laws to keep industrial skill at home. The exportation of specified kinds of tools and machines to the colonies or elsewhere was prohibited, and skilled artisans were forbidden to leave the country.

The rum industry, it will be recalled, was of great importance. There was no restriction applying in a specific way to the making of rum, but the Molasses Act of 1733 and the Sugar Act of 1764, by taxing the raw materials of rum and promoting the use of imported liquors,[1] indirectly affected one of the most important of colonial industries. If the Act of 1733 had been obeyed, the industry and the trade connected with it would have been disrupted.

CONTROL FOR SECURING STAPLES

English policy was not made up exclusively of "thou shalt nots." It was hoped that by keeping the colonists engaged in ways that harmonized with English industry, they could more easily be kept out of mischievous forms of trade and manufacturing, and that at the same time some of England's economic needs might be supplied. The idea of diverting colonial capital and energy from forbidden into favored channels runs throughout the documents and the writings of the age.

One of the methods used was the granting of bounties. An act of 1705 provided the following sums per ton beyond the market price: hemp, £6; tar and pitch, £4; ship timbers (masts, yards, bowsprits), £1. Late in the colonial period, bounties were also offered for silk and for coopers' materials.

The idea of preferential imperial tariffs, so ardently advocated by Joseph Chamberlain in the late Victorian era, was adopted as early as 1642. Goods taken from England to the colonies or from the colonies to England in British vessels were virtually free from duties. This general ar-

[1] See below, pp. 109, 110.

rangement was soon abandoned, but in specific cases it was utilized from time to time, as by the repeal in 1700 of duties on English woollens exported to the colonies, and by the removal of tariffs on colonial lumber sent to England in 1722 and on iron in 1750.

Indirectly, the colonists were encouraged to devote their energies to favored industries by repayment of duties (drawbacks) on imported goods. Among the commodities reexported from England to the colonies on which drawbacks were allowed were calicoes and other goods imported into England by the East India Company, and foreign hemp, china, and linens. A report of the Board of Trade in 1733 notes a complaint that the people of the colonies "have an advantage over those of Great Britain in the drawback allowed for all India and other goods exported thither which pay a duty in Great Britain, but are subject to no duty of importation" in the colonies. But the advantage of drawbacks was often more than nullified by the disadvantage of being compelled to go to England instead of having direct access to the goods in the country of origin.

By such devices as bounties, preferential tariffs and drawbacks, colonial subordination was sugar-coated, but it remained a bitter pill. It was distasteful, if not because it was an economic disadvantage then simply because it was subordination and not equality. But it should be remembered, as Sir Josiah Child observed, that such was "the policy of the Dutch, Danes, French, Spaniards, Portugals, and all nations in the world," and that Americans inside the empire had privileges they learned to covet when they were on the outside.

GENERAL PRINCIPLES OF IMPERIAL POLICY

The policies of "all nations in the world" having colonies exhibited certain characteristics in common. They were not formulated in a logical, comprehensive system of thought, but were implicit in laws and practices and in the writings of men versed in "political arithmetic."

There was generally what now appears to have been an exaggerated emphasis on metallic money. Europe was emerging from feudal economy, wherein revenues had consisted largely of rents and feudal services, and wherein interchange had often been mere barter. But modern credit instruments were as yet so inadequately developed that a money economy prevailed. How could money be most readily secured? In lieu of gold and silver mines, or of booty captured from one's enemies, the essential method is to sell more than one buys and thus have a favorable balance of trade. But how solve the problem of selling more than one buys? Buy cheap raw materials and sell dear manufactured goods. Build ships and carry your own goods and if possible, goods for others, charging freightage. But how make sure of cheap raw materials, dear manufactures, and shipping? At last the riddle is unraveled: have colonies to produce your raw materials, to consume your manufactures, and to employ your shipping.

But it was soon discovered that the effectiveness of the scheme depended on the character of the colonies. "New England," complained Josiah Child, "is the most prejudicial plantation to this kingdom." The people, he says, are frugal, industrious, temperate, with promise of a "wonderful increase of people, riches, and power." But "since it is the duty of every good man primarily to respect the welfare of his native country, . . . I cannot omit to take notice of some particulars wherein Old England suffers diminution by the growth of these colonies settled in New England." New Englanders, he complains, raise corn and cattle, as do Englishmen; they engage in manufacturing and fisheries; they build ships; they compete with England for the trade of the other colonies. In a word, the industries of New England, unlike those of other colonies, compete with English industries instead of complementing them.

Thus it was held that the *raison d'être* of colonies was to furnish the cheaper materials of basic industries, along with exotics such as rice or indigo, in return for the dearer manufactures of the owner of colonies. By natural inclination and interest of colonials or by imperial authority, the economic activities of colonials must be kept in supplementary and not competitive relations with the center of empire.

It is as true today as it was in the days of mercantilists that the value of dependent territories to an imperial power varies directly with the extent to which they complement the economy of the imperial power, and inversely with the extent to which they compete with it. During the régime of *laissez-faire* and free trade, the prevailing idea was, let nature take her course. If natural conditions in India, for example, favor a complementary relationship, so much the better for England; but if Indians find that manufacturing and trade in competition with England are best for their own interests, then it is England's ill luck. But *laissez-faire* and free trade, failing of general acceptance, have been replaced by a new mercantilism, perhaps in method more urbane and subtle but hardly less effective.

Englishmen, in the contemplation of the failure of eighteenth-century mercantilism in America, have at least one consolation. Had it not been for the Revolution, England would now be a subordinate part of the Empire. Witness the satirical tirade of an Englishman against American insubordination in 1776: "What! an island! a spot such as this to command the great and mighty continent of North America! Preposterous! A continent whose inhabitants double every five and twenty years! Who, therefore, within a century and a half will be upwards of an hundred and twenty millions of souls!—Forbid it patriotism, forbid it politics, that such a great and mighty empire as this, should be held in subjection by the paltry kingdom of Great Britain! Rather let the seat of empire be transferred; and let it be fixed, where it ought to be, *viz.*, in Great America!"

CHAPTER IX

INDEPENDENCE

DAMMING THE STREAM

A revolution is a removal of obstructions in the current of change. In the case of the American Revolution, the analogy of the stream becomes readily apparent.

When the colonies were first planted and while they were small and weak, subordination to England was natural and inevitable. As they grew older and became large and lusty and with England's assistance put an end to the threat of French ascendancy, they naturally no longer thought of themselves as weak and subordinate parts of the empire. In place of subordination, the natural substitute seems to be coordination. For no nation liveth to itself and none dieth to itself. But in place of the development of old-world and new-world nationalities along coordinate lines, the substitute for subordination virtually forced upon the colonies was a sudden severing of relations and the establishment of a separate and independent nation.

"Your grievance," said an Englishman, berating the colonists in 1776, "is the sovereignty of Great Britain; for you want to be independent." He exclaims that an American "will ever complain and smuggle, and smuggle and complain, 'til all restraints are removed, and 'til he can both buy and sell, whenever and wheresoever he pleases. . . . But, my good friend, be assured that these are restraints which neither the present nor any future ministry can exempt you from. . . . In short, while you are a colony, you must be subordinate to the mother country."

If the England of 1763 had had the wisdom of the England of 1783, there would probably have been less talk of subordination of colonials and of their subjection to the restraints of England. But the price of such wisdom seems to have been the experience which made it useless—the loss of the colonies. The England of 1763, instead of moving with the current which was inevitably away from subordination, undertook the hopeless task of trying to stop the stream.

A more rigorous enforcement of colonial subordination to England was suggested in 1763 by a number of circumstances. The French had been conquered and Englishmen were free to turn their attention to making profitable use of the empire. Nationalism and a sense of power, intensified by the victorious war, now found expression in a domineering attitude toward the colonies. The colonial merchants had continued to carry on extensive trade with the enemies of England during the war, and natural resentment in England suggested measures of discipline and control. The cost of the war had been so great that the national debt had practically doubled, amounting to what was then the enormous sum of about £140,000,000. The government was desirous of having the colonies pay as much as possible of the costs of the war. Another circumstance connected with the new policy, undoubtedly overemphasized by many writers but not unimportant, was George III's coming to the throne in 1760, and his insistence on the royal prerogative, at home and in the colonies. William Pitt, who was ousted by George III, was more imperialistic than the king himself. But Pitt saw the danger of a consistent application of imperial theory. George III saw only his prerogative. Pitt was brilliantly inconsistent; George III was stupidly consistent.

George won the quarrel and lost an empire. But the king's rôle has been exaggerated. The Stamp Act, for example, was signed by a commission during the king's insanity.

OLD RESTRICTIONS ENFORCED

The policy of more rigorous enforcement found expression in several ways.

The list of "enumerated articles," consisting of goods to be sent only to England, was increased by the addition of such important items as lumber, iron, pot and pearl ashes (potash and potassium carbonate), whale fins, raw silk, hides and skins. In 1766, exports not "enumerated" were to be sent only to England or Ireland or to countries south of Cape Finisterre (northwestern Spain). It seems that when colonials took their goods to northern European countries they were too much tempted to carry home with them cargoes of foreign goods. This regulation about non-enumerated articles was therefore made as an aid in enforcing the law requiring the colonists to use goods imported from England.

Masters of ships were put under new and rigorous regulations concerning bonds and particularly concerning certificates from a customs office. Customs officials who had been living in England and delegating their work to proxies were replaced or sent back to their posts. New letters of instructions were sent to the governors. Speedy and well-armed vessels were stationed in large numbers along the coasts in charge of naval officers with instructions to seize any vessel suspected of engaging in illegal trade. Seizure was made attractive by the promise of profits by confiscation of ships and cargo. Conviction was made easier by the extension to the colonies of the practice of granting writs of assistance to customs officers. Ordinary search warrants were limited to a specified place and to specified articles. A writ of assistance enabled the holder to use his own discretion as to the premises (house or ship) to be searched, and gave him full authority to make forcible entry, forcible search, and forcible seizure of goods. It was hoped that by this means the popular support of smugglers could be overcome.

NEW RESTRAINTS IMPOSED

At a time when the current of colonial opposition to subordination was naturally strong, the English were not content with invigorating the enforcement of existing restraints; they proceeded to impose new restrictions and to seek additional sources of profit and revenue.

Closely connected with the policy of more effective enforcement was the Sugar Act of 1764; for it was a revival in modified form of the law of 1733 commonly known as the Molasses Act. The import duties levied by the older act on non-British (mainly French and Spanish) molasses were so high as to force the continental colonies either to evade the law or to buy only from British planters. Evasion resulted, the authorities conniving. Thus the British planters were not protected, nor were the customs revenues augmented.

In 1764 it was decided that the law should be revised and enforced. Loud remonstrances were of no avail. The law taxed non-British molasses threepence a gallon, prohibited the importation into the colonies of non-British rum, and permitted the free importation of British molasses and rum. Among various other provisions, the law also placed new restrictions on the importation of Madeira and Fayal wines, popular among the wealthy as was rum among the poorer classes.

Another policy which had already been formulated but which had not been applied before the Seven Years' War except to New England was the control of colonial currency. Restraint of tendencies toward inflation was highly desirable. The English government, however, was in a glass house. Its own policy had been in part responsible for inflation. It had tried to keep the colonies dependent on the home country for manufactures, and had expected colonials to pay for manufactures either in staples not produced in England or else in money. The constant draining of specie from the colonies to pay for English manufactures had been perhaps the principal factor in the disastrous experiments of the colonies with paper money.

The situation was expressed by an Englishman in 1764 when he said that the colonies "have not, within themselves, the means of making money or coin. They cannot acquire it from Great Britain, the balance of trade being against them. The returns of those branches of commerce in which they are permitted to trade in any other part of Europe are but barely sufficient to pay this balance." Such were the circumstances which made particularly annoying the Currency Act of 1764, "to prevent paper bills of credit hereafter to be issued in any of his majesty's colonies or plantations in North America."

NEW TAXES LEVIED

The policy of more rigorous enforcement of the acts of trade, while primarily for the regulation of trade, was secondarily for the increase of the public revenues. The Sugar Act of 1764 had a similar connection with taxation. With the passage of the Stamp Act of 1765, the government adopted a policy of taxation not primarily for regulation of trade but rather for revenue. The occasion was the decision to keep an army in the colonies. The tax was to be collected from users of "skin, vellum, parchment, or paper" for almost every conceivable legal purpose and for newspapers, pamphlets, playing cards, etc. Thus the official stamp or mark on a pack of playing cards was to cost one shilling; on a lease, contract, bill of sale, indenture of apprenticeship, etc., two shillings and six pence; on a college diploma, two pounds; on a license for selling wine, four pounds.

The failure of the Stamp Act due to colonial opposition was followed by its repeal in 1766. The repeal was accompanied by an act asserting the complete authority of parliament over colonial taxation, and by a clever arrangement for collecting in England instead of in the colonies the tariffs on textiles imported by the colonies. During William Pitt's illness, Lord Townshend came forward with new plans to vindicate the authority of England and augment the revenue. His proposals included the reorganization of the customs service by sending Commissioners of the Customs to the colonies. The new taxes proposed consisted only of duties on imports, but these were such commonly used articles as glass, lead paints, tea, and paper. Enforcement was to be secured by legalizing the use of general search warrants or writs of assistance. The revenues were to be used to pay the salaries and other expenses of royal officials in the colonies, thus rendering them less dependent on colonial legislatures. Renewal of colonial agitation was followed in 1770 by the repeal of the duties on glass, paints, and paper, the tax on tea being retained. The tea tax, trivial in itself, occasioned events that were far from trivial.

FRONTIER EXPANSION OPPOSED

Whenever economic or political disturbances had earlier generated discontent, there had been two ways of escape for the disgruntled elements: the sea and the frontier. They could go to sea, or, if men of wealth, fit out a vessel and send it to sea with reasonable assurance of a lucrative illegal traffic; or they could turn frontiersmen and with reasonable ingenuity live in crude comfort.

During the Seven Years' War English policy was rapidly generating discontent. The sources of foreign specie were being dried up, an increasingly unfavorable balance of trade was draining specie into England, and at the same time the issue of credit money was forbidden. The accustomed channels of trade open hitherto by British connivance were now being closed in spite of loud remonstrances and protestations of ruin. New tax policies were becoming less fruitful of revenues than of riots.

Under these circumstances, if England was to prevent a colonial explosion, the frontier safety valve was especially needed. And yet with England in undisputed control alike of the sea ways and of the vast unsettled areas embracing Canada and Florida and extending to the Mississippi, colonials were paradoxically more than ever restricted, not only at sea but in their westward advance. A proclamation of 1763 prohibited settlements to the west of the Atlantic watershed, and the so-called Quebec Act of 1774 subjected the regions between the Mississippi and Ohio rivers to the government of the Province of Quebec. By the former act, land grants and even surveys in the regions beyond the headwaters of eastward flowing streams were forbidden. Settlement was prohibited, and settlers already there were ordered out.

Bold frontiersmen might push their way westward and depend on "tomahawk" claims or "squatter's" rights. But speculators and promoters of colonization were seeking formal grants and looking forward to the time when legal title would be essential to the maintenance of rights. Washington, Franklin, and others later prominent in the Revolution were interested in securing land grants now forbidden.

BREAKING THE DAM: A FLOOD OF OPPOSITION

England, flushed with the pride of imperial triumphs, was inclined to build high the dam against colonial insubordination. Colonial resentment found expression with undisciplined and rude energy. But the violent rejection of Britain's change of attitude was not apparent till after the passage of the Stamp Act of 1765. Colonial agents in England even applied for appointments or made recommendations for appointments to office for administering the Stamp Act. The extent to which the agents of the colonies as well as officials of the English government had misjudged the colonial temper soon became apparent. Agitation assumed the proportions of a flood that menaced the dam and threatened the entire system of English control.

There was recourse to the skull and cross bones in place of the official stamp. Oaths were taken by some to resist the use of stamps—except for bonfires. There was resort to the hanging, beheading, and burning of effigies. Officials were coerced into abandoning their duties in administering the law. Unpopular officials, notably Chief Justice Hutchinson at Boston, were mobbed, their homes invaded, their property destroyed. Colonial legislatures passed fervid "resolves." The excitement led to the first intercolonial assembly (the Stamp Act Congress) not initiated by officials of the Crown. Most influential, probably, were the nonimportation agreements in New York, Massachusetts, Rhode Island, and Pennsylvania, for boycotting English goods.

The nature of the Stamp Act can hardly explain all this. The act was the occasion, but the causes lay deeper. In the commercial communities, the smuggler had long been honored and even the pirate had often been protected. In the frontier communities, the law of Britain was held in repute only in so far as it coincided with the rough-and-ready frontier ideas of justice. The war which had just come to a close in 1763 had been perhaps unusually effective in disrupting economic life, as by inflation of currency, and in demoralizing society, as by the sudden shift of masses of men from the conditions of primitive warfare to the routine of shop and farm or to the uncertainty of unemployment.

The Stamp Act gave the various restless and discontented elements a convenient and common outlet for their emotions. Their troubles were often of purely colonial origin, but the Englishman was a convenient scapegoat. The old restrictions had been recognized as legal, and to object to their enforcement was not entirely defensible. But the Stamp Act was an innovation. It was furthermore an innovation affording politicians a magnificent slogan—"no taxation without representation." It was an innovation affecting colonials of all sections individually and directly. A direct tax is something tangible—and more than likely, something monstrously unjust. Internal conditions following the war, combined with the various English policies already in effect, had put colonials into a state of high tension. The Stamp Act merely touched a peculiarly sensitive "pocket" nerve, and caused the tension to find relief in action.

The action produced its reaction in the repeal of the Stamp Act. When this in turn was followed by the Townshend Acts, imposing duties on certain English manufactured goods, the cue for colonial action was not hard to find. Why not do without English manufactures? The decline of importations from England following the passage of the Stamp Act had been a leading factor in the repeal of the Stamp Act. Formal non-importation agreements were entered into from 1767 to 1769, and riotous methods such as had been used to prevent the enforcement of the Stamp

Act were now used to prevent the importation or use of British manufactures. Merchants who had unwillingly signed the agreements, or who had refused to sign them, were burned in effigy, insulted, mobbed, tarred and feathered. Customs officials were treated in a similar manner. In New York non-importation cut down the imports from £482,000 in 1768 to £74,000 in 1769.

Such tactics at length again brought results. In 1770 the Townshend duties on English manufactures were repealed, and the tax on tea, which remained, was so low that tea could be bought more cheaply in America than in England.

After 1770, discontent subsided. Imports from England had fallen from £2,250,710 in 1764 to £1,336,119 in 1769. They then rose rapidly, and in 1771 amounted to £4,202,472. Extremists in Massachusetts and Virginia, to be sure, kept up the fight and used every opportunity for fanning the embers into flame. Their decisive opportunity came in 1773. The East India Company in 1772 found itself in trouble financially, with more than twenty million pounds of unsalable tea in stock. It appealed to the government for aid, and at the same time brought pressure to bear through a large number of members of parliament controlled by it. The government came to its rescue handsomely, by means of a loan, a remission of payments to the government, and the privilege of sending its tea to America without paying customary auction and export duties.

This meant cheap tea in the colonies. But it meant also that smuggling would be less profitable. Furthermore, smugglers and legitimate dealers alike were outraged by an attempt on the part of the East India Company to dispense with American middlemen with the exception of those who were known to have remained submissive in the late controversies. These, together with the sons or dependents of certain Englishmen whose political influence was desired by the company, were made the consignees. And thus the powerful mercantile classes, who, after the repeal of the Townshend duties, had been favorable to reconciliation, were once more alienated by discrimination and the threat of ruin. The fate of the consignments of tea, as at the "Boston tea party," was the fate of English authority in America.

PROBLEMS OF INDEPENDENCE

With the aid of foreign powers, the Atlantic Ocean, and a bungling English government opposed by many of the English people, the colonies passed successfully from subordination to sovereignty. But the struggle itself gave rise to many serious economic problems unsolved at the end of the war, and peace brought with it other problems no less grave.

Not the least of the questions demanding attention was the condition of public finance. Scarcity of specie had prompted several disastrous colonial experiments with paper money based upon unsupported public credit, and these experiments led in turn to the English Currency Act of 1764 for restraining emissions of credit notes. But the colonial governments, convinced against their will, were of the same opinion still. Under the conditions existing in 1776, it is difficult to see how resort to credit money could have been avoided.

As the shrewd Franklin phrased it, the colonies, at the beginning of the war, "had neither arms nor ammunition, nor money to purchase them or pay soldiers. The new government had not immediately the consistence necessary for collecting heavy taxes; nor would taxes that could be raised within the year during peace, have been sufficient for a year's expense during war." They, therefore, he explains, resorted to the printing of paper bills. Depreciation naturally followed. "The excessive quantities which necessity obliged the Americans to issue for continuing the war, occasioned a depreciation of value." He goes on to explain that the depreciation "has operated as a gradual tax," which he thinks "has fallen more equally than many other taxes, as those people paid most who, being richest, had most money passing through their hands." To an economist the argument of Franklin concerning the effects of inflation may sound more like special pleading than the philosophy for which the Doctor was noted. But his explanation of why the colonies resorted to "the printing of paper bills" is beyond dispute. Bills of credit authorized by the Continental Congress amounted to nearly a quarter of a billion dollars. The actual income of the government from these vast issues, in terms of specie, amounted to less than $40,000,000. After being paid out by the government to meet its obligations, the bills further depreciated till the value was ultimately but a fraction of $40,000,000.

The Continental Congress was newly organized and had no tax-collecting power save by appealing to the states. The state governments continued the tax-collecting function along with the other functions exercised during the colonial period, but without imperial limitations. And yet the states, although in full possession of the taxing power, also resorted very largely to paper notes for financing their part in the war. Their issues amounted to more than $200,000,000.

Depreciation of Continental notes began soon after the adoption of the policy of issuing them, and at length, in 1780, Congress officially admitted that one silver dollar was equal in value to forty dollars in paper. Depreciation continued till the older notes were no longer accepted as currency. They were only "worth a Continental."

With such a medium of exchange, and with no available

security as a basis for loans, domestic or foreign, the upkeep of the armed forces was almost impossible save by requisitions of supplies on the basis of certificates of indebtedness. These in turn were passed on by the holders for whatever could be secured, and thus were added to the volume of depreciated paper. Washington is reported to have said that a wagon load of paper was necessary for a wagon load of flour. Virtual foraging alone kept the armies from starvation even in the midst of plenty.

The effects of the financial situation on the relations of private creditors and debtors, employers and employees, buyers and sellers, were mitigated somewhat by extensive dependence on barter. Thus a storekeeper would accept a farmer's produce in exchange for a craftsman's goods, retaining as compensation a part of what both had for sale, and thus all three got along with a minimum of money. But those who had no readily exchangable goods to offer and received a fixed money income, either for services or for investments, were hard pressed, as were creditors who had to accept payment in depreciated money.

Victory and peace, instead of bringing a solution of the financial problem, brought exaggerated expectations rapidly succeeded by discontent and alarm; a dissipation of the spirit of unity; further resort by states to inflation; the failure of tax plans; and the bankruptcy of the Confederation. Were officials in charge of finances blameworthy, or was the debacle inevitable? If war was to be waged, Franklin's conclusion as to the necessity of inflation seems inescapable. In the words of a noted modern student of the question, "If the result is disastrous, war means a measure of disaster and loss!"

Thus independence from English restraints concerning currency ushered in no monetary golden age, literally or figuratively. Similar disillusion followed escape from other restrictions. The new basis of commerce with England and her surviving possessions was far from pleasing to contemplate. Americans had been inside the empire and wanting to get out. They were now on the outside, but in a commercial sense wishing to be in again. Trade was hampered not only by having now a foreign status in imperial markets but by the chaotic monetary system. Manufactures had sprung up like mushrooms during the operation of the non-importation agreements and while the war cut off English imports, but with the return of peace and of intercourse with England, many of the manufacturing industries disappeared like mushrooms. In their place was unemployment, discontent, maladjustment.[1]

THE ECONOMIC BASIS OF THE CONSTITUTION

It was believed by many that a strong government able to secure favorable commercial treaties, to levy protective tariffs, to impose retaliatory discriminations, and to reorganize finances would suffice to restore prosperity. But when the strong government was in operation it was found that such treaties could not be concluded; discriminations were then in the nature of boomerangs; and the inability of the country to pay for foreign manufactures operated perhaps more effectively than protective tariffs to bar foreign goods. Depression was aggravated by the unsound monetary system; but the causes of depression are traceable to economic forces not primarily connected with public policy.

Nor was the passing of the crisis due so much to political as to economic causes. Americans presently began with characteristic initiative in economic matters to look for trade in new channels. Thus Washington wrote to Jefferson in 1788 that "notwithstanding the shackles under

[1] For an account of trade and manufacturing, see pp. 128–133.

which our trade in general labors, commerce to the East Indies is prosecuted with considerable success. . . . The voyages are so much shorter, and the vessels are navigated at so much less expense that we hope to rival [Europe] and supply, at least through the West Indies, some part of Europe with commodities from thence." Manufacturing, too, was regaining much of its lost ground. Washington refers also to this phase of economic recovery before the new government was in operation. Of certain articles of manufacture, the quantity is "incredible," and the quality "excellent."

Washington, indeed, had less of illusion concerning the relation of government to prosperity than most of the hero worshippers of later times, who have attributed the economic and the political salvation of the people to the Constitution and to the man who was first in charge of the constitutional machinery. Writing in 1788, when it was becoming apparent that enough states would ratify the constitution to put it into operation, he remarked that "many blessings will be attributed to our new government, which are now taking their rise from that industry and frugality into the practice of which the people have been forced from necessity. I really believe there never was so much labor and economy to be found before in the country as at the present moment." Various blessings which he mentions "will be referred to the fostering influence of the new government. Whereas many causes will have conspired to produce them." Again he wrote, before the adoption of the Constitution, that the people are already "emerging from the gulf of dissipation and debt into which they had precipitated themselves at the close of the war. Economy and industry are evidently gaining ground."

Washington recognized, of course, that an "energetic government" would promote industry by making people feel "secure"; that it would be useful in acquiring "equal advantages in commerce"; and that it could aid in relieving the country from "the embarrassments in which it is entangled through want of credit." Such objects were sufficiently important, and there were other economic reasons for ending the political confusion of thirteen sovereign states united merely by an advisory Congress.

The Constitutional Convention was occasioned by an interstate economic problem—the navigation of the Potomac. The Constitution framed by the Convention included among its provisions the control of coinage and of legal tender, of interstate and international commerce, of treaties, and of the public domain, by the Federal government; and extensive powers of taxation were accorded the central authority, including control of import duties. Particularly important in connection with the financial policy of the new government was the provision that "all debts contracted and engagements entered into before the adoption of this Constitution shall be as valid against the United States under this Constitution as under the Convention."

The Constitution begins, "We the people of the United States." It has long been recognized that a very large minority if not an actual majority of the people opposed the "ordaining and establishing" of the Constitution. Students have also come to realize that abstract political theories played no great part in popular estimation. People were influenced for or against the Constitution largely by real or imagined economic interests. The division was largely but not of course exclusively between the various "moneyed interests" on the one hand, and on the other, the farmers and others engaged in relatively self-sufficing industry, whose main concern with government was to be let alone.

Washington privately stated that unless the claims of holders of Continental and state debts could be satisfied, thereby "to retrieve the national character, . . . we may well recur to the old Confederation." The Constitution was the work of these holders of public obligations, together with the classes mentioned by John Adams: "substantial citizens along the line of the seaboard towns," slave-holding planters, army officers, propertied classes; "the moneyed interest, which ever points to strong government as the needle points to the pole."

ECONOMIC POLICIES OF THE NEW GOVERNMENT

What should be done with the debts incurred since the separation from England? This question for a time overshadowed all others. The debts had been incurred in several ways. The loans secured from foreign countries were not a subject of controversy. The domestic debt consisted of ordinary loans represented by formal certificates of indebtedness (Loan Office certificates, corresponding to later bonds); of certificates of indebtedness issued informally in various connections, particularly by purchasing agents in return for supplies; of bills of credit (paper money); and of various obligations incurred by the states.

Hamilton as Secretary of the Treasury favored the taking over or "assumption" of the obligations other than paper money incurred by the states, and the funding of these, together with the debts incurred by the Congress, except its paper money, and repayment at face value. The certificates were negotiable, and had depreciated along with paper money, though not to the same extent. Many of the original holders had disposed of their certificates, in large degree from necessity, at varying stages of depreciation. When Hamilton's plan was being formulated many business men of the cities and many politicians learned of the prospects of redemption at face value, and bought up certificates cheaply from those less informed or less confident. The certificates had originally been owned most extensively in the cities, and by the time Congress acted on Hamilton's plan, urban capitalists and politicians had acquired nearly all of them. A Boston paper favorable to Hamilton's plans tauntingly observed: "They who are in—Grin. They who are out—Pout. They who have paper—Caper. They who have none—Groan."

Congressmen from states most largely agricultural, and owning fewest of the securities, objected that redemption at face value under such conditions was not an honest recognition of obligations but was twofold robbery. In the first place the sacrifices of the original holders, who had accepted a dubious promise to pay in return for aid in winning independence, were ignored in favor of the speculations of capitalists, who had secured the certificates cheaply in many instances by means of "inside" information. In the second place, the agricultural classes would be robbed by taxation to enrich the capitalistic holders of the certificates, or, euphoniously, to add to the fluid capital of business men.

Complete avoidance of repudiation and confiscation would have required redemption at face value of the surviving paper money also (the bills of credit). Paper money was in effect repudiated by redemption at only one per cent of the face value. But Hamilton as Secretary of the Treasury was not interested primarily in avoiding repudiation. He had three main objects. One of these was to establish the credit of the government with business men and with foreign governments; and the redemption of paper money was not necessary for the attainment of this purpose. A second object was to gain for the government the continuing support of moneyed men. To this end he favored funding and a permanent debt instead of outright payment of the certificates, so that business men would have a perpetual stake in the government as its creditors. His third main object was to add to the fluid capital available for industry, especially for urban business. The government obligations, held by business men and secured by taxation, could be used by them admirably for financing business enterprises.

After a hard struggle, objections were overruled. The Congressmen who favored Hamilton's plans were mostly holders of certificates and at the same time were in most cases representatives of regions where urban business, greatly favored by the plan, was most prominent. Thus they were able to combine personal interests with the demands of their influential constituents.

Hamilton's objects in establishing a national debt owned largely by the "moneyed and trading people" were apparent also in his plan for a national bank. The plan called for the use of stock in the public debt for financing the bank. "The chief object of this," he writes, "is to enable the creation of a capital sufficiently large to be the basis of an extensive circulation, and an adequate security for it." That is to say, subscribers to bank stock were to pay for it largely by transferring shares of stock in the public debt. The bank, in turn, was to have power of issuing notes to circulate as "active or productive capital."

The bank as established at Philadelphia in 1791, with branches in other cities, had a capitalization of $10,000,000. One-fifth was subscribed by the government. Three-fourths of the privately subscribed stock was paid for in shares of stock in the public debt. One-fourth was supposed to be paid in specie, but was in large part a matter of credit. Thus the bank's extensive issues of notes were based mainly on stock in the public debt secured by taxation, and on deposits. Patrons of the bank, as well as its stockholders, were mainly either government creditors or members of the economic group to which they belonged. Thus Hamilton was remarkably successful in building up a compact and powerful group of "moneyed and trading people" who could be depended on to support the new government. But sectional and class conflicts ensued, culminating in the Jeffersonian and later the Jacksonian revolts against eastern capitalism.

Hamilton's "moneyed and trading people" were the classes most vitally interested in the public debt, banking, currency, and the "augmentation of fluid capital." Their triumph in these matters seems less incongruous than their control of the public land policy. This was peculiarly the concern of the classes at the opposite pole from the urban capitalists. Yet the early land policy, as well as the other economic policies of the government, was decidedly favorable to eastern capitalists.

During the Revolution, Congress issued warrants for land bounties to encourage enlistment; and these warrants were later bought up extensively by capitalists and army officers. Settlement of new land by individual initiative was opposed. In 1785 the western settlers were described as "uninformed and perhaps licentious people," a menace to security of property, for whom there should be "a strong-toned government." In 1787 the cabins of Ohio squatters were destroyed by soldiers. The government refused to sell less than 640 acres. Purchase had to be made at Philadelphia. A premium was put on the sale of land in large tracts to speculators and promoters.

Among numerous large grants was one in 1787 to the Ohio Company, of Boston, which secured about 1,500,000 acres. Speculation ran riot. The price of land holdings was raised by that "augmentation of fluid capital" which Hamilton had so much at heart. Land speculation was a factor in the ruin of more than one of the great figures of early American history, as Robert Morris, financier of the Revolution, and Colonel William Duer, both intimate friends of Hamilton. Both found themselves at length in debtors' prisons.

Neither speculation nor fraud was confined to eastern capitalists and politicians. Professional men, particularly lawyers, throughout the country became heavily involved. Georgia, which was hostile in the extreme to Hamilton's financial policies, granted vast areas of land to a group of Virginians, including Patrick Henry, whose alleged frauds caused the cancellation of the grant. In 1795 a grant of 30,000,000 acres was made by Georgia to the Yazoo Company. Every member of the legislature who voted for the grant, with a single exception, was interested in the scheme. But in general, the agricultural states and classes were in favor of a liberal policy of selling land directly to the settler, and of securing money in this way rather than by taxation and funded securities, to pay the national debts.

The new government also undertook to encourage trade, shipping, and manufacturing. Here, too, Hamilton was an outstanding influence, though less dominating than in finance. In connection with these phases of post-Revolutionary economic activity, it was soon discovered that the Revolution, instead of bringing independence, had meant merely the continuance of interdependence in altered forms.

CHAPTER X

INTERDEPENDENCE

TROUBLES OF THE THIRTEEN "SOVEREIGN" STATES

"What right had they [in the Constitutional Convention] to say, *We the people?* . . . Who authorized them to speak the language of, *We the people,* instead of, *We the states?*" Thus thundered Patrick Henry against the Constitution. The political doctrines of the time included the theory of absolute sovereignty. Before the adoption of the Constitution, the thirteen "sovereign" nations were insistent that nothing should impair their sovereignty. Even during the war, in 1781, when the revolutionary forces were in direst need of financial backing, the right of levying an import duty of five per cent was denied the Continental Congress, Virginia, for example, first conceding the right and then retracting it in order to avoid a surrender of sovereignty.

But it was soon found that independence unqualified was not producing anticipated results. Congress, though prevented by its lack of power from infringing on the rights of states, was from the same cause unable to free the western posts from British control and to secure desired commercial concessions from foreign powers. Pennsylvania, which early began its career as a center of protection, met with frustration in its tariff policy because of smuggling of duty-free goods from New Jersey. Levying duties on goods from one state to another resulted mainly in vexatious routine and petty jealousy. Virginia and Maryland found that the Potomac, far from being a severing channel justifying separate sovereignties, was a medium of intercourse demanding common action. In a word, it was soon discovered, paradoxically, that unlimited sovereignty had its limitations, and that the "consolidated" government implied by the phrase "We the people" was more nearly in accord with the facts of daily business.

COMMERCE AND THE REVOLUTION

With the Revolution, political subordination to England was at an end. In the state of mind then existing on each side of the Atlantic, political coordination was unthinkable; it was difficult enough in the relations between the states. As for England and America, complete political separation seems to have been, psychologically speaking, the only recourse. But in retrospect it is readily to be seen that economic relations demanded a coordination of political relations between the two nations as well as between the several states. In response to this need all that could be done was to effect an interchange of diplomats. And an eminently respectable European tradition made diplomats little more than spies concealed by the mask of official urbanity.

English colonial policy had striven to keep the colonies engaged in supplying England with needed staples of food and raw materials in return for manufactures. Nature, with some notable exceptions, was on the side of British policy. A new country with abundance of natural resources and scarcity of population and skilled labor turned naturally to agriculture, fisheries and lumbering. An old country with dense population, skilled labor, and plenty of fluid capital, turned naturally to manufacturing. But insistence that the one type of economic life must be accompanied by political subordination and the other by political domination tended to the frustration rather than the forwarding of the forces of nature. The forces of natural adaptation and economic interest inherent alike in the older and the younger societies continued to operate after political subordination was displaced by independence. But natural tendencies were now frustrated by lack of political coordination as seriously as earlier by undiscerning domination.

Temporarily, the advantage was decidedly with the English. Americans were awakened rudely to the realization that in England and the West Indies, where their trade had been most extensive, their ships were no longer accorded the privileges of British vessels. The Navigation Acts closed the West Indies to American vessels and cut off one of the largest branches of American trade. The St. Lawrence was closed to Americans by England, as was the Mississippi by Spain. Preferential duties, bounties, and other advantages previously given to Americans in English markets were no longer granted. Spanish, Portuguese and French tobacco, for example, now in large degree supplanted American tobacco in English markets. Difficulties, indeed disasters, also overtook the fur trade. Flourishing during colonial days, for a time it was ruined by the Revolution. The retention by England of the northern posts from Michilimackinac on western Lake Huron to Dutchman's Point on Lake Champlain, and the shifting of shipping centers to Canada, gave almost complete control to England.

Continental nations had flirted with the colonies during the Revolution, but were coy thereafter. The Revolution, so largely a protest against commercial restrictions, gave rise in America to an ardent desire for reciprocal relations with other peoples. Sweden in 1783 and Prussia in 1785 made liberal treaties. But other powers, with colonial interests and far more important commercial relations, preferred to continue the system of restriction and monopoly.

Of all the situations of American traders resulting from the Revolution, the most curious and diverting if not the most serious was in the Mediterranean. England, Spain, and other modern imperial powers have tried to rope off particular sections of the world for their own exclusive use. In northern Africa the Barbary States (Tripoli, Tunis, Algiers and Morocco) claimed to be "the sovereigns of the Mediterranean." But instead of reserving the Mediterranean for their exclusive use, they were generous enough to allow to others, upon the conclusion of treaties of peace, the privilege of navigating their sea. England had secured such privilege, and as long as Americans were subjects of the English crown, they shared the rights of Englishmen. But Americans, having assumed the rights and powers of sovereignty, must also shoulder its obligations,—including a recognition of Barbary sovereignty. They were reminded of the reciprocity of sovereignty. Did Americans wish to navigate the Mediterranean? Then let them make a treaty of peace, suggested the ambassador of Tripoli at London. The cost?—only thirty thousand guineas to each of the four states, and a little compliment of three thousand guineas to himself. At that time America had no money either to pay for the "treaty" or to wage a "war." And so the Mediterranean trade, another large and flourishing branch of colonial commerce, was lopped off.

Strenuous and ultimately successful efforts were made to open up new channels of trade with China, the East Indies, and Russia, as well as with countries nearer home, and some progress was made soon after the Revolution. But in spite of obstructions trade soon returned in large proportion to the old pre-Revolutionary channels. This was due to British kinship, larger British credits, and smaller British costs. Their intimate knowledge of American markets and of the peculiarities of American taste gave to the English an obvious advantage over Frenchmen or others with different language, habits, and modes of preparing and handling goods. The scarcity of specie and of fluid capital in America made credit relations particularly important, and English merchants profited by American needs. As for the lesser costs of English goods, this advantage of Englishmen is indicated by the case of the French loan for buying clothing for American soldiers during the Revolution. Instead of the money being spent in France, it was taken to Holland and used for the purchase of cloth made in England. The progress of machine technology and of *la grande industrie* gave to England an advantage in cost of production long unchallenged.

MANUFACTURING AND THE REVOLUTION

American manufactures in the colonial period became important enough in a few instances, as was earlier indicated, to attract the unfavorable attention of English authorities. But they were largely confined to homespun cloth and related products of household industry; and to crude, unfinished goods, as iron, lumber and leather, for further fabrication for the most part by European craftsmen.

The first powerful stimulus to manufacturing was the non-importation movement of 1765 to 1770, when the colonists were fighting the Stamp Act and the Townshend Acts. But the manufactures thus brought into being were for the most part of temporary character, in households and small shops, and involved no large or permanent capitalization. The rapid revival of importations from England (the value of imports in 1771 being greater than in any other year preceding the Revolution) indicates the avidity with which colonial consumers returned to English goods.

Then came the non-importation agreements in 1774, and

soon thereafter the war cut off a large part of continental European as well as English manufactures, though even English goods found their way into the colonies to some extent, as in the case of English cloth for the Revolutionary soldiers, bought in Holland with money loaned by the French. Manufacturing in general was powerfully stimulated by non-importation and war. Some of the wartime establishments became the nuclei of permanent towns and industrial communities.

The coming of peace in 1783 was marked by a widespread reversion to English goods. But this rapidly drew out of the country the specie that had accumulated during the war, and since the export trade of colonial days was now largely cut off by the operation of the Navigation Acts, the Americans found themselves presently without means of paying for imported manufactures. This crisis operated, as had the non-importation agreements and the war, to force Americans either to do without manufactures or else to procure them at home. Thereafter the growth of manufacturing was so steady and consistent that Hamilton in 1791 in his famous *Report on Manufactures* was able to enumerate seventeen main branches of manufacturing "which are carried on as regular trades [in contrast with household industry], and have attained a considerable degree of maturity." Each of these seventeen branches represented, in turn, a considerable variety of manufactures, as for instance, the third in the list: "Of wood—Ships, cabinet wares and turnery, wool and cotton cards, and other machinery for manufactures and husbandry, mathematical instruments, coopers' wares of every kind."

But by the time of Hamilton's report, the reviving export trade was providing a basis for paying for manufactures, and England with her new machines and factories was competing strenuously. The natural advantages of farming, fisheries, lumbering, and trade again asserted themselves and for a time once more completely overshadowed manufacturing. The next of the mutations of manufacturing occurred after 1808, and was due to the exigencies of neutrality and war connected with the French Revolution.

REVOLUTION—EUROPEAN STYLE

The French Revolution began, as other revolutions have begun, as a breach in a dam athwart the stream of social change. In France the greater nobles and churchmen were virtually free from taxation, while having the right to appropriate from their dependents and inferiors virtually all their earnings except a subsistence. Lesser churchmen usually lived in their assigned parishes, and minor nobles on their inherited estates, and rendered services to society more or less valuable, no doubt, in return for their income. But many of the greater churchmen and most of the wealthy noblemen enjoyed vast income and almost unlimited privileges without commensurate obligations or services. These few thousand members of the privileged First and Second Estates were the gilded ornaments of a corrupt and bankrupt autocracy.

Beneath—far beneath—the autocratic royal circle, the nobles, and the clergy, there were about twenty million members of the Third Estate. Within the Third Estate was the dominant group of well-to-do business and professional men of the towns. The growing wealth, ambition, and intelligence of the Third Estate and especially of its dominant upper group constituted the prevailing tendency—the stream of social change. The obstacle in the way was the rock of privilege occupied by royalty, nobility and clergy. Removal of the obstacle was by the dynamite of revolution.

"After us the deluge." Many Frenchmen of the privileged classes realized that something unpleasant was about to happen. But they hoped that it could be put off. And so when the explosion came, the deluge of liberated waters engulfed them. Bedraggled aristocrats who managed to crawl out of the flood went about Europe bemoaning their fate and bemeaning their countrymen. It was not long till the other governments of Europe, still dominated by such classes as had lately been so unceremoniously humiliated in France, decided on intervention for the restoration of the old régime in France.

So the revolutionists had to fight again in self-defense. Their revolutionary ardor for liberty, equality and fraternity turned them into missionaries; and because of the concerted opposition of European governments, their missionary zeal soon found expression in wars of liberation. With the rise of Napoleon the tremendous energies liberated by the destruction of the fetters of the old régime were diverted into the older channels of militarism and imperialism. In contrast were the navalism and imperialism of England. Thus the magnificent beginnings of revolutionary idealism degenerated into the closing episodes of the Second Hundred Years' War between England and France.

BITTER FRUITS OF INTERDEPENDENCE

During the quarter century of conflict in Europe initiated in 1789 by the French Revolution, America repeatedly changed rôles. First came the part of the interested spectator trying to decide whether or not to take sides. Then came the rôle of the more or less disinterested neutral. There was no time to change costumes till America found herself playing the part of the innocent and injured bystander. Finally, and anomalously, came the part of the enemy of England without being the friend of France.

With European countries at war, Americans found their

trade to be expanding so rapidly as to dwarf colonial trade in its palmiest days. The total exports in 1769 are estimated to have been worth about £2,850,000, and total imports about £2,600,000. In 1790, the value of exports totaled about $20,000,000, and of imports about $23,000,000. Both exports and imports rose consistently, except for the brief interlude of peace at the opening of the century, till in 1807 the value of exports totaled more than $108,000,000, and of imports more than $138,000,000. Europeans called for American foods and raw materials and for manufactures in the preparatory stages; they also called for the services of American shippers in the carrying trade. Vast quantities of goods were brought in for reexport. At one time reexports even exceeded the imports retained for use at home.

A map showing the ramifications of American trade during the first two decades of the Republic is virtually a map of the world. The Barbary states, the "sovereigns" of the Mediterranean, were induced by means less gentle than the purchase of "treaties" of peace to open the Mediterranean to American ships. France early in the wars of her revolution opened her colonies to Americans. As Holland and Spain in turn had their ships destroyed or driven from the seas, they also welcomed American aid in maintaining continued access to their colonial goods and gold and silver. Even England, at times hard pressed for ships and sailors, relented and allowed Americans a fleeting access to their old-time haunts of trade in the British West Indies.

Americans ranged southward through the Gulf and the Caribbean and the Atlantic and through the Straits; thence northward along the western coasts of the Americas, and westward in the wake of Magellan and of Drake to the Orient, turning the Southwest Passage at last into a highway of trade. In the other direction, they sailed across the

Atlantic to the northern waters; and through the Mediterranean; and southward following the historic route of the Portuguese along the island stepping stones and the coastal slaving centers, and around the Cape, and thence across the Indian Ocean to China and the Islands, where those going westward met the eastbound ships.

Goods gathered in far places were exchanged in Europe for fabricated wares demanded at home and for reexportation. Or they were bartered on the way to Europe, as in the West Indies, West Indian goods in turn being sold in Europe. Particularly extensive was the carrying trade between European belligerents and their colonies.

It was the fruit of the carrying trade that, seeming at first so fair, began first to turn to dust and ashes. England early in the wars began to make trouble. Since France and other countries at war with England had barred Americans from their colonies before the war, the opening of their colonies to Americans during the war (said Englishmen) was merely a wartime measure justifying reprisals on the part of England.

Then it was that Americans resorted to an effective device for "neutralizing" goods secured in the territories of belligerents. "The fabrics and commodities of France, Spain, and Holland," complained an Englishman in 1805, "have been brought under American colors to ports in the United States; and from thence reexported, under the same flag, for the supply of the hostile colonies. Again, the produce of those colonies has been brought, in a like manner, to the American ports, and from thence reshipped to Europe." He went on to complain that Americans even went so far as to destroy all documentary evidence of the place of origin of the goods and even to issue fraudulent certificates and affidavits.

In the view of Englishmen, Americans were blameworthy

not only for trading with the colonies of England's enemies but for doing so with the aid of English mariners who had been encouraged to leave their own vessels in favor of service under American masters. "We not only allow the trade of the hostile colonies to pass safely, in derision of our impotent warfare, but to be carried on by the mariners of Great Britain. This illegitimate and noxious navigation, therefore, is nourished with the life blood of our navy." In the absence of international agreements to the contrary, Americans could hardly be blamed for seizing an opportunity for profitable trade. Nor were inducements to English sailors in the form of better pay, pleasanter service, escape from war and opportunity for naturalization as reprehensible on the part of Americans as they were vexatious to English masters and officials of government. Britannia, encountering difficulty in ruling the waves, indulged the easy retort that America was waiving the rules.

Legitimate freedom of the seas for neutrals—that, so Americans contended, was the basis of their trade. The American point of view then emerging and more or less consistently maintained throughout American history, may be briefly summarized. (1) Free ships (the ships of neutrals) make free goods (even if originating in belligerent countries) except in the case of contraband of war. (2) Belligerents must grant immunity from confiscations or molestation to private property at sea except in cases of contraband carrying and blockade running. (3) Contraband of war must be defined by mutual agreement and limited primarily to munitions of war. (4) Blockade, with its privilege of confiscation of blockade runner's goods and vessel, must be so limited in extent as to be reasonably effective.

As long as war is war, laws and treaties will become scraps of paper. Each major conflict among the nations becomes more ruthless and destructive than the last. In the battle of the giants of the days of Napoleon and Pitt, by blow and counter blow the body of the law was dismembered. England's final thrust was in 1807 when she declared that France and countries aiding France by excluding the British flag were in a state of blockade. Neutral as well as belligerent vessels were barred except those that stopped at English ports, secured licenses, and made various payments to the English government. Otherwise, vessel and cargo were subject to seizure and condemnation. British officers were given further powers to impress neutral sailors adjudged to be Englishmen into the British navy. Then came Napoleon's *coup de grâce.* In the grand manner, "Napoleon, Emperor of the French, King of Italy, Protector of the Confederation of the Rhine," not only proclaimed the British Isles to be in a state of blockade, but declared that any vessel submitting to search by the English or conforming to English regulations denationalized itself and subjected itself to confiscation by the French or their allies.

Pity the poor neutral between the devil and the deep sea and unable to decide which was which. From the issuing of these decrees and orders in council in 1807 to the declaration of war in 1812, about 850 American ships were seized. These losses were suffered in spite of the Embargo Act of 1807 for keeping American vessels at home (applied in 1809 only against England and France), and the Non-Intercourse Act of 1809 for keeping French and British goods out of America. These defensive and retaliatory measures proved ineffective, partly because of extreme hostility at home, especially in New England. The abnormal prosperity and activity of the trading centers was now replaced by a sudden cessation of business and collapse of prosperity. Among the various conflicting solutions proposed, war became increasingly popular. But war with whom? Logic called for war with neither or for war with both. But if in purpose England had not been the chief of sinners against American rights, she had at least been more successful. And France had but recently come to the aid of America against England—not, to be sure, because she loved America more but England less.

English orders in council, Napoleonic decrees, embargo, non-intercourse, war, post-war competition—these were the winds that withered the most flourishing branches of American business. But the blight of trade was the fructification of manufactures. Capital accummulated by trade was rapidly transferred to manufacturing, and the cutting off of imports gave hope of ready sale with large profits. Old industries revived and new industries took root. In textile manufacturing, progress was especially rapid. It was estimated that the number of bales of cotton used increased from 1,000 in 1805 to 90,000 in 1815, and factory methods were being introduced.

But the end of the war and the sudden influx of English manufactures upset the calculations of business men once more, and helped to bring on the panic of 1819. It was thought at the time that the problem of competition was largely a matter of general post-war readjustments. But soon there came the realization that a new and continuing force was in operation—the competitive power of the machine. Until America could make adjustments to this new factor, the fruits of interdependence would remain unpalatable.

ATTEMPTED ISOLATION

With the signing of the treaty of peace in 1814, there remained a number of problems for later adjustment. A commercial convention with England adjusted trade on a basis of nominal reciprocity, but the exclusion of American vessels from the West Indies gave England a decided advantage. English vessels were commonly used even in the export of American lumber and foodstuffs. Other agreements with England concerned boundaries, fisheries, and the navigation of the Great Lakes. From Spain Florida was secured in 1819, and the first international treaty line to the Pacific was run to the forty-second parallel and thence due west.

Whatever Europeans may have thought of Americans, it is apparent that by the end of the Napoleonic period Europe inspired Americans with no excess of confidence or esteem. The influence of the course of events in Europe on American business during the early years of the Republic was even more decisive than had been the influence of English authority on colonial business. With the coming of peace and with the adjustment of the more important problems of trade relations and fisheries and boundaries, Americans were willing to accept the advice of Washington about European entanglements in business as well as in politics. The new orientation was soon apparent in a number of ways.

The decline of shipping, after the momentary flood of imports from 1815 to 1818 had subsided, greatly reduced the registered tonnage. In 1810 there were 984,269 registered tons; as late as 1840, the tonnage was less than 900,000.

While foreign commerce, especially the carrying trade, was contracting, there was corresponding internal expansion. The most vital weakness in the plan of isolation was dependence on foreign manufactures. The more than tenfold increase in importations between 1814 and 1816, largely of manufactured goods, threatened to destroy a large part of the plants established during the preceding decade. Personal interests, combining with popular desire to escape from European contacts, resulted in the tariff of 1816 and subsequent protective measures, though more effective than protection was the introduction of improved methods.

Finally, the new orientation following the War of 1812 resulted in the Monroe Doctrine. Americans were to be protected from European contacts by preventing the further "intrusion" of Europeans in the Americas.

PART IV

SECTIONS AND CLASSES

CHAPTER XI

FRONTIERSMEN AND FARMERS

SECTION VERSUS CLASS

Throughout American history, but especially during the half century preceding the Civil War, the division of the country into sections is a fact of striking importance. Less conspicuous but no less important is the division of the population into economic classes.

The student of industrial history must recognize both class and sectional cleavages. If the intention is to emphasize the influence of natural factors, or to think of man as a creature of environmental forces, then it is appropriate to set the picture in a geographical frame. If, on the other hand, it is desired to stress the human rôle in the utilization of natural resources, or to emphasize the relations of men to each other instead of to nature, it would appear that economic groups provide a more appropriate setting.

THE EXPANDING DOMAIN

When the thirteen colonies won their independence, some found themselves possessed of extensive unsettled western lands, and some had none. There were many conflicting claims. The ensuing quarrels and jealousies added seriously to the problems of Congress and of the states in their relations with each other. But among the outstanding accomplishments of the period of the Confederation preceding the adoption of the Constitution was the cession of a large part of their lands by the states to the Congress of the Confederation. By 1802 all the state claims had been surrendered.

Between 1783 and 1803, the only territorial changes were the transfers of claims by the states to the national government, and adjustments of disputed boundaries. In 1803 came the acquisition of Louisiana territory. President Jefferson's insistence on the cession of Louisiana by France to the United States was largely a result of the pressure of settlers west of the mountains, who had been making the free navigation of the Mississippi a condition of their allegiance to the government of the United States. Furthermore, Jefferson was convinced that the country must remain predominantly agricultural if it was to maintain democratic institutions, and with the addition of Louisiana there were potential agricultural areas to offset for a long time to come the growth of trading, manufacturing and commercial classes on the seaboard.

The Louisiana purchase treaty left the boundaries ill-defined, and subject to Spanish claims and Spanish treaties. The question of immediate concern was the boundary between Louisiana and West Florida. Many Americans were making their way into the Florida country, and were exposed to the Indians and to the somewhat capricious policy of Spanish officials left practically without supervision by the home government, on account of the European problems of Spain during the Napoleonic era. Spanish control so near the mouth of the Mississippi, with a disputed boundary, was resented even after the purchase of Louisiana as a menace to the unimpeded navigation of the Mississippi. The impulse to secure the Florida country was further strengthened by knowledge of intrigues between the Spanish authorities and the frontiersmen of the southwest. After various questionable episodes, as the invasion of East Florida by the impetuous Jackson in 1818, in pursuit of a band of Seminole Indians, a treaty was signed in 1819 by which, for the payment of not more than $5,000,000 of Spanish claims, the legal title to the Floridas passed to the United States.

At the same time, the western boundary of Louisiana was fixed at the Sabine River, and the possible claim of the United States under the Louisiana purchase treaty to the region between the Sabine and the Rio Grande was surrendered to Spain. Texas had once been under the French flag; in 1819 it was a part of the Spanish dominions. Shortly thereafter the revolt of Mexico put it under the Mexican flag. After the Texas Revolution of 1836, Texas for a time became a republic under its lone star flag. Texans desired annexation to the United States, but the question of slavery in the territories was retarding the policy of expansion. It was not till 1845, when British intervention was used as a club against the anti-slavery party, and the question was associated with the occupation of Oregon, that annexation was finally accomplished.

Mexico had never recognized the independence of Texas. Annexation, she declared, meant a declaration of war, and diplomatic relations were severed. Then came the Mexican War of 1846–1848. And thus it was that the boundary of Texas was fixed at the Rio Grande, and that California and New Mexico were acquired by the United States.

The northern boundary of California had been fixed by treaty with Spain in 1819 at the forty-second parallel. Russian claims had been surrendered south of 54° 40′ by treaty with the United States in 1825. In 1818, England and the United States agreed to extend the boundary line between the United States and Canada westward along the forty-ninth parallel to the Rocky Mountains. The Oregon country west of the Rocky Mountains, north of 42°, and south of 54° 40′ remained in dispute. In the early 'forties Americans in large numbers moved westward along the Oregon Trail, and propaganda for the Russian treaty line of 1825—50° 40′—afforded the supporters of Polk for president an effective campaign slogan—"fifty-four forty or fight." As is often the case after a political campaign, Polk, the successful candidate, had a sober second thought. So did the English authorities. The result was the treaty of 1846, agreeing to the forty-ninth parallel.

Thus the years 1845 to 1848 witnessed the annexation of Texas, the occupation of Oregon, and the acquisition of California and New Mexico. The Gadsden Purchase of 1853 was merely a minor extension of territory at Mexico's expense, for the purpose of securing a more favorable right of way for a transcontinental railway. This tremendous outburst of imperial ardor rounded out the country's contiguous frontiers, furnished problems of assimilation that brought on the acute indigestion of Civil War, and gave ample room for many decades of pioneering.

DISPOSING OF THE DOMAIN: THE PUBLIC LAND POLICY

Not all of the unoccupied land in the territories mentioned in the preceding survey of territorial expansion belonged to the federal government. Particularly is this true of Texas. But the unalienated domain held by the central government has been so vast as to dwarf state lands and policies. The Federal land policy has been a factor of utmost influence in American history. Its earlier importance pertained primarily to pioneering and the colonizing of the continent. Its later importance is due more largely to its connection with the control and utilization of natural resources.

A notable achievement under the Articles of Confederation was the adoption of the rectilinear survey system. In the main this concerned the technique of handling the public domain. More important economically were larger questions of policy. It will be recalled that in colonial times the plan adopted was to make large proprietary and charter grants; a policy which found expression in the late colonial period in the great land companies, notably the old Ohio Company with 500,000 acres. It will also be remembered that with the acquisition of western lands from the states by Congress, the policy of large grants was continued, and a similar policy was adopted by the government under the Constitution. The purpose was to sell in large amounts, to capitalists only, and not to actual settlers. An act of 1796 provided for the sale of specified areas in tracts of not less than a section, the price to be not less than two dollars an acre. A minor concession to the demands of would-be settlers was the opening of land offices at Pittsburgh and Cincinnati as well as at the capital.

The law failed to stimulate the settlement of the west or to appease the men of small means who wanted land. In 1800, with the turn of the tide against the financial interests up to that time dominant in the government, a more liberal land law met in part the demands for a democratic policy. The size of tracts was reduced to 320 acres. The minimum price remained two dollars per acre. Four additional offices where land could be bought were opened in the west. The important element of credit was introduced, purchasers being allowed four years in which to pay. The credit policy, combined with the abnormal European war-time demand for American produce, brought on an era of over-expansion and speculation, with later deflation and collapse. The next formulation of policy, in 1820, omitted the credit feature but reduced the minimum price from $2.00 to $1.25, and also the minimum quantity from 320 acres to 80 acres.

Lands were not offered for sale until they had been officially surveyed and blocked out into the rectangular system of sections and townships. But the frontiersman was unwilling to wait for the surveyor and the proclamation of sale. A pioneering type arose, half farmer, half hunter,—a reversion to the primitive,—with an aversion to neighbors. In addition to such individualistic frontiersmen, communities of farmers were sometimes formed in advance of actual sale of lands. Many who were unable to meet the conditions of the earlier land laws, either as to making payment or as to visiting the place of sale, took matters into their own hands by settling on lands of their choice without title. The irregular occupation of lands in advance of survey and sale caused trouble alike for the settlers, for the government, and for purchasers. As the idea of democratic sale and settlement gained ground, the pressure on the government for protecting the trail blazers and illegal occupiers resulted in preemption laws. A settler able to show actual residence on the land, and actual cultivation of a portion of the tract claimed, was looked upon as having preempted the land as against the claims particularly of speculative purchasers. The preemption system, or legal recognition of "squatter's rights," was formulated in a long series of legislative acts and executive orders, beginning as early as 1801, and culminating in the act of 1841.

There was a natural and not very abrupt transition from the preemption system to the homestead act of 1862. It was made a party issue by the Free Soil Democrats in 1852, in a declaration to the effect that the public land should not be sold to individuals or to corporations, but "should be granted, in limited quantities, free of cost, to landless settlers." Under the preemption laws, to be sure, there was ultimate payment for the land, but the amount was small, and the preemption system operated as a credit system by which payment was deferred until improvement of the land made payment no heavy burden. The size of a homestead was a quarter section. The condition of acquiring title, aside from paying a small fee, was actual residence on the land for five years. Even aliens upon declaring their intention to become citizens could make entry but title depended on full citizenship. A homestead was exempt from foreclosure for debts incurred previous to acquisition of title.

The public land policy included also the granting of lands for special purposes; most prominent among these was education, as when every sixteenth section was reserved for public schools in the states admitted before 1848. The lands thus reserved were handled in various ways, in some cases advantageously, but often at a sacrifice. Grants of land or of percentages of money from land sales were also made for road improvements, canals, and railroads.

It is to be noted that no distinction was made in land titles between agricultural resources and special resources such as minerals. The contrasts between the two became increasingly important. Agricultural resources are permanent, and even if exhausted by improper use, are renewable. Most of the other resources of the land are temporary and non-replacable, as oil or iron. The utilization of agricultural resources may be, and generally has been, individualistic and small-scale in method. The utilization of special resources is more likely to require corporate organization and large-scale methods, as in drilling oil wells or developing coal mines, and in marketing the output. Farming is by nature competitive, due to the wide diffusion of productive soils and the relative ease with which farming may be undertaken. The exploitation of special resources lends itself more readily to monopoly due to the limited areas where a particular article of commerce, as oil, is found, and to the impossibility of individual exploitation. There is a final contrast, of utmost importance historically and in contemporary society. The liberal sale and free distribution of farming lands has promoted equality of opportunity and the wide diffusion of wealth. The liberal sale and free disposition of titles to special resources has promoted inequality of opportunity and concentration of wealth. The number of farms at the disposal of the government was long sufficient to meet all demands. The quantity of land containing such special resources as oil, iron and gold was unknown, but had it been known it obviously would have been inadequate to meet more than a fraction of the demand.

The government could either have reserved from sale, and developed publicly or under lease or contract, such lands as were known to have special resources or values; or it could have granted lands with title limited to agricultural resources. But when the public domain was being alienated, no one knew, in respect to most of the land, what portions contained special resources or potential value for townsites; and apparently no one thought seriously of limiting the title to agricultural purposes. The idea of distinguishing between agricultural rights on the one hand and subsoil and water-power rights on the other hand has recently been adopted. After the best cars have been stolen the garage is locked.

PIONEERS' PARADE

In all the world's history what is more epic than the movement of the frontier across the American continent? What materials for Homeric tales in the grand manner! If only Americans, like the Greeks, were without self-consciousness and historical iconoclasm, perhaps their

Homer would yet arise to sing the glories of their gods and heroes. But modern scientific civilization, whatever may be its advantages, robs us of a pleasing epic simplicity and of capacity for mistaking the mellowing illusions of sunset for the realities of midday.

The first frontier was formed by Virginia gentlemen who soon gave up their courtly manners for Indian etiquette, and by Puritans whose aptitude for prayers was quickly supplemented by equal skill at potshots. By the end of the seventeenth century, the advancing European tide had forced its way in many places to the fall line but rarely except in the case of fur traders was there any attempt to go back of the navigable waters of eastward flowing streams.

The areas between the fall line and the Appalachian gateways were extensively occupied before the Revolution. The exhaustion of tidewater tobacco lands; monopolizing of tidewater lands by earlier settlers, and especially in the south by the great planters; the coming of Germans, especially the "Pennsylvania Dutch," and of the Scotch-Irish; the transportation of convicts, as for instance the twenty thousand sent to Maryland from 1750 to 1770; the freeing or fleeing of indentured servants;—these were the principal factors in filling the uplands from Pennsylvania to South Carolina and Georgia before the Revolution. From 1700 to 1775 the population increased from about a quarter of a million to about three millions. For a time the frontier was checked at the Appalachian barrier, nature there being reenforced at first by the hostility of the Indians and the French and after 1763 by the opposition of the Indians and the English.

The frontier, on the move again, made its next advance through the Appalachian gateways and in the form of a wedge to the Mississippi. This movement extended approximately to 1820. New Yorkers and New Englanders occasionally found their way westward up the Mohawk to the lake country or by a cross-country route to the Alleghany valley and thence to the Ohio. But a simpler and less dangerous route was by water to Philadelphia or Baltimore and thence by land. In Pennsylvania the military road cut by General John Forbes in the French and Indian War by way of Lancaster and Bedford to Fort Pitt was extensively improved and made the chief gateway to the west. From Baltimore as well as from Philadelphia a road led direct to the Ohio, by way of Fort Cumberland on the Potomac and thence by Braddock's Road to Fort Pitt, or by the National Road to Wheeling, lower on the Ohio. The Cumberland Road also tapped the Shenandoah valley of Virginia. Virginia, the Carolinas and Georgia had a network of roads, with more than one gateway across the mountains. But most of the roads gave access to the Wilderness Trail through the Cumberland Gap between the Tennessee and Cumberland rivers. Through this gap and down these rivers coursed the flood of emigrants from Georgia, the Carolinas and southern Virginia:

> "Some to endure and many to fail,
> Some to conquer and many to quail,
> Toiling over the Wilderness Trail."

The streams of the western Appalachian watershed from southern New York to the Carolinas flow in an ever narrowing depression till they converge in the Ohio. The valleys of the Ohio, the Cumberland, and the Tennessee comprise a gigantic triangle. The movement of population, beginning at the Appalachian base of the triangle, filled the triangle, forming a wedge. Having penetrated to the Mississippi, the wedge was flattened against the core of the continent till it extended northwestward along the Mississippi and the Missouri, and southward to the Gulf. In the

Gulf region it spread over southern Louisiana and West Florida. In the meantime people were reaching Lakes Erie and Ontario by moving directly westward or northward from New England, New York, Pennsylvania, and Ohio, and were reaching the Gulf by moving directly southwestward or by detouring by water around Florida. But in the main the movement was in western wedge formation to the Mississippi and thence along the Great River.

By 1821 these population movements had led to the admission of eleven states: Vermont, Kentucky, Tennessee, Ohio, Louisiana, Indiana, Mississippi, Illinois, Alabama, Maine, and Missouri.

Slowly after 1820 the frontier moved directly westward, and more rapidly after about that date there were parallel northwestern and southwestern frontiers.

The rapid advance of the northwestern frontier was due to several circumstances. The Appalachian barrier was pierced by the Erie Canal, constructed from 1817 to 1825. By treaties with the Indians between 1816 and 1830, a stretch of Indian lands extending from Lake Erie to the Missouri River was ceded to the government. Steam navigation on western lakes and rivers facilitated emigration and trade. The capture of the extensive fur trade from Canadians by Astor's American Fur Company, aided by American legislation in 1816 expelling foreign fur traders from the United States, called attention anew to the regions east and west of Lake Michigan. Fur traders were followed by miners attracted in hordes by the rich veins of lead to be tapped by shallow "diggings" with little labor. As early as 1823 an operator arrived with an outfit extensive enough to employ a hundred and fifty slaves. As the miners followed the fur traders, so the miners were followed by farmers, craftsmen, and permanent homeseekers. But before stable conditions were attained an Indian war was fought, new cessions were secured from the Indians, and the soldiers who engaged in the war (the Black Hawk War of the early 'thirties) carried home with them news of the wonderful northwest. Most vital of all the factors promoting the advance of the northwestern frontier was its ease of communication eastward by the lakes and the Erie Canal and the later railroads, and southward by the Missouri and Mississippi rivers. Sign and symbol of this was Chicago, first gaining a place in the census in 1840 and springing into a city of more than a hundred thousand before the Civil War. The western limit was the semi-arid belt beginning near the ninety-fifth meridian in eastern Kansas.

While the northwestern frontier was moving rapidly toward the semi-arid western plains, there were several factors also favoring the southwestern advance. First in importance was the acquisition of Florida (1819). While treaties were being made with the Indians of the northwest, similar cessions were being secured from the southwestern Indians. In 1835 they gave up all of their lands east of the Mississippi and agreed to removal to the Indian Territory. Ample room for expansion was afforded by the acquisition of Louisiana and Florida and the virtually unimpeded settlement of Texas. The main motive for expansion was to supply the growing demand for cotton due to the industrial revolution. Expansion was facilitated by the abundance of navigable streams flowing into the Mississippi and the Gulf, and by the development of steam navigation. In contrast with independent small-scale farming in the northwest was the plantation system projected westward from the seaboard tobacco states. The limit of plantation settlement was the semi-arid belt extending westward from central Texas.

But the pioneers of the cattle industry were gradually extending the frontier still farther westward.

Thus for a generation after the central wedge had penetrated to Missouri, the northwestern and southwestern frontiers rapidly advanced and the midwestern frontier moved slowly toward what was supposed to be the Great American Desert. The region extending from western Minnesota and Iowa, eastern Kansas, Indian Territory, and central Texas westward indefinitely to the mountains was looked upon as hopelessly barren: "The Creator seems to have said to the tribes of emigrants that are annually rolling toward the west, 'Thus far shalt thou go and no farther.'" As late as 1856 a western explorer told the Association for the Advancement of Science that "these plains west of the one hundredth meridian are wholly unsusceptible of sustaining even a pastoral population until you reach sufficiently far south to encounter the rains from the tropics." Its one advantage apparent to the settlers was in affording a convenient area for disposing of the Indians without having to wage wars of extermination.

In contrast were the attractions of the Pacific. Unpleasant experiences caused explorers and frontiersmen to paint the adjacent plains in hues too somber; while to the scene beyond the mountains, distance lent enchantment. To motives of adventure and of gain were added the jingo tendencies of the 'forties, when "fifty-four forty or fight" roused unwonted interest in the Oregon country, and when the war with Mexico focussed the attention of the nation on California. To the impulse of patriotic pride and to the attractions of climate and soil and access to the sea was added the lure of gold.

And so in the 'forties and 'fifties the question that agitated the people of migratory tendencies from Florida to

Minnesota and from Maine to Texas was the question of getting to the Pacific coast. A popular route from the western frontier left the Missouri River in the region of Independence and Leavenworth, led across the plains south of the Platte River, crossed the mountain pass to the west of Fort Laramie, reached the Snake River, tributary of the Columbia, at Fort Hall, and then diverged northwestward as the Oregon Trail and southwestward as the Northern California Trail. A southern route having advantages particularly of relative freedom from snow was the Santa Fe Trail long in use to Santa Fe and continuing as the California Cut-off and the Spanish Trail to Los Angeles. From the region of Great Salt Lake a number of routes found precarious courses over the deserts and through the various passes. Some sought the coast by following substantially the trail of Lewis and Clark to the north of the Oregon Trail. Others, especially among the 'forty-niners and their successors, found their way across Mexico and Central America. By way of Panama a monthly service was organized. Easterners in large numbers went by way of the Horn, even chartering ships for the four months' voyage. William H. Seward, on his way to Washington in 1849 as newly elected senator from New York, remarked that "the world seems almost divided into two classes, both of which are moving in the same direction; those who are going to California in search of gold, and those going to Washington in quest of office."

Thus it came about that in the mid-century era there was added to the midwestern, northwestern, and southwestern frontiers the Pacific coast frontier. But in a few years the coast was peopled and measurably civilized, and the new frontier began its eastward march to meet the older westward moving frontiers and to conquer the last and mightiest obstacles of desert and mountain.

THE LIFE OF THE FRONTIER FARMER

The types of farming that developed during the colonial period,—plantation, village, and farmstead,[1]—continued throughout the era of frontier expansion, but the New England village type of economy was virtually supplanted by the separate farmstead. In the southern areas adapted to cotton culture, new plantations were often established without the frontier farmstead intervening. In the more favorably located areas of the east and of the Ohio drainage basin, farmsteads passed from the stage of self-sufficing subsistence farming to the production of marketable surpluses to supply the growing towns and the southern plantations. But the vast majority of farmers remained substantially self-sufficing.

Old men recalling their boyhood days even in such a favorably situated region as Illinois and Indiana speak of going to town two or three times a year and depending largely on such products as hickory nuts and maple syrup for money. With zest they tell of gathering and hulling eight or ten bushels of hickory nuts during the season and selling them at a dollar a bushel, and of maple syrup time and the sale of a few surplus gallons at seventy-five cents a gallon. From the formal records of history the reconstruction of the life of the frontier farmer is virtually impossible. But there are not only the memories of old men; there are occasional diaries and records of travel; and there are stories that exhibit a sense of realism and a respect for historical verity, notably the writings of Hamlin Garland and O. E. Rölvaag.

When viewed as a whole and in restrospect, glamorous, dramatic, even epic in quality was the movement of the frontier across the continent. The life of the individual

[1] See above, pp. 50–55.

farmer, when viewed at closer range, reveals abundant courage and occasional adventure but a mode of life that was crude, harsh, depressing, and severely limited in its possibilities.

FRONTIER INFLUENCES

It is often said that America is materialistic. The term is vague and much misused. But if it is intended to indicate merely a preoccupation with problems of the natural environment, it may perhaps be properly applied to America. There has been an unremitting struggle with material forces—the subduing of wild beasts and wilder men, the clearing of forests, the piercing of mountains, devising means of transportation over magnificent but perplexing distances, and acquiring a technology adapted to ever varying and expanding environmental conditions. Such problems have no doubt given to Americans a bias, an outlook, that those of older societies and of traditional and urbane patterns of behavior may naturally consider materialistic. There has been a constant opening up of new economic opportunities with fortune recurrently favoring even the humblest with chances to "strike it rich" in gold or oil or unearned increment or clever handling of the real or fancied wants of their fellows. The bigness of economic opportunities, the bigness of environmental problems, the bigness of the American scene as measured by the continent-embracing frontier—all this has given an exaggerated value to bigness as a quality. There is a tendency to make bigness the measure of greatness and of value and to place the stamp of approval on big farms, big fortunes, big businesses, big cities, even big institutions of art and learning, simply because they are big.

In subduing the continent, enormous obstacles have been overcome. In the triumphant progress of American pioneers, a ruthless and masterful temperament has been evolved. The great American motto might well be the words inscribed on the wagons of early emigrants to Colorado: "Pike's Peak or Bust." Masterful and uncompromising methods first used in gaining ascendancy over nature have been readily transferrable to human relations. This tendency, accentuated by the influx of Europeans accustomed to servility in class relations, has been destructive of democratic relations between classes, supposedly promoted by the frontier.

Among frontiersmen there was usually at first a crude democracy based on relative equality of opportunity, but this was short-lived. Extreme individualism was the outstanding trait of frontiersmen; and this was little more compatible with equality of opportunity than was the old-world system of aristocratic government which the frontiersmen sought to escape. Aside from questions of differing capacities, unregulated individualism soon destroys equality of opportunity. Fortunes even of unborn generations are made or marred by accidents of location in relation to future trade routes or town sites, or undiscovered subsoil resourccs, or adaptability of the land for supplying market demands as yet non-existent and unforeseeable. Maintenance of equality of opportunity, one of the great American myths, depends in frontier and rapidly growing communities even more than in older, stable societies on rational, group control of such matters as the unearned increment and profits derived from localized and limited natural resources.

Obviously the frontier has been the outstanding factor in the rate of growth and the distribution of population, and in the manner of investing surplus capital. In the initial stage the pioneers were largely self-sufficing; then followed the stage of contacts with older societies and the exchange of their surplus goods for such essentials as salt, weapons, and tools; and later still came the stage of dependence on outside capital as well as markets. The development of economic relations between the frontier and the succession of communities left in the wake of the advancing frontier is a factor of primary importance in American industrial history, and particularly so during the period of sectionalism culminating in the Civil War. In our study of the southern planter and of the capitalist of the north, the theme will more than once recur.

CHAPTER XII

MASTERS AND SLAVES

SLAVERY: HISTORIC EBB AND FLOW

The south's "peculiar institution" was in fact older than civilization. Its origins go back to tribal war and conquest and the utilization of captives as laborers in place of extirpation or use as food. A servile class being thus created, its maintenance was promoted not only by new conquests but by the survival value of servility as opposed to assertiveness. In all early civilizations, slavery seems to have been prominent. But in the evolution of modern industrial society in Europe, slavery was displaced by serfdom because the latter was economically more efficient; and from a similar cause, serfdom was in turn supplanted by tenant farming and wage labor.

While the wage system was being established in Europe and Europeans were looking to the new world as a land of limitless opportunity, there was a reversion to slavery in America, land of liberty. By the end of the eighteenth century southerners themselves quite commonly wanted to get rid of slavery. Early attempts to end the slave trade were frustrated by the traders of England and New England, but by 1800 it had been forbidden by most of the southern states. Various proposals were made for abolishing slavery as well as the slave trade. Among the leading southerners who desired to find a way of escape from the system were Washington, Jefferson, and Madison.

While southerners rather idly proposed the abandonment of slavery, a young New Englander unwittingly disposed of the problem by making slavery profitable. Philosophical ideas of equality and democracy disturbed the minds of some, but planters generally were concerned with the cost of maintaining their slaves and with the belief that their labor "is neither so productive nor so cheap as that of day laborers or white servants." Tobacco culture was ruinous to the soil and the demand was limited and almost at a standstill. Rice and indigo were suited only to limited areas. The profitable use of slaves was confined to the production of some staple making possible a form of gang labor simple in nature and readily supervised. Cotton was such a staple, except that the excessive cost of separating the lint from the seed limited the demand. With the introduction of Whitney's gin for mechanically separating the lint from the seed, the cost was so reduced that the ensuing demand made cotton the greatest of the staples. With the progress of mechanical spinning and weaving in factories, the demand was virtually unlimited.

The increased productivity of slave labor gave to slaves an added property value, which was further augmented by the cessation of slave importations in 1808. The rapid expansion of the cotton country meant a constant and growing demand for slaves. On the new plantations, under experimental conditions, with ruthless overseers and drivers attempting the utmost returns, the death rate was high. Under these conditions, even the owners of the decadent older plantations found reluctant profits in disposing of their surplus slaves to the barons of the Cotton Kingdom. A Virginia newspaper stated in 1836 that about forty thousand slaves valued at about twenty-four million dollars had been exported from Virginia alone during the preceding year. Such estimates have little value except that cumulatively they give evidence of an extensive trade. In 1832 a prominent advocate of slavery described Virginia as "a negro raising state for other states." The extension of slavery due to the profits of cotton culture is indicated by the fact that aside from increase of domestic consumption, the value of cotton exported increased from $5,250,000 in 1800 to more than $44,000,000 in 1830, and to more than $204,000,000 in 1859.

PLANTATIONS

From varied sources the ranks of the planters were recruited and rapidly their domains were extended till the more fertile and more accessible areas from Maryland to south central Texas were occupied by masters and slaves. There was long a relatively easy transition from the small-farmer class to the planter class. Many a farmer from adjacent regions bought or preempted a tract of land suitable for cotton and bought a slave or two at a time, and at first, as a planter in the making, shared with his slave the manual labor of the farm. In the newer sections, life was unconventional and robust, with few of the scruples of the Puritans and fewer of the aristocratic amenities of the Old South of colonial fame. Horse racing, gambling, drinking French wines or more frequently corn whiskey from the mountains, barbecues, informal dueling with ever-present weapons, concubinage—these were the favorite recreations, the popular evidences of success among the planters on the make in the newer sections. By degrees there was a tendency to imitate the social manners as well as to duplicate the economic arrangements of the older and more cultivated plantation societies.

Over the vast area occupied by the planters there were innumerable variations, even when social conventions and economic methods had hardened into the régime of the Cotton Kingdom. But there were distinctive characteristics. A plantation was a tract of land large enough to employ group labor rather than merely the labor of the owner or tenant; and in order to make the group labor profitable, it must be used for the production of a staple, or at least of marketable commodities. The plantation is thus distinguished alike from subsistence farming associated with the frontier and with regions where farm produce could not readily be sold, and from small-scale independent farming for markets prevalent wherever markets were accessible.

Decades of experiment with cotton culture by slave labor evolved the view that the ideal plantation should contain about a thousand acres and employ about a hundred slaves. But the cotton barons in many cases owned a large number of such plantations, often widely scattered. Joseph Davis, brother of the president of the Confederacy, was reputedly a millionaire. Thus absentee landlordism developed, with the various units ruled by overseers. Under the overseers were bosses ("drivers") to direct the work of the different gangs.

Cotton culture, supplemented by corn and oats, poultry and gardens, kept all hands busy "thirteen months a year." January was a convenient season for making repairs to fences and implements, clearing away dead trees or fallen limbs (the trees being "deadened" by "barking" them near the base). Late January and February were devoted to plowing, and in the far south to planting corn. A month later, cotton planting began, the seed being drilled in rows perhaps seven feet apart in exceptionally fertile soil. When the cotton was up, broad hoes were used to "chop" out all cotton except bunches fifteen to twenty inches apart, and to clear the row of weeds and grass, thus keeping it from getting "foul." A second "chopping" further cleared and thinned the row. Plowing continued at intervals for two or three months, when finally the cotton was "laid by." Before the cotton was ready to "pick," there were varied tasks as cutting of oats or wheat, and "foddering" of the corn (stripping the stalks of their leaves before they began to wither). By August the earlier planting of cotton was beginning to open, and unless the white, fluffy balls protruding from the bolls or burrs were "picked" before exposure to rains and wind, they would be lost or their quality damaged, and so repeated pickings were required. Then followed sunning and ginning and packing or baling, and hauling to river landing or railway station or local town market. Picking should be over by Christmas, but sometimes there was a sprinkling of white other than snow in the fields in January. Thus there was sometimes an overlapping of the work of season's end and season's beginning, giving rise to the saying that cotton growing required thirteen months a year.

With increasing profits from cotton, and with improvement in transportation giving readier access to markets, there was a tendency to abandon supplementary crops and craft work, but on the older plantations there was an economic diversity somewhat resembling that of the villages farther north. One reads of plantation slaves trained as weavers, tailors, tanners and shoemakers, as turners, carpenters, wheelwrights and smiths. The slaves in many places were given gardens and poultry yards and often their work was according to the task system, allowing them time of their own after completion of their allotted tasks. They were graded according to age and strength as full hands, three-quarter hands, half-hands, and quarter hands. The house of the planter or of his overseer, the tool sheds and other plantation buildings, and the cabins of the slaves were concentrated in old-world manorial manner. Household servants living with the planter's family were in a different world from the ordinary slaves, and contacts with negro mammies and Uncle Remuses, especially in their idealized literary forms, give impressions perhaps no more adequate or typical than those derived from pictures of the more brutal of the slave drivers.

THE PLANTER AND HIS NEIGHBORS

The best land was owned in large tracts by a few planters. But the criterion of wealth was not so much the number of acres as the number of slaves. The concentration of wealth was not so extreme as in later urban society, but for a newly developing agricultural country it was sufficiently remarkable. In 1850 there were more than six million whites in the slave holding states. Of these, approximately 350,000, or between five and six per cent of the white population, owned at least one slave. But about 175,000, or fifty per cent of the slave holders, including prosperous small farmers and men of the professions, owned only from one to four slaves. Of those who owned fifty or more of the three and a half million slaves, there were less than eight thousand.

Most of those who had no slaves, or only one or two, or perhaps a family, were small farmers. Near the plantations they often produced supplies demanded by the planters, whose quest of cotton profits led them to neglect such things as corn growing and hog raising. Some of the immediate neighbors of the planters were their tenants. On poorer lands away from streams, or on exhausted plantation lands, or in the mountains or the piney woods, were "red necks," "hill billies," and "crackers," farmers resembling the backwoodsmen of other regions. But their relative isolation and the poverty of their soil made them seem primitive in their crude self-sufficiency. In so far as they had economic relations, these were largely with the plantation towns, where they disposed of surpluses of corn and wheat in the raw state or as pork and whiskey, and of peach and apple brandy. Transportation by mountain trails and roads and the abundant streams was naturally toward the plantations. By a system of roads and later of railroads, supplemented by shipping around the coast, the tobacco country was connected with the cotton country. The almost universal use, even among slaves, of plug tobacco for chewing and of snuff tobacco for "dipping" even more than for "snuffing" afforded the tobacco planters an important market, and at the same time the constant growth of the cotton industry carried off the surplus negroes of the east.

The non-agricultural neighbors of the cotton planters were mainly merchants and lawyers. The three principal classes of inhabitants of colonial Charleston were described by a traveller as lawyers, planters, and merchants. The description is applicable to later towns of the cotton country. The lawyers of Charleston were described as being "far above priests and bishops," and disdaining "to be satisfied with the poor Mosaical portion of the tenth." Conditions throughout the country were described as increasingly favorable to lawyers: "In another century, the law will possess in the north [*i. e.,* the northern portions of the new world] what now the church possesses in Peru and Mexico." A fee of $50,000 to a lawyer in a single case in a Mississippi court is evidence of the lawyer's enviable position in southern life, but in fact even the legal profession, powerful as it was, like other professions was bound securely by economic ties to the cotton barons. The legal and political machinery was fashioned by the lawyers to the order of the planters. Many planters became lawyers, and many more were politicians. A philosophy to give intellectual and moral support to the southern system was largely the work of lawyers, preachers and teachers. Chancellor William Harper of the Supreme Court of South

Carolina wrote his *Memoir on Slavery* in 1838, and even earlier Thomas Dew of William and Mary College told the planters in persuasive terms why they no longer needed to pay even lip service to the equalitarian doctrines of Jefferson.

Merchants, like lawyers, were clever enough to divert an ample percentage of planters' profits into their own pockets. But they were subordinate none the less to the plantation system. Many of the great planters, like those of colonial times, had river landings of their own. But ocean-going and even coasting vessels were now so much larger that a class of middlemen collected the cotton in small boats for concentration at market towns and shipping centers.

In addition to merchants of the towns who collected and shipped the cotton and brought in supplies of manufactured goods, there was a considerable and rather curious group of middlemen, "the nomads of the south," who maintained connections between cotton planters, back-country farmers, and tobacco planters. They handled back-country products, especially whiskey and brandy and homespun for slaves, in exchange for southern cotton and eastern tobacco, odds and ends of manufactures, and exotics such as coffee. They disposed of cotton not only for domestic manufactures but as well for the new cotton mills of Virginia and the Carolinas; and they brought supplies of eastern tobacco to the cotton country. These nomadic wagoners with their interesting jugs and casks and bales and boxes of plug, snuff, twist and leaf tobacco, and other items no doubt savory and sightly to the isolated slaves and small farmers, and with their no less interesting tales of planters for mountaineers and of mountaineers for planters, were an important and relatively independent class, helping to bind the various elements together in subordination to the cotton barons. Less pleasing and picturesque but influential in the expansion of the plantation system and in uniting eastern and western planters, were the slave traders.

LIMITATIONS OF SLAVERY

Many of the limitations attributed by abolitionists to slavery were of course the limitations of race—not so much of racial inferiority in the biological sense but of ineradicable racial differences under inescapable social disadvantages. One of the causes of the continuance of slavery in the old south was the social question involved in radical racial differences.

But as long as there was an abundance of fertile soil on which an easily grown and readily marketable staple could be produced, a servile working class afforded many economic advantages to the landlords. While expansion was still practicable in the contiguous areas of the south, even the older regions whence cotton was receding profited because of the demand in the newer areas for slaves, tobacco, corn, and other products of the older south. As long as there was an abundance of good new cotton land, the barons of cotton and slaves appeared invincible and with a few significant exceptions were loud in their praise of slavery.

Their overmuch profession of confidence was in part an attempt to convince themselves and in part a protective armor against outside attacks. For southerners were beginning to sense the coming effects of the end of expansion. When new areas were no longer being opened up, the older areas could no longer be sustained by sale of slaves and of supplies dependent on expansion. As the relative size of the older, less productive regions increased in proportion to the newer, more fertile regions, the former could depend less on the latter even with continuing expansion. With an end of expansion, the comparative crudeness and wastefulness of servile labor would no longer have been counteracted by opportunity to exploit new areas. Slavery would have been turned back upon itself to work out its own salvation unaided by prodigal nature in the form of virgin lands.

The final outcome, if there had been no external interference, is necessarily hypothetical but is clearly implicit in the economic situation. "When the small remainder of the suitable climatic zone had come to be occupied—dealing now with the prospect in 1860—opportunity for enhancing fortune by migration must have dwindled, and pressure to improve methods must have increased upon all the population." Thus remarks an outstanding student of the old south, Professor Phillips, who continues: "This need not have brought a decline of the plantation system, though it would impinge upon the régime of slavery. . . . The economic problem as regards personnel put emphasis of course upon rewards as well as opportunities for skilled work by slaves, and thus suggested the relaxation of the restraints of slavery. That more was not accomplished in this line was due in part to the abolition agitation, the repercussion of which in the south put reactionary emphasis upon the race problem and police."

The uninterrupted working out of internal forces would necessarily have tended away from slave labor—in an evolutionary, not a catastrophic manner. The leisure-class ideal, particularly prominent in the caste system of the old south, would have succumbed to the hard realities of decline of revenues even for consumption goods. Already there were bitter complaints of "southern wealth and northern profits." Sacrifices would have diverted wealth from consumption goods into capital goods for stimulating plantation productivity and for utilizing non-agrarian sources of income. Otherwise the cost of maintaining slaves would have increased with increasing numbers and the productivity of their labor would have declined with the declining fertility of the soil. To stimulate production and alleviate the burdens of supporting the slaves, it seems apparent that slave labor would ultimately have been abandoned in favor of some modified arrangement imposing on the workers larger responsibility for their maintenance and affording more effective incentives for skill and initiative essential to the reclamation and more effective use of the lands and the diversification of industrial life.

With the impending occupation of "the small remainder of the suitable climatic zone," the slow-moving internal forces, barring external interruption, would inevitably have speeded up. But northern interference obstructed the working out of natural tendencies. The outcome implicit in southern economy was at first unwittingly retarded by external propaganda and then precipitated by external force.

CHAPTER XIII

BUILDING OF INLAND TRANSPORTATION

ECLIPSE OF CAPITALISM

The "dismal science" of economics (tending to confine things within the walls of definitions) defines a capitalist as one who uses what has been saved by himself or others from consumption for the purpose of additional production. Applying the definition somewhat literally, one finds that the frontiersman who turns his cattle into beasts of burden and the cannibal who turns his captive into a slave are capitalists. It is convenient to limit the term in ordinary usage to those who finance such larger industrial undertakings as banking, trade and transportation, mining and manufacturing.

During the earlier decades following the break with England, and especially during the era of Hamilton, the sun of capitalism was hardly more than dimmed by passing clouds. The beginning of eclipse was the Jeffersonian revolt of the debtor-farmer-planter group. Then followed the decline of trade beginning with the struggle of Napoleon against British domination of the sea. Capitalistic manufacturing, which made headway during periods of interrupted trade, was disrupted by resumption of trade. The government refused to recharter the Bank of the United States on the expiration of its charter in 1811, and the second bank of 1816 was far from satisfactory to the financial interests. Disgust with foreign pressure led to the ideal of isolation. Removal of foreign pressure in 1815 gave opportunity for westward expansion and internal development. The day of the farmer, the planter, and the frontiersman had come.

THE CAPITALIST LOOKS WESTWARD: INLAND TRANSPORT AND TRADE

With the movement of population westward there was at first little contact maintained with the east. The first great opportunity of the capitalist after his eclipse early in the century was in developing transport facilities and in financing interchange between the settlers and the people of the older sections. Where navigable streams existed, the financing of transportation was not difficult. For this reason the flow of western goods was for a long time largely southward. To solve the problem of transportation beyond the reach of navigable streams, there was first a resort to toll roads. In 1792 the road between Philadelphia and Lancaster came under control of the Philadelphia and Lancaster Turnpike Road Company. The company sold shares and built the road, a distance of sixty-two miles, of crushed rock, at the tremendous cost, in that era of limited capital, of $465,000. But the tolls netted an excellent return on the investment. The road was part of a plan proposed by the Society for the Improvement of Roads and Inland Navigation for connecting seaboard Pennsylvania effectively with the west and the northwest. It was the first road of its kind, and its success inaugurated an era of efforts to improve transportation facilities by private initiative, which long continued to absorb a large proportion of capital and enterprise. During the first two decades of the nineteenth century, more than a thousand miles of roads were constructed, mostly by private initiative. The construction of bridges was ordinarily undertaken by separate companies. Capital was secured by ordinary stock sales, by governmental purchases of shares, and by lotteries.

Privately constructed roads often proved to be unprofitable. There was an increasing demand for roads where it was known that the excessive costs of construction or the relatively light traffic would prevent private financing. In addition, toll paying was hardly popular. In consequence there was an increasing demand for public subsidies and for public construction. Private capital continued to be used in connection with such projects, but more largely in the form of investment in government bonds. The most extensive federal undertaking was the National Road, begun at Cumberland, in northern Maryland, in 1812, and extended, during the next quarter of a century, to Vandalia, Illinois. Aside from the National Road, some of the roads most important alike in the westward movement of population and in the maintenance of trade were the following: the road up the Mohawk valley to western New York; the road through Pennsylvania to Pittsburgh, commonly called the Forbes Road because it followed the line cut by General Forbes in the French and Indian War; and the Wilderness Road through the Cumberland Gap to the region of the old southwest.

CANALS

The cost of transportation by road before the building of railroads ran from twenty cents to sixty cents per ton-mile; the railroad rate fell to three cents. In 1818 Virginia farmers complained that the price received for a bushel of wheat would carry only two bushels to seaport markets eighty miles away. Baltimore and Philadelphia were able to supply the west with essentials not produced there, and to pay prices high enough to attract certain western goods, as furs, whiskey, and ginseng, but the principal trade of the west was by means of the Mississippi and its tributaries. Inversions of values due to transportation costs are illustrated by the case of the bushel of salt exchanged for a cow and calf. By reducing their corn to whiskey, westerners could make a small profit by sending it to eastern markets. Seaboard cities, and through them, European markets, were reached by the primitive method of having live-stock transport itself across the mountains. The National Road and the Wilderness Road were thronged with droves reaching into the thousands. Live-stock passing through the toll gate on the Wilderness Road at Cumberland Gap in 1828 was estimated at far above a million dollars in value. But with the increasing demand for western hogs, mules, horses, and cattle in the newer cotton-growing regions of the south, the east-bound movement, even in this primitive manner, declined. The cost of transportation by roads had been effectively brought home to Boston during the War of 1812. The usual price of flour in Boston was seventy-five cents per barrel more than in New York, due to the boat haul from New York. When the British cut off the coastwise trade and flour had to be secured by overland freight, the difference in cost mounted to about five dollars.

The outstanding need for capital after the collapse of the inflated trade of the first decade of the century was for the financing of inland transportation facilities by water. The need was met in two ways: the construction of canals and the building of steamboats.

Canals local in character and relatively inexpensive in construction were financed by private companies. But with the demand for capital regularly exceeding the supply, it is not surprising that the cost and the uncertainty of the larger enterprises, such as connecting the Hudson River with Lake Erie, made skeptics of investors. It remained for Governor DeWitt Clinton to become the moving figure in constructing what was known as Clinton's "ditch"—undoubtedly the most important of American canals.

The Erie Canal ran northwestward from the Hudson at Albany through the Mohawk valley to Rome, and thence generally westward not far from the shore of Lake Ontario but avoided the lake because of its contact with eastern Canadian trade centers, and because the main objective was to tap the country west of the mountains and south of the lakes, not for Montreal but for New York. With Montreal and the St. Lawrence there was separate connection directly northward from the Hudson by way of Lake Champlain. Ending at Buffalo on the Erie side of the Falls, the Canal traversed a length of 363 miles, with about seven hundred feet of lockage. The beds of streams were avoided to escape seasonal floods. Begun in 1817, it was finally extended to Buffalo in 1825, at a total cost of about $8,400,000.

In place of a hundred dollars per ton from Buffalo to New York, the cost was now reduced to less than eight, and the time, an equally important element in the case of many goods, was reduced from twenty days to six. Only eight miles of carriage by land intervened between New York and Pittsburgh. Freight from Philadelphia to Columbus was eighty dollars a ton; from New York it was fifty. Wheat grown in Georgia in 1827 was kept from the Savannah market by the competition of wheat produced in New York. By means of the Erie Canal and the Champlain Canal, the Hudson valley, the St. Lawrence, the Great Lakes, and the Mississippi were joined together. By means of the canal and its heir, the railroad, the prophecy of Clinton was fulfilled: when advocating the construction of the canal, New York, he said, "will in the course of time become the granary of the world, the emporium of commerce, the seat of manufactures, the focus of great moneyed operations, and the concentrating point of vast, disposable, and accumulating capitals, which will stimulate, enliven, extend, and reward the exertions of human labor and ingenuity, in all their processes and exhibitions. And before the revolution of a century, the whole island of Manhattan . . . will constitute one vast city.''

The unfavorable location of New York as compared with Pennsylvania and Maryland in maintaining commercial contacts with the west resulted in the Erie Canal. The spectacular success of the canal stimulated the people of the region of Philadelphia and Baltimore to undertake competitive canal systems. Philadelphians complained that New York could send goods 750 miles to central Ohio by water, via the Erie Canal, Lake Erie, and the Ohio Canal, more cheaply than Philadelphians could send the same goods 140 miles by overland freight to central Pennsylvania.

In 1826, the year following the opening of the Erie Canal, the state of Pennsylvania began work on its rival enterprise. There were two canals, one on the east and one on the west of the divide, the canal boats being drawn over the crest of the mountains by means of a portage railroad—inclined planes, wheeled cars for the boats, and cables—operated by stationary engines. In addition to the canals and the portage railroad, there was a stretch of railway about eighty miles in length between Philadelphia and Columbia on the Susquehanna River. This cumbersome system was not completed till 1834. It cost the state more than ten million dollars. But in spite of its cost and cumbersomeness, it enabled the Pennsylvanians to regain much of the trade that had been diverted to the Erie Canal and to develop a vast new trade. A similar attempt of Baltimore to reduce the cost of access to the west was not so successful.

Other canals of chief importance were west of the mountains and in the lake region. The government of Ohio in 1822 formulated plans for a canal to connect the Ohio River with Lake Erie at Cleveland. This project, known as the Ohio Canal, was finished in 1833, and immediately transformed Cleveland into an important shipping center, more than 250,000 bushels of wheat alone being freighted to the town by the canal during its first year of operation. In 1830 a plan was projected to connect Lake Michigan with the Mississippi River, but there were many delays, and the canal was not opened till 1848, when boats first moved between Chicago and Ottawa on the Illinois River. This ninety-mile Illinois and Michigan Canal transformed Chicago from a mud-splattered and wind-swept village into a metropolis. In 1855, after the expense of blasting through solid rock, a canal was opened at St. Mary's River between Lakes Huron and Superior, and five years later 117,000 tons of iron ore, and thousands of tons of iron, passed eastward through the canal, from a region which Henry Clay, ardent advocate of internal improvements, had described only twenty-five years before as so remote from civilization as to be "in the moon."

Innumerable other projects were undertaken. By 1837, not less than a hundred million dollars had been invested. State debts incurred for canals amounted in 1838 to more than sixty millions, thus affording individuals an opportunity to invest without responsibility for the enterprise. State governments and private companies alike overshot the mark. Many of the projects were abandoned or put into operation in an unfinished condition. The riot of enthusiasm produced a speculative fever, which was cooled by the financial crisis of 1837. Furthermore, the railroad was becoming the favorite object of popular enthusiasm for transportation facilities. But before railroad construction is considered, another phase of inland transportation by water demands attention—namely, the use of the steamboat. Together, the railroad and the steamboat made an end of the great age of canal transportation—the former by outrivaling canals as arteries of traffic, and the latter by becoming so large as to render the canals unusable except in connection with costly transhipments.

THE STEAMBOAT

As viewed through the haze of travellers' tales and folklore, there are few phases of American history more glamorous than the age of the flatboat on western rivers, and of the crews who manned them, those curious compounds of strength, agility, and crude wit, the "alligator-horses." In actuality the life of these men, as for instance of Mike Fink, the Mississippi "Snag" and the Ohio "Snapping Turtle," must have been hard, cruel and brutalizing. On the western rivers there were not only boatsmen by trade but innumerable homeseekers, and farmers in quest of markets for their surplus. Most of the traffic was downstream, but in some almost miraculous manner the hardy frames, steel muscles, and quick wit of the "alligator-horses" propelled many of the "floating tubs" upstream a mile an hour with freight of half a hundred tons. An important aspect of river navigation by steam was the full utilization of the river upstream as well as down.

It has been suggested that the year 1817 has a threefold significance in the history of inland transportation, due to the crossing of the Alleghanies by the National Road, the beginning of work on the Erie Canal, and the successful use of steamboats for upstream traffic on the Mississippi. But the introduction of steam power for navigation was far from sudden or sensational. It came about gradually as a result of the work of literally hundreds of inventors and innovators.

Among Americans, the most interesting pioneers in steam navigation were James Rumsey with his curious contraption of steam-operated poles and other devices that attracted the interest of Washington and of Franklin; and John Fitch with his endless chain, side paddles, rear paddles, crude screw propeller, and experiments as at "Conjurer's Point" on the Delaware, culminating in several extensive trips by steam power more than a decade before Robert Fulton's *Clermont* rode the Hudson to Albany. Robert Livingston, who became Fulton's partner, carried on extensive experiments in Europe and America, and acquired, for himself and Fulton and Nicholas Roosevelt, a monopoly of steam navigation rights in New York. Fulton's main contributions consisted of his improvement of the side paddle wheel and his insistence on an English engine as superior to anything elsewhere obtainable. The engine was encased in masonry in the *Clermont,* which was one hundred and thirty feet long, with paddle wheels fifteen feet in diameter. The trip to Albany, in spite of opposing winds, averaged nearly five miles an hour.

The successful voyage of the *Clermont* on the Hudson in 1807 by no means resulted in immediate transition to steam power. It was not the *Clermont* but the *Washington,* built in 1816 by Henry Shreve at Wheeling on the Ohio, that was in reality the prototype of the steamboat of western rivers. The new type was in a sense indigenous. It was an adaptation of the flatboat long used on the shallow and shifting currents of the level western plains. It has been said that if La Salle should now retrace his course of two hundred and fifty years ago down the Mississippi, most of his voyage would be on dry ground. The shifting of the mid-channel of many western streams may occur almost overnight. The deep draft and the hold of boats adapted to such a river as the Hudson had to be abandoned. Shreve cleverly combined steam propulsion with characteristics of the familiar flatboat—a flat-bottomed boat having a shallow draft and an upper deck to take the place of the hold. When Captain

Shreve reached Louisville in 1817 on his return voyage from New Orleans, there was "a great stir" in the west, and he was acclaimed as having solved the problem of upstream navigation by steam. His model soon won almost exclusive favor. The Mississippi and its tributaries for a time contained more steamboat tonnage than the Atlantic seaboard, more even than the British Empire.

In 1817, the epochal year of Captain Shreve's return voyage up the Mississippi, the first attempt at steam navigation on the Great Lakes met with disaster. The *Walk-in-the-Water* of 1818, with side paddle wheel and stern steering wheel, survived local lake voyages for three years, when it also was wrecked. Several steamboats were launched during the period of renewed interest in the settlement of the northwest attendant upon the opening of the Erie Canal, and the typical cargo of these earlier vessels was described as consisting of "men, women, children, beds, cradles, kettles, and frying pans." But with the opening of the canals in the Ohio valley, between Lake Michigan and the Mississippi basin, and between Lakes Michigan and Superior, and with the exploitation of mines as well as farms, the handling of freight called for constantly increasing fleets of lake vessels —a traffic which was augmented rather than diminished by the building of railroads.

RAILROADS

The great age of canal and river transportation merged into the railway age beginning about 1830. The locomotive, like the steamboat, had been the subject of innumerable experiments in various parts of the world. One of the earliest locomotives was put together by William Murdoch, an employee of James Watt, in 1784. Put in operation on a Sunday night in Murdoch's village near Birmingham, the "fiery and hissing little monster" is said to have frightened the village clergyman into the belief that he had encountered Satan in his native guise. Watt, so optimistic about the stationary engine, had oddly enough no faith in steam locomotion, and turned Murdoch back into routine channels. Oliver Evans operated a locomotive on the streets of Philadelphia in 1802, and later offered wagers that he could run a steam carriage on rails over level ground at the speed of fifteen miles an hour. Englishmen took the lead in the application of steam power to land transportation, as did Americans to transportation by water. Various "horseless carriages" were run experimentally, but not commercially till George Stephenson in his "Rocket" of 1829 hit upon a successful combination of devices and improvements made in the main by his predecessors. The first American locomotive engine, like the engine for Fulton's *Clermont*, was imported from England.

Devising an efficient locomotive was of course the first essential step, but long experimentation alone could effect a successful use of even the most efficient engine. Should the tracks be of wood or iron? What was the best shape, and the best width? What degrees of curve and of grade are permissible? How should the fuel and water supply be managed? How avoid collisions, especially on one-way tracks? These and scores of other technological problems must be solved, largely by trial and error. Applied science was in its infancy and common sense had its limitations. Probably the principal single contribution to the technique of railway operation was the telegraph opportunely invented by S. F. B. Morse and put into effective use in 1844, with fifty thousand miles in operation before the Civil War. Another particularly important innovation that won general favor about the same time was the iron rail.

Almost as perplexing and perhaps more important were questions of finance and organization and right of way and rates and relations to governments, local and national. A railway was viewed at first as a new kind of turnpike, with tolls and private carriages. A recognition of the monopolistic character of railroads, combined with the opposition of certain vested interests, as the stockholders in canals, innkeepers along turnpikes, and the stagecoach people, led to some slight attempts at public regulation. But in general the mania for railroads enabled corporations to secure almost unlimited powers.

For a quarter of a century before the first steam railway was in operation, experiments had been made with railways for hauling coal and ore from mines and stone from quarries, the cars being propelled by men or horses or gravity. There were various advocates of such railways for general use in place of canals. It was argued that the cost would be less, that a single horse could draw an immense load on a road with tracks, and that such a road could be used more readily in winter when canals were likely to be closed by ice.

The first steam railroad was opened in 1833. It was the Charleston and Hamburg Railway from Charleston to the Savannah River opposite Augusta, Georgia. But the great national revolution in transportation was inaugurated by the business men of Baltimore in a desperate effort to keep pace with New York and Philadelphia in the race for western markets. The first lap of the race had been won handily by Baltimore. The opening of the National Road from Cumberland to Wheeling on the Ohio in 1817 had enabled Baltimore, with insignificant expenses for roads to Cumberland, to outbid even Philadelphia. The National Road connected in this way with Baltimore became the principal traffic artery to the west. Philadelphia with its turnpikes to Pittsburgh was a close rival. But New York, by means of the Erie Canal, completed in 1825, forged quickly ahead of both, and won the second lap of the race. Philadelphia, by means of its system of railroad, canals, and portage, although unable to overtake New York, quickly left Baltimore in the rear. To add to the plight of Baltimore, the Chesapeake and Ohio Canal up the Potomac valley was projected, and its value to Baltimore depended on tapping it by means of a lateral canal from the Potomac valley to Baltimore. Otherwise Washington and not Baltimore would be the future mart of western trade south of Philadelphia.

The business men of Baltimore and sympathetic public officials of Maryland, realizing the inadequacy of the National Road, set about devising ways and means of escape from the dilemma. The Maryland Canal Company was formed, for constructing the lateral canal to connect Baltimore with the Potomac valley, in cooperation with the Chesapeake and Ohio Canal Company. Soon the men of Baltimore had a vision transcending even a canal to the Ohio. Their ambition encompassed a gigantic interstate project connecting Maryland, Virginia, western Pennsylvania and Ohio with the Great Lakes,—a project to be financed by the joint resources of the states and the federal government. The soaring ambition was brought rudely to earth by the unfavorable reports of the engineers concerning the canal to the Ohio; and even the lateral canal from Baltimore to the valley of the Potomac was pronounced unfeasible. The problem was further complicated by divided counsels. Some argued that the canals should be undertaken despite the adverse engineering reports. Others proposed what must have seemed to all except the most daring a counsel of desperation, namely, a railroad across the mountains.

It was under these circumstances that the Baltimore and Ohio Railroad came into existence. The canal company continued with its plans; and those favoring a railroad formed a separate company. Both companies began operations on July 4, 1828. The quarrels continued, the canal company having advantages of exclusive right of way along the Potomac, the only feasible route for the railroad. The canal, in spite of large expenditures, both public and private, was extended only to the foot of the mountains. The railroad company at length overcame its various handicaps and in 1853 reached Wheeling on the Ohio.

But already the mountains had been conquered, to the north and to the south. As early as 1842 a series of ill-jointed links later to form the New York Central had extended to Buffalo, but it was not till after the middle of the century that the handicaps of disunion and of tolls on freight to protect the Erie Canal were entirely overcome. In 1851 the Erie Railroad reached Lake Erie at Dunkirk. To the southward, Savannah, Charleston, and Atlanta were connected in 1850 with Chattanooga on the Tennessee River. In 1852, the year preceding the extension of the Baltimore and Ohio to Wheeling, the Pennsylvania Railroad reached Pittsburgh. New Englanders, long without adequate connection with the west, and left out of the running in the age of canals, entered the race with vigor in 1841 by means of the Boston and Albany Railroad giving connection with the Erie Canal, and later with the railroads from Albany to the lakes. The region of the St. Lawrence was tapped by means of a series of lines extending in 1850 to Ogdensburg on the St. Lawrence near Lake Ontario.

The goal of leading railroad builders in the east during the first and second decades of railroad history (the 'thirties and 'forties) was the navigable waters of the west—the lakes and the westward flowing rivers beyond the mountains. This goal was reached in the 'fifties and a new goal was set—the main artery of mid-continental traffic from the lakes to the Gulf. This goal also was reached. Railroads were extended from Buffalo to Chicago by 1853, and to St. Louis by 1855. In the far south, Charleston and Memphis were connected in

1859. Pittsburgh and Wheeling and other Ohio valley towns were connected by a network of roads with the Mississippi and the Great Lakes. But westerners were concerned not only with gaining access to the east but with facilitating north-and-south commerce, with gaining access to the regions west of the Mississippi, and with developing their own varied industrial life independently of outside contacts. Southerners were making almost frantic efforts to retain their hold on the west by cheapening the transportation of western produce to the cotton country.

By 1840, 2,818 miles had been built; the mileage increased by 1850 to 9,021; and in the final decade before the war, to 30,626. The cost of railroad construction during the 'fifties was estimated to have been more than $1,134,000,000.

FINANCING OF INTERNAL IMPROVEMENTS

In the growth of transportation facilities and of trade, resources and capitalistic organizations of unprecedented scope were necessary. The favorite method of securing funds and of carrying on such enterprises was the method still prevalent—the organization of a stock company and the selling of shares. Since "hard" money was often scarce, banks were tempted to excessive issuing of notes and extending of credit. States and municipalities bought shares, after the example of the federal government in owning shares in the Bank of the United States. Maryland and Baltimore, for example, bought half the shares of the Baltimore and Ohio Railroad. Governments often undertook the full ownership and management of such enterprises, as in the case of the Erie Canal. But whether they owned outright or merely subscribed to the stock of corporations, state and local governments ordinarily met the larger part of the expense by issuing bonds. These were particularly popular (before the repudiations resulting from the panic of 1837) with foreigners. From 1802 to 1835, during the high tide of agitation for internal improvements, the federal government spent only $9,520,000 on roads and canals. But state and federal governments often subsidized private corporations by means of land grants or other favors, as when Congress assigned 750,000 acres of land in aid of St. Mary's River Canal, connecting Lakes Huron and Superior. In their eagerness to secure the benefits of transportation facilities, individual business men, local groups, and municipalities frequently made outright donations, one community often bidding against another. As early as 1830, mill owners of the Merrimac suggested the building of a railroad from Boston to Lowell, and subscribed a "bonus" of $100,000.

Wasting of money in unsound projects, and excessive investment in enterprises affording no immediate returns, helped materially to bring on the panic of 1837. This event in turn affected the future financing of such enterprises. It dried up the federal government's source of revenues, and, by putting an end to surplus income, gave effect to President Jackson's policy of discouraging federal internal improvements. More important, it involved the states and municipalities in such financial straits that the resort in some cases was repudiation of public debts. In general, the result was dissatisfaction with governmental participation in such enterprises. Progress was more cautious after the panic and after the more costly experimental stages had been passed. Private corporations felt surer of profits, and were willing for governments to refrain from undertaking enterprises where risk was slight and profit large. Some of the state constitutions were amended to forbid further governmental business ventures. Thus it came about that after the panic of 1837 private financing by joint-stock companies was more largely depended on than before. But the companies continued to seek the aid of state and federal subsidies in the form of land grants, tariffs, etc., and to welcome local subscriptions and "bonuses."

In the era of disillusion following severance from Britain, the capitalist suffered eclipse and the popular trend was toward individualism and economic independence in farming and pioneering. But the ensuing unparalleled movement of population quickly created demands which brought the capitalist into prominence again. First was the need of transportation facilities for reaching the west and for maintaining contacts with the east. The extension of transportation facilities led in turn to a succession of opportunities, which culminated at length in the restoration of ascendancy to the capitalistic group.

CHAPTER XIV

INTERVENTION OF CAPITAL IN BASIC INDUSTRIES

MILLING, DISTILLING AND BREWING

Among the opportunities for the intervention of capital attendant upon the extension of transportation facilities, first in natural sequence, but overlapping others, was the development of such basic industries as milling, lumbering and mining.

As long as the advancing population was limited by primitive methods of transportation, a self-sufficing economy was necessary. The advance guard resembled the seaboard colonists of earliest days. A modicum of seed and live-stock, tools, implements and weapons they managed to take with them or to import. They produced their own food as a matter of course. They fashioned from the forest their own crude timbered houses, heavy furniture, and other necessary wares of wood. They tanned their own leather and made their own shoes, harness, and other leather goods, and after transportation facilities with the south were established, farmers of adjacent regions long continued to make brogans or "negro shoes" for the southern trade during idle seasons, as a principal source of money income. In their own hand mills or in small and crude community power mills they ground their own flour and corn meal.

The ease with which corn and wheat could be grown, and the universal demand not only for bread but for beverages and meats dependent upon cereals, gave first importance to the intervention of capital in the utilization of grains. The value of flour and meal alone in 1860 was $224,000,000, almost twice the value of any other group of manufactures included in the census. Small mills widely dispersed account for a large proportion of the output, but there was a decided tendency toward large-scale enterprises. The largest mill in 1860 was in western New York and had an output of three hundred thousand barrels valued at $1,500,000. The western output for market was at first sent down the rivers, but the declining costs of transportation led to a progressive increase in the export of western flour and grain to the east.

Because of relatively high costs of transportation, the west could more effectively compete with the east in grain raising by turning the grain into beer and whiskey and provisions. In consequence the making of spirituous liquors and later of beer shifted westward. By 1850 Ohio had the principal distilleries. The older practice of household distilling went out of vogue except in the remoter mountainous areas—the "moonshine" regions of later days. By the middle of the century there were distilleries with an annual capacity of two million gallons, and soon thereafter there were breweries with an output of two hundred thousand barrels a year. The value of malt and spirituous liquors produced in 1860 was about $43,000,000. The retail price of whiskey was often as low as twenty-five cents a gallon—a fact that has elicited from some one the meditative remark that with whiskey at such a price and with cigars at half a penny apiece, convivial indulgences when the last century was young could be easily financed.

PACKING

One of the distinctive features of western business was the packing industry. The vast areas of land adapted to corn growing in the Ohio valley and beyond could be used in only a small degree for local needs and for supplying distilleries. The markets for corn and corn meal were limited. For raising hogs, corn was unexcelled. The extension of cotton culture in the south meant a constantly enlarging market accessible by cheap river transportation. The result was an unparalleled expansion of hog raising and of the packing industry.

By the middle of the century, about a million hogs were being slaughtered for market in Ohio, Indiana, and Kentucky, approximately a third being at Cincinnati, the "Porkopolis." Slaughterers and packers were employed by men with large resources, who bought the hogs in local markets and managed the sale of the provisions. Butchers, following an old custom, received the offals as wages, but with the increasing value of by-products they often offered bonuses. The main products were salted pork, bacon, and lard. The increased demand for salt led to the capitalistic development of that industry. Minor products and by-products included bristles, glue, prussiate of potash, fertilizers, and oil or grease for soap making, for lubrication, and for lighting in lamps and candles.

With the extension of population to the regions of natural pasturage for cattle, the packing of beef, with its various by-products, began to rival the pork industry. The principal centers were Chicago and St. Louis.

LUMBERING

The use of barrels, tierces, and hogsheads by the packers created one of the innumerable demands upon the lumbering industry. In comparison with the great drovers who hired the butchers and packers and marketed the products of the packing industry, the lumbermen generally were petty capitalists. Saw mills, like grist mills, followed quickly in the wake of frontier settlements. As early as 1819 there were eight saw mills and sixteen grist mills in Washington County, Missouri. The use of small, inexpensive steam engines enabled sawyers and millers to escape from the limitations of water power. But even the smaller engines required considerable capital. Engines made in 1812 by Oliver Evans of Philadelphia, of ten to twenty-five horse power, capable, so it was claimed, of sawing 5,000 boards or grinding 240 bushels a day, cost $6,000.

Both lumbering and the wood working industries which utilized lumber continued as in colonial days to be carried on extensively as supplementary or part-time industries by farmers. But the extremely rapid expansion in the demands for lumber tremendously increased the large-scale, capitalistic exploitation of forest resources. It appears, from incomplete census data, that during the middle decades when expansion of output was most rapid, there was a decline in the number of saw mills and planing mills. In 1860 the number was about twenty thousand, with an output of lumber averaging in value about $5,000 per mill. In the 'thirties, Maine was the principal source of lumber. The two hundred mills in the vicinity of Bangor in 1832 had an average daily capacity of 7,500 feet. The output of Maine continued to increase, but there was a more rapid expansion in western New York and the pine belt farther west. Before 1860, Chicago became the leading lumber market, the receipts of lumber other than shingles and laths from 1850 to 1860 averaging about 300,000,000 feet a year. Lumbering was being developed on an increasing scale in the south, but the finer grades of forest products were commonly imported from the north. Among primary manufactures, lumbering in 1860 ranked second in value of output, being exceeded only by milling.

TANNING

In some places a by-product of lumbering was tanner's bark. Among the by-products of the beef-packing industry were hides. The tanning and currying industry came to be one of the country's outstanding primary manufactures, due to the importance of leather goods and the effective development of the reproductive leather-working industries. Tanneries, observed Secretary Gallatin in his famous report on manufactures in 1810, are "on a very large scale—the capital employed in a single establishment amounting to one hundred thousand dollars." A few hides were exported, as well as a great deal of leather, but the industry was so well established that a great many hides were imported. The census report of 1860 resembled Gallatin's report in emphasizing the amount of capital invested and the fact that tanning "feeds an active branch of the import trade." In value of output, tanning in 1860 ranked third among primary manufactures, being next in importance to lumbering.

MINING AND SMELTING OF LEAD AND COPPER

The French early discovered lead deposits in the hills southwest of St. Louis, and even mined a small amount. The first American to undertake operations seems to have been a New Englander later known to fame in the settlement of Texas—Moses Austin. In 1797 he secured a grant of land and set about the mining and smelting of lead and the erecting of a shot tower. He sank a shaft to a depth of eighty feet. But most of the newcomers after the purchase of Louisiana were without resources save pick and shovel, bucket and hand windlass, and muscular power to operate them. They undertook nothing but shallow "diggings." They sold their ore (averaging perhaps a hundred pounds a day at two dollars per hundred) to men who owned the furnaces. The furnaces were extremely crude and wasteful, costing from about fifty to a hundred dollars, and requiring the attention of only three men. The lead pigs were made into shot or sold to merchants. The shot from the Missouri mines came to be used extensively throughout the region and played no small part in the conquest of the valley and of the country beyond. It was estimated in 1819 that the value of lead mined up to that time was equal to one-third of the purchase price of Louisiana.

But the Missouri mines were soon reduced to relative unimportance by the discovery, in the 'twenties, of the Galena lead deposits of northern Illinois and southern Wisconsin. The mines of this region underwent a period of crude, small-scale and wasteful exploitation such as those of Missouri had experienced. But larger capital and more efficient methods were soon introduced, and by 1845 they attained the maximum production of 54,495,000 pounds. Most of the output was first shipped down the Mississippi but later a larger part of it was diverted eastward.

Somewhat farther north, in the Lake Superior region, one of the richest copper deposits in the world was opened up in the 'forties, and large-scale, capitalistic methods were introduced. Production was relatively slight till after the Civil War, but after the opening of the St. Mary's River Canal in 1855 the output increased from 3,100 to 8,000 tons. In the same region were found the gigantic iron deposits which were later to revolutionize American industry.

COAL AND IRON

The expansion in the "raising" of "fossil fuel" by the bushel was the subject of somewhat awed comment by the census authorities of 1860. The output, it was stated, had increased in value since the census of 1850 from about seven million dollars to "over nineteen millions." The forests continued to supply the country with most of its fuel as well as lumber, but with the exception of charcoal burning, the fuel business was generally incidental either to farming or to lumbering. In an amusing way it was sometimes incidental to transportation. One of the diversions of travellers who could afford the leisure without annoyance was to watch the firemen of steamboats and locomotives replenish their fuel from streamside driftwood or trackside débris. It was not till the 'thirties that coal was used in place of charcoal for smelting.

The dependence of mining on transportation facilities is especially obvious in connection with the anthracite coal of Pennsylvania. There was an inkling of the value of anthracite in the eighteenth century. The Lehigh Coal Mine Company was organized in 1793 for the purpose of mining and transporting anthracite from the Mauch Chunk region near the Lehigh River. Difficulties of transportation over nine miles of stones and stumps to the Lehigh, and along the shallow, rapid current of the river, prevented coal from reaching Philadelphia for twenty years. Of seven boat loads sent on their way down the stream in 1813, only two reached their destination. At twenty dollars a ton, the promoters lost money. But some of the consumers gained enthusiasm for the "fossil fuel," and the result ultimately was the formation of two stock companies. One was the Lehigh Coal Company capitalized at $55,000; and the other, the Lehigh Navigation Company, at $150,000. Thirty years after the organization of the original Lehigh Coal Mine Company of 1793, Mauch Chunk coal was successfully marketed at Philadelphia. Then followed a network of canals, these being supplanted in turn by railroads, with rapid extension of markets, new uses for coal, and capitalistic organization of mining.

Bituminous coal was mined in a small way for local use in various parts of the country from early colonial times. Before transportation opened up western resources, the seaboard depended on Virginia mines or on imported coal. But by 1860 western Pennsylvania and Ohio were supplying most of the demands for soft coal. Anthracite was more extensively used for smelting, and its output was still greater than that of soft coal.

Before the development of iron mining in the Lake Superior region, the mining and smelting of iron were carried on in the vicinity of the fuel used. Until the 'thirties of the last century, charcoal was used. With the using up of the forests on the seaboard, iron was in part imported and in part produced in widely scattered areas for supplying local needs. The finest iron was produced in the bloomeries of the Lake Champlain region. Furnaces for pig iron and crude castings were located even in the remotest regions penetrated by any considerable number of settlers, if iron ore was available, for the abundance of wood for charcoal solved the fuel problem. Such primitive iron mining and smelting was long maintained in various regions. But in the 'thirties and 'forties there was a remarkable concentration and localization of the iron industry. Transportation opened up the anthracite coal mines. Improvements in smelting led to the use of anthracite as fuel. The result was the rapid outrivaling of the scattered, antiquated charcoal-burning furnaces (despite a brief revival due to the protective tariff of 1842), and the centralization of iron mining and smelting in the anthracite region.

After a century of smelting by coke in England, Americans began experiments in the use of coke made from the abundant supplies of soft coal in western Pennsylvania and the Ohio valley. The experiments were successful, and by 1860, 122,000 tons of iron were smelted with soft coal and coke. Iron ores were abundant in the same region. These factors, combined with the building of railways, heralded the early ascendancy of the Pittsburgh region in mining and smelting.

But even before its ascendancy was established, events occurred which foretold the shifting of the source of iron to a distant region and the dispersion of smelting over wide-spreading bituminous areas. These events were the accidental discovery of the remarkable deposits of the Lake Superior region, and the opening of the St. Mary's River Canal. A government surveying party headed by William A. Burt was using Burt's own device, a solar compass. Unaccountable variations in the compass led to an investigation which revealed the presence of virtually unlimited quantities of high-grade ore. The opening of the canal between Lakes Superior and Huron in 1855 was followed by the eastward flow of ore to the coal regions and the geographical separation of iron mining from smelting. But in 1860, the amount of ore shipped eastward was still relatively unimportant—117,000 tons.

In that year the total output of pig iron was less than a million tons—meager in comparison with later figures, but the official estimate for 1820 places the output at only 20,000 tons. The increase had been largely due to the demand for railroad rails, which in turn had been the basis of improved transportation and the stimulus for better methods of smelting. Since colonial days there had been about a twelve-fold increase in the capacity of the best furnaces—from twenty-five tons to three hundred tons a week. The colonial iron "plantations" had been outstanding examples of the "big business" of those days, but in comparison with some of the corporate undertakings of even the earlier days of smelting with coal, they were pigmies. Several factors combined to make more profitable such a concentration of capital as was illustrated by the Brady's Bend Iron Company in western Pennsylvania in the 'forties. Its investment amounted to a million dollars. It combined under one management the several processes of mining and coking coal; of extracting iron, limestone, and furnace materials; of reducing the iron to rails or other forms demanded by consumers; and of marketing its output without the intervention of middlemen. Hundreds of company houses for workers formed one of the early industrial towns of the iron and coal regions. The new industrial baronies were already in the making.

CHAPTER XV

LARGE-SCALE MANUFACTURING AND TRADE

FACTORS FAVORING CAPITALISTIC MANUFACTURING

Capitalistic intervention in the later stages of manufacturing was promoted by many influences. In the first place, the primary or basic industries already discussed provided abundant materials, as leather, lumber, iron, and cotton. The ginning of cotton was a primary manufacture no less than the tanning of leather. But it was a process so obviously inseparable from the plantation and so obviously necessary in giving value to cotton, that elaboration is needless. A second factor was the development of transportation facilities. Manufactures, being relatively valuable, could stand the costs of bad transportation facilities more readily than could the bulkier products of basic industries; but those who produce the latter must be able to dispose of them in order to be able to buy the former. A third factor was the sectional specialization whereby the south produced cotton, and the west engaged mainly in supplying provisions, lumber, hides, leather, and in general the output of basic industries. The middle states of the east, and to a less degree New England, during the period immediately following the Napoleonic era, found that their most profitable or promising opportunities for investment were in aiding the westward movement, especially by promoting transportation projects. But New Englanders, because of their location, found little opportunity to profit by westward expansion except by going west, and even this for them was relatively difficult. They could produce no staples demanded by other countries, because their economic life, instead of complementing, competed with the industry of Europe. New Englanders had considerable accumulations of capital, surviving especially from the high tide of commercial prosperity of the first decade of the century. They had abundant water power. The population was relatively dense in numbers and at the same time educated and adaptable. They had to send their manufactures by sea to New York, Philadelphia, or Baltimore, but transportation by sea was cheap, and they were able to compete with the middle Atlantic states in western markets. The west sent its goods to the south and received specie with which to meet the unfavorable balance of trade due to the prohibitive cost of sending its products eastward.

In addition to these more obvious conditions underlying the capitalistic development of manufacturing to supplant the import trade, the household crafts, and shop industry, there were other factors which call for special consideration. These were technological advances; the recruiting of the labor supply by immigration; and protective tariffs.

TECHNOLOGICAL ADVANCE

The peoples of antiquity, wrote Francis Bacon, made gods of inventors (as Prometheus, teacher of the art of using fire); "while to those who had done good deeds in civil affairs (as the founders of cities and empires, . . . subverters of tyrannies, and the like) they only decreed the honors of heroes. And certainly if one rightly compares them, he will find this judgment of antiquity to be just. The benefits of discoveries can pertain to all the race of man; civil benefits only to certain sets of men." By way of illustration, he mentions "printing, gunpowder, and the needle [of the mariner's compass]. For these three have changed the face and state of things in all the world." Had he lived two centuries later, he might very well have mentioned such "mechanical discoveries" as his own countrymen were bringing to light at the time of the American Revolution. The work of the revolutionary heroes conferred "civil benefits" on "certain sets of men"; while makers of the steam engine, the spinning mule, the power loom, and the coke-burning furnace have wrought a transformation in the daily affairs of virtually "all the race of man."

The English government tried in vain to monopolize inventions. Patent laws and treaty arrangements gave almost no protection to an inventor outside of his own country. American patent law was based on the principles of the English Statute of Monopolies of 1624, which, while hostile to monopolies in general, made an exception in the case of inventions. But the meaning of the term invention was likely to include a new industry or business, as well as a new device or technical process. From 1793 to 1836, the patent law was extremely lax, and virtually no attempt was made to verify the claims of inventors. A mere statement of the number of patents issued means little. Americans freely introduced the technology of foreigners, oftentimes patenting "inventions" which were merely importations.

The adaptation of the steam engine to transportation on American inland waters and railroads has been already considered. Knowledge of steam power, centuries old, had been revolutionized by the mind of James Watt and the money of his partner, Matthew Boulton, in their world-famous plant at Soho near Birmingham. Among Watt's improvements were fuel-saving devices and a practicable rotary or "sun-and-planet" motion by which power could be transmitted not only to the up-and-down strokes of water pumps but to the wheels of factory machinery. Americans, because of the abundance of water power, and because of their greater interest in transportation as compared with factory industry, were at first more concerned with the steamboat engine and the locomotive. But crude stationary engines, as has been seen, soon carried lumbering and milling beyond the limits of water power. In the meantime, the age-old pitchback principle for utilizing simply the weight of the water and turning the wheel backward toward the fall continued to be the principal source of power in manufacturing till near the middle of the century. In the 'forties, a French turbine wheel on exhibit at the Franklin Institute at Philadelphia was used as a model for the first successful American turbine. The principle having been learned from foreigners, the development and standardization of the turbine and its efficient application to industry were more largely effected by Americans than by foreigners.

This tendency to acquire the principle from abroad and to outrival the old world in its practical use, is characteristic of Americans in the textile industries, in smelting, in road building and canal construction, and in other phases of technology. "These very Americans," wrote de Tocqueville, "who have not discovered one of the general laws of mechanics, have introduced into navigation an engine which changes the aspect of the world."

Franklin was a scholar who received world-wide recognition. But he was typically American because he wrote *Poor Richard's Almanac* and invented a stove. The distinctive passion among Americans, so de Tocqueville and others tell us, was for physical comfort. De Tocqueville's explanation is implicit in the title of his famous book,

Democracy in America. In an aristocratic society, a few inherit the means of physical comfort and give the matter little thought. The lower classes likewise pay little heed to improving material conditions of living because their inheritance accustoms them to a mode of life devoid of all save necessaries and to a mode of thought which sees no possibility of improvement. In America, in spite of limitless opportunity, home-seeking and the quest of fortune were harsh experiences. Once established, men found that wealth for a comfortable living was readily obtainable; and in a crude, uncultured community, wealth had little other value. Those who came to America were willing to struggle through harsh experiences but their natural goal was to escape therefrom into a comfortable existence.

American ingenuity naturally found expression most distinctively in ministering to the "ruling passion" for physical comfort. "The great glory of the Americans," wrote an Englishman in 1861, "is in their wondrous contrivances—in their patent remedies for the usually troublous operations of life. In their huge hotels all the bell ropes of each house ring on one bell only; but a patent indicator discloses a number, and the whereabouts of the ringer is shown. One fire heats every room, passage, hall, and cupboard, and does it so effectually that the inhabitants are all but stifled. Soda water bottles open themselves without any trouble of wire or strings. Men and women go up and downstairs without motive power of their own. Hot and cold water are laid into all the chambers; though it sometimes happens that the water from both taps is boiling, and that, when once turned on, it cannot be turned off again by any human energy. Everything is done by a wonderful new and patent contrivance; and of all their wonderful contrivances, that of their railroad beds [berths] is by no means the least. . . . Looking at the bed in the light of a bed—taking, as it were, an abstract view of it—or comparing it with some other bed or beds with which the occupant may have acquaintance, I cannot say that it is in all respects perfect. But distances are long in America.''

Perhaps the chief distinction of American technology, even in the earlier stages of capitalistic manufacturing, was mass production to meet the demands of a democratic and rapidly growing country. Selling at ''a low price to all'' rather than at ''a high price to a few'' was described as early as the paradoxically democratic ''reign'' of Andrew Jackson as the characteristic feature of American business. It was observed that one result was a lowering of the quality of goods. When only a few wealthy people had watches, these were mostly good ones; with a watch in everybody's pocket, there were few good ones. But undoubtedly with increase of output, price declined more rapidly than quality. In any case, desire ''to sell at a low price to all'' has been a factor in the unprecedented development in America of standardized, large-scale production.

Such an evolution of industry was based in part on the application of power in the operation of machinery in manufacturing. But the making of efficient steam engines and spinning machines and other devices depended on power-operated machine tools. On account of the lack of such tools, the cylinders of many of Watt's engines, even after he had the facilities of Boulton's plant, often varied more than an eighth of an inch, and in attempts to make them steam-tight they were stuffed with cork, putty, paper, and felt. The limitations of mechanical methods are further illustrated by the fact that bolts and screws were chipped and filed by hand, with infinite variations in size and pitch or number of threads per inch.

In the field of machine tools, as elsewhere, Americans profited, especially in the initial stages, by the work of foreigners. Particularly important were Henry Maudslay's improvements of the lathe. The turner's lathe, one of the oldest of mechanical devices, was capable from early times of beautiful and varied creations. Minor variations, in fact, were unavoidable. Even the most expert turner could not so guide his tool by hand as to make an exact duplicate. Nor could the speed of the revolving material to which the tool was applied be materially increased in order to reduce the cost. Henry Maudslay's innovation, known as the slide rest, was a mechanism for the automatic control of the cutting tool as well as of the material to which the tool was applied. With innumerable variations, the principle of mechanical control of cutting, planing, grinding, drilling and boring tools made possible the production of articles or parts of articles, whether of metal or of material not so stubborn, on a scale of measurement so exact as to vary only in an infinitesimal fraction of an inch. Mechanical speed decreased the cost as well as increased the accuracy. Exact duplication of parts gave rise to the system of interchangeable parts and made possible a vast reduction of costs and cheapening of repairs.

Samuel Smiles, who, in his biographies of English engineers, idolized machines and the makers of them, contrasts the mode of operation of engines of the old and the new type. "We have heard of a piece of machinery of the old school, the wheels of which made such a clatter that the owner feared the engine would fall to pieces. The foreman who set it agoing, after working at it until he was almost in despair, at last gave it up, saying, 'I think we had better leave the cogs to settle their differences with one another: they will grind themselves right in time.'" When an engine was first set up, it was induced to go to work with utmost difficulty. Often the foreman of the factory where it was made was called in, and "would almost live beside the engine for a month or more; and after easing her here and screwing her up there, putting in a new part and altering an old one, packing the piston and tightening the valves, the machine would at length be got to work. But now," he goes on to say, and he was writing in 1863, "the case is quite different." By means of machine tools, variations are kept within a thousandth of an inch. The five thousand parts of the oscillating engines of the *Warrior* were made by workmen "who knew not the places they were to occupy, and fitted together with such precision that so soon as the steam was raised and let into the cylinders, the immense machine began as if to breathe and move like a living creature, stretching its huge arms like a new-born giant, and then, after practising its strength a little and proving its soundness of body and limb, it started off with the power of above a thousand horses to try its strength in breasting the billows of the North Sea."

Machine tools were particularly important in making machinery for use in the production of standardized goods. Before the end of the eighteenth century an American invented an automatic nail-making device. About the same time, mechanical lathes were introduced for turning flat, round, or oval handles and standardized gun stocks. Early in the nineteenth century, the idea of interchangeable parts was applied by Eli Whitney, inventor of the cotton gin, to the making of muskets. Within half a century, rifle and revolver making was so highly standardized that in the rifle factories machines of a hundred kinds were used, so largely automatic that one workman supervised a considerable number of them. Samuel Colt, who died in 1862, established one of the most remarkable factories of his age and perfected the standardized manufacture of the revolver to such an extent that in England, the birthplace of modern technology, he was paid the sincerest form of flattery. By 1860, standardized watches were rivaling the output of European craftsmen; harvesters and other machines for farmers far excelled those of any other country; and the sewing machine had begun to transform the clothing and leather-working trades. These are but a few outstanding instances of technological advance made possible by machine tools.

LABOR

Foreign observers often commented on American ingenuity in mechanistic industry, and sometimes accounted for it by lack of labor. "In the States," observed an Englishman who made an official report in 1854, "the labor market is higher than with ourselves, especially as respects skilled labor. It has, therefore, been a principal aim as much as possible to apply machinery for the purpose of supplying this want, and, as the consequence, it will be seen that some of the principal achievements of American inventors have been acquired in this department. To this . . . may be attributed the extraordinary ingenuity displayed in many of their labor-saving machines, where automatic action so completely supplies the place of the more abundant hand-labor of older manufacturing countries."

Other observers noted the independent spirit of American workers. "It must not be dissembled," wrote another Englishman in 1823, "that there are circumstances which render it disagreeable to carry on manufacture in America. The workmen are under very little subjection: sometimes they are absent from their work for several days, to the great detriment of the employer; but should they be reprimanded, it might cause the proprietor to be insulted; and the indignation of the working people, in this land of equality, is really to be dreaded. Those workmen who are attentive, and of economical habits, soon acquire a little property; and with this they will buy land and quit their former employers, for all species of servitude is disliked in the United States.''

The opportunities of employees to secure cheap land or to make a living as independent shopkeepers or craftsmen gave to the workers a sense of security which, from the point of view of employers in quest of cheap and subservient labor, no doubt had its disadvantages. The advantages of free labor, which northerners so often claimed in contrast with the disadvantages of slave labor, ought to apply, so it would seem, to their labor in contrast with the ''cheap'' and subservient if not servile labor of their European competitors. But it was generally held that ''free'' labor must not be too ''free'' or else manufactures could not thrive. Franklin, like Englishmen of his time, went so far as to say that ''manufactures are founded in poverty. It is the multitude of poor without land in a country, and who must work for others at low wages or starve, that enables undertakers to carry on a manufacture, and afford it cheap enough to prevent the importation of the same kind from abroad, and to bear the expense of its own exportation. But no man who can have a piece of land of his own, sufficient by his labor to subsist his family in plenty, is poor enough to be a manufacturer,[1] and work for a master.'' Such views in time became a part of the foundation of international socialism—in a manner hardly foreseen even by the shrewd Franklin.

During the middle decades of the century, American

[1] Note the older use of the word manufacturer, common before the rise of mechanized industry.

laborers were far from starvation and cheap land was far from exhaustion. But conditions from 1840 to 1860 were tending decidedly toward the creation of a mass of dependent workers who could not readily be absorbed by agriculture or by mining, lumbering, and other basic industries.

One of these conditions was the subsiding of westward expansion as the frontier approached "the great American desert" and the choicer intervening areas were settled. There was a certain disillusion and a weeding-out process by which many were turned back from the pursuit of fortune by way of the west. The unhealthy speculation in land brought fortune to a few but loss of savings and of opportunity for home-building to many more. A sarcastic Englishman remarked that not more than one-half of one per cent of the Yankees who started west intended to cultivate the soil. Their aim was to make fortunes by dealing in "the great western staple—the Progress of the Country." In this grander aim they had even learned to scorn the selling of cheap clocks and wooden nutmegs. Times of stress, and especially the panics of 1837 and 1857, forced many of the vast numbers who engaged in land speculation to give up at a sacrifice even their valid holdings. Another Englishman as early as 1843 observed the conditions which were inevitably tending to create a class of industrial laborers. He noted the abundance of fruit and provisions for which there was no market, and continued: "The same evil exists in the western states of America, as respects agricultural produce, as we find in England as to manufactured goods; excessive competition, and consequent reductions in wages, have driven so many from the eastern states, to cultivate land in the west, added to the shoals of emigrants daily arriving from other countries, that the produce is so abundant it can scarcely be sold for the expense of taking it fifty miles to market, and prices will still go lower and lower as more and more land is brought into cultivation." This tendency was soon to be accentuated by the use of labor-saving farm machinery.

The most important source of labor for manufactures was immigration. There was little of this during the first feud with England and on through the maladjustments of the early republic, the European wars, and the War of 1812, to the fourth decade of the century. Nor was the flow considerable during the era of most rapid expansion westward. The number of immigrants nevertheless increased from less than ten thousand in 1820 to about eighty thousand in 1844. Then came famine and rebellion in Ireland. Year by year the number doubled and trebled and quadrupled till in 1850 more than three hundred thousand came. Most of them fled from starvation and coercion in Ireland. In the meantime the revolutionary movement in Europe beginning in 1848 was running its course. Liberal and democratic elements, especially in Germany, were being harassed by reactionary governments and were suffering disillusion as to the liberalizing and unifying of Germany as a result of the Revolution of 1848. The number of immigrants therefore continued to increase till 1854. In that year the number was about 425,000. Then began a temporary decline.

The immigration from 1820 to 1860 included 872,317 who were classed as laborers. This classification excluded farmers (764,837), mechanics (407,524), servants (49,-494), and varying numbers of miners, mariners, and craftsmen in the principal fields of skilled industry. The Irish, numbering almost a million from 1820 to 1860, engaged largely in unskilled labor connected with agriculture and with the innumerable construction and transportation enterprises. They thus relieved (or ousted) Americans from such forms of labor and made them available for employment in manufacturing. Germans, numbering almost a million and a half, engaged more commonly in farming, in which they often outrivaled Americans, and in the trades requiring skill and patience.

It was the coming of the Germans, and particularly of the Irish, which created in America a laboring class in the European sense. But no "labor problem" in the sense of serious conflicts between employers and employees resulted even from this vast inflow of workers. Many of the factory workers were girls who were not entirely self-dependent, and who expected presently to marry. Workers continued to hope for a turn of fortune that would bring them wealth and independence; and although in most cases the hope was destined to be illusory, it led them to view their jobs with complaisance as makeshifts or as temporary instruments for acquiring capital. Employees were likely to think of themselves as capitalists in the making or as housewives to-be. Employers therefore had the advantages of an adequate supply of laborers who were inclined, to be sure, to change jobs freely but who were reasonably industrious and rarely inclined toward organization or group action.

PROTECTION

When the mid-century Irish tide was setting westward, American protectionist orators were turning with fervor to the argument that high tariffs mean high wages. "It is a protective tariff," ran an argument of 1846, "which gives to American industry the only effectual guaranty that it will not be brought down to a level with the degraded labor of Europe. It furnishes the only security that our standard of wages is not to be measured by the cost of production in those countries where the life of the laborer is but an incessant struggle for bread.'' The controversial character of the subject, and the shifting of arguments with shifting of group alignments, are illustrated by the case of Daniel Webster. When New England was against protection, he attempted to prove the natural affinity of high wages and free trade. When capital in New England was turning to tariff-shielded industries, he was equally sure of the beneficence of protection in promoting labor's welfare.

Americans had rebelled against the old protective system of England even more than against a recognition of the sovereignty of the English crown. But some of the features of the system were copied by them, and one of these features, the levying of duties on imports, has been so intensively developed that, to an American, protection ordinarily means simply the levying of import duties for the avowed purpose of protecting American industry.

The refusal of the states to permit the Congress of the Confederation to levy import duties was a factor in the calling of the Constitutional Convention. One of the first measures of the new government was the enactment in 1789 of a tariff which is commonly described as having been merely for revenue, but which was certainly intended in part for the encouragement of American industry. From 1808 to 1815, when foreign trade was largely cut off, protection by tariff was of course inconsequential. Tariff duties were increased mainly to aid in meeting the costs of the War of 1812. But the pleasing taste of wartime monopoly experienced by manufacturers from 1808 to 1815, combined with fears of English competition on the resumption of trade with England, stimulated the demand for protection by tariff duties. The act of 1816 and subsequent acts to 1833, particularly those of 1824 and 1828, were frankly protectionist. They aimed especially at the promotion of the cotton, woollen and iron industries. In the meantime the question was acquiring the partisan and controversial character it has since then continued to exhibit. By a compromise arrangement in 1833, protective duties were to be retained but gradually reduced. Tariff policies from 1833 to 1857 were subjected to many fluctuations, but the prevailing tendency, as in England during the same period, was in the direction of free trade.

Tariffs, it can safely be said, influenced the way in which capital and labor were applied. The real or supposed advantages of protection to the manufacturer naturally attracted capital in a measure into protected channels. But since the country was consistently classed among the debtor countries and was regularly experiencing a deficit of capital, the use of capital in one industry meant the withdrawing of capital from some other field of investment. Funds diverted by tariffs from consumption into manufacturing were probably inconsequential, and were at least in part counterbalanced by higher prices of consumption goods in protected categories. The net result of tariffs, therefore, was the stimulation of certain industries by the attracting of capital and labor, and retardation of other industries by the withdrawal or the withholding of capital and labor. The degree of stimulation and retardation, and the resulting advantages or disadvantages to the country—these are questions to which controversy has given a disproportionate interest and importance.

The tariffs of the epoch, in the judgment of economists as distinguished from public officials, demonstrate the influence of protection not so much on the development of manufactures as on the evolution of popular thought. The tendency has been to view the problem of promoting manufactures in solid colors of black and white. To one school of thought the tariff has been the scapegoat; to another, the cure-all. Public officials are naturally among the most vocal of all classes. Nor are they timid in making claims as to the beneficence of their own and the maleficence of their opponents' policies. Individuals or groups whose interests are served by a particular policy find it much easier to convince themselves and others that the policy should be adopted if it can be made to appear essential to the welfare of all. Those who refuse to be convinced are likely to go to the other extreme of attributing to such a policy the destruction of the public welfare. Tariff controversies were more influential than the intrinsic effects of tariffs in aggravating the group cleavages which culminated in the Civil War and which are presently to be considered.

EXTENT OF CAPITALISTIC INTERVENTION IN MANUFACTURING

In America as in England, the earliest and most complete instance of the supplanting of household and handicraft shop industry was the spectacular rise of capitalistic cotton manufacturing. Samuel Slater, an English artisan who defied the English authorities by emigrating to America, and who has been called "the father of the factory system in America," was less influential than is commonly supposed. The first practicable mill for spinning was put up under his direction, to be sure, in 1790, from his memory of spinning machinery in England, but conditions were then unfavorable, and little progress was made till after the interruption of trade in 1808. Thereafter, mills were rapidly built, and Slater, among others, profited by the ill wind that blighted commerce. By that time, too, the cotton gin was having its effect on the supply of raw material. Francis Lowell, a New England merchant, was one of those who turned idle wartime trading capital to good account in the cotton industry. He had made a study of the new system of manufacturing while visiting in Manchester, and upon his return he put to use the knowledge acquired abroad by perfecting a power loom and forming a company for combining in a single plant the various processes of cloth making. After him was named "the Manchester of America," the new industrial city that sprang up at Pawtucket Falls on the Merrimac.

For the early decades of the century, statistics are extremely deficient. But the general trend is apparent. It is supposed that the amount of cotton consumed in 1790 was 5,000,000 pounds. By 1815 it had grown to about 20,000,000 pounds. The amount used in 1860 was nearly 423,000,000 pounds. The number of spindles in factories in 1805 was about 4,500; in 1815, about 130,000; and in 1825, about 800,000. By 1860, the number of spindles had grown to about 5,235,000. The increasing size of factories is shown in part by the increasing number of spindles per factory. According to Secretary Gallatin's report of 1810, the number of spindles per factory in 1808 was only about five hundred; fourteen of the sixty-two mills were so small as to be operated by horse power. The number consistently increased till by 1860 the average per factory was about 4,800. There was also a tendency to combine the various phases of cloth making in a single plant.

In a similar manner but more slowly in woollen manufacturing the factory system encroached upon household and handicraft shop methods, long firmly established in the woollen industry. Capitalistic woollen as well as cotton manufacturing was localized largely in New England, and especially in Massachusetts.

The introduction of the sewing machine stimulated the capitalistic organization of the clothing trade. In this industry, there had grown up in the cities the outwork or "putting-out" system, by which workers received materials and did the work in their homes. The sewing machine, which came into use in the late 'forties, gave a great impetus to the use of ready-made clothing. The outwork system continued, but with it the number of clothing factories for performing certain parts of the work increased, and at the same time, the "boss" system developed, by which portions of the work were done in small shops under "bosses," who, in turn, were engaged by the "master tailors" or factory owners to supplement the work done in factories. The business was thus carried on by a combination of factory, shop, and household work, but under the direction of capitalists. The output in 1860 was valued at $69,000,000, ranking third among reproductive manufactures. The industry was extensively developed in thc west, especially at Cincinnati, its basis there being in the demands of the cotton country.

Even more valuable in output, as well as more capitalistic in nature, was the boot and shoe industry. This industry and other leather-working trades, as well as clothing, were affected by the sewing machine. Indeed, machines for cutting, shaping, and sewing leather lent themselves more readily to factory organization than did machines for sewing cloth. Only one branch of reproductive manufactures (cotton goods) had an output of greater value in 1860 than the boot and shoe industry. The output of a single establishment in that year was valued at $750,000, and this was one of five factories operated by the same proprietors. These five plants produced more than a million pairs of footwear worth $1,300,000. Machinery operated by steam power, so the census authorities observed, was coming into vogue. As in textiles, New England took the lead, though the output at Philadelphia exceeded that of any other one town.

In value of output, the leading industries in 1860 (aside from basic industries) were cotton, boots and shoes, clothing, woollen goods, and machinery. The making of machinery was promoted by several factors, some of which were peculiar to America. Growth of machine-using industries; the desire to sell cheaply to every one instead of at a dear price to a few; the invention of machine tools; the scarcity of labor; the vast amount of engineering and construction work: these and other factors account for the remarkable development in America of this important branch of manufacturing. In machine making, New England was overshadowed by New York and Pennsylvania. In the west, Ohio and Kentucky held the places of preeminence, due in large part to demand for engines for steamboats and to the growing market for farm machinery.

An index of progress toward capitalistic manufacturing is found in the decline of household industry. Statistical evidence is fragmentary, to be sure, but as to the general trend it is conclusive. The value of household manufactures per capita in 1840 is estimated to have been $1.70; in 1850, $1.18; in 1860, $.78. By the last named date, the output of houschold industry in New England and the middle states was negligible. In many parts of the south the system continued in virtually unabated vigor. The output per capita in Tennessee in 1860 was valued at $2.86 as compared with $.19 in Pennsylvania. In the regions which were settled after 1840, household industry gained only a precarious and temporary hold. This is explained by the fact that transportation facilities were keeping pace with settlement and making possible an inter-dependent economy in place of a self-sufficing economy. The proportion of population in 1860 engaged in specialized manufacturing in New England was about one to eight; in the central states, one to fifteen; in the west, one to forty-eight; and in the south, one to eighty-two. The absence of capitalistic manufactures in the south is further instanced by the fact that in the "Cotton Kingdom" in 1860 there were less than three hundred thousand spindles out of a total of nearly five and a quarter millions in the country, and of those in the south, few were in the main area of cotton culture.

A final bit of evidence as to the extent of capitalistic intervention in manufacturing is an estimated expansion of investment from fifty million dollars in 1820 to a billion dollars in 1860. To be sure, there is no differentiation in this estimate between primary and reproductive manufactures, but undoubtedly the latter made relatively greater progress in the interval than the former.

REVIVAL OF FOREIGN TRADE AND SHIPPING

Capitalistic manufacturing waxed as household industry waned. But the tremendously rapid increase in the output of factories was absorbed in small part only by markets made accessible by receding household industry. The cheaper cost of machine-made goods created new demands not met by the output of household and shop industries. With growing wealth and population, new tastes were formed, new wants experienced. Many of these were for luxuries and finer goods not native to America or not economically produced at home. The basic industries afforded increasing surpluses for export. In consequence, the eclipse of foreign trade beginning with the Napoleonic wars was temporary.

The sudden influx of goods after the Treaty of Ghent of 1814 was a prime factor in the panic of 1819. Bad financial conditions combined with westward expansion and protective tariffs kept foreign trade from prospering for more than a decade. By 1837 there was a lively trade in exports and imports alike, but the panic of that year had results resembling those of the panic of 1819. It was not till near the middle of the century that there was consistently rapid expansion. For comparison we may take the years 1816, 1846, and 1860.

Exports: 1816, $81,920,000; 1846, $113,489,000; 1860, $400,122,000.

Imports: 1816, $147,103,000; 1846, $121,692,000; 1860, $362,166,000.

The figures of 1846 had been exceeded, but only in a sporadic manner. After 1846, there was a consistent growth. The carrying trade, which figures to some extent in both exports and imports, declined in relative importance.

Accompanying the increase in exports and imports, there was a corresponding growth in shipbuilding and in tonnage of American ships for foreign trade. Shipbuilding flourished. This was the golden age of the sailing ship, soon to be supplanted by British ingenuity and initiative in building ocean-going ships of steel propelled by steam. The registered tonnage or tonnage intended for foreign trade amounted in 1810 to 984,269 tons. The tonnage of 1840 was actually smaller—899,764 tons. But by 1860 it had grown to 2,379,000 tons. The gross tonnage of entrances and clearances in 1846 was 6,300,000; in 1860, 17,067,000. The prominence of American capital in this unprecedented increase of trade is shown not alone by growth of shipbuilding but by the fact that in 1860 American vessels carried, in value, 66.5% of the imports and exports, and made, in gross tonnage, 71% of entrances and clearances.

What is the explanation of this remarkable intervention of capital in foreign trade at a time when capital and labor were being so extensively directed into other channels? A factor of importance, but undoubtedly by some exaggerated, was the work of the 'forty-niners and their successors in the expansion of the gold supply and of credit based thereon. The Opium War of 1841 was another factor of some importance, as it hastened the opening up of Chinese trade. England in 1845 repealed her Corn Law restricting the import of grain, and allowed her vast industrial population unhindered access to American supplies. Her historic Acts of Trade were finally repealed in 1849. About the same time, a series of free-trade budgets removed the principal duties on imports into England. The southern planters were experiencing their heyday of prosperity in their expansion over the choicest lands of the cotton belt. The ever-increasing output of the fleecy staple bulged the outgoing ships and furnished the money for buying foreign goods. The opening up of transportation facilities to the west brought western grain and other goods to eastern marts for export and took European as well as eastern manufactures to the west. These developments appear, viewed superficially, to be conclusive evidence of abounding national well-being. But in them is discernible the fatal culmination of group cleavages—the end of the liaison of western farmer and southern planter.

PART V

CONFLICT

CHAPTER XVI

GROUP CONNECTIONS AND CLEAVAGES

CREDITOR-DEBTOR CONFLICT

The group relations which culminated in mid-century violent conflict went through an evolution traceable to the creditor-debtor conflict beginning in the early days of the republic.

The legendary view of the founders of the American republic was of men on pedestals. Washington, Jefferson, Adams, and even Hamilton were arbitrarily detached from the concrete problems of individual and group interest from which no man can escape and retain his influence on the course of political events. With the appearance of such books as the studies by Professor Charles A. Beard on the early economic history of the republic, the legendary view is giving way to a frank recognition of the fact that the government of the republic was forged, as it has continued to be tested, in the fires of economic conflict.

In 1788, Washington wrote of the gulf of debt in which the people had been floundering. A noted American historian has asserted that if the debtor laws had been rigorously enforced after the Revolution, two-thirds of the people in parts of the country would have been in prison. It is not difficult to understand why such a division of the population into debtors and creditors existed. The testimony of

Washington is an indication that the Revolution was no exception to the general rule that war affords unusual opportunities for concentration of wealth by questionable means. "Speculation, peculation, engrossing, forestalling," he complained, "afford too many proofs of the decay of public virtue." But without questioning the motives or virtues of the participants in the events of the time, it can readily be seen that economic forces were tending toward the enrichment of some and the impoverishment of many others.

Agriculture had been seriously disrupted, especially in the regions occupied by troops, and in lieu of money, credit was required for restoration to normal conditions. The same is true in varying degree of a number of other industries. Workers were in a bad way. Prices had risen rapidly; wages lagged far behind. The disbanded soldiers added to the unemployed. Congress had no money to pay off the army. The officers, after exerting pressure accompanied by some show of disaffection, were liberally treated with five years' full pay. The privates were unable to secure adequate arrangements even for back pay, and whenever they were fortunate enough even to secure credit, they swelled the ranks of debtors. As an alternative they could only heed the call of the wild. In lieu of pay some of them were given "land scrip." But large numbers bartered away their rights to land in order to meet immediate needs, and thus promoted the tendency toward control of western lands by capitalists and land companies. With the choicer regions thus preempted, soldiers and workers were faced even in the west by the threat of dependence on the creditor-capitalist group.

The rise in prices which so adversely affected the laboring population was largely due to inflation of the currency. Those who had only their labor to sell were likely to have to accept depreciated money at a high valuation and to dispose of it in making purchases at a low valuation. Not only wage earners but also those with fixed incomes in salaries and in returns from certain forms of investment were likely to have to accept depreciated currency and to pay inflated prices. People with poor means of knowing what was going on, especially the farmers in contrast with those in the centers of trade, being unable to keep in touch with fluctuations, were at an obvious disadvantage.

ASCENDANCY OF THE CREDITOR-CAPITALIST GROUP

It will be recalled that the vast quantities of paper money issued by the Continental Congress and the states depreciated rapidly. Holders of notes, mortgages, and other formal instruments of credit would of course have been at a disadvantage if they had been required to accept from their debtors the depreciated currency at face value. On the other hand, the failure of the government to recognize the validity and legal tender nature of its own money meant repudiation and confiscation. Creditors preferred repudiation and confiscation. Their view was adopted and was given final recognition in 1790 by the fixing of the ratio of 100 to 1 for the redemption of currency.

There was another kind of government obligation,—the certificates of indebtedness or bonds. These, like the money, had depreciated. They often changed hands at five per cent of their face value. But they were not legal tender, and debtors could not use them at face value for paying off any form of debt. The creditor class, which had generally favored repudiation of the government's obligations in the form of money, opposed the repudiation of the certificates or bonds. Here again they won. The certificates were to be redeemed, by means of taxes, at their face value. At the same time, they were made the basis of financing the country's principal institution for controlling currency and credit—the Bank of the United States.

Sources of wartime wealth, as government contracts, privateering, and greater bargaining power in connection with fluctuating economic conditions, particularly prices, had given to eastern capitalists an initial advantage. The certificates of indebtedness were so extensively bought up by them cheaply on the eve of the adoption of the policy of repayment at face value that they held an overwhelming proportion of the securities at small cost. Massachusetts held more than Virginia, North Carolina and Georgia combined. Bank stock, too, was similarly held, largely by virtue of the use of debt securities to purchase bank stock. In 1791, only three of the twenty-five directors were from the south; and at the next election, only two southerners were chosen. Such were the results of the assumption, refunding, and bank bills.

The same group of moneyed men, it was now recognized, was in control of shipping, trade, and manufactures, and was in a position to make profits on the business of the planters—profits which often appeared to the planters to be not payments earned but tributes levied.

Many of the grievances of the planters were also grievances of the small farmers, who found it even more difficult to escape from debt than did the planters. They and the frontiersmen had an added grievance—the engrossment of western lands. J. A. J. Fauchet, French minister to America in 1794, observed the grumbling attitude toward the policy by which "vast and fruitful domains" were "sold in whole provinces to capitalists who enrich themselves with great profits by parceling out to the cultivators land which they themselves never saw."[1]

[1] For accounts of the early financial and land policies of the government, see above, pp. 122–126.

REVOLT OF THE DEBTOR-PLANTER GROUP

The planters, to be sure, had tried, but with few exceptions not very successfully, to rival the capitalists in the engrossment of western lands. They had helped to frame the Constitution and to put the federal government into operation. As Hamiltonian policies one after another were adopted, the planters became increasingly wary, but were reassured by the presence of the greatest of the planters in the executive chair. With Washington no longer president, and with some of the effects of Hamiltonian policies becoming apparent, there developed a sufficient community of interest among planters and small farmers and frontiersmen to enable the planters to veer away from their former capitalistic associates in the making of the new government and to seek an alliance against them for the control of the government.

In the person of Jefferson the movement found an effective leader. He had not been a member of the Constitutional Convention. His connection with Hamiltonian policies had been plausibly clear of commitments, in spite of his deal with Hamilton for supporting federal assumption of state debts in return for placing the capital on the Potomac. His philosophical doctrines of equality and his interest in the extension of small-scale agriculture as a basis for democracy, equipped him for gaining the ear of the small farmers and frontiersmen. And so, under Jefferson's direction, there arose, in the words of Fauchet, "a declared opposition between the agricultural and the moneyed interests."

Jefferson, who won the election of 1800, avowed his agreement with the predominant element, "the agricultural part of our citizens," but he recognized the limitations of practical politics. Referring to Hamilton's policies, he said, "We can never get rid of his financial system." In respect to other matters he expressed the hope of being able "by degrees to introduce sound principles and make them habitual." But "what is practicable must often control what is pure theory."

What was "practicable" turned out to be a simultaneous reduction of taxes and of the national debt by paying off the principal of the debt contrary to Hamilton's idea of a permanent debt; the reduction of expenses for public offices and for naval armaments desired by the commercial interests but regarded as useless by agrarians; the purchase of Louisiana, affording territory for the expansion of agriculture to counteract the growth of urban interests; and a slight curbing of the Bank of the United States by utilizing "Republican" banks or banks at least willing to acquiesce in "the reformed order of things" for handling public finances. Local banks were likely to be partisan because the chartering of banks was a prerogative of the state legislatures, and banking privileges were under the spoils system even earlier than public offices. Under Madison, upon whom fell the Jeffersonian mantle, the bank was refused a renewal of its charter. But chaotic financial conditions resulted in 1816 in the chartering of the second Bank of the United States. The earlier fear of the central government when under Federalist control was now diminished, though insistence on state rights continued among agrarians.

Jefferson's desire to conciliate the capitalistic interests and to utilize them in support of "the reformed order of things" found further expression in his allowing the tariff to stand, and in his support of the claims of the Yazoo land companies. These claims grew out of rather exceptionally corrupt and offensive land speculations in the region of the Yazoo River in what is now western Mississippi. Southern Republicans were generally hostile, but many northern Republicans favored the claims. Most of the stockholders lived in the north. Jefferson's view finally prevailed, but not till 1814. So successful was the party of Jefferson in wooing and winning business interests and at the same time in retaining the support of the agrarians that parties for a time gave way to mere factional differences within the Republican party. The tendency was facilitated by the solvents of war and of westward expansion. But realignments were soon to appear.

REVOLT OF THE "COMMON MAN"

It is apparent not only from the original text of the Constitution but even more specifically from the writings of Hamilton, Adams, Madison, and others, that the makers of the Constitution had in mind a society controlled by an untitled aristocracy of wealth. "The property and liberty of the rich" were to be secured, said Adams, "against the encroachments of the poor in a popular assembly," the House of Representatives, by means of an "independent" senate, an "independent" judiciary, and a president whose selection was to be beyond the reach of popular control.

But who are the rich? The Hamiltonians believed that among the rich, the capitalistic elements or the "moneyed men" should prevail. To strengthen these elements, he inaugurated his far-reaching financial plans which put an overwhelming part of the fluid wealth of the country into the hands of a few holders of debt securities and bank stock. These were the rich men—"the aristocracy of paper [stocks and bonds] and patronage," as an opponent in derision called them. The Jeffersonian party was inclined, at least in the person of Jefferson, to theorize about equality and democracy. But even Jefferson himself was disinclined to remove the property qualifications for voting or to amend the provisions of the Constitution for safeguarding the power of the propertied classes. To the Jeffersonians, the propertied classes most worthy of power were the landed classes. To them the moneyed classes cherished by Hamiltonian policy were at first anathema. But as has been seen, the Jeffersonian party came to terms with men of moneyed property. There was a reconciliation of the business men with the agrarian government on the basis of their acquiescence in "the reformed order of things"—which meant not a whole loaf as under Hamilton but a goodly portion.

But in the meantime, while Jeffersonians in philosophical moments were toying with the theory of democracy, the unlettered pioneers were building democratic societies from the mountains to the Great River. Even in the strongholds of Hamilton's "moneyed men," the working classes were becoming self-conscious and demanding the ten-hour day, the vote, and the free public school. The planters, to whom the democratic dogmas of Jefferson had been a matter of mild amusement, were at last engulfed by the rising tide of manhood suffrage. Politicians who had denounced the demands of the masses for the suffrage became converted to the cult of the common man. In public an extreme simplicity of dress was affected. Daniel Webster had joined with John Adams and others of the old guard in Massachusetts to stop the onset of the democratic hosts. Later he was glad to claim the reflected glory of having older brothers and sisters who had been born in a log cabin. "If ever I am ashamed of it, may my name and the name of my posterity be blotted from the memory of mankind."

In 1828 began the "reign" of Andrew Jackson, "Old Hickory," the frontiersman. In the presidential campaign of 1840, the Whigs, heirs of the Hamiltonian tradition, represented General Harrison, their candidate, as living in a log cabin, wearing a coonskin cap, and drinking hard cider. He was in fact a Virginia "gentleman" who had moved to

Ohio, built a country mansion, and maintained a rather antiquated interest in classical literature. And so the campaign of 1840 was in reality a demonstration of the possibilities of burlesque and of publicity buncombe in utilizing the cult of the common man for partisan ends.

There was no consistent body of thought or public policy associated with the Jacksonian revolt because there was no economic unity or cohesion among the common people as distinguished from those who had previously controlled the government. Pretensions to prestige or influence based on wealth or inheritance and family connections were subjected to scorn. The capitalistic interests of the east were particularly suspect, and the second Bank of the United States was not rechartered because of a belief that it was being utilized unfairly in the interest of men whose fortunes were already made and to the disadvantage of men on the make. There was no objection to banking as such or to private capitalism as such. The predominant ideal was to make money by approved eastern methods of stock jobbing and land speculation as well as by farming or trade. Men of all classes, in the west even more than in the east, shared the frenzy of speculation in land, in bank credit, and in corporation stocks preceding the panics of 1837 and 1857. There was a pervading passion, wrote de Tocqueville, who lived in America at the height of the democratic cult, for wealth and physical prosperity. "I never met in America with any citizen so poor," he remarks, "as not to cast a glance of hope and envy on the enjoyments of the rich, or whose imagination did not possess itself by anticipation of those good things which fate still obstinately withheld from him."

There was no conception of ordered ranks and classes under aristocratic sway. Nor was there to be found, except in a few rare cases, a conception of the basic and complicated problems of working together and living together in society as being community problems. Individualism, almost to the point of anarchy, prevailed, especially in the newer communities. The individual "common man" either viewed himself as a potential capitalist, or planter, or wealthy farmer, or else in an unquiet acquiescence he made the most of fate.

STRANGE BEDFELLOWS

Out of this welter of individualism and horse-play politics emerged a fateful alignment between the ultra-democratic "common man" of the west and the most aristocratic of all Americans, the southern planter.

In a sense it was a renewal of the planter-debtor liaison which had overthrown the Federalist party of Hamilton and had given power to the Republican party of Jefferson. But in the meantime there had been the long period of confused and shifting issues and party alignments, during which the outstanding questions of public policy centered around Henry Clay's "American System" of protective tariffs for eastern manufacturers and of internal improvements for opening the east to western produce and the west to eastern manufactures.

Planters were in a bad way politically. They had an unconquerable aversion to protection because they exported cotton, rice, and tobacco, and imported manufactures. They were by no means enthusiastic for internal improvements as projected by Clay, for these, by facilitating interchange of eastern manufactures and western produce, would tend to tie together the eastern capitalists and the western farmers. To be sure the Whig party abandoned its principles in quest of power, but this hardly endeared it to the planters.

As for the Democratic faction of the old Republican

party of Jefferson, Madison, and Monroe, it had come under the sway of what seemed to the heirs of the Virginia Dynasty the harum-scarum elements, under the crude and domineering Jackson, who had even gone so far, in connection with the tariff and nullification, as to insult and manhandle the aristocracy of South Carolina. But the Virginia Dynasty had come to an end and something must be done.

As for the "common man" of the east, there had been in the 'thirties an outburst of humanitarianism and reforming zeal, with a tendency toward independent political action by labor groups. But there was no impelling economic motive for independent political action, and there was little of choice for these classes between Democrats and Whigs.

But western farmers and merchants, especially after internal improvements by the federal government ceased to be an issue, had reasons for aligning themselves with the planters. One cause was the dependence of both westerners and southerners on the credit, shipping, and other services furnished by eastern capitalists, with the accompanying feeling that the latter were tribute takers. The more conservative business men who were already wealthy and firmly established favored the Bank of the United States with centralized control and policies of stabilization. New men, capitalists in the making, and planters, believing that the bank was being used to their disadvantage, were for decentralization of banking and of governmental patronage of banks. These sentiments of opposition to the Bank of the United States, while not confined to the west and south, were naturally more commonly experienced there than in the east.

A more important issue, or at least an issue more persistently controversial, was the question of protective tariffs. Early in the history of the Republic, a small measure of protection as a nationalistic policy was not opposed by the south. New England, then more largely engaged in shipping and trade than in manufacturing, was the principal center of opposition to protection. With the growth of manufacturing and the decline of foreign trade, the capitalists of New England and the middle Atlantic States looked with increasing favor on protection. The planters of the south became extremely hostile. Westerners were inclined to flirt with Clay's "American System" of internal improvements and protective tariffs. But a series of vetoes, culminating in Jackson's famous Maysville veto of 1830, checked the extension of federal aid, and the panic of 1837 put an end for a time to state as well as federal grants. Thereafter federal internal improvements, except in connection with the later railroad land grants, figured little in national politics. Should westerners continue to favor tariff subsidies to eastern manufacturers without equivalent aid for the improvement of western transportation facilities? The western vote in 1824 had been almost unanimous for protection, while the southern vote had been overwhelmingly against the tariff bill of that year. As early as 1833 the drift of the western vote was apparent, and it continued in the 'forties in the direction of the southern free-trade position.

On the question of slavery in the territories, the western vote was far from unanimous or consistent, but the doctrine of popular sovereignty supported by the planters was at first in harmony with prevailing western sentiment.

But these and other political evidences of accord between the southern planters and western farmers and capitalists are merely superficial indications of an economic liaison which motivated political tendencies. This economic alliance was based on the imperative need of the west for a market. It was this need which, in the early days of the republic, had caused a threat of secession on the part of settlers beyond the mountains unless the federal government succeeded in opening up the Mississippi River to the unimpeded use of Americans. It was this need which formed the basis of Clay's abortive "American System." By the time it became apparent that the union of tariffs and internal improvements was to be unfruitful, the expansion of the plantation system over the lower Mississippi basin, east and west, had revealed the possibilities of a farmer-planter alliance.

"Cotton is King!" exclaimed a writer of the time. Cotton goods, he observes, may be seen freighting in almost every vessel of Christian nations that traverses the seas of the globe. They fill the warehouses and shelves of merchants everywhere. Why is it possible for stockholders in cotton corporations to receive their dividends, operatives their wages, merchants their profits, and civilized peoples everywhere their cheapest and most comfortable garments? It is because of the labor of slaves on southern plantations. Nearly all of the cotton consumed in the world is the product of American slave labor. While the cultivation of cotton outside of the southern states of the union has declined or has been at a standstill, the consumption of cotton in Europe from 1835 to 1845 almost doubled.

The writer goes on to say that it is this virtual monopoly that has given commercial value to slaves and has led to the rapid extension of slavery from Virginia, the Carolinas, and Georgia westward to the Mississippi and beyond. At the same time, through Ohio, Indiana, Illinois, and Michigan, free labor has been spreading with equal speed. Slaves cannot satisfactorily produce diversified crops; their *raison d'être* is the great commercial staple, cotton. The plantations, therefore, require vast quantities of provisions, clothing, and other supplies. Farmers of the free-soil states have long looked to the manufacturers of the east in vain for markets. At last by means of the steamboat on their river courses they have found the markets requisite for their prosperity on the southern plantations. The planters in turn sell their cotton to English manufacturers. Slavery thus "attains its importance to the nation and to the world by standing as an agency, intermediate between the grain-growing states and our foreign commerce. As the distillers of the west transformed the surplus grain into whiskey, that it might bear transport, so slavery takes the products of the north and metamorphoses them into cotton, that they may bear export."

In this way there "was a tripartite alliance formed, by which the western farmer, the southern planter, and the English manufacturer became united in a common bond of interest: the whole giving their support to the doctrine of free trade."

That this arrangement, thus clearly and in general accurately described by a writer of the time, had elements of weakness as well as of strength is apparent. The outstanding feature of the economic conflict preceding the Civil War was the struggle of southern planters to maintain the alliance and of eastern capitalists to disrupt it. The issue of this conflict was in reality the "impending crisis." The economic defeat of the planter was attested politically by the election of 1860. This in turn was the prelude to the appeal to arms.

CHAPTER XVII

VICTORIOUS CAPITALISM

NORTHWESTERN BRIDGE OF BOATS

Beyond the Appalachians lies the Great Valley. Upon the abounding prosperity of southern planter and western farmer, the eastern capitalist looked with envy. The first Hannibal who led the hosts of eastern capitalism across the divide was not himself distinguished as a capitalist but as governor of New York. His achievement was not by private initiative and investment but by public enterprise. Paradoxically, his conquest of the mountains was by a bridge of boats. South of the Erie Canal were the principal strongholds, but within a quarter of a century the main passes had been captured by the onset of the locomotive, and the Great Eastern Divide no longer divided the people.

The people of the west, by virtue of their sale of produce by floating it downstream, had been able to pay the heavy costs of carrying lighter and more valuable manufactures over the mountains, especially after the federal government had built the Cumberland Road, but virtually none of their produce could bear the charge of eastward transportation. This was altered by the Erie Canal, but only for those portions of the west which had access to the Great Lakes and only for certain kinds of goods. By the construction of the Pennsylvania Canal, the area of the western basin accessible to the east was enlarged, but the cumbersome and costly inclined-plane arrangement across the crest of the Alleghanies limited the canal severely. In 1844 through freight amounted to only 75,000 tons in contrast with 350,000 tons on the Erie Canal. Grain, for instance, could hardly bear the cost, and eastward-moving goods were far from equal to the westward flow.

The Erie Canal and the steamboat on the lakes made possible the development of a vast new region to the northwestward—a region too remote from the navigable southward flowing streams to enter successfully into the north-south system of trade. The main significance of the bridge of boats by way of the Erie Canal and the lakes was not the tapping of the Mississippi basin but the building of an empire in the otherwise isolated northwest. This region was bound from the first to northeastern capitalism by the flow of capital, by credit facilities, and by sentiment, as well as by the one line of communications that prevented isolation and made advancement possible.

WESTERN BANDS OF IRON

By means of canals connecting the Mississippi with the Great Lakes, a considerable diversion of traffic from the north-south system was possible. To be more exact, the possibility of sending goods eastward without loss meant that additional goods were produced. At the same time, the main flow southward was constantly increasing in volume. The alignment of southern planter and western farmer held. Competition of the east tended to raise the prices of western provisions, but southern planters were able to pay the added costs, and western farmers took a larger portion of the planters' gross profits. In another way canals affected but did not seriously impair the economic relations of planters and western farmers. By cheapening the cost of transporting from the east the manufactures needed in the west, the upstream traffic on the Mississippi was impeded, and the triangular trade was greatly increased. Western produce moved southward on the river courses. Western provisions not used in the south and southern cotton were exported or taken to the east by eastern shippers. Eastern and foreign manufactures moved westward by canal and river and to some extent southward by way of the west to the plantations.

Eastern capitalists were hardly disadvantaged by this arrangement, since they were in a position to share the profits accruing alike from southern cotton and from western provisions. But with the building of railroads they had an overwhelming advantage, especially over the planter. Canals were measureably effective as arteries for sending the life-blood of commerce westward, but not as veins for completing the circulatory system. The round-about triangular trade was the result. Railroads were veins as well as arteries.

Western provisions, even grain for eastern mills, could now be drawn eastward to compete with the output of seaboard farms. Thus eastern capitalists were able to lower the costs of maintaining the laboring population of the factories and the market places; and they were able to compete in European markets with the venders of the produce of the plains of Russia. Western hides and wool and lumber could now be made to feed the factories and fill the ships of seaboard capitalists. All this was facilitated by conditions abroad. By the repeal of the Corn Law and the Navigation Acts and the adoption of free-trade budgets in the 'forties, English markets were opened up. There were bad harvests in Europe immediately preceding and following the middle of the century. The rapid growth of urban population in England and on the Continent as well as in eastern America meant an augmentation of demand for western food and raw materials.

By examining a railroad map of the United States in 1860, one observes at first glance three main features. First, there was a seaboard network of lines extending from Washington and Baltimore to north of Boston. Secondly, in the west there was another network, much more extensive, from Pittsburgh, Wheeling, Cincinnati, Louisville, and St. Louis on the south to the ports of the Great Lakes between Milwaukee and Buffalo on the north. Thirdly, there were the four great trunk lines, the New York Central, the Erie, the Pennsylvania, and the Baltimore and Ohio, connecting the two networks. The triangle made by lines drawn between Baltimore, Memphis, and St. Louis was almost devoid of railroads, as was the lower Mississippi basin.

In viewing the conquest of western markets by eastern capitalists, the case of Cincinnati is particularly instructive. The southern trade had made the city. From a river town of about 25,000 people in 1830, it grew into the "Porkopolis" of the west, a city of 160,000 in 1860, a close rival of New Orleans, which was the leading city beyond the mountains, with less than 170,000 people. Cincinnati's trade had been overwhelmingly with the south. By 1855, the east had captured an almost equal share. Before the Civil War, the balance was heavily weighted in favor of the east. In the case of flour, the shipments from Cincinnati in 1850 had been almost exclusively southward. During the three years from 1857 to 1859, southward shipments of flour amounted to only 273,053 barrels out of a total of 1,648,662 barrels.

"The mighty tide of the Mississippi and its ten thousand tributaries," exclaimed DeBow, the most noted of southern publicists, as early as 1851, are being rolled back "until their mouth, practically and commercially, is more at New York and Boston than at New Orleans." By 1860, northern capitalists had crossed their Alps and conquered their Italy.

Economic connections of the upper Mississippi basin with the south had been absolutely essential to the prosperity of the western farmers because only in the south could they dispose of their produce. Now they could sell their provisions and raw materials as well as buy their manufactures and luxuries in the east. The conditions of trade promoted the shift, for easterners advanced goods to western merchants on credit. Eastern capitalists also financed the construction of canals and railways and extended formal loans. Thus because of credit as well as of commerce, the people of the upper Mississippi basin were rapidly becoming less dependent on the planter and more dependent on the eastern capitalist.

"SOUTHERN WEALTH AND NORTHERN PROFITS"

Traffic on the Mississippi continued in reality to increase till 1860. But in comparison with the tremendous expansion in the flow of trade by railroad, lake, and canal, the growth in river trade was insignificant. The advantages of east-west traffic by the railroads newly built or in process of construction were so obvious as to make it apparent that an economic revolution was going on. But alike before and after this revolution, while eastern business men were building their bridge of boats to the northwest and forging their bands of iron for the west, they were finding ways to tap the wealth of the planter.

Some northern capital found its way into the south in buying of plantations and slaves and in building of factories. In the 'forties, for instance, New England capital established a successful manufactory of machinery in Alabama for making mills and cotton gins. In 1860, about 200,000 bales of cotton were spun in southern mills, and there was a decided tendency on the part of New Englanders to build additional mills where water power, raw materials, and cheap white labor from the hills and ridges and worn-out tobacco and cotton lands could easily be combined.

But the main sources of northern profits were not from northern capital transferred to the south but from capital retained in the north and used for meeting southern needs. Cotton and other southern staples formed approximately two-thirds of the country's total exports, and were the principal sources of money for imports. But exportation and importation were by northern business men in northern ships, or else by foreigners. Nor was the route a direct one: exports and imports alike were assembled in great part at New York for distribution. Exports from New York totaled about one-third of the exports of the entire country, while the city's imports ran as high as two-thirds of the country's total imports. Cotton manufactured in America immediately preceding the Civil War amounted to about 800,000 bales a year. There was little manufacturing in the south, and virtually none not financed by northerners. For buying manufactured goods and selling his produce, the planter depended not only on manufacturers and merchants and ship owners in the north but as well on northern bankers. At the time of secession, southern debts to northern merchants are supposed to have amounted to two hundred million dollars.

Allies of the planters, the southern merchants and ship owners, had maintained a considerable traffic on the Mississippi and other rivers, and had been able to draw southward much western produce without the intervention of eastern capital. The building of railroads was rapidly reducing them to insignificance.

energies to destruction. Those who sell have, therefore, an exceptional bargaining power. It is natural, indeed inevitable, that in a society motivated by the profit-making spirit, patriotism will in some way be reconciled with profits. If there is united support of the war, if the government is powerful, and if public officials are both efficient and incorruptible, there is a theoretical possibility of holding in leash the ordinary economic motives and forces. In the Civil War, not even this theoretical possibility existed. There was lack of unanimity. The government was dependent on those who controlled the supplies it needed. The bargaining power of contractors was augmented by an abnormally large demand for goods; by the relative inefficiency of government agencies unaccustomed to the performance of economic functions; and by the government's lack of funds to meet its obligations. The result, in the words of Colonel Olcott, government prosecutor, was "the war's carnival of fraud."

PROFITS OF WAR FINANCE

The weakness of the government in its bargaining power subjected it to the mercy of financiers as well as of contractors. There was much to be said in theory for the government's paying its way by means of current taxes. But extensive taxation was impracticable. It would have converted the widespread latent discontent into active hostility to the war. The classes most able to bear taxation were in a position to raise a hue and cry in the press and to organize themselves into an effective agency of opposition.

Virtually no provision was made for war taxes till past the middle of 1862. The tariff act of March, 1861, was merely a fulfillment of Republican protectionist promises. In July of 1862 an internal revenue bill was passed for levying moderate excises on a bewildering variety of articles, activities, and occupations. Income taxes were levied for a time, but the yield was insignificant till after the war had ended. From 1862 to 1865, inclusive, the taxes amounted to about $667,000,000. Almost half of this amount was in the form of tariff duties, but excises came to be the main reliance. Sales of land and miscellaneous receipts increased the revenues to about $730,000,000. There was a further increase of revenues from taxes after the war. This was partly due to sales taxes, tariffs, and other duties imposed upon the "conquered provinces." Part of the rise in tax payments was merely nominal because of the declining value of money.

Currency inflation was one of the attempted methods of meeting expenses without taxes. From 1862 to 1865, inclusive, expenditures totaled almost $3,350,000,000. The $667,000,000 received in taxes, and the small additional revenues, as from land sales, covered only about one-fifth of the expenditures, about four-fifths being on the credit of the government. Paper money authorized by Congress amounted to $450,000,000. The legal tender notes or "greenbacks" thus issued were not redeemable in coin. But the first two issues, totaling $300,000,000, were convertible up to January 1, 1864, into six per cent gold bonds. Furthermore, vast quantities of short-term treasury notes were issued, bearing interest in currency, but subject to conversion into gold bonds. Many of the treasury notes at maturity became legal tender and swelled the volume of depreciated currency. The privilege of exchanging depreciated greenbacks for gold bonds, and of buying short-term treasury notes with depreciated currency and converting them into gold bonds, promoted the sale of bonds but at a heavy cost.

The main recourse of the government in securing funds

was by selling bonds. The privilege of converting the depreciating paper money and many of the treasury notes into gold bonds has already been mentioned. Since the money was reissued upon its return to the treasury, it might be used repeatedly for conversion into bonds. A bond issue of $500,000,000 was authorized by the same law which, in February of 1862, made provision for the first greenbacks. These bonds, the so-called five-twenties, ran for twenty years, redeemable after five years if desired by the government, and bore interest at six per cent in gold. This was the most noted bond issue, partly because of its connection with greenbacks, and partly because of the spectacular methods pursued by Jay Cooke, Philadelphia banker and fiscal agent of the treasury, in popularizing the bonds. There were several other bond issues and a great variety of securities representing short-term loans. In its earlier borrowings, the government was forced to sell its bonds and short-term notes at a heavy loss. During the summer of 1861, six per cent bonds to the extent of $60,000,000 sold at an average discount of 10.91 per cent. Bonds which were sold by the government at ninety-two cents to the dollar early in the war were worth $1.14 to the dollar in March of 1864. The six per cent gold bonds rapidly increased in value. At the end of the war the obligations of the government were so varied and confused that with the exception of such issues as the five-twenties popularized by Jay Cooke, only an experienced and expert stock broker understood their legal status and market values. In a period of inflation and faltering confidence, a tremendous difference in value resulted from an obscure provision in the law permitting conversion of a particular type of securities into gold bonds. Such conditions naturally played into the hands of professional investors and brokers.

The financial problems confronting the government may now be summarized. Extensive taxation was impracticable early in the war because of the danger of opposition not merely to any specific tax policy but to the war policy in general. Paper money was at best a temporary expedient for a particular emergency. In the uncertain state of public confidence, a more extensive resort to unsecured currency would have meant disastrous depreciation, repudiation, and, at best, the results associated with the disordered finances of the Revolution.

Short-term loans and bond issues were inevitable. With an inflated currency, was the government to sell its bonds for paper money or specie? It was decided that paper money (or bank paper measured in value not by gold but by paper money) would be accepted. The next question was, shall purchasers of government bonds receive interest and principal in paper money or in specie? If interest payments and redemption were to be in paper money, the bonds must be sold at a depreciated price, with declining faith in the government. It was decided that the bonds should bear interest in gold or specie and be redeemable in terms of gold.

But since the government accepted paper money and non-gold-bearing treasury notes for them, this meant a golden harvest for investors—that is, unless, as some expected, the government would ultimately default or become bankrupt. By receiving payment in inflated paper and promising payment in gold the government was able to maintain by an artifice the appearance of par value and thereby to bolster up the faith of its citizens. This process gave to holders of government obligations after the war a mighty economic lever, which was immeasurably strengthened by a decision of the Supreme Court to the effect that obligations of the national government were not subject to state or local taxation. Thus ironically enough the holders of public securities were relatively free from tax burdens and at the same time were deriving their profits from tax payers by means of a transfer of wealth from tax payers to security holders. But far more important than their direct profits from public securities were the influences the creditors of the government were able to exert on public policy.

AGENCIES FOR HANDLING SECURITIES

The Civil War period wrought a revolution alike in the extent and in the mode of handling of financial operations. But the buying and selling of securities in contrast with commodities had long been familiar to Americans.

The joint-stock association was an institution which the colonists brought with them. It might even be said that many of the colonists were brought to America by joint-stock companies. The varied certificates of indebtedness issued by the states and by Congress during the Revolution, and the funded obligations of the government after the Revolution, familiarized the wealthier classes of the east especially with the possibilities of stocks and bonds. The extension of colonization westward, the building of the early toll roads, canals, and railroads, and the financing of many of the larger manufacturing enterprises, entailed the formation of corporations and the sale of their stock.

The states, in their rivalry to secure capital and promote business, imposed virtually no restrictions on corporations. The granting of individual charters by special act of public authorities had commonly been superseded by incorporation under general laws requiring nominal fees. The limitation of the liability of stockholders to the amount of stock held had commonly superseded the old common-law rule of unlimited liability of business associates.

The formal organization as early as 1817 of the New York stock exchange, consisting of an association of brokers, gave evidence of the increasing importance of the joint-stock association. But there was relatively little of the later rapid sale and resale for speculative purposes, and relatively little utilization of stocks and bonds as collateral in big financial transactions. Most of the stock was held by persons actively connected with the business enterprises represented by the stocks, or by persons who desired a continuing, interest-bearing investment. The most popular form of speculative investment was real estate, especially western lands. The earlier predecessors of gold-brick and blue-sky stock-and-bond salesmen were the pedlars, traditionally Yankees, of "cheap clocks, wooden nutmegs, and apple parers," these, in turn, being largely displaced by dealers in the great staple of the west, "the Progress of the Country."

The quantity of bonds and short-term paper issued by the government during and shortly after the war was prodigious. In September 1865, the national debt, not counting the legal tender notes (greenbacks) and fractional currency, amounted to about $2,300,000,000. Extensive loans and parts of loans had already been paid off. There was constant conversion of bonds and other obligations from one form of instrument into another, with frequent change of ownership. By the various funding operations carried on after the war, the volume of business in the sale and conversion and frequent resale of bonds was tremendously increased. There were also gigantic increases in state and municipal debts.

Public securities, unparalleled as they were in volume, were outrivaled by the stocks and bonds of corporations. It has been estimated that by the end of the war the capital of the newly formed petroleum companies exceeded half a billion dollars. At length the buying and selling of oil stocks became so vast that at Titusville, Pennsylvania, an imposing oil exchange building was erected. The capital stock of twenty-eight railroads on May 1, 1869, totaled about four hundred million dollars. The group of railroads dominated by Vanderbilt in 1870 had a capitalization of about a quarter of a billion dollars. The formation of new companies and the expansion of the stock of old companies deluged the country with shares. During the last war year Wall Street brokers alone handled a volume of business amounting to about six billion dollars.

There had long been stock brokers operating in a moderate way. There were now organized a number of banking firms, later to attain international celebrity, devoted largely to the handling of public and corporation stocks and bonds. On account of the unsettled currency and because of the extensive foreign market, they had money changing facilities, and made handsome profits in handling currency as well as stocks and bonds. The most noted of these firms, though not the oldest, was Jay Cooke & Company. The firm had offices in Philadelphia, Washington, New York, and London. Cooke, who was dubbed a modern Midas and a Napoleon of finance, had the exclusive agency for marketing one of the most important bond issues of the war, the five-twenties. Later he undertook the sale of the seven-thirties, treasury notes paying interest in currency at 7.3 per cent but fundable at maturity in 1867 in six per cent gold bonds. Under his direction the issue of seven-thirties amounted to $830,000,000 in six months. He made the loans "town talk." Cooke's brother at Washington wrote him about an interview with Horace Greeley, who "was very curious to know how we got up the furore." He employed thousands of local agents. He issued hand bills and posters. He flooded the mails with circulars and "follow ups." He paid large sums for newspaper advertisements and publicity. He employed a staff of newspaper agents for "the manufacture of editorials, letters, notices," and other propaganda. He found ways of displaying the results of his work so as to impress newspapermen, Congressmen, treasury officials, and "Old Abe" himself. Cooke seems to have been a "super-salesman." "He take me in a room," said a fellow banker, a Frenchman, "and before I go out he make me do what I wish not to do." His firm has a prominent place in the history of modern advertising and "high-pressure" salesmanship. After the war, similar methods were used in promoting corporate undertakings, particularly the financing of the Northern Pacific Railroad. It was in connection with this undertaking that the firm went to the wall in the panic of 1873. Thus the field was left to Drexel and Company, the house of Morgan, and other firms that during this period of unexampled bond and stock expansion began to play leading rôles in national and international finance.

REORGANIZATION OF BANKING AND CURRENCY

General banking as well as the handling of securities underwent a transformation. The first Bank of the United States, it will be recalled, was a semi-public institution, with the government as a share holder and with federal bonds as a basis of capitalization. It was so intimately connected with Hamiltonian politics and with the ascendancy of the eastern "moneyed people" that on the expiration of its twenty-year charter the Jeffersonians refused to recharter it. The financial chaos of the period of war ending in 1815 constrained the followers of Jefferson to establish in 1816 the second Bank of the United States. But the Jacksonians, as we have noted, were no better pleased with centralized banking in control of eastern capitalists than had been the Jeffersonians. A fight was waged against it and its virtual overthrow was accomplished even before the expiration of its twenty-year charter. The funds of the government were withdrawn and placed in the more dependable of the state banks, known to the opposition as "pet" banks.

Banking functions generally were exercised by private institutions operating under state charters or state laws. Political influences in the several states were often decisive in the granting of banking privileges. The most important privilege was the issuing of bank notes as money. Such issues became very extensive. They were often unsecured or inadequately secured. They were extremely varied in form and value. The country was flooded with currency rivaling that of colonial times.

The government's deposits, being in state banks, were indirectly subject to the caprice of state authority. The government encountered criticism alike from advocates of a national banking system and from state banks not favored with deposits. As a result, it adopted in 1840 a plan known as the Independent Treasury or the Sub-Treasury. Government funds were deposited partly in the treasury at Washington and partly in government vaults in various other places. Thus the federal government washed its hands, as it were, of the banking problem.

In the meantime something had been done to remedy the almost intolerable chaos in banking under state authority. Corporation law passed in part from the caprice of charters granted in individual cases for political purposes to charters secured by conforming to general laws regulating incorporation. Legal restrictions remained extremely lax, but improvement was made by private initiative. The Suffolk Bank of Boston introduced a plan of administering for other banks a redemption fund by which their notes would be redeemed at par. Banks throughout New England adopted the plan, and their bank notes gained wide repute. New York, after the opening of the Erie Canal, rapidly became the outstanding financial as well as trading center. In 1853, a clearing house was established. Daily settlements and up-to-date knowledge of the status of each bank promoted caution and stability. At the same time, the use of clearing-house certificates reduced the interchange of money by facilitating balancing and cancellation of accounts. Thus mobility of resources no less than stability of policy was promoted. Other cities soon adopted the clearing-house plan.

The Independent Treasury had disadvantages, as for example the immobility and idleness of public funds. More serious were the disadvantages of leaving to uncoordinated state authorities the control of banking and particularly of the issuing of bank notes to be used as money. The system of national banks originating in 1863, whatever may have been its own deficiencies, had some effect in remedying the shortcomings of state-controlled banking.

An immediate object in the authorization of national banks was the sale of government bonds. A bank established according to the law of 1863 might issue currency secured by government bonds. In spite of this liberal provision, the opportunities elsewhere for profitable investment were so great that the results at first were disappointing. The profits made by those who ventured into the field proved to be so satisfactory (the First National Bank of Washington, for instance, paying a dividend of ten per cent in gold on six month's business in 1864) that others were induced to adopt the plan. In 1865 the taxing of notes issued by state banks was authorized. This forced their notes out of circulation, and made possible a uniform and more dependable currency.

NEW NATURAL RESOURCES

The war brought on a vast expansion of financial operations, and vital changes in financial institutions. The extremity of the government proved, as during the era of disordered Revolutionary finance, to be the opportunity of the capitalist. Another source of prosperity for triumphant capitalism, less dependent on the war but stimulated by it, was the exploitation of new natural resources.

America has an almost unparalleled variety of resources. And yet from early times there were precursors of modern world-wide interdependence, as when colonial New Englanders brought in molasses for making rum. An important phase of this interdependence goes back to a discovery made in 1839 by Charles Goodyear—the vulcanizing of rubber. The process was patented in 1844, and was made the basis of an industry of some importance by the time of his death in 1860. In that year rubber valued at $1,427,000 was imported. By 1870 the amount had grown to $3,460,000. Little change was required in the basic vulcanizing process for the later expansion of the industry, but the great day of "elastic metal" awaited the coming of the automobile.

Beginning in 1866 with a ten-acre million-dollar plant at Philadelphia, the making of paper from wood pulp wrought a revolution by cheapening paper and multiplying its uses. In keeping with the love of the sensational which is commonly associated with the cheap newspapers made possible by the new process, the promoters of the factory gave a public demonstration of a five-hour transformation of a nearby tree into print paper for the entertainment of printers and publishers invited from various parts of the country.

By the end of the war, the inexhaustible resources of

the Lake Superior region were supplying an eighth of the iron smelted in America. From 1870 to 1880, the proportion increased to a fourth. In the Lake Superior region, and in Arizona and Montana, the output of copper was rapidly increasing, but the new age of copper awaited the age of electricity. The discovery of the Comstock lode in 1859 inaugurated a frenzy of speculation and exploitation in silver mining. From a negligible output at the beginning of the war, the amount rose rapidly till 1890. But silver played a larger part in politics than in business.

Of the various other distinctive developments in the use of natural resources, by far the most important in the era of the war was the sudden emergence of the petroleum industry.

Wells drilled for salt in western Pennsylvania had often been abandoned because of oil, which was less valuable than salt. Its use as a medicine had been taught to the whites by the Indians, who had skimmed the oily surface of pools or dipped their blankets in the pools, wringing out the oil. Samuel Keir, a Pittsburgh druggist who owned a salt well containing oil, conceived the idea about the middle of the century of selling the oil as a newly discovered panacea which would inaugurate "a new era in medicine."

> "The healthful balm from nature's secret spring
> The bloom of health and life to man will bring;
> As from her depths the magic liquid flows
> To calm our sufferings and assuage our woes."

About the same time, Canadian shale oil was being used for lighting purposes, as a substitute for candles and whale oil.

Here were two ideas which, put together, were of utmost importance: commercializing petroleum for illumination, and securing it in large quantities by drilling for oil instead of for salt water. On August 27, 1859, William Smith and his sons, salt-well drillers, in the employ of the Pennsylvania Rock Oil Company and under the supervision of E. L. Drake, a New England railroad conductor, reached a depth of about seventy feet in a well on Oil Creek near Titusville, Pennsylvania, and lost their drill. To their surprise, oil rose in the well, and Drake by pumping secured about twenty-five barrels a day. Few events in American industrial history have had more revolutionary effects.

The 'forty-niners of California were hardly rivaled by the 'fifty-niners of Pennsylvania, but in 1861 there was an oil boom of large proportions. The drilling of wells to the lower oil-bearing strata or "sands" turned a crude and unproductive region into a land of "flowing gold." But flowing wells expanded the production to unimagined figures, and the price fell to ten cents a barrel.

It was known, however, that petroleum had many possible uses. The scientific study of the subject seems to have been initiated by George H. Bissell, an alumnus of Dartmouth College. While on a visit to his alma mater in 1854, he was shown a bottle of petroleum as a curiosity. He wondered if it might not have unrecognized possibilities. A specimen was taken to a chemist. The chemist reported that petroleum was a "raw material from which, by simple and not expensive process," many valuable products might be made. This was in 1855. It was Bissell who, in 1854, had promoted the organization of the Pennsylvania Rock Oil Company which in 1859 employed Drake to supervise the drilling of the first well. From the report of the chemist in 1855 to the present, there has been an uninterrupted development of knowledge and extension of uses.

One of the first uses, after illumination, was lubrication. Almost immediately its value was recognized abroad. Exports by 1865 amounted in value to $15,766,000, and by

1870 to $32,669,000. Output increased from 21,000,000 gallons in 1860 to 1,104,000,000 gallons in 1880.

With the release of energies by the end of the war, and with new uses and expanding exports, the speculative frenzy resulting from "oil on the brain" infected multitudes far distant from the oil towns. With a combination of luck and skill a few drillers were able to penetrate the rocks and tap the oil sands. With ease the innumerable fraudulent promoters evoked a flow of gold from every stratum of society. The unrestricted private exploitation of one of the rarest gifts of nature brought wealth to some but to many more it meant demoralization or financial ruin or both.

NEW AGENCIES OF COMMUNICATION

It is not without a sense of relief that one turns from the riotous and wasteful exploitation of nature's gifts to a contemplation of man's deliberate and rational use of his own creative powers. Innumerable devices for transmitting intelligence range from Indian signals by fire and smoke to radio and television. The telegraph was the culmination, as are most of the great inventions, of a long series of studies and experiments by various men in different countries. The instantaneous charging of wires with electrical currents and the discernment of the charge by the breaking of the circuit had been familiar to European scientists. In 1832 an American artist, S. F. B. Morse, while returning from Europe, had a casual conversation with a scientist, and these electrical phenomena were discussed. Their significance for the communication of intelligence had apparently never seriously impressed any one. The idea struck Morse with such force as to lead to his giving up his profession in order to devote himself to the problem. Years of toil and poverty ensued. At length, with the aid of scientists and of a Congressional appropriation in 1843 of thirty thousand dollars, he was able to build an experimental line from Baltimore to Washington. Its first use, even before its completion, was to send news of the Whig Convention of 1844 from Baltimore to an intermediate point, where the messages were relayed to Washington. The code of dots, dashes, and spaces was manipulated simply by varying the length of time the circuit was left open.

Then came commercialization. The government was offered the inventor's rights for a hundred thousand dollars. The offer being refused, the right to use the invention was sold by Morse and his associates to private companies. Competing companies were formed, some of them using devices other than Morse's. Speculation ran riot. Consolidations and elimination of the weaker companies were followed by charges of monopoly. Congress intervened, and this was followed by charges of corruption. By 1866 the Western Union was emerging triumphantly with a virtual monopoly. Already in 1862 a wire had been completed to San Francisco. Another company with Congressional sanction began in 1864 to construct a rival line but in 1866 it, too, capitulated to a combined attack of legal obstructions and financial inducements. It was not for many years that transcontinental service was satisfactory.

No other invention was so largely responsible for the speeding up of the tempo of business and of life. When railroad and telegraph reached St. Joseph on the Missouri River in 1859, two thousand miles and two months intervened between the western terminus and California. By a marvel of speed and coordination the time required for communicating with California was later reduced by the Pony Express to twelve days.

Perhaps the most urgent need of the telegraph was in railroading. The maximum use of trackage and the evolution of complicated train schedules would otherwise have been impossible.

The application of the Morse telegraph to under-water use was made practicable by the introduction in 1843 of gutta percha from the Far East. Permanent cable communication between Dover and Calais was established in 1851. Three years later plans were under way for a trans-Atlantic cable.

> "Bold Cyrus Field, he said says he,
> I have a pretty notion
> That I can run a telegraph
> Across the Atlantic Ocean."

Beginning a successful quest of fortune in New York at the age of sixteen, Field by the middle of the century was preparing to retire when the idea of submarine telegraphy intrigued him to begin the career that gives him a place in history.

The Atlantic Telegraph Company which he promoted secured extensive stock subscriptions and public aid alike in England and America. To their war ships, the *Niagara* and the *Agamemnon,* the American and British governments assigned the duty of laying the cable under the direction of the company's officials. After many mishaps, communication was established in August, 1858, between Newfoundland and the west coast of Ireland. There was world-wide jubilee. "Their line is gone out through all the earth and their words to the end of the world." But while the cable was still the talk of the town the signals faded and failed. Almost a decade more of international effort, with Field continuing as guiding spirit, was at last rewarded in 1866 by permanent success. An earlier cable which had been lost was recovered from the ocean's bed and also put into operation. A "cable fever" followed, with the usual inflation and over-expansion of companies, and ultimate stabilization.

RAILROADS AND LAND GRANTS

In railroad building after 1860, many of the distinctive traits of the era found embodiment. The triumph of the capitalist over the planter found expression in the pledge of the Republican party to promote a transcontinental railway north of the southern Pacific route proposed by the planters. The triumph of business men in northern politics was reflected in the granting of public subsidies to private companies. Widespread public and private corruption found perhaps most notorious illustration in railroad finance. Railroad construction revealed in a striking manner the prosperity of business men, their exuberance, their capitalization of the future, their speculative tendencies, and the over-expansion which had its debacle in the panic of 1873. Finally, the history of railroads reveals a prominent cause of the renewal of traditional antagonism of farmers toward business men. Some of these aspects of railroad history will become apparent in the discussion of later topics. Matters of immediate concern are the coordination of seaboard and mid-western lines, the extension of railroads to the Pacific, and the public subsidizing of private companies.

The first great age of railroad building ended with the conquest of the Appalachians. But before effective use of the roads for through traffic was possible, many obstacles had yet to be overcome. An official report on railroad consolidation stated that in the 'fifties seven transfers were required in transit from New York to the Mississippi River. The Erie, which was the first unified line or trunk line to reach the middle west, was dependent on the unsatisfactory shipping facilities of the sandy harbor of Dunkirk. It was not till 1863 that it secured direct communication with Cleveland by means of a road through northern Pennsylvania. Thereafter other connections were easily effected. The New York Central consisted at first of an uncoordinated group of local lines. By the early 'sixties there was unified service from New York to Buffalo. The Pennsylvania Railroad and the Baltimore and Ohio, by reaching the Ohio River, were able to tap the river traffic, but they found that many years were necessary for making effective connections with the mid-western railway network.

It was not till about 1870 that satisfactory through connections to Chicago were established by the eastern trunk lines. The processes of making consolidations by the joining of local lines, end to end, often necessitated excessive financial compensation to lesser lines absorbed by the greater, but competition was thereby reduced. But with the formation of several trunk lines bidding for through traffic, an era of cut-throat competition began. This in turn brought on an era of pools or agreements as to rates and allotment of traffic or of profits. Then came problems of monopoly, of western discontent, and of public regulation.

Before the consolidation of eastern branch lines into trunk lines had been completed, work was begun on a transcontinental trunk line. In 1832, when the first blundering efforts were being made to build local railroads, when California was part of Mexico, and when Oregon was claimed by England, a bold westerner of the territory of Michigan proposed a railroad from New York to the mouth of the Oregon. He envisaged "an immense city at the mouth of the Oregon," mart of trade with the Orient, united with New York "by a railway by which the traveller leaving the city of New York shall at the moderate rate of ten miles an hour place himself in a port right on the shores of the

Pacific." As the author predicted, people laughed at the proposal. But by the beginning of the Civil War, any one who opposed a transcontinental railroad was viewed as hopelessly antiquated.

The planters' choice of routes was naturally through Texas and the southern part of the lands acquired from Mexico. But southern cities, as Memphis, Charleston, and New Orleans, had trouble in agreeing as to the eastern terminus. In the north there were bitter controversies as to the most appropriate route. Sectional jealousies thus defeated every effort at public intervention, and the magnitude of the task, as well as the difficulty of agreement about the route, kept private enterprise from taking hold of the problem.

The Civil War eliminated the planters and made possible a compromise among the northern business men. By Congressional authority granted in 1862, President Lincoln fixed the main eastern terminus at the village of Omaha on the west bank of the Missouri, opposite Council Bluffs, Iowa. The nearest railroad connection was at St. Joseph in northwestern Missouri, which had long been a rendezvous for those who were venturing westward across the plains, and which had recently become the starting place of the Pony Express. Branch lines to be built by public aid were to radiate from Omaha, with trunk-line connections eastward by way of Chicago. The trunk line was built westward from Omaha by the Union Pacific Company, and eastward from Sacramento by the Central Pacific Company, the latter chartered by California. Subsidies included not only the right of way but title to alternate sections of a strip of land forty miles wide, or 12,800 acres adjacent to each mile of road. The government also agreed to extend bond subsidies to aid in financing the work, the bonds to be secured by a second mortgage on the road, private purchasers of the company's securities thus having first claim on the property. For construction on the plains, bonds were to be advanced to the value of $16,000 per mile; for desert country, $32,000 per mile; and for three hundred miles of mountainous country, $48,000 per mile.

To the accompaniment of artillery salutes and public jubilation, a construction gang began its work at Omaha December 2, 1863. At Sacramento work had already been undertaken. For construction at the eastern end, machinery and supplies could be had at Pittsburgh and intervening points and shipment could be made by steamboat by way of the Ohio, the Mississippi, and the Missouri. For work at the western end, most materials, including iron, were sent by water from the Atlantic seaboard—a dangerous war-time voyage of many months. The passive resistance of nature and the active hostility of man on the plains and deserts offered sufficient obstacles, but these were dwarfed by the problems of river and valley and mountain. Surveyors, bridge gangs, tunnel diggers, graders, and track layers (mainly Irish in the east and Chinese in the west) succeeded each other, with supply trains following in the wake of the trackmen and at successive points establishing supply stations. In the wake of the supply trains was a motley crew resembling the underworld of the great cities, preying upon the construction gangs as they returned to headquarters for supplies and for relief from their dangerous and exhausting work. "Hell on wheels" the migratory town was called.

Rivalry of the two companies in securing land grants and loan subsidies promoted the speedy completion of the line. At Promontory Point near Ogden, Utah, on May 10, 1869, the last tie was laid. The final spike, made of California gold, was driven with a silver hammer by the alternate strokes of Leland Stanford of the Central Pacific and

Thomas Durant of the Union Pacific. By telegraph the news was flashed to east and west and celebrations everywhere proclaimed the joining of eastern and western shores.

There was little tendency at the time to count the cost. The homestead law had offered free homes to settlers. The settlers needed railroad facilities. Popular criticism of land grants was thus allayed. The grant of more than twenty million acres to the Union Pacific and Central Pacific companies, combined with bond subsidies, encouraged other interests to look for large favors. The grants promised to the Northern Pacific were described by Jay Cooke, promotor of the company, as an "empire" of farming, forest, and mineral resources—"a broad fertile belt from Wisconsin through the richest portions of Minnesota, Dakota, Montana, Idaho, Oregon and Washington to Puget Sound." On the basis of returns from land grants to other companies, he estimated that the Northern Pacific would be able to realize from the lands a sum ranging from $165,000,000 to $550,000,000. More than two hundred million acres were promised by federal and state governments to railroad companies, but in some cases the companies failed to comply with the conditions of the grants.

The public costs of railroad building were not confined to land and loan subsidies. Over-expansion by the use of too large a proportion of capital to build railroads beyond current needs and to finance ventures of speculative or fraudulent nature precipitated the devastating panic of 1873. When the first enthusiasm of great achievements and greater ambitions had waned and western farmers had begun to realize the disadvantages of dependence on monopolies, there was a revival of animosity against eastern business men. This was aggravated by revelations which pointed to the most serious of all the costs of railroad building—public and private corruption.

CHAPTER XIX

REBELLIOUS FARMERS

PROFITS OF PATRIOTISM

"Designing, unprincipled or speculative characters in the latitude of Washington [are] as thick as autumnal leaves (only all the year round)." Thus wrote one banker to another in 1864 while in a nearby latitude the soldiers were falling like autumn leaves in patriotic devotion to the Union. After the war there seems to have been no abatement of such nuisances acting under cover of patriotism, either in Washington or in other parts of the country. Among them were men connected with the railroad to the Pacific. This was viewed as a patriotic national undertaking. Its completion was heralded as not inferior "in its national significance to the Declaration of Independence." Ironically, as the centennial of the Declaration approached, there came astounding revelations of a "carnival of fraud."

The financing of the road had been aided, it will be recalled, by extensive land grants and loans. It was intended that the company, as recipient of these aids, should finance the building of the road by selling stocks and bonds. But its main dependence was on bonds. The principal stockholders formed a second corporation, known as the Credit Mobilier, for the actual work of constructing the road. These "inside" stockholders, instead of selling stock for cash in accordance with the terms of the charter, issued large amounts to public officials for political influence and to themselves in alleged payment for constructing the road, in spite of the fact that the costs of construction came out of bond sales. In a word, the "inside" stockholders paid for the road largely out of bond sales, gave shares of stock to influential persons, retained handsome construction profits, and kept for themselves the permanent control of the railroad, with profits and millions of acres of public lands. A quarrel among the "insiders" was responsible for the facts being made known. The result was a political explosion which wrecked many national reputations. Many other "great" men "saved their virtue at the sacrifice of their intelligence."

The investigation of the company's affairs was undertaken by the December session of Congress in 1872. The tide had turned—"a very dirty tide." A surprising action by the same Congress in its last moments gave impetus to the opposition. A retroactive law was passed for increasing the salaries of public officials. Congressmen increased their own salaries from $5000 to $7500, authorizing the payment of the larger sum for the two years of the expiring Congress. This was almost universally denounced as the "salary grab" or the "back-pay steal." Then followed a series of investigations and revelations of widespread corruption, giving ample food for cynicism by extending to the Centennial celebration of the Declaration of Independence and beyond. "The people having for years acquiesced in the most villainous and corrupt legislation by Congress, the members began to believe that they had become so thoroughly debauched that they would submit to any outrage." Thus in 1873 confided a prominent Republican to a friend. But now there were stirrings of revolt. Nor was corruption or the revolt against it confined to national politics, as witness the "rings" in the cities, especially the Tweed ring in New York and the Philadelphia gas ring. There was an insistent demand that public officials should regard public office not as "a private perquisite" but as "a public trust."

LOADED DICE OF INFLATION AND DEFLATION

While investigations of corruption were under way, the pressure of hard times became heavy. The panic of 1873 was followed by years of depression. The principal sufferers were farmers of the west and south, who naturally associated hard times with political corruption. In reality, the most vital causal connection between political measures and hard times was to be found in the processes of inflation and deflation.

Inflation of currency was from several sources. Up to the taxing of state bank notes in 1865, these notes were issued virtually without restriction. The federal government issued almost half a billion dollars in paper money unsecured except in part by the privilege of conversion into gold bonds. The government also gave legal tender status for a time to many of the short-term treasury notes. But a more extensive inflation was in the issue not of currency but of public and private securities. As has been noted, the country was flooded with government bonds with interest and principal payable in gold, or with a provision for later conversion into gold bonds. As the quantity of these bonds increased, the drain on the gold that was coming into the treasury, mainly through the customs, aggravated inflation and depreciation of currency by preventing the building up of a gold reserve as a basis for the resumption of specie payments.

There was a phenomenal increase in corporation stocks and bonds. The "watering" of stock began on a large scale during the same era. The term is said to have been derived from the fact that live-stock dealers were credited with increasing the weight of hogs and cattle before sale by giving them free access to salt and water. It was commonly held that corporation stock should represent the actual paid-up investment of the stockholders. The corporation, it had been held, should sell goods or render services at prices no higher than necessary to earn a fair profit on the paid-up investment. The paid-up investment should be used only for purposes actually contributing to the production of goods or services, and not for buying out competitors or buying unused franchises or influencing public policy or creating a monopoly. But such ideas came to be viewed as antiquated. Mergers, especially of railroads, were commonly occasions of a vast expansion of stock without additional investment. Stock was often issued to public officials virtually without value received (except indirectly). Oftentimes the payments for stock were made out of dividends. Stock was issued to purchasers of bonds as an added inducement to buy bonds. Fraudulent promoters often sold bonds in this way and then by resort to bankruptcy or to flight evaded payment of interest on the bonds. One of the best known illustrations of stock inflation is the case of the Erie railroad described particularly well by Charles Francis Adams in his *Chapters of Erie and Other Essays.*

A time of currency inflation is primarily advantageous to debtors who have fixed obligations which can be paid off when, on account of inflation, money becomes cheaper and goods dearer. But at the beginning of the period of wartime inflation, there was relatively little indebtedness. Government officials had only recently boasted of a surplus. Taxpayers, therefore, were not benefitted by being able to pay off any extensive government obligations with inflated currency. Some advantage undoubtedly accrued to those who owed mortgages, corporation bonds, and similar securities, but the losses of creditors who held such securities seem not to have engendered any widespread alarm or discontent.

There is another group, besides debtors, which is likely to be benefitted financially by inflation of currency. A period of inflation is necessarily a period of readjustment, and it seems inevitably to be a period of speculation. The Secretary of the Treasury complained in 1865 that inflation "is converting the business of the country into gambling." Those who had fluid resources combined with knowledge and boldness were able to profit by rapid and speculative operations. Such men were mostly eastern business men. There was a speculative increase in farm values, but the speculative tendencies of farmers were usually confined to buying gold-brick or blue-sky stock.

Aside from speculators, the chief beneficiaries of inflation were those who financed the war. Bonds were sold in terms of cheap money and redeemed in gold. While business men were by no means the only purchasers of bonds on these conditions, they were the principal beneficiaries. As for inflation of stocks, this obviously was made the basis, where possible, of profits which, under cover of capitalization popularly supposed to represent an active investment, would be less likely to arouse hostility on the part of the paying public than would a smaller quantity of stock paying higher dividends. Such hostility was later to be allayed by the popularization of stock-sales among consumers themselves.

Deflation was primarily concerned with currency. Its object was the establishment of all currency on a parity with gold. The method adopted was contraction of the amount of money in circulation. Treasury notes were deprived of legal tender quality. The quantity of greenbacks was reduced. By taxation of state bank notes, they were driven out of circulation almost entirely after 1865. The amount in circulation on July 1, 1865, was about $143,-

000,000 as compared with about $20,000,000 a year later. The circulation of national bank notes was confined to an almost constant level after 1866 by the rising price of federal bonds. These bonds, which were required as security for note issues, were being redeemed and were commanding such a high price as to make their purchase and later even their retention as security for notes unattractive. The circulation of money of various kinds per inhabitant on July 1, 1865, was $31.18; in 1870, $20.10. The lowest point was $16.25 in 1878. Thereafter there was a gradual rise to Civil War levels and beyond. Greenbacks reached parity with gold in December, 1878, and payment of gold in return for paper money on demand was resumed the following month.

The restoration of confidence in the currency by the elimination of unregulated state bank notes and of unsecured money of every kind was a desirable move of utmost importance. But inflation and consequent depreciation had resulted, it must be remembered, not so much from the amount of money issued as from its character. There was an increasing need for currency. Aside from coinage, the federal government had left the problem to the states. They in turn had allowed almost unrestricted power to private banks. When the federal government faced the problem, it merely resorted to the issue of paper money. The unregulated state bank notes and the federal greenbacks issued during a time of wavering faith naturally declined in value irrespective of the quantity issued. Because of the tendency of "bad" money to drive out "good" (Gresham's "law"), the quantity of gold declined and attained a factitious value.

It is apparent that during and after the Civil War, with the vast increase in public and private business, there was a real need of an expanding quantity of money. This need was felt peculiarly by the farmers because of poor banking and credit facilities in the regions of rapid agricultural expansion. Farmers, furthermore, had little knowledge of the machinery of credit operations. Their assets were immobile. They, therefore, had to pay exceptionally high interest rates. To these were added various fees, oftentimes needless if not fraudulent, for examination of titles and preparation of legal instruments connected with security for loans. Beyond question the quality of money needed improvement. That the best method of effecting improvement was a radical contraction of the amount of money in circulation is an unproved assumption.

Why, it may be asked, was the government unable to improve the quality of money without a too serious reduction in the quantity? Taxes, other than customs, were generally payable in depreciated currency. Gold was received in the form of customs duties, but it was paid out largely to bondholders in connection with the government's policy of selling bonds for depreciated paper and promising payment of principal and interest in gold. The gold that might otherwise have been made the basis of a sound currency was thus constantly drained off to pay the bondholders.

But gold having once been allowed its factitious value, the resulting high prices also had a factitious quality. The policy of financing the war by means of inflated currency and gold bonds having been put into effect, there was inevitably a process of robbing Peter to pay Paul. In the case of the public creditors *versus* the government—that is, the bondholders *versus* the taxpayers—there was theoretically a way of escape from the dilemma. This was the taxing of the bonds in such way as to cancel the excessive profits accruing from the purchase of the bonds in cheap money. But since the government was controlled by the group which was profiting from gold bonds bought with cheap money, the way of escape was theoretical only. As a matter of fact, the bonds, as has been noted, were exempt from state and local taxation. Even the federal government depended on forms of taxation, particularly customs duties, which left its bonds relatively free even from federal taxes. As a result, the incidence of taxation aggravated rather than mitigated the process of robbing Peter to pay Paul. The bondholders' advantage was secure whether currency was deflated or not. But as long as inflation continued, they enjoyed the advantage, confined largely to them, of an income in gold.

Hostility to deflation assumed the form of the greenback movement and later of the free-silver movement, both most prominent among farmers. The point of view of the farmer as debtor during deflation was undoubtedly in many ways unsound, but it has more often been subjected to caricature than to adequate analysis. To those who make no effort to see things through the farmer's eyes, his demand for greenbacks or for free silver is likely to be viewed as the ignorant vagary of a western "clodhopper." To them, Bryan's "cross of gold" speech is merely the windy rhetoric of a demagogue in the person of "the boy orator of the Platte."

Consider the hypothetical case of John Smith, erstwhile coachman, and in 1865 a discharged soldier returning home to Pennsylvania. Everyone hails him as a savior of the union, but no one seems to need his services as a coachman or even as a man of all work. He hears the cry, "go west, young man," and responds by going to Illinois. He acquires a quarter section of land, a wife, and a debt. He arranges with local dealers to buy implements and supplies on the security of his forthcoming crop. Each year he finds it necessary to secure credit on this basis, and since he buys on credit, prices are higher than for cash. At the same time, with contraction of currency, the general level of prices is declining. There is one level when he buys his goods in winter and spring and summer, and there is a lower level when he sells his crops in the fall to pay for past purchases. He notes, too, that there is a tendency for the price of what he sells to go down faster than the price of what he buys.

In the course of time, children arrive. One year there is costly sickness; another, a poor crop; another, a cyclone destroys his barn. The remedy? A mortgage. There is the legal red tape with fees and what appear to him to be dishonest charges running the already high interest rate to a level far above the rate required of business men. In the meantime, prices of farm produce continue to fall. He sometimes finds it more profitable to use his corn as fuel than to haul it to market. Prices of things he buys also fall but not so rapidly, and he perhaps observes that they are protected by a tariff which fails to reach his produce, for corn and wheat and hogs are not imported. Each year the interest on his mortgage remains nominally the same, but mounts in reality to higher and higher rates, for when the mortgage was placed, money was cheap and each year it becomes dearer. When the mortgage is due, the amount is nominally unchanged, but since money is dearer, his added obligation is perhaps fifty per cent of the face of the mortgage.

He knows little about politics and finance, but he hears rumors about reducing the amount of money. Anyway he has less. He hears also about the government bonds. He has never seen one. He is told that the people who have money to loan on mortgages have most of them. He hears they were bought while he was away at war to save the union. They were bought, so he is told, when there was plenty of money, and the interest and principal, he hears, are being paid in gold. How does the government get the gold? By taxes. Who pays the taxes? He is rather hazy about it, but some one tells him he has to pay a tax every time he buys a pound of sugar. He hears that he pays a tax either to the government or to those who have bonds and sell mortgages and run factories every time he buys a plow or a yard of cloth. It is all a puzzle to him—he is too busy or too tired to try very hard to figure it out. But one thing he knows—he doesn't like the feel of the hot end of a poker.

He is convinced that there is a robbing of Peter to pay Paul. He is equally sure that the Peter in the case is himself and that Paul is the capitalist who holds mortgages, runs factories and railroads, and owns bonds. And he is equally convinced that the capitalist is a wicked man.

In reality, the capitalist, even the bondholder, was merely fortunate in being able to capitalize the wartime needs (and perhaps indiscretions) of the government. In a society motivated by profit-making, his actions were for the most part natural and consistent with prevailing morality, including that of the farmer. Even the abnormal corruption was a part of the price that society inevitably paid for its indulgence in war.

PROBLEMS OF MARKETS AND MIDDLEMEN

Before the war the farmer of the west had attained a favorable position. Economic and political alliance with him had been the aim of planter and capitalist alike. The planter had not always seen eye to eye with the farmer, but with the exception of slavery in the territories, there had been substantial agreement on decisive issues. The prosperity of the planter and the expanding area of cotton culture created an increasingly valuable cash market for western farm products in the south, and long nullified the opposition of the farmer to the extension of slavery. The opening up of communication by canal and railway with the east and the rapid growth of eastern cities gave to the west the advantage of an eastern market competing with the planter for the farmer's produce, and affording a market in addition for raw materials of manufacture not needed in the south.

War sadly altered matters for farmer as well as planter. It permanently impaired alike the planter's political influence and his purchasing power. The south was forced to depend more largely on its own produce, thus forcing the farmer of the west to depend primarily on eastern markets for the sale of his produce as well as for the buying of manufactures. Politically, after the war the farmer found himself to be a subordinate factor in the new political alignment, which was dominated by the capitalist more completely than the old alignment had been dominated by the planter. In the old arrangement, the planter had to walk warily in order to avoid antagonizing the farmer and forcing him into alliance with the alert and increasingly powerful capitalist. In post-war politics, the planter having been in effect eliminated politically, the capitalist found the farmer's opposition, deprived as it was of the potential support of the planter, an easy problem to solve.

With the coming of the railroad, the farmer's hopes had run high. Even in regions remote from rivers he would be able to grow staples for market instead of having to maintain a self-sufficing economy. He would be delivered from bondage to waterways. He would have an eastern market as well as a southern. To secure railways, many sacrifices were made. Bonuses were paid. Stock was bought, often not so much as an investment as an encouragement to railway promoters.

But the new conditions of marketing introduced by railroads proved to have unforeseen disadvantages. In the processes of merging the local roads into trunk lines, and in the general manipulation of railroad stocks during the post-war speculative era, small stockholders frequently were made to suffer. The completion of competing trunk lines often reduced rates on through traffic below a profitable level. But farmers rarely traveled as passengers except between local points, and as for through freight, not the farmers but the middlemen were the principal beneficiaries. The railroads undertook to make up for low competitive through rates by means of excessively burdensome noncompetitive local rates. As usual, the farmer was the chief burden bearer. To penalize or to favor certain communities, discrimination in rates was not infrequent. Having undertaken the growing of cash crops for market in place of the self-sufficing, frontier type of farming, the farmer found himself to be dependent on cash markets to lift his mortgage or pay his other debts; and for access to cash markets he found himself to be dependent on the railroad. Briefly, he had engaged a servant who turned out to be a master.

With the change from self-sufficing agriculture to dependence on cash crops, the farmer experienced other complications. He must depend on railroads not only to haul his crops to market but as well to bring him his implements and other manufactures from cities more or less remote. If rates were excessive in the one case, they were equally burdensome in the other. The manufacturer could add the freight rate to his price, with perhaps an added profit, and thus pass along the cost of transportation to the farmer as buyer. To the freight rate was added a goodly sum made possible by the tariff duties, as indicated by the fact that farm implements were frequently sold more cheaply abroad, after payment of the various costs of exportation, than at home. In the sale of his own goods, the farmer found no means of passing on the freight rates to those who bought his produce. Nor could he add a tariff. He sold his goods in a competitive market and purchased manufactures in a protected market. The profits of middlemen intervened, alike in selling his produce and in buying manufactures. His was the weakest bargaining power in the process of interchange.

A basic problem which farmers after the Civil War found most puzzling and most difficult was the too rapid expansion of the farm area. Expansion was stimulated by the homestead law, combined with the prolonged agitation for the settlement of the territories by free-soilers to prevent the extension of slavery. The advantages of the west were exaggerated. Propaganda of railroad promoters and land agents and town boomers found support in Horace Greeley's apparently disinterested but unduly emphatic advice to the young man. Even before the war was at end there was renewal of immigration. From about 92,000 in 1862, the number of immigrants grew to nearly a quarter of a million in 1865, and to almost half a million in 1873. The new comers during this era were overwhelmingly from northern and western Europe. They were predominantly German and Scandinavian. Many of them tarried in the cities of the east, but the usual goal was a homestead in the west. The tide was swollen by discharged soldiers and sailors and workers in the war industries.

While the number of farmers was increasing inordinately and the farming area was rapidly expanding, the productivity of farms was increased by the introduction of machinery and improved methods. The scarcity of labor and the unusual demand for goods during the war promoted the use of machinery. The reaper had already been introduced, and it was now popularized. Competitive conditions after the war gave advantage to those who could afford to buy machinery and to those whose land was adapted to the use of machinery, and this in turn made the struggle harder for others. During the twenty years beginning in 1860, the estimated output of corn more than doubled, and of wheat almost trebled.

These, then, were some of the troubles that beset the farmer. Official corruption added to his tax burdens, and surrendered the government, so he was convinced, to groups that opposed his interests. Inflation, with its immense transfer of wealth, mainly to non-agrarian groups, and its creation of debtor and creditor classes, was followed by deflation, with the farmer bearing the main burden, directly or indirectly, of debt payments, public and private. New conditions of marketing, which seemed at first so promising, involved the farmer in the loss of a large part of his market in the south. In addition, he found himself dependent on powerful and clever middlemen and on monopolistic railway corporations. His produce he had to sell in a competitive market, while manufactures had to be bought in a protected market. The one traditional remedy for the discontented or the oppressed—western land—was now contributing to his misfortunes.

With the transition from subsistence farming to the growing of cash crops for market, the farmer entered definitely into the increasingly complex and interdependent economy of interchange. The "independent farmer" took his place among the great American myths. Even his interdependence was strangely like dependence.

NON-POLITICAL REMEDIAL MEASURES

The farmer is more intimate with nature than with man. While he may talk about the weather, he knows very well in spite of the rain-makers that there is nothing he can do about it. Something of this attitude carries over into his relations with men. There is the vast and mighty economic system that seems almost as impersonal and almost as immune to his influence as is nature. Normally, he is inclined to be a fatalist. Whether it is a crop failure or a mortgage foreclosure, the best he can do is to grin and bear it.

But the state of the farmers as described in preceding pages became so exceptionally calamitous as to bestir them at last into trying to do something about it. Their first action was non-political. It took the form of the Granger movement.

The Grange, or as its organizers called it, the National Grange of the Patrons of Husbandry, had origin in the mind of Oliver Hudson Kelley. This interesting Yankee—he was once described as "an engine with too much steam on all the time"—was born in Boston. In approved manner he went west when a young man and became a Minnesota farmer. Later he secured a clerkship at Washington under the Commissioner of Agriculture, who sent him in 1866 to secure first-hand knowledge about southern farming. The conditions he observed were so depressing to his ardent temperament as to set up a train of reflections concerning causes and remedies. The outcome of his reflection was a full-fledged plan for a farmers' organization, not merely for the south but for the nation.

His plan was an adaptation of the Masonic order. The Grange was to be secret, ritualistic, social, and educational. A so-called national organization was first formed, with Kelley as secretary, entrusted with the organizing of local Granges. He was voted a salary of two thousand dollars a year, to be derived from fees of local Granges as yet non-existent. The first of these was organized not among farmers but among employees of the government at Washington. Kelley set out boldly in 1868 without funds, resolved to earn his salary or at least his traveling expenses by forming a chain of Granges from Washington to Minnesota. He had the curious idea of organizing farmers in the cities, and naturally came to grief till he reached his own farmstead and began to work among "dirt" farmers. At the same time he made extensive use of optimistic if not deceptive methods of publicity, assuming in his articles and advertisements that a great national organization was rapidly coming into being.

To his optimism and ardor were presently added other influences which enabled him to transform his visionary scheme into a practical and successful movement. What the farmers needed, in their own opinion, was in the main an agency for improving not so much their intellectual and social status as their economic well-being. Men whom he had interested in the movement began to talk about the Grange as an agency for helping them to buy more cheaply, to sell their crops at higher prices, to checkmate the middleman, and to bring pressure to bear on railroad rate makers.

Even with these added purposes of an economic nature, the Grange could hardly have overcome the isolation, individualism and apathy of the farmers as a class had it not been for the rapidly increasing gravity of the farm problem. The burden of inflation and deflation, the difficulties of inequitable prices and freight rates, the farmer's inferior bargaining power, the revelations of official corruption, the panic of 1873,—these and other causes of agrarian unrest enabled the sponsors of the Grange to point to it as an instrument of protest and of self-help.

That the strength of the movement was in the spontaneous demands of the farmers for agencies of their own to promote their group interests is apparent. In addition to the Grange, innumerable other farmers' clubs were coming into being in the early 'seventies. These were at first local and independent and were later federated into state organizations. The Grange itself made little headway except in connection with its promise of relief for bad economic conditions. The spontaneous character of the movement, in spite of its appearance of artificial or accidental origin in the mind of its principal promoter, is perhaps indicated by the fact that similar tendencies were observable in European countries.

After its early slow and discouraging progress, the Granger movement spread over the plains like a prairie fire. By 1874, thirty-two states and territories were represented at the annual meeting of the national Grange. The membership by the end of that year was estimated at three-quarters of a million. There were more than twenty thousand local units. Indiana soon had an average of two Granges for every township.

The objects were set forth in the official Declaration of Purposes. The home life of the farmer and his family was to be made more attractive and comfortable. Diversified and systematic farming (later to be known as scientific farming) was to be encouraged, and agricultural education was demanded. Cooperative buying and selling was approved. The credit system was opposed, together with tendencies toward prodigality and aping of the "fashion system." Monopolies, particularly in freight rates and transportation, were denounced. The Grange as an organization was to refrain from political action, but its members should perform their civic duties and Granges might discuss the political aspects of farm problems.

Farmers rallied to the Grange and to the farmers' clubs mainly because they hoped thereby to be able to sell their produce and buy manufactures more advantageously. The principal obstacle in the way appeared to them to be monopoly. Railroads maintained monopolistic rates. Middlemen fixed the prices of farm produce. Manufacturers, in alliance with merchants, and aided by the tariff, arbitrarily controlled the prices of manufactures, especially of farm machinery. Banks determined the amount of money in circulation and the conditions of credit.

Such a view of the situation led inevitably to an idea of the intimate connection between politics and the farmer's economic problems. This in turn directed the Grangers toward political action. The farmers' clubs were commonly organized with a frank avowal of political aims. But our present concern is with the non-political aspects of the movement.

In the farming regions, and especially in the grain-growing and cattle-raising areas, farm life was relatively isolated and individualistic. Before the days of good roads, automobiles, labor-saving devices for household work, rural mail delivery, telephones, and radios, the farmer and his family had extremely meager opportunities for social intercourse and intellectual contacts. There were visits to the usually drab and uninviting market town, and on Sunday the none too genial services at church in the old-time atmosphere of repression and brimstone theology; but such diversions did little to relieve the tedium of exhausting toil or to minister to social, intellectual, or esthetic needs. The mingling of men and women (for women also were members) in the local Granges was a wholesome and exhilarating experience of incalculable value aside from any interchange of economically useful ideas and experiences.

More definitely related to the solution of the economic problems confronting the farmer was the development of cooperative enterprises. For the marketing of their crops, cooperation was not very extensively undertaken. The baffling mechanism of shipping and storage facilities, credit arrangements, and commission houses in the larger trading centers interposed an insurmountable obstacle. But attempts were made to handle wool and tobacco by means of cooperative agencies, and cooperative elevators and creameries achieved a moderate success. More popular was cooperative buying, particularly of farm machinery. There are no dependable figures of the number of stores and other agencies, or of the volume of business, but such enterprises were undertaken throughout the country, especially in the west and south. Members of a local Grange, without any formal merchandizing organization, often pooled their orders and secured a discount. Local orders were often combined into a single order by the county Grange, and these in turn were sometimes consolidated into a system of buying by the state Grange. Arrangements were sometimes made with specified merchants by which a discount was secured on purchases by members. State Granges entered into agreements with firms at Chicago, St. Louis, San Francisco, Memphis, New Orleans, and other cities for handling the business of the Granges.

A form of cooperation almost universally attempted was mutual fire insurance. There was an occasional venture in life insurance. A beginning was made in cooperative banking. Milling and packing were also undertaken, though not extensively. The most ambitious and at the same time the most disastrous enterprise was the making of farm machinery. In Iowa the Grange officials encountered such opposition from the manufacturers of harvesters in securing wholesale rates that cooperative manufacturing was undertaken. About two hundred and fifty harvesters were made and sold at a greatly reduced price. The problem of patent rights and other difficulties led to the failure of the plan in Iowa. The national Grange projected unsuccessfully an even more ambitious plan for making farm machinery.

The most successful form of cooperation was the simpler retail cooperation adopted from the Rochdale Equitable Pioneers. The Rochdale plan had originated at Rochdale, England, in 1844. Twenty-eight weavers pooled their savings and established a small store for the sale of staple goods. In order to keep from being squeezed out of business by the concerted competition of ordinary dealers, the store sold goods at prevailing market prices. The surplus was used for expanding the business, for providing the members of the society with social and educational advantages, and for paying a small refund in proportion to purchases. The management was democratic but centralized and efficient. The business had modest beginnings, utilized accumulating experiences, and grew into a large and varied enterprise affording a model for innumerable other cooperative ventures in England.

Unfortunately for American cooperation, the Granges in a majority of instances ignored the experiences of the English. Other factors contributed to the decline of the movement. The rapid increase in the funds of the Granges during the period of expanding membership gave an exaggerated view of their financial resources. Plans were too ambitious, hopes too exalted. Inexperience meant costly mistakes, not serious in small beginnings but fatal in larger enterprises of manufacturing and of marketing the farmers' crops. Dishonesty was not unknown, and it, like inexperience, was serious in proportion to the scope of the enterprises. Many Granges were not careful in the choice of members, and some were admitted whose aim was "to make money not from the farm but from the farmer." Local dealers, manufacturers, and middlemen became increasingly hostile as the cooperative plans expanded. Bankruptcy overtook some of the enterprises, and in order to escape responsibility for debts incurred by some of the central agencies, many of the local Granges disbanded.

Many successful cooperative enterprises survived, but in agrarian economy at large they had little importance. What remained was chiefly an experience which has profited later cooperatives mainly in the avoidance of mistakes. In the meantime, one of the causes of the decline of cooperation, the use of farm organizations for political purposes, was of paramount importance.

THE POLITICAL REVOLT OF THE FARMER

To the student of politics, the story of the political revolt of the farmer is long and complicated and no doubt important. To those whose attention is focussed on economic phenomena, the revolt is relatively unimportant, save as to its causes, which are already apparent. It was essentially a futile effort on the one hand to throw off the burden of paying for the war and on the other hand to escape from a condition of economic inferiority imposed by the triumph of capitalism.

The first phase was the diversion of the Granger movement into an attempt to control railroads by means of state legislation. This phase was the only one that was even measureably successful. Success even here was limited by the failure to secure uniform state regulation or adequate interstate control, and by the disruption of the Grange.

The eagerness of the west for railroads, combined with unscrupulous political influence exerted by railroad promoters, had been responsible for the initial error of a too liberal policy of *laissez-faire* in the public regulation of transportation. The abuses during the period of speculative expansion and official corruption following the war caused little opposition in the larger cities, especially in the east, for competition in through traffic profited the cities at the expense of rural sections, and investors in the cities feared the effects of regulation on the value of stocks. The initiation of railroad regulation was therefore the work of the farming communities.

When farmers were offered fifteen cents a bushel for corn and were told they could "take it or leave it," while at the same time corn was selling for six times that price in the east, and when coal was so dear that corn was found to be a cheaper fuel, there was the inevitable cry of "down with monopoly." The attack on the monopoly of the middlemen assumed the form, as has been noted, of cooperation. But on the monopoly of transportation, cooperation had no effect. This was the decisive influence in the diversion of Granger activity into politics.

Illinois was then the outstanding state in the production of wheat and corn. In 1869 a law was forced through the legislature for the regulation of railroad rates, but it was worded so vaguely as to be of no avail. Revision of the state constitution was being undertaken at the time, and farmers assembled in a Producers' Convention and brought pressure to bear for a constitutional mandate to the legislature. This resulted in three laws basing rates on mileage, fixing maximum rates, and establishing a commission empowered to secure information and to supervise the carrying out of the laws. Farmers of other states were quick to follow suit. By 1874 there were "Granger laws" in Minnesota, Iowa, and Wisconsin.

But the railroads had weapons "by the carload." The laws were often inconsistent and unworkable. This was due in a measure to the inexperience of the legislators and the lack of precedents. It was due in part to the influence of railroad lobbyists. When a bill could not be killed, the next best thing, from the point of view of the corporations, was its emasculation or its reduction to such form as to make its enforcement burdensome or inequitable. Passes were issued to legislators, judges, and other officials. In one state there was resort to the device of withholding passes from officials who were not "friends" of the companies. Provisions that might facilitate judicial nullification were welcomed. In Illinois an adverse decision by the court was followed by the defeat of the judges at the next election.

But whether the laws were nullified or not, resort to the courts cost time and money and could more easily be endured by the companies than by the farmers. The laws were often ignored, and when plaintiffs by court action sought redress, reprisals were not infrequent. On some specious plea that veiled and yet revealed its motive, the company could readily refuse at the crucial moment to deliver a plaintiff's order for farm machinery or to haul his crops to market or expedite their movement in transit.

The judicial attack on the laws was based on two main assumptions. One was that a railroad charter was a contract and that regulations altering the nature of the contract without the consent of both parties was illegal. Another assumption was that by the reduction of rates by legislation the state was depriving the owners of railroads of property "without due process of law," which was forbidden by the Fourteenth Amendment. Thus early after its adoption in 1868 did that famous amendment, which was supposedly a weapon for insuring liberation of the slaves, become an instrument of business. These two assumptions of opponents of railroad regulation reached at length the highest court of the United States in its review of the "Granger cases." A railroad charter, it was held, except in so far as it might contain specific provisions which were violated by a regulatory law, could not exempt a railroad from the operation of such a law. A charter must be interpreted in terms of the state's general law of incorporation, and in the light of the powers allowed to the state government by the constitution of the state and by that of the nation. Concerning the second assumption—based on the "due process" clause—it was held that well-established custom at home and abroad gave to legislative bodies power of regulating businesses "affected with a public interest." A railroad, it was affirmed, was such a semi-public business, and might therefore be subjected to legislative regulation.

The farmers thus initiated legislation by the states and decisions by the courts which prepared the way for later more effective state laws and commissions and the comprehensive act of Congress of Cleveland's first administration, establishing the Interstate Commerce Commission. Though hampered by an increasing tendency toward judicial hostility, the federal commission survived until at length its reorganization made it a measureably effective and universally accepted agency of regulation.

But in the meantime the "Granger laws" had been so effectively opposed by the railroads that most of them were repealed. The companies themselves were engulfed by the panic of 1873, which had been in large measure of their own making. The farmers, tiring of the unequal fight against the railroads, or contenting themselves with the illusion of victory, turned their attention to money and credit.

The greenback and free-silver movements were in reality mere phases of a single movement. The circumstances already described resulted in a burden of debt, public and private, which weighed most heavily on the farmers, and especially those of the west.

What remedy, if any, was available? The farmers attacked the tariff but without effect. They opposed in a fumbling manner the payment of the bondholders in gold and were met with charges of trying to destroy the credit and integrity of the government. They tried to better their condition by checking the power of monopolists through cooperation and railroad regulation, and because of their own inexperience and individualism as well as because of the more efficient tactics of the middlemen and the railroad corporations, they met with virtual failure. When they began to realize that the increasing value of the dollar meant for them increasing obligations to their creditors, they fixed upon cheap and plentiful money as the "paramount issue," and began to attach to it an exaggerated importance as a cure-all. The demand for paper money (greenbacks) was succeeded by the cry for "the free and unlimited coinage of silver at the ratio of sixteen to one."

They were embittered by their burdens and by the failure of attempted methods of relieving them. They were misled by inadequate knowledge of economics. The group which, at the time, was loudest in professions of superior knowledge had inaugurated or sanctioned the adoption of the policy of fiat money. The farmers were merely advocating a continuance of that policy. Their doing so was peculiarly unfortunate for themselves. Leaders of the opposing group have never ceased on occasions of conflicting political opinion to point with scorn to the western farmer —so wild-eyed and dangerous as to be capable even of advocating bad money. The immediate results of his greenback and free-silver misadventures were a diversion of attention from possible measures of relief and the continued bearing of a plainly inequitable part of post-war economic burdens.

CHAPTER XX

PROSTRATE PLANTERS

WAR'S DEVASTATION

In the north there were many who refused a full measure of devotion to the policy of coercing the south to remain in the union. In the south there was opposition both to secession and to war for making secession effective. But secession came. War came. Northern armies came. The instinct of self-defense became the basis of a degree of devotion not often paralleled in history. The devotion was the more fervent as the cause became more desperate.

While gold bonds were being bought in the north with paper money, gold and silver hoards and ornaments were being exchanged in the south for virtually worthless currency and rapidly depreciating bonds. Ornaments and articles of use that were not indispensable were converted into munitions of war. Consumption goods and instruments of production alike were devoted almost without reservation to the war. The result was that at the end of the war there was almost everywhere in the south a serious deficit.

In such places as Richmond, Atlanta, and Charleston there had been a measure of skill, some equipment for manufacturing, and relatively adequate transportation facilities. Had they been undisturbed, such centers could have turned from the making of swords to plowshares and could have aided materially in the true reconstruction of the south. But the existence of their meager facilities helped to provoke not only their own destruction but the devastation of extensive adjacent areas. Earlier, Sheridan had spared no effort to reduce the magnificently fertile Shenandoah valley to a state of such barrenness that "a crow must carry his rations" if he wished to cross it. Later in the war, Atlanta, Charleston, Columbia, and innumerable lesser places, as well as many of the finest of the plantations, were left in ashes in the track of Sherman's march. Pianos riven with axes, family portraits on the walls pierced with union bayonets—little things were these, and yet large. For to war's destructiveness they added the desolation of spirit and the bitterness of hatred.

With the collapse of the Confederacy, its obligations were valueless. With emancipation, slave property vanished. With the restless movements of negroes in quest of free food and shelter from the government without work, which they commonly believed was the meaning of emancipation, the land itself was deprived of productive labor and was therefore at the moment of little value. Vast quantities of goods, especially cotton, and much land, were declared confiscated because of claims by the Confederate government.

Railroad finances, trackage, and rolling stock were in a hopeless condition. In places the invading unionists had torn the wrought-iron rails from the ties and twisted them about the trees along the tracks, and had even dug up the ties and burned them. Cars had been run along sidings and into fields, where they were used as dwellings.

There was virtually no circulating medium. Gold and silver were almost unknown and the Confederate currency was worthless.

To levy ordinary taxes would have been futile, and so the unionist authorities imposed upon the "conquered provinces" a tax on sales. The all-important article for sale of course was cotton. A twenty-five per cent sales tax, a revenue tax of two to three cents a pound on cotton, and certain other taxes enabled the government to collect from the south a considerable surplus beyond the costs of federal "reconstruction" during the three years following the war.

But of the taxes paid the government received by no means all. Secretary McCulloch of the Treasury Department paid his respects to his own agents in charge of the cotton taxes. "I am sure I sent some honest cotton agents south," he said, "but it sometimes seems doubtful whether any of them remained honest very long." With the added burdens of heavy federal taxes dishonestly administered, many southerners, already staggering, fell by the wayside.

"CARPETBAGGERS" AND "SCALAWAGS"

Secretary McCulloch's agents in the south were dishonest, so he himself affirmed, but they at least were responsible agents of the federal government. Their peculations at the expense of the government and their extortions at the cost of the people perhaps subjected them to little danger of being brought to book. But fear of official retribution must have been a restraining influence in limiting both the nature and the extent of their dishonesty.

But in the south there were other northerners who had no official responsibility to any one, and at the same time had the support of the dominant group in the federal Congress and of the federal commanders in the south. This dominant group at Washington was unwilling to take complete charge of the south by means of federal agencies (though there were army units, Freedman's Bureau agents, and others with specified functions in the south), and instead sought to gain their ends under cover of the fiction of autonomous local rule by "loyal" citizens. But "loyal" citizens were confined, so far as whites were concerned, to those who had not fought for the south and who were willing to accept new state constitutions giving to negroes not only freedom but the right to vote. Such restrictions meant that few southern whites could (and fewer still would) have anything to do with the "loyal" governments. There were a few who were willing to cooperate on the basis prescribed by Congress. Some of these may have been honest and honorable. Unquestionably most of them were turncoats and opportunists. Many of them had been advocates of secession. Foreseeing its failure, or being unable to gain their ambitions as secessionists, they trimmed their sails for the wind from the north. Events proved them to be interested mainly in the opportunity to burglarize their helpless country in the name of loyalty and patriotism. By their fellow southerners they were called "scalawags"—the "mean, lousy and filthy kine that are not fit for butchers or dogs."

Working with the "scalawags" (except when quarrels arose over division of the spoils) were the "carpetbaggers" from the north, with their worldly goods (until their fortunes were recruited in the south) carried from place to place in cheap traveling bags made of stout carpet cloth. Some who went south, to be sure, were zealots rather than plunderers—men like the fierce abolitionists of pre-war days—simple-minded men who had no thought for the complex realities of life and who believed with fervor that the immediate and compulsory freeing of the slaves was a divine command and an instantaneous solvent of age-old problems. The negroes, in spite of their slave-bred ignorance, were wiser than their self-appointed deliverers. Many of the negroes soon discovered the real nature of the northern "invasion." "A carpetbagger," ran a definition attributed to a negro preacher, "is a man who came down here from some place and stole enough to fill his carpet bag full; but the scalawag knew the woods and swamps better than the carpetbagger did and he stole the carpetbagger's bag and ran off with it." Most of the "carpetbaggers" were indeed like most of the "scalawags" in being opportunists and self-seekers. The majority of whites who accepted the "reconstruction" or "loyal" governments in any save a passive manner were "carpetbaggers" from beyond the south.

Under joint control of "scalawags" and "carpetbaggers," negro suffrage became an agency not for the genuine emancipation of the negroes but a more or less transparent façade behind which negroes and their former masters alike were exploited by the "political drill masters" to enrich themselves. In one after another of the secession states the "loyal" governments were set up, and virtually without exception there ensued, along with the enactment of some constructive and serviceable legislation, an astounding record of graft and misrule.

At first there was merely petty graft, extending from trivial instances to a riotous carnival. Cigars and wines and other personal articles were charged to the public treasury. Articles were bought at exorbitant prices. Excessive mileage (as eighty cents, for instance, in Louisiana) was allowed to officials, and the distance traveled was "estimated" with "generosity." Many members of the legislatures and conventions could neither read nor write but they were lavishly supplied with stationery and newspapers.

From indulgence in relatively trivial thefts of public funds, there was a rapid and bold advance to an orgy of corruption. Immense sums were paid as subsidies to railroads and other companies often wholly fraudulent in character. Public approval was given to "blue-sky" bonds for the purpose of enabling "insiders" to sell them. Imaginary public buildings, as school houses, were paid for out of public funds. Contracts, especially for printing, absorbed uncounted millions of dollars in graft. A frequently cited instance is the case of South Carolina. Its printing bills from 1790 to 1868 amounted to $609,000; and from 1868 to 1876, to $1,326,589.

In order to secure funds, tax rates were doubled, trebled, and multiplied. A moderate illustration is the case of Louisiana, where the increase was about eight hundred per cent. There was a monstrous piling up of state and local debts. The debt of New Orleans was multiplied twenty-five fold. In 1873, the debt of South Carolina was increased from $7,600,000 to $29,000,000. The land sold for unpaid taxes in the one state of Mississippi amounted to six million acres. Property values declined. Private mortgages were added to the burden of public taxes and debts incurred by "scalawag" and "carpetbag" misrule.

PROBLEMS OF HOME RULE

After the World War of 1914 to 1918, there was everywhere in the United States a wartime spirit of lawlessness and intolerance and a craving for secret and violent adventure born of war. In the cities these tendencies found expression in riotous living, a carnival of jazz and exotic dancing, a mania for speed and dizzy experiences; and in the underworld they took the form of "bootlegging," "hijacking," and "racketeering." In rural sections the primitive traits unleashed by war and suppressed by the return to peace found vent in secret conclaves, an ardent quest for menaces and missions, the carrying out of missions in whippings, hangings, hooded parades, burning crosses, and shadowy escapades, some harmless, others direful in the wreck of reason and of justice.

After the Civil War there was a similar cycle of maladjustments in the transition from war to peace. In the eas[t] was "high carnival" among the rich, and an exodus of th[e] less fortunate as frontiersmen and "carpetbaggers." In th[e] west and among the farmers generally and the poorer classes of the cities, many of those in whom the coming of peace confined the passions and violence of war found release for their inquietude of spirit on the frontier and in the turbulent railroad construction gangs. In the south alone did the return to peace mean so great a suppression of primitive man who is uppermost in war as to call for secret and shadowy modes of expression. And in the south of "reconstruction" years, there was no necessity of searching for justifying menaces and missions. These were at hand. The menaces were the men from the north (the "carpetbaggers"); the renegades of the south (the "scalawags"); and the misguided negroes who were being used by their "political drill masters" for venal and vicious ends, playing with fire that might have started a consuming conflagration.

Thus the release of the primitive expressed itself among "carpetbaggers" and "scalawags" in exploitation of the south; and among other whites in the south in checkmating that exploitation by the only means available—depriving the "drill masters" of negro votes as political tools. The first phase of the original Klan movement met with almost universal support among the whites. When its one legitimate aim was attained (the wresting of governments from the "drill masters") the Klan degenerated into an agency more nearly resembling later groups of similar form—an agency for the mere expression of primitive desires and passions declared to be illicit by the laws and conventions of peace.

During the celebration of the centennial of independence the last of the "political drill masters" were defeated, and in the following year the withdrawal of federal troops gave tacit approval to the beginnings of real reconstruction by southerners themselves. But the problems confronting the "home-rule" governments were appalling. There was the question of the franchise. The alternatives were harsh. The negroes were legally enfranchised by federal and state constitutional enactments. They were ill-prepared for so sudden a shift, and many arguments were adduced against their immediate and complete enfranchisement. In any case the minds of the whites were even less prepared for acquiescence than were the minds of the negroes for voting and office holding. But since enfranchisement already existed by constitutional enactment as a price of autonomy, the alternatives were acquiescence or evasion. Artifices were devised by which the letter of the law might abide the killing of the spirit. There was a formal acceptance of despised and violated constitutional and statutory laws—a condition foreshadowing later experiences with the laws relating to alcoholic beverages. In the latter case the tables were turned—the south was the decisive factor in imposing on the urban centers of the north the laws by them despised and violated.

There were other problems, as the debts incurred during the war and the era of "carpetbag" rule. There were the problems of inflation and deflation, markets and middlemen, tariffs and taxes—problems common to the south and the west. There was the problem of trying to restore relations, economic and political, with the west. This in turn involved the problem of restoring the political equilibrium of economic groups, disturbed by the ascendancy of the capitalists after the war. Finally, there was the problem, overshadowing others in urgency and importance, of adapting the agriculture of the south to free labor.

NEW SYSTEMS OF LABOR

The south was confronted with the problem of a thoroughgoing reorganization of its labor system during a period of economic disorganization after a disastrous military defeat. Its problem was complicated by other grave influences. The negro was quite apparently unequal to the white in many ways. Modern scientific thought tends toward an explanation connected with differences of opportunity and environment rather than toward an explanation based on racial or hereditary traits. But the post-war south was not a scientific laboratory. Southern prejudice magnified the negro's inferiority, attributed it to inherent racial traits, and took for granted a social system based on the assumption of negro inferiority. Northern prejudice ignored the negro's inferiority and tried to force by military power a sudden transition the nature of which was largely determined by the misconceptions of an outsider and by the arrogance of a victor. Not failure but the measure of success attained in such disheartening circumstances is the surprising feature of southern post-war economy.

The south's first attempted solution of the problem of transition from slave to free labor was embodied in the "Black Codes." These were enacted by southern legislatures before the heavy hand of the military commander intervened for the maintenance of "carpetbag" and "scalawag" rule. The "Black Codes" can be judged only in the light of the events immediately preceding their enactment.

After the defeat of the south there was a political interregnum. For several months there was virtually no recognized government in a large part of the south except the military government in the neighborhoods of the army encampments. It was during this interregnum that the former slaves were "testing their freedom" by the two-fold process of changing their names and leaving their habitats of bondage. The late summer and the autumn of 1865, the harvest season, was a time of crucial importance. The harvest would be meager at best, and the exhaustion of food and reserve supplies at the end of the war was expected to create a critical situation even with the harvest well in hand. But the negroes were on the move with no thought of the coming winter's menace of famine and of pestilence. They had been encouraged by northern propagandists to insist on freedom and to look to the invading armies for protection and even for maintenance. There was a widely held idea that the lands would be divided. For every one there would be "forty acres and a mule." Plantations lay idle. Negroes who made contracts to work for wages impulsively forgot their agreements and often left their families for their former masters to support. Serious as were the economic consequences for an already utterly exhausted region, such a situation involved social dangers even greater. Thievery, unregulated relations of the sexes, pestilence, were among the more obvious dangers. Suppose the multitudes of restless, unemployed, and irresponsible vagrants, who were inevitably to be disappointed in their impossible anticipations of food and leisure without labor—suppose they should become not merely migratory and restless but unruly and violent? The danger was increased by the widespread view of the negroes that the plans of the federal government for taking care of them were to find fulfillment toward the end of the year. What would be the outcome of the inevitable disappointment? Such chaotic conditions gave rise quite naturally, especially in the regions of preponderant negro population, to a state of mind commonly described as the "Black Terror." Among the "Black Codes" of the political interregnum, the most repressive were those of South Carolina, Mississippi, and Louisiana, enacted during the "Black Terror" of '65.

To put an end to the migratory tendencies of the negroes, and to set them to work again, vagrancy laws were passed. Vagrancy was variously defined. But the definitions were more or less obviously applicable to negroes moving about without sanction or employment. Penalties included fines or imprisonment, or labor on public works, or labor for private employers for a specified period under conditions which at least technically afforded protection to the vagrant. Other offenses besides vagrancy were subjected to penalties of a similar nature, the aim being to substitute compulsory paid labor for slave labor.

Convict labor and the hiring out of petty offenders are methods by no means confined to negroes and to the south. Nor can it be asserted that the southern laws in their extremer forms were intended as a permanent solution of the problem. Many of their provisions were extreme and impolitic. But northerners have long since realized that the harsh and impetuous condemnations of the time arose from misconceptions of the problems confronting their vanquished foes.

As soon as emancipation became an accepted fact, the planters commonly resorted to contracts with their former slaves. They further sought special legislation to legalize, standardize, and enforce these contracts. Necessarily in such legal matters, the employer had great advantages, but these were counteracted in some degree by the scarcity of laborers. In some of the states apprenticeship laws and laws restricting the negroes to specified kinds of work were also passed.

Professor Dunning asserted (and there have been few more competent than he to pass judgment on the subject) that "this legislation [embodied in the 'Black Codes'], far from embodying any spirit of defiance towards the north, or any purpose to evade the conditions which the victors had imposed, was in the main a conscientious and straightforward attempt to bring some sort of order out of the social and economic chaos which a full acceptance of the results of war and emancipation involved." But this view, quite commonly held by later northern writers, is exactly the reverse of northern views at that time. Even Carl Schurz, moderate as compared to many, was misled by his preconceptions of immediate and unqualified economic equality for the negro. He "declared for an economic and social revolution to be enforced by legislation and the army in European fashion. . . . Legislation backed by the bayonet should obliterate class distinctions."

The policy of coercion was attempted by the federal Congress by means of the Freedman's Bureau and the army. The work of the Bureau was in theory most vitally concerned with the conversion of the former slaves into independent farmers or tradesmen, mainly by the distribution of lands. In practice it came to be concerned mainly with the supervision of the system of labor contracts by which the southern whites were already working out the problems of transition. Probably the chief value of the Bureau was in bringing northerners into contact with the details of the problem of emancipation. Thus their minds were prepared for acceptance of the inevitable—the leaving of the problem to the southerners themselves.

The government failed utterly to carry out the plan of distributing land among the negroes and establishing them as independent farmers. Nor was the initiative or ability of the negro able to surmount the obstacles in the way of his acquiring lands independently of governmental aid. The semi-compulsory system of labor contracts was the transitional substitute, as we have seen, for slave labor. Out of the contract system there at length emerged the prevailing forms of farm labor in the south since the war—share tenancy or "cropping" and the wages system.

Share tenancy seems to have grown up spontaneously, supplanting the formal labor contracts of the transition period, and being preferred to the informal wage agreements of northern free labor. Usually the tenant furnished only his clothing, his food, and his labor. The landlord, in return for providing land and houses, garden plot, live stock, implements, and seeds, received one-half of the crop. There were variations, as the "third-and-fourth" plan, the landlord furnishing only the land and the house and receiving one-third of the corn and one-fourth of the cotton.

After their first taste of the doubtful sweets of free locomotion, most of the negroes calmly settled down into the routine of farm labor, accepting first the contract system and then the share tenancy arrangement. But some insisted on changing from place to place. Reconstruction of railroads, towns, and farms gave impetus to the wages system. Farmers had need of seasonal workers, as cotton "choppers" in the spring and pickers in the fall. Some farmers preferred to hire men for cultivating their farms. Share tenancy and the wages system thus grew up together as substitutes for slavery.

An Englishman writing in 1871 on the basis of extensive knowledge of conditions in the south attested the widespread adoption of share tenancy and praised its effects on the negro. But his pleasing picture of the economic status and opportunities of the negro is marred by the admission that at the end of the year the tenant was nearly always in debt. Under the new economic conditions it was this burden of debt perpetually bearing down on the negroes that formed their gravest handicap in achieving genuine economic emancipation.

The negro share tenant was required to furnish only his labor, his clothing, and his food. But since he was entirely without resources, his food and clothing could be had only by means of credit. He was not only without resources; he was utterly without training or experience in a provident regard for the future. Nor was he well equipped by education or by nature for protecting his interests against any who might seek to take advantage of him. As a result of this combination of circumstances, small stores arose throughout the south, on the plantations, at the crossroads, and in the towns. These stores were often owned by the landlords. In any case it was a simple matter to extend credit to a negro tenant with his part of the crop as security. The negro knew nothing of bookkeeping and little of prices. The situation afforded a tempting opportunity for excessive prices, exorbitant interest, and extortionate mortgages. But irrespective of the willful fleecing of the negroes, many of them, simply because of lack of foresight and discretion, became hopelessly involved in debt.

> "Nigger work hard all de year,
> White man tote de money."

The system of share tenancy and mortgaging of crops included white tenants in various regions of the south. It was difficult enough for whites and virtually impossible for negroes to break out of the vicious circle and achieve a genuine economic emancipation. Nor was the system without its disadvantages to landlord and merchant. Not the least of these was the temptation to dishonesty and oppression of the tenant. Losses due to illness or dishonesty or removal of tenants were not infrequent. Landlords and merchants rarely had sufficient capital to advance supplies to tenants and were dependent on the bankers. These in turn were interested only in receiving cash for their loans and were likely to be dictatorial as to the crops to be planted. Cotton crowded out other crops and diversified farming was retarded.

SIGNS OF REVIVAL

"Since the war," wrote Sidney Lanier, "pretty much the whole of life has been merely not dying." The noblest poet of the south was himself stricken in his youth. But the achievement of home rule and of ordinary honesty in government and the peaceful transition from slave labor to free labor gave the younger generation something to sustain them besides the will to live.

Economically, King Cotton still ruled. After 1875 the output regularly exceeded the pre-war crop. In the Black Belt of alluvial soil and large plantations tilled by negroes, cotton remained virtually the only crop. The expense of maintenance was less than under slavery, but the yield per acre under free labor was disappointing. The principal signs of progress in agriculture were in the regions less fertile but more commonly owned in small tracts by whites who were themselves tillers of the soil. Agricultural education encouraged by the Grangers early began to have some influence. Travelers began to observe diversified farming, fertilization, road improvement, and other indications of revival and progress.

There was also a renewal of railroad building. Railroad mileage in the whole country trebled during the two decades from 1860 to 1880, and merely doubled in the secession states, but thereafter the rate of construction in the south exceeded the general rate. There was a resumption of cotton manufacturing on a larger scale. Lumbering began to flourish. A beginning was made in the smelting industry in Alabama, where, on opposite sides of a valley, coal and iron and limestone awaited the furnace fires.

Southern problems, and those of the north and the east and the west, were beginning to meet and merge in a new crucible of industry.

PART VII

CRUCIBLE OF INDUSTRY

CHAPTER XXI

TECHNOLOGY

MENDING THE FRACTURES OF WAR AND POLITICS

An ingenious observer of American politics, noting the tendency to ascribe prosperity or adversity to the party in power, conceived the clever idea of comparing variations in rainfall with changes in party control of the government. He discovered a curious correlation of adverse weather conditions and adverse balloting. The mythical view of the influence of politics is illustrated by the factitious place of the tariff. Since the days of New England's right about face toward protection and South Carolina's attempted nullification of protection, the government's tariff policy has been at once the panacea and the scape-goat of American politics. The responsibility of the government for prosperity or adversity is grossly exaggerated. One should be cautious, therefore, in assessing the economic seriousness of the wounds of politics. Political differences are more likely to be economic effects than causes.

So long as government refrains from direct participation in productive processes, its economic rôle must remain largely negative. But its negative rôle may assume considerable importance. Its tariff policy or the incidence of its taxation may depress one group or section and correspondingly stimulate another. Jackson's administration, in destroying the second bank and failing to substitute a policy of constructive control, was negatively responsible for chaotic and unsound banking and currency. The coordination of banking by the Federal Reserve System of Wilson's régime undoubtedly checked the operation of forces which made for extremes of expansion and contraction and thereby stabilized industry.

So long as the government refrains from direct participation in productive processes, its rôle remains essentially that of arbiter to promote fair play, or concert master to coordinate the several types of instruments and maintain concord. The success of the government in this rôle depends on a relative equality of strength on the part of the participants in the game, or on a proper proportion of the various types of instruments. In a word, the success of the government in the economic rôle to which it is limited in a system of private capitalism depends on the maintenance of an economic balance of power.

Before the Civil War, capitalism was becoming constantly more powerful and aggressive. As a result of the war its triumph was rendered overwhelming. This triumph disturbed the balance of power of the economic groups, and subjected the planter and the farmer to the political domination of the capitalist. Government was utilized inevitably, then as in other times of disturbed balance of power between groups, primarily in the interest of the dominant group, with loud professions, of course, of identity or unity of group interest with the interest of society. The wounds of war were inflicted mainly on the planters. The wounds of post-war politics included the farmers.

In accord with the exaggerated view of the responsibility of government for adverse conditions, there was overemphasis on the efficacy of political remedies in the healing process. Important, of course, were the recovery of home rule in the south, the local political successes of Grangers and Populists, and the turn of the tide in the 'eighties toward the Democratic party. But the healing of the wounds was essentially not a political but an economic process. To change the metaphor, the fusing of the group and sectional elements into a genuine national unity was not in the caldron of politics but in the crucible of industry. Too much mending of the fires of the boiling caldron of politics retarded, in fact, the work of fusion in the crucible of industry.

FORGING NEW IMPLEMENTS: THE AGE OF STEEL

During the era of railroad construction preceding the Civil War, the production of pig iron increased from about 165,000 tons in 1830 to about 820,000 tons in 1860—somewhat less than a five-fold increase in spite of the tremendous demand for rails, engines, and other products of iron. Three decades later, in 1890, the output was more than 9,200,000—more than eleven times the output of 1860. Advancing another thirty years, the output in 1920 was nearly 37,000,000 tons—about a four-fold increase.

After the Civil War, the fact of main importance was not the quantity of iron produced but the transformation of industry by transition to the age of steel. Before the introduction of the Bessemer-Kelly process, the output of steel was in quantity negligible. It was not until after the Civil War that the first Bessemer converter was installed. The output of steel in 1875 was only about 390,000 tons. By 1890 the total output of steel ingots and castings by the Bessemer, open-hearth, and crucible processes was 4,277,000 tons, almost an eleven-fold increase. The total output in 1920, mainly by the open-hearth and Bessemer processes, was more than 42,000,000 tons, almost ten times the output of 1890. By 1928, the post-war depression had been overcome, and the output reached a new high level of about 50,500,000 tons.

This marvelous expansion in the output of iron and steel was in response to new demands. Such articles as knives, axes, swords, and in general the finer hand tools had long been made of steel. Damascus in the ancient Orient and Milan in medieval Europe were noted for their steel. With the coming of the steam engine, of machine tools, and of power-operated machinery, the demand for steel was greatly increased, and was made insistent by the growth in size of machinery demanding a stronger material in order to keep the physical dimensions within reasonable limits. By the end of the nineteenth century the transition to the age of steel was well under way. Steel rails and engines and cars, steel subways, steel bridges, steel fences, steel frames for the gigantic buildings that have sprung into being in the course of days as compared with the centuries given to the great structures of medieval times—these, together with steel machines of unexampled size and number, are the more striking illustrations of the modern use of steel.

An understanding of the complicated technology of iron and steel making requires the professional attention of highly trained engineers. Our attention is demanded by only a few of the more significant phases of the technological revolution.

Mining of the ore and also of the fuel coal has been largely mechanized. Coal mining is largely underground. Many mines have electric elevators and trains, compressed air drills, steam shovels, and other mechanized equipment, with highly efficient devices for handling the coal above ground as well as in the mine. Iron mining is mainly from open pits. A visit of the president to one of these pits in 1927, in the Lake Superior region, occasioned the following account by a reporter: "The chief executive rode by train to the edge of the great open-pit mine. . . . He gazed into an enormous treasure trove one and one-half miles wide and seven miles long, along the sides of which, on spiral tracks, steam shovels gnawed the rough sides of the hole and lifted sixteen-ton mouthfuls of ore into waiting cars. . . . Mr. Coolidge was heard to say the pit was infinitely larger than anything he had ever imagined. He looked with fascination into the bottom of the crater, eight hundred feet down, where the cranes and trains looked like playthings on toy rails. Moving from his original stand, the chief executive was taken to another viewpoint of the same pit, about two miles away. . . . 'How many tons a year do you get out of this one mine?' he suddenly asked. He was told 10,000,000 tons."

The steam shovels that mine the ore dump it onto cars for shipment. There are even more remarkable mechanical facilities for shipment across the Great Lakes, for transfer to railroads, and for deposit by the railroads at the gigantic blast furnaces at Pittsburgh and other smelting centers. Improved coking ovens permit the salvaging and economical utilization of the gases. Coal tar, formerly a nuisance, is an increasingly valuable by-product. Slag from the blast furnace is turned in part into track ballast and cement. Gases from the furnace are used in the power plant. From 1850 to 1925 the output by the blast furnaces of the country increased, according to estimates by the federal Bureau of Labor Statistics, more than 7000 per cent, while the number of employees increased less than fifty per cent.

Much of the pig iron turned out by the blast furnaces is used as such for making iron castings. The first extensive utilization of pig iron for making steel was by the Bessemer process, or the Bessemer-Kelly process. An Englishman, Sir Henry Bessemer, and an American, William Kelly, seem to have arrived independently at the basic idea of the modern process of steel making, namely, the burning out of impurities, particularly carbon, by the introduction of a blast of air through molten cast iron contained in a vessel called a converter. Bessemer's process was more efficient, however, and his patent had been first allowed. In 1866 the Bessemer and Kelly interests compromised their conflicting claims, and steel output rapidly expanded. Bessemer steel cost little more than iron and was made in less than an hour, whereas the old crucible process of steel making devised by Benjamin Huntsman in 1740 required months.

In the Bessemer process, the oxygen of the air, as it was forced by the blast through the molten pig iron, induced combustion which burned the carbon out of the iron. Carbon was then reintroduced to give hardness to the metal, the amount depending on the hardness desired. But Bessemer steel could not be tested in the process of making it to determine the content of carbon or other elements. The resulting steel was not absolutely uniform or dependable. A broken rail or cable or girder due to a flaw in the steel might result in catastrophe.

The increasing demand for greater uniformity of content and quality led to the adoption of the open-hearth process. An open-hearth furnace is fed by a charging machine which has been described as almost human in its uncanny manipulation of materials. The steel, instead of having to be poured out of a pear-shaped, movable converter, as in the Bessemer process, is drained off, in the open-hearth furnace, from the side of the furnace opposite the feeding mouth. The impurities are burned out substantially as in the Bessemer process. But tests by ladling, impossible in the Bessemer process, are made to determine the content; and desired ingredients are added, as carbon and manganese. By a modification of the lining of the converter, chemical processes are set up which remove sulphur and phosphorus, impurities not oxidized by the Bessemer process. The output of the open-hearth process is a remarkably uniform and dependable steel. In 1890, the output of open-hearth furnaces was only about 12 per cent of the total; by 1926 it was about 84 per cent.

Corresponding to the changes in mining, smelting, and steel making are improvements in forges, rolling mills, and machines of giant power and fairy-like precision for the transformation of steel into myriad forms of actual use, from the hair-like spring of a lady's watch to the gigantic blowing engine of a blast furnace.

NEW INSTRUMENTS OF POWER

The handling of the Titanic operations of modern mining and smelting and forging, and of the machinery called into being by the age of steel, necessitated advances in power beyond the dreams of James Watt and Matthew Boulton.

The reciprocating engine of Watt's time was enlarged and improved, but in principle it remained unaltered for a century. The principle was in essence the utilization of the expansive energy of steam in forcing a piston reciprocally back and forth through a cylinder, the reciprocations of the piston being transformed into the rotary motion of a shaft by the interposition of a connecting rod and a crank. During the last two decades of the nineteenth century the ingenuity of inventors, particularly of Sir Charles Parsons and of Gustaf de Laval, created the turbine, a new type of engine in which the reciprocating piston was supplanted by revolving blades, the energy of steam being utilized to produce directly the rotary motion of the shaft. A great advantage of the turbine is its small size in proportion to its power. Indeed it is generally agreed among engineers that the power delivered by a modern turbine of say 60,000 kilowatts capacity could not be duplicated by a reciprocating engine because of physical limitations. Particularly important in modern shipbuilding is the marine turbine. With the increasing use of electric power for the operation of the machinery of factories and the need for large quantities of low-pressure steam for process work in such plants as paper mills, steam turbines have been introduced to combine the functions of driving an electric generator and of furnishing steam for some phases of factory work. Turbines of this type are called "bleeder" machines.

Somewhat similar in principle but more revolutionary in its effects is the water turbine. One of the oldest of devices for using mechanical power is the water wheel. During uncounted centuries the water wheel had utilized the direct energy of water on the wheel's outer rim. The float wheel was turned simply by the force of a flowing stream on the lower rim submerged in the stream. In the usual types of overshot and undershot wheels, the weight of the water, or its weight combined with the added energy of its fall, effected the revolution of the wheel. Only a small part of the wheel's rim can be acted on by the force of the water at any one time. In the turbine, the blades or vanes are located on the interior, and the water, passing through the turbine, transfers its energy to all the blades or vanes at once. The energy is derived not from the mere force of water flowing against the wheel or falling on its rim but from the equally distributed pressure transmitted from impounded water and from a sudden change in the direction of the water's flow. The turbine is more efficient, more readily controlled, and smaller in proportion to its power than the old-fashioned water wheel.

In the development of the hydraulic turbine, Frenchmen hold a prominent place. The Jonval turbine was patented in 1841. Several Americans during the mid-century period were interested in the problem, and during the Civil War James Leffel established in Ohio a successful factory for the making of turbines. But the earlier turbines were not only crude but inconsequential. They merely effected certain improvements in the direct transmission of water power to the machinery of mill and factory. The revolutionary effects of the water turbine awaited the development of electrical knowledge and of demand for electricity generated by water power. The beginnings of commercial generation of electricity by water power occurred in Colorado and at Niagara Falls in the last decade of the nineteenth century. By that time the dynamo, the electric motor, and transmission devices had come into being.

The dynamo in its crude and experimental form goes back to the 'thirties of the last century. Faraday in England, Pixii in France, and Joseph Henry in America, as well as a long line of scientists going back to Doctor William Gilbert, physician to Queen Elizabeth, contributed to the discovery of the principle and to the invention of the device for transforming mechanical energy into electricity. Numerous improvements followed, and by the 'seventies the problem of the commercial dynamo was solved. The building of transmission lines quickly followed, though these at first were limited to the immediate vicinity of the generating plant. The use of water turbines for generating electricity increased as the transmission system became more efficient. Beyond the range of transmission lines from water-power sites, the steam turbine came into use, and since electricity may be transmitted more cheaply than coal can be transported, there is a tendency to locate the generating stations near supplies of coal. Partly because of unsettled controversies over the control of hydro-electric power, steam generated electric power increased more rapidly after 1922 than hydro-electric power. The dynamo takes mechanical energy, as of water, and transforms it into electricity; the electric motor takes electricity and turns it into mechanical energy, as in operating a pump. A dynamo, in fact, is readily convertible into a motor. It follows, therefore, that the development of the dynamo for generating electricity meant also the development of the electric motor for converting electricity into mechanical power.

But one of the most important uses of electricity—illumination—depended on the invention of entirely different devices. In the 'eighties and 'nineties the arc light, burning carbon sticks connected in a series with a dynamo, came into common use. The most successful of these were the Brush lights, named after Charles Brush. They were first introduced at Cleveland, Ohio, and street lighting by the electric arc soon became popular. But for indoor lighting and ultimately for street lighting, the solution of the problem was found to be the incandescent lamp. This, like most other great inventions, was the cumulative result of the labors of many scientists and inventors. Final success was the reward of Thomas A. Edison. The carbonized filament lamp was perfected by him in 1879. The carbon soon burned out, however, and more than a quarter of a century passed before a satisfactory substitute was found in the form of a metal filament. Tantalum was first used and this in turn was supplanted by tungsten.

The most revolutionary of all the recent instruments of power is probably the internal combustion engine. It is this invention which has filled the highways with automobiles and is filling the sky with airships. Here as in many other details of technology, Europeans have been the originators and Americans have excelled in subsequent improvements and in the manufacture and popularization of new devices. Among the names most prominently connected with the evolution of the internal combustion engine are Huyghens, a Dutchman; Barber, an Englishman; Lenoir, a Frenchman; and Otto, Daimler, and Diesel, Germans.

The most successful internal combustion engines use gasoline derived from petroleum as a fuel. They are of the reciprocating type, but the piston is operated not by the pressure of steam on the piston, but by the explosive force of the vaporized and ignited gasoline within the piston chamber. The usual type requires a cycle of four strokes of the piston, one for intake of gasoline and air, one for compression of the air and the vaporized gasoline, a third for transmission of the explosive energy (induced by ignition from an electric spark) to the crankshaft, and a fourth for expulsion of the products of combustion. The successful development of the internal combustion engine awaited not only the perfecting of the mechanism itself but the refining of gasoline from petroleum, the vulcanizing of rubber for tires, and the working out of subsidiary electrical devices.

REVOLUTIONS IN TRANSPORTATION

Perhaps the most interesting of the revolutionary changes in transportation are connected with the internal combustion engine. But a due regard for the sequence of events reminds us first of recent changes in older methods of transportation.

During the decade before the Civil War, American shipbuilding attained an output in gross tonnage not equaled till after the turn of the century. The brief interlude of American ascendancy in shipbuilding was during the period of transition from sail to steam engine and from wood to iron and steel. The retarding influence of the Civil War, combined with England's readier acceptance of the new construction material and the new motive power, gave England an overwhelming advantage in later marine shipbuilding and shipping. In 1840 the iron steamship *Great Britain* was equipped with a single-screw propeller. The paddle wheel for ocean-going vessels was soon abandoned. In 1888 the twin-screw propeller proved its superiority. After many experiments, the turbine engine in the early twentieth century made possible another advance in size, power, and speed of ships at sea. Now comes marine propulsion by electricity. In all these changes, with the exception of the last, Americans have had relatively little part. But the revolution in marine transportation has been influenced by the gigantic increase in the volume of traffic due to American imports and exports and American travel habits; and Americans have been the principal beneficiaries of technical improvements whether made by themselves or by Europeans.

If in marine shipbuilding Americans were laggards, in the technology of railroad construction they forged ahead. The great age of railroad expansion was in a sense a phase of the age of steel. The discovery of the secret of cheap steel made possible steel engines, steel rails, steel cars, steel bridges, steel automatic machinery for the gigantic engineering tasks of crossing the rivers and penetrating the mountains and maintaining free from obstruction the half a million miles of track enmeshing the cities and far flung across the continent. The more important trunk lines have double and in places quadruple tracks. The early diversities gave place to standard gage tracks four feet and eight and a half inches wide and to standardized rolling stock. The size of recent engines and cars gives to early equipment a pigmy, smile-provoking stature. In spite of rapidly increasing size and speed, the relative number of accidents has been diminished as a result of the automatic air brake originated by George Westinghouse in 1868; the automatic block signal system; the automatic coupler; the telegraph; and the system of interlocking switches, kept free from ice and snow by electric heat and controlled in groups by tower operating devices. The smooth working of a complicated railroad system, especially in a great terminal yard with its vast network of trackage and its intricate maneuvering of trains, is one of the marvelous achievements of modern technology. Adding to the comfort and convenience as well as to the safety of travelers and transport workers are Pullman sleeping cars; dining cars in place of bedraggled roadside kitchens; vestibule cars with internal passageways for passengers from car to car; electric light in place of sputtering and uncertain oil or gas lamps; steam heat in place of dangerous wood stoves or coal stoves; and the electric motor or the internal combustion engine gradually displacing the noisy and dirt-dispensing steam engine.

The first applications of electricity to transportation were in the limited areas of towns, for vertical traffic in buildings as well as for horizontal locomotion on the streets. Hydraulic power, long used for freight lifts and to some extent for passenger elevators, was supplanted largely in the building of skyscrapers by the electric motor and electric control devices.

Just as there were hydraulic lifts before there were electric elevators, so there were street railways with steam-propelled, cable, or horse-drawn cars before there were electric traction railways. The modification of the dynamo for use as a motor soon suggested its possibilities for traction purposes. Among the earliest experimental electric railways were those of Siemens at Berlin in 1879 and of Edison at Menlo Park in 1880. Frank Sprague, apprentice of "the wizard of Menlo Park," constructed an electric railway for actual use at Richmond in 1887. In the course of the following quarter century, electric traction was widely adopted in the leading cities of the world for surface, elevated, and subway transportation. The coming of the electric railway rapidly extended the suburban movement and tied adjacent cities together with interurban lines.

But within half a century of the Menlo Park experimental

traction line, many electric railways were being abandoned. In connection with subway and elevated railways in the cities, and in connection with railways originally built for steam power, electric traction has continued to extend its usefulness. But the surface lines in the cities and the suburban and interurban lines have found it hard even to hold their ground. In 1890, the trackage operated by electricity amounted to 1,262 miles. In a dozen years it had grown to about 22,000 miles. In another decade it had almost doubled with nearly 41,000 miles in 1912. From 1917 to 1922 the mileage decreased from 44,676 to 43,789.

The main cause of decline is the automobile. The revolution wrought by the internal combustion engine and the auxiliary technical developments connected with automobile manufacturing can only be described as astounding. During the final year of the last century, the production of motor vehicles in the United States was about five thousand, and the total number registered was about eight thousand. Within a quarter of a century, annual production of passenger cars had mounted to nearly four million and of trucks to nearly half a million. The number of cars registered and taxed with a state registration fee had grown by 1926 to more than twenty-two millions.

The gigantic expansion of transportation and travel by private automobiles and public omnibuses and trucks was made possible by two main technological developments. One of these was the perfecting of the internal combustion engine, already described; the other was the system of mass production to be discussed in a later chapter.

In the development of navigation in the air, as in the evolution of the automobile, the internal combustion engine was a preliminary technological achievement. But there was another even more serious technical problem—in the words of Wilbur Wright, "the soaring problem." Soaring had teased and baffled the ingenuity of the mechanics of antiquity as well as of modern times. The first important step was taken in the year of the victory of the thirteen colonies over England. In 1783 two Frenchmen made a successful balloon flight with Benjamin Franklin as one of the spectators. On his being asked the value of such a device, Franklin is said to have replied, "What is the use of a new-born child?"

In the subsequent development of dirigible lighter-than-air machines, the Germans, especially Count Zeppelin and his associates, were ultimately to take the lead. But in the solution of the problem of bird-like soaring and control of heavier-than-air machines, Samuel P. Langley and the Wright brothers, Orville and Wilbur, and various others, have given prominence if not preeminence to America. Propellors, curved surfaces to take advantage of the buoyant pressure of the air, devices for stabilization, the earth inductor compass; but chiefly, persistent and intelligent practice by men scientifically selected because of their adaptability to "soaring"—these have been the essentials of successful navigation in the air. "The soaring problem," said Wilbur Wright, "is apparently not so much one of better wings as of better operators." After long and patient calculations and laboratory work, Orville Wright, at Kill Devil Hill, North Carolina, on December 15, 1903, made the first flight in a self-propelled machine. The time was twelve seconds; the distance, 120 feet. On the same day, Wilbur Wright flew 852 feet in fifty-nine seconds, but wrecked the machine.

Those who live in the midst of a revolution are not likely to be competent judges of its outcome or significance. Early proponents of railroads believed that a speed of a hundred miles an hour would be practicable. Enthusiastic spirits undoubtedly look to the navigation of the air for impossible feats. But unless men's daring and ingenuity strangely fail them, the future has in store for aircraft a major rôle as an agency of transportation.

Revolutionary changes in transportation had been inaugurated alike in England and America by canals. In the rage for speedy and spectacular methods, the relatively slow and plodding use of inland waterways, whether natural or artificial, suffered a decline. Early canals and navigable streams were frequently abandoned because of the shallowness of their channels or because of the competition of railroads. But the tortoise later gained on the hare. Europeans took the lead in a return to canal construction for larger vessels. The Suez canal was opened in 1869 and later enlarged. Other notable recently constructed canals are the Corinthian canal, severing the Morea from northern Greece; the Baltic canal, terminating at Kiel, for avoiding the circuitous and tortuous course around the Danish peninsula; the Cronstadt canal, giving St. Petersburg (Leningrad) access to the sea; the Amsterdam ship canal; and the Manchester ship canal.

Most notable, perhaps, of earlier ship canals in the United States, aside from the Erie canal, which was for small vessels only, was the St. Mary's River canal for connecting Lakes Huron and Superior—a project which came to be chiefly valuable for the transport of Lake Superior ores to the furnaces. But it was not till the twentieth century that there were evidences of an American renaissance of canal construction. The Cape Cod canal, completed in 1914, afforded a much more direct and a safer route for coastwise traffic north and south of Cape Cod. In the same year the Houston ship canal was opened. The reconstruction of the Erie canal into a canal large enough to accommodate thousand-ton barges was begun in 1904 and completed in 1918. The mileage as well as the capacity was enlarged, and light houses, gigantic terminals, and other improvements were added. In magnitude of engineering problems, in cost, and in economic importance, by far the greatest of all canals is the Panama canal, constructed from 1904 to 1914. The efficient and successful completion of this unparalleled undertaking is a magnificent tribute to the possibilities of governmentally conducted economic enterprises. It is the beginning of what is confidently expected to be a series of governmental canal and river projects. Among these are the control of the flood waters of the Mississippi valley, the harnessing of water power at Boulder Dam and elsewhere, and the opening up of continuous transportation facilities by water for larger vessels from the cities of the Great Lakes to the cities of the Gulf on the one hand and to those of the Atlantic seaboard on the other. These are some of the projects that are expected to inaugurate a new era of transportation by water joined significantly with the control of flood waters and the utilization of water power.

THE MODERN HERMES

The Greeks in their lusty youth, which was the youth of civilization, invested their gods with traits which they no doubt desired for themselves but deemed beyond the range of human limitations. At the command of Zeus, Hermes, herald of the gods, binds beneath his feet his golden sandals, which bear him alike over the wet sea and over the limitless land, swift as the breath of the wind. The messengers of modern man require no sandals, they are infinite in number, and their speed is not the snail's pace of the laggard wind but the flash of radiant energy that leaps from world to world and in a moment encircles the earth.

There are men now living who were born at a time when the messengers of men were not even equal to the messengers of the gods of Hellas but were like the messengers of the

Greeks themselves. In the 'forties of the last century, the occupation of Oregon was discouraged by some because of the distance. It was urged that if Oregon should become a state, the issues which required attention at the national capital would be beyond the ken of the people of Oregon until after they were decided, and that the representatives of Oregon would require so much time in reaching Washington that representatives from other parts of the country would have met and transacted their business and returned to their homes. Marcus Whitman, noted pioneer in the Oregon territory, left Pittsburgh on March 15, 1836, and reached Walla Walla on September 2. In 1843, his voyage from his home in New York to his post in Oregon extended from April to October. The migration of 1843, with expert guides and careful organization, required four and a half months to travel from Independence in northwestern Missouri to its destination in Oregon. Within four score years after the organization of the Oregon territory and within three score years and ten after the admission of Oregon as a state, a presidential candidate spoke to the nation by radio in New York; held conferences in the east as late as November 1; traveled in a leisurely manner westward to his home on the Pacific coast, making several speeches on the way; delivered an address on November 5 at his home on the western coast with the whole nation and many beyond its limits as his audience; and before taking the oath of office as president, made a tour of the countries of Central and South America with his every move recorded day by day in the newspapers of the world.

In the communication of ideas and impressions, the methods that are culturally or economically significant are either visual or auditory. In primitive times the visual methods included gestures and signals; the auditory methods consisted of sounds which evolved into articulate speech. With the emergence of the art of writing, culminating in the phonetic alphabet of the Greeks (from which our own is derived), language as an instrument for communicating ideas became more significantly visual than auditory.

No further progress is observable till we reach the age of the printing press, which was introduced into Europe in the fifteenth century. Even this device was for centuries severely limited in its possibilities. The art of mechanically reproducing written ideas remained essentially a system of block printing with the type set by hand and adjusted by hand and even the necessary pressure exerted by hand power till the era of the industrial revolution. More revolutionary in effect than the initial introduction of the printing press was its transformation, since the middle of the nineteenth century, into the mechanically operated cylindrical or rotary press with its auxiliary processes. The typewriter, reduced to practical form by Remington under patents granted in 1871 to Christopher Sholes and James Densmore, facilitated the preparatory stages of printing, but was of course far more than a mere auxiliary of the press. Processes more largely subsidiary to printing were paper making from wood pulp; mechanical typesetting; and photo-engraving.

The first form of writing was picture writing. Pictures remain in many ways the most effective vehicles for the communication of impressions. Methods were early discovered for reproducing pictures as well as words by means of the printing press. But the pictures were drawings or sketches and not photographs. A world without photographs and mechanical reproductions of photographs is now not easily visualized. And yet it was not till about the middle of the nineteenth century that the photographic process was discovered (though the daguerreotype was somewhat earlier), and it was not till much later that the mechanical reproduction of photographs was reduced to practical form. Then came photo engraving, and color photography, and the perfecting of mechanical color printing, with suddenness and significance truly revolutionary.

By means of the printing press, typesetting machines, cameras, and other devices, the recording and duplicating of linguistic and pictorial symbols for conveying visual impressions have largely been mechanized. The mechanizing of printing extended over many centuries. The mechanical recording and duplicating of sounds had apparently engaged the serious attention of no one till the age of Edison, and his phonograph or "sound-writing" machine of 1877 was in a sense a by-product of his laboratory. The mechanism was relatively simple: a drum or cylinder covered with tinfoil (later with wax); a delicate recording instrument susceptible to minute sound vibrations in the air; and a device for retracing the course of the vibratory indentations and thereby reproducing the vibrations, that is, the sounds.

After the invention of the camera and the phonograph, it is not surprising that "motion writing" or the recording of action should have become the object of inventive ingenuity. The cinematograph or "action-writing" machine is in reality a modified camera mechanically equipped to take a series of pictures in rapid succession. But the taking of such pictures results merely in a series of pictures with minute, progressive variations. The mechanical problems of projecting the films on a screen in a realistic manner were not solved till the turn of the century. At length, as a culminating phase of the mechanical recording of images, motions, and sounds, came their union in the "speaking movies."

Throughout these inventions there is a sequence in the evolution of methods of communicating impressions. Picture writing merged into phonetic writing and phonetic symbols were at length mechanically recorded and duplicated by the printing press and auxiliary devices. The making of pictures by manual drawing or painting was supplemented by mechanical recording of images by the camera and their mechanical reproduction by the printing press. The mechanical recording of sounds and multiplication of sound records resulted from the perfecting of the phonograph and the phonographic record. A similar achievement in respect to action was the motion-picture camera and projector. And finally, in the "speaking movie," action and voice, after their unnatural separation, are again united.

It is to be noted that in all of these developments there is no instantaneous conquest of space, and there is no direct contact between the person who produces and the person who receives the impression. The printed book or the picture on the screen must be before one's eyes; the phonographic record or the "speaking pictures" must be within one's natural range of hearing. Borrowing a familiar metaphor from the modern dietary, one may say that books, photographs, phonographic records, and moving-picture films contain "canned" goods, "canned" ideas and impressions. While these devices were coming into being, other discoveries and inventions were making possible the instantaneous projection through space alike of auditory and of visual communications.

These developments were made possible mainly by means of advances in electrical phenomena. Their forerunner was telegraphy, already discussed. The telegraph is literally an instrument for the projection of writing, or for writing at a distance. Varying intervals of time between closing and opening the electric circuit, with varying combinations of the intervals, formed the telegraphic alphabet. The ideas being sent by the telegrapher, spelled out by his handling of the key, were recorded at the other end by the clicking of the receiving instrument and by an automatic writing device (a part of the receiver) for transforming the code of intervals in the circuit into a code of dots and dashes.

The use of wires and the electric circuit for the projection and literal reproduction of sound goes back to the centennial year of American independence. A transmitting instrument susceptible to sound vibrations, a vehicle for the projection of the vibrations, and a receiver for reproducing the vibrations—these are the essential features of the telephone as devised and perfected by Alexander Graham Bell and his associates and successors. No batteries or generators were used, the circuit being established by means of magnets. The transmitter and the receiver were at first identical, but stress of competition due to a superior transmitter invented by Edison led to improvements in the Bell system. Thousands of other technical improvements followed.

At first the telephone was viewed as a toy. Its progress is illustrated by the fact that in 1900, at approximately the end of the first quarter of a century of its history, the number of telephone stations of the Bell system was about 850,000; while at the end of the first half century the number had grown to more than 17,500,000. The United States, with about one-sixth of the world's population, had about sixty per cent of the world's telephones. The economic and social consequences are apparent from a momentary effort to visualize a world without the telephone.

For the use of electro-magnetic currents the telephone depends on wires. Researches by scientists in various parts of the world resulted in a cumulative knowledge of electricity which has made possible the control and utilization of waves or "oscillatory motions" without wires. First came the projection of telegraphic signals in Europe by Marconi during the last decade of the nineteenth century. Later experiments by him and various others in America established wireless telegraphy on a commercial basis.

Just as the wireless telegraph projected the signals of the

telegraphic code, so the wireless telephone or the radio broadcaster projected sounds, the direct agencies of auditory impressions, instantaneously through space. Nor does the wizardry end there. Radio photography and television are being perfected for ultimate union with the broadcasting of sound, in a manner comparable to the union of the cinematograph and the phonograph in the "speaking movies."

From the invention of the mariner's compass to the projection of the human voice thousands of miles through space, men have more or less casually and acidentally blundered into knowledge of the invisible waves of energy that bathe and penetrate the earth. Men's empirical and individualistic advances are at last giving place to scientific, organized, coordinated and successful efforts to achieve a sovereignty over a domain of knowledge and of power worthy of the envy of the ancient gods.

THE SCIENCE AND THE BUSINESS OF INVENTION

Samuel Crompton, inventor of the spinning mule, secluded himself in his country house, called "Hall in the Woods," and his epochal, world-stirring invention was locally called the "Hall-ith-Woods" machine. An inventor of the older type was popularly viewed as a person who devised a complete new machine, as the cotton gin, or an integral process, as the vulcanizing of rubber. It is true that most of the great inventions have resulted from the cumulative work of many minds. The steam engine was not invented by James Watt. Certain important improvements only were devised by him. Crompton's mule derived its curious name from the fact that it was viewed as a hybrid offspring of the spinning jenny and the water frame. These in turn were modifications of earlier devices. And yet, in the days of handicraft methods and of transition from them to machines, complete and integrated machines or processes, empirically conceived and individually evolved, were often feasible. Even in the more complex conditions of the age of machinery and of intangible chemical and electrical processes, an individual inventor working independently occasionally achieves noteworthy results.

But most of the recent advances, alike in pure science and in its technological applications, have resulted from coordinated and carefully controlled researches. The modern trend was happily described by President Hoover in his address at the fiftieth anniversary celebration of the invention of the incandescent lamp in the Edison laboratory. Mr. Edison, he said, exemplified "the modern method and system of invention, by which highly equipped, definitely organized laboratory research transforms the raw material of scientific knowledge into new tools for the hand of man. In earlier times mechanical invention had been the infrequent and haphazard product of genius in the woodshed. But science had become too sophisticated to be wooed in such surroundings. Nowadays a thousand applied-science laboratories, supported by the industries of our country, yearly produce a host of new inventions."

Just as the secluded, individualistic inventor, such as Crompton, has generally given place to the large research organization, so invention itself has extended farther and farther beyond its older meaning. National and local agencies of government, educational institutions, societies, foundations, and business organizations have undertaken rapidly expanding programs of research. Despite monopolistic limitations on the nation-wide use of the resulting technological knowledge and skill, America has been thrust into the unifying crucible of industrial research.[1]

[1] This important subject is further discussed in the concluding chapter in connection with the rationalizing of industry.

CHAPTER XXII

CAPITAL

INCREASING FLUIDITY OF CAPITAL

The beginnings of modern economy, or as Sombart, the great German economist, would have it, of modern capitalism, are traceable to the processes by which rents were transferred from landlords and public officials to business men, and thereby from the purchase of consumption goods to the establishment of productive enterprises. These processes of transforming landed income into the capital goods of mercantile, mining, and manufacturing enterprises marked the beginning of the modern fluidity and mobility of wealth. They made possible the more effective use of existing wealth for the production of new wealth in Europe and for the acquisition of wealth created by peoples outside of Europe. To the riches of Europe were added the booty of conquest, the products of slave labor, and the profits of trade. Incidental to the new mobility of wealth was the colonization of America.

In the expansion of the American people over their present vast extent of territory, capital was needed in ever increasing quantities for the development of transportation facilities and for financing the interchange of manufactures and the products of the farm, the forest, and the mine. Thus the original fluidity of capital evident in the financing of colonizing enterprises continued in varying forms with the expansion of the areas of settlement.

The peculiar fluidity of capital in America has been associated in a measure with the financing of American wars. In the redemption and funding of the Revolutionary debts, Alexander Hamilton repeatedly emphasized the importance of an "augmentation of the fluid capital" of the country. The amount of the indebtedness incurred by the states and the Continental Congress had been vastly increased by the decline of public credit. The securities had been taken over largely by business men at greatly depreciated prices. The funding of the securities at face value meant a vast increase in the resources of business men by the transfer of the scattered and more or less immobile resources of the country, through taxation, to the security holders. These, in turn, utilized their securities for the financing of banking and trade and manufacturing. Thus there was brought about the Hamiltonian "augmentation of fluid capital."

By a somewhat similar process, the financing of the Civil War tended to transfer the scattered and relatively immobile resources of taxpayers to the holders of gold-bearing securities, consisting largely of business men. But in the case of Civil War finance, the intensive propaganda and efficient organization for the sale of government securities widely extended the market for securities and accustomed large classes of people to the idea of making small, interest-bearing investments. The way was thus prepared for the later tendency to invest in the stocks and bonds of business enterprises. But a relatively small area of the country was thus affected by Civil War finance. Large groups in the north were unwilling or unable to invest in public securities and were later aggrieved by the government's financial policies. As for the south, the failure of the Confederacy swept away the investments there made in public securities.

Far more influential and nation-wide in scope was the influence of the World War. The federal interest-bearing debt on June 30, 1916, was less than a billion dollars. In 1919, it was more than twenty-five billion dollars. The securities included thrift stamps and treasury savings stamps in fractions of a dollar. The security holders ranged from the great corporations of the cities to the farmers and farm workers of the remoter districts and to children in the schools. The agencies for promoting the investment of savings in public securities formed virtually a roll call of public and private institutions and organizations, political, social, and cultural as well as financial. Buyers of securities in smaller quantities were often influenced by the pressure of propaganda, and were forced in many cases to dispose of their holdings at a sacrifice during the temporary depreciation accompanying the post-war depression. But there was nevertheless an unprecedented expansion in the number of bona fide investors.

It has been urged that public securities diverted capital from productive enterprises and therefore adversely affected the real fluidity of capital. This view was suspiciously associated with the propaganda against the taxing of industrial profits on the ground that it drove investments into public, tax-free securities. Undoubtedly the financing of the war promoted the fluidity of capital. In the first place, there was an expansion of credit instruments available as collateral for business enterprises. Secondly, and even more significantly, the investing of small savings in securities was fixed as a habit among large classes of people and the habit was later readily transferred from public securities to the stocks and bonds of business corporations. Nor were business men slow to capitalize the habit. The selling of stocks and bonds was organized with rare efficiency and was extended to the application of stimuli to employees and consumers. The reduction of taxes on industrial profits was followed by the flow of capital into stock-market transactions in such gigantic volume as to overwhelm all former records and to bring on a reaction in November, 1929, in the temporary collapse of the market.

The use of capital in business in the earlier history of the country was facilitated by the simple, small-scale nature of business enterprises. But with the increasing use of machinery, the growth of widely separated and interdependent communities, and the undertaking of projects calling for long-time investments based upon the prospective growth of population and demand, the independent business enterprises of individuals and small groups were inadequate. The mobilization of a large number of small investments was therefore increasingly important. The solution of the problem was found in the joint-stock company. This was long essentially a partnership. At common law, the liability of a partner is unlimited. Shareholding therefore involved serious risks of jeopardizing not only the amount individually invested but additional assets to meet any liabilities incurred by the company from misfortune or mismanagement or fraud. To overcome this obstacle in the way of the fluidity of capital, the statutory device of limited liability was introduced. New York adopted the principle of limiting the responsibility of stockholders to the amount of stock held as early as 1811, and other states gradually followed suit. Rivalry among the states in attracting capital led to increasingly favorable legislation. The later decades of the nineteenth century were marked by an increasing tendency to restrict the powers of stock-issuing organizations, but a more liberal policy, particularly in the judicial interpretation of the laws, was apparent after the World War. Thus public policy reenforced the investing habit resulting from the sale of public securities.

The popular tendency to invest in private securities found expression after the World War in an unprecedented increase in the number of stockholders. On the basis of a study made in 1925 and presented to the Academy of Political Science, it was estimated that from 1918 to 1925 there was an increase of at least 3,500,000 in the number of stockholders, made up of about 500,000 employees, 1,000,000 customers, and 2,000,000 investors from the public at large. In addition, it was estimated that the number of bondholders had increased by about 2,500,000, and that about 1,800,000 farmers had become financially interested in cooperative buying and selling.

The industrial mobilization of small savings was brought about not only by the direct investment of savings by individuals in securities but perhaps even more extensively by indirect means. Savings banks, building and loan associations, fraternal orders, educational, religious, and philanthropic institutions, insurance companies, and even labor organizations have brought together innumerable small sums and invested them extensively in the stocks and bonds of business corporations. Thus on November 1, 1928, the Treasurer of the American Historical Association reported the ownership of corporate securities amounting to $194,900. Such institutional investments are almost universal.

In 1895 the assets of building and loan associations were $624,700,000. In 1910 they totaled less than a billion dollars. By 1925 they had grown to more than $5,500,000,000. During the three decades the number of members increased from about a million and a half to almost ten millions.

As late as 1910 the savings deposits in banks and trust companies amounted to less than $7,000,000,000. In 1925 the total was more than $23,000,000,000. The number of depositors had more than doubled. In the meantime, corporations employing large numbers were developing savings fund facilities for their employees, and the postal savings system was being extended.

The total income of life insurance companies in 1880 was

$80,538,000; in 1900, $400,603,000; in 1925, $13,017,800,-000. The number of policies in force at the end of 1880 was 923,000; at the end of 1900, 14,395,000; and at the end of 1925, 97,629,000. Liabilities, which consisted almost entirely of the element of ownership by policy holders, amounted, in 1900, to $1,493,379,000; and in 1925, to $10,-867,475,000. It was reported in 1929 that "life insurance companies operated in this country for seventy-nine years before the first $50,000,000,000 worth of life insurance was written. The second fifty billion has been placed in force in a little over six and one half years." These figures do not include government war-risk insurance, large amounts of fraternal insurance, and vast increases in other forms of insurance with premiums collected from innumerable holders and invested largely in corporate securities.

By means of these and similar indirect devices there was brought about an unparalleled fluidity of capital and ease of its mobilization for business purposes.

REORGANIZATION OF BANKING AND CURRENCY

The modern bank is a vital agency in maintaining the fluidity of capital and in facilitating its mobilization. The reorganized banking system based on the Federal Reserve Act of 1913 was a prominent factor in the subsequent coordination of finance and integration of capital.

A bank is a central reservoir. Into it flow innumerable scattered and individual resources of money and credit. On the basis of deposits of patrons and of its paid-in capitalization, the bank is able to make loans and to advance money at a discount on credit instruments. On the fulfillment of prescribed legal conditions, the bank is able to use a part of its resources as a basis for the issuing of notes to circulate as money. The immense resources at the command of banks have tended toward emphasis on still another banking function—the investment of their funds or the funds of their patrons in securities. Large corporations are even formed for the sole purpose of buying securities and forming investment trusts for their stockholders. Some banks emphasize one function, others another function. But their position in modern economy is basically dependent on their maintenance of the fluidity of money and credit.

The reorganization of the banking system in connection with Civil War finance eliminated many of the defects of earlier banking, but the strain put upon the banking system in times of crisis proved to be greater than it could bear. The provisions connected with the issuing of bank notes proved to be inelastic and unsuited to the solution of the currency problem. There was no adequate method of centralized control or of mutual coordination. State banks with inadequate resources and over-extended credit multiplied in numbers. During recurring periods of rapid expansion, credit was extended on the basis of inadequate reserves; and call loans, frozen assets and speculative investments helped to precipitate crises which in turn still further demonstrated the inelasticity of banking.

The reorganization of banking undertaken by the administration of President Wilson resulted in one of the outstanding legislative enactments in American economic history. The Federal Reserve Act of 1913 provided for a banking corporation to be known as a federal reserve bank, with a minimum capital of $4,000,000, in each of twelve specified districts. The stockholders of the corporation were to consist of the national banks of the district and of any state banks and trust companies which might wish to enter the system under prescribed conditions. Six of the nine directors of each federal reserve bank were to be chosen by the member banks and three by the Federal Reserve Board. This board consisted of seven (later eight) members appointed by the President of the United States, including the Secretary of the Treasury and the Comptroller of the Currency. There was also a board of governors, consisting of the chief executives of the district banks.

The chief duty of a district federal reserve bank was to mobilize the reserves of the district. Member banks were required not only to buy stock but to maintain specified deposits with the district bank. The district bank served as a clearing house for member banks. Credit was made more flexible, with less likelihood of speculative expansion or contraction, by a measure of control over rates for handling notes and other credit instruments. By such methods the district bank was able to mobilize the reserves and to coordinate the more important activities of the member banks.

Similarly, the Federal Reserve Board was able to bring about a national integration of banking and also of currency on a stable yet flexible basis. By the provision that one federal reserve bank must rediscount the commercial paper or credit instruments of another bank when requested to do so by the board, there was possible an equalization of credit and of available funds among the several districts. A special need of funds, for example, in the wheat belt to aid in the harvesting and marketing of wheat might be met by the handling of Minneapolis or Kansas City credit instruments at Boston at a specified rediscount rate, thereby transferring relatively idle seaboard funds to the area of immediate need. The clearing system, extended to the entire country, effected a gigantic canceling of mutual obligations, reduced the dangers and losses of unpaid checks, and minimized the costly intersectional movement of currency. The national bank notes were supplanted by a far more elastic system of federal reserve notes. The amount of commercial paper deposited with a district bank, plus a gold reserve, constituted the basis of the expansion or contraction of the federal reserve notes. The withdrawal of commercial paper from deposit was to be followed by the withdrawal of corresponding quantities of federal reserve notes. The quantity of commercial paper on deposit was an imperfect barometer of business conditions, but as compared with the bond deposits of the national bank note system, a relatively high degree of elasticity was possible.

Soon after its adoption the system was tested severely by the titanic problems of the World War and of the post-war alternations of expansion and depression. Its acceptance by the financial interests of the country was indicated by the fact that large numbers of state banks entered the system, augmenting the capital of the regional banks, by May 25, 1927, to $129,030,000,000. Thereafter the increasing emphasis on investment banking promoted a flow of capital into state banks to escape from federal regulation of the handling of trust funds and securities.

The belief persisted in the farming regions that the great power of the rulers of the system was utilized during the World War to bring about an inflation of currency and immediately after the war to force upon the agricultural interests a disproportionate share of the burdens of deflation. By many, the federal reserve officials were blamed in part for stock speculation and the subsequent collapse of November, 1929, on the ground that they failed to exercise their statutory powers of controlling credit. Whatever may be the ultimate judgment of economists as to the validity of these beliefs, there can be little dissent from the opinion that the coordination of financial activities by the federal reserve system is on the whole decidedly preferable to the chaotic antecedent conditions.

INCREASING SIZE OF BUSINESS UNITS

Those who formulated the Federal Reserve Act intended that the new banking system should promote decentralization and the maintenance of competitive units in business. But the tendencies toward the enlargement of business units received therefrom at most a merely temporary setback.

It is apparent that to the term business unit more than one meaning may be attached. From the point of view of the immediate productive process there has been an increase in the size of the farm, the factory, the mine, the store, the bank, and various other units. From the point of view of the financing and administering of enterprises, there has been an even more impressive enlargement of administrative corporations and associations. The Federal Reserve System, in spite of the purpose of its organizers to promote the decentralization of finance and to prevent unfairness in the financing of small businesses, is itself an outstanding illustration of the administration of business on a nation-wide scale, to be discussed presently in connection with combinations and trade associations.

In using statistical data concerning the increasing size of establishments or industrial plants, there is difficulty in arriving at a comparable basis for different periods. By way of illustration, the definition of an "establishment" varies in successive censuses. Concerning business as a whole, exact comparison is virtually impossible. For many major branches of industry, however, the known facts are adequate. The enlargement of plants before 1905 is shown admirably in a series of statistical tables compiled by the late Professor Van Hise in his noted book on *Concentration and Control*. He pointed out, for example, that from 1870 to 1905 the number of plants in the iron and steel industry decreased from 808 to 606, or 25%, while at the same time the average capital per plant increased 938.8%, the value of output per plant increased 482.8%, and the tons of product per plant increased 1,323.6%. In relatively recent industries there was naturally a rapid increase in the number of plants as well as in their size. In electrical machinery, apparatus, and supplies, there was an increase in the number of plants, from 1880 to 1905, of 931.7%; the capital per plant increased 1,017.7% and the value of the output per plant increased 414.1%. Similar tendencies were observable in the branches of industry which had first been affected by the industrial revolution. In the combined textiles, including dyeing and finishing, the number of plants increased 50.8% from 1850 to 1905, while the capital per plant increased 691.5% and the value of products increased 525.5%. But the most significant change in textiles was after 1870. The number of plants in 1870 was greater than the number in 1905, but between those years the capital per plant increased from $62,000 to $294,000. With variations in degree, the enlargement of units of production ran generally through the business world.

During the decade after 1905 the tendency continued but with abated force. During and after the World War there was a marked acceleration. The number of establishments in 1914 was 271,822, and in 1925 only 187,390. And yet, in spite of the large decrease in the number of plants, and with it an increase in the use of labor-saving devices, the number of wage earners increased with the general population from 7,015,136 in 1914 to 8,384,261 in 1925, thereby entailing a vast increase in the number of workers per plant. Primary horse power increased from 22,264,343 to 35,772,628; and the value of products (to be discounted by rising prices) increased from about $24,000,000,000 to about $63,000,000,000, —the number of plants, it is to be remembered, in the meantime decreasing.

In 1925 the manufacturing establishments with outputs valued at $500,000 or more were only 10.8% of the total number but they employed 70.3% of wage earners and their output was 78.6% of the total output. With the enlargement of plants, the handicraft shops and household industries virtually disappeared. By 1921, establishments with outputs ranging in value from $500 to $5,000 produced only three-tenths of one per cent of the total output and employed only six-tenths of one per cent of the total workers in manufacturing. Obviously, machinery entailing greater initial expenses and greater ultimate economies encroaches more and more on small-scale enterprises. The populations of all sections of the country are merged in a common dependence on standardized commodities produced in "bigger and better" plants.

FORMS OF BUSINESS COMBINATION

The enlargement of units of production is much more readily reducible to statistical form than is the movement toward business combinations and associations. An industrial plant is a tangible entity. Though technological changes are rapid, an industrial plant stays put for a measurable time, and when it is reconstructed or given over to the wrecking crew, its fate is apparent. But changes in the ownership and control of business enterprises are not under one's eyes. Unpublished arrangements, inaccessible accounting, legal fictions, fluidity of stock-market and private transactions, the mercurial influence of personalities,—these and many other shifting and elusive forces render the exact measurement of the combination movement impossible.

Business, when conducted by independent and competing individuals or by partnerships or by the ordinary local share-issuing corporation, results in lack of coordination, that is to say, in varying degrees of disorder extending to the chaos of bankruptcies and of panics. To the desire to remedy the ills of uncoordinated business were added the expectations of larger profits from economies of management and the lure of gain from monopolistic prices.

To secure these and other advantages of combination, various railroad companies as well as a number of manufacturing companies entered into pooling agreements. These, though not unknown before the panic of 1873, were particularly popular as an antidote for the evils of unrestricted competition associated with the panic. Railway pools were agreements including such provisions as a division of traffic between competing lines and the maintenance of specified rates. The underlying ideas of the railway pool were applied to various businesses. The allocation of output, of markets, and of profits, and in some cases the fixing of prices, were the usual subjects of pooling agreements. A pool might not get beyond the stage of a gentleman's agreement. But any degree of stability or effectiveness demanded a formal agreement embodying acceptance by the several business units of a common agency for enforcing the terms of the agreement. Such arrangements were generally held to be conspiracies in restraint of trade and were therefore unenforceable in the courts. As a result, the effectiveness of pools was likely to depend on exceptional or temporary conditions. They have persisted, but their era of chief importance was in the 'seventies and 'eighties, preceding the rise of trusts.

The trust is a legal device of long standing. But as a form of business combination it originated with the Standard Oil Company's changes of organization in 1879 and 1882. In the formation of a trust, the shareholders of constituent companies surrendered their shares to trustees and received in place of them certificates of ownership from the trustees. The legal authority of trustees might vary indefinitely, but they were generally given supervisory powers over the companies whose stock they held in trust, as to nature and quantity of output, marketing arrangements and prices. Each constituent company remained a legal entity. Various businesses soon flattered the Standard Oil trust by imitation. The passage of the Sherman Anti-Trust law in 1890 and of anti-trust legislation in most of the states during the closing years of the century, finally checked the trust movement and led to the devising of other forms of combination. To most of these the term trust was popularly applied.

The next stage in the evolution of formal industrial combinations was the holding company. It owed its origin to the grace of the state of New Jersey. The holding of stock of one corporation by another had generally been adjudged illegal till in 1889 New Jersey passed a law which legalized it. Thereafter the competition among the states for corporation fees and taxes led to the enactment of similar laws by most of the other states. With the increasing legal obstacles in the way of trusts and with the waning of the panic of 1893, the movement toward combination was resumed, in the closing years of the century, in the form of the holding company. Among innumerable instances were the Standard Oil Company, the United States Steel Corporation, and the General Motors Company. The holding corporation, unlike the trust, became the owner of the securities of the companies affected, and these companies became subsidiaries. The new type of organization had the advantages of the trust in the unification and coordination of management, and was able to weather more successfully the legal and political storms that menaced the trust. The device came to be used also in the organization of subsidiary companies for utilizing by-products, for transportation, for marketing, and for various other purposes. There are instances, too, of the holding company as a device for the pooling of patent rights.

It was necessary, of course, for the holding corporation to secure only a controlling interest in a company it wished to reduce to subordination. The control of business by financiers and by stock speculators was thus promoted. The holding corporation long remained the outstanding type of formal business combination. But a later tendency was in the direction of calling in and canceling the stocks of the constituent companies and the issuing of equivalent shares of the central corporation. This is in reality a process of integral consolidation or merging of companies. Recent combinations among competing units have tended to assume the form of the merger rather than of the holding company. Combinations, largely in the form of mergers, accounted for the disappearance, from 1919 to 1928, in manufacturing alone, of about six thousand companies. But the center of the financial stage was held by the consolidation of light and power interests, the service industries, and banks.

Corporate finance has become so varied and intricate that those interested in the control and coordination of a particular industry may depend in part on mergers, in part on the holding-company device, and even more largely on various informal arrangements.

INFORMAL AND FUNCTIONAL INTEGRATION AS AN ANTIDOTE FOR COMPETITIVE CHAOS

Formal combination by pooling agreements, or trust agreements, or holding corporations, or mergers, or by more than one of these methods at the same time has aimed at the integration of a particular industry or of related industries. In the terms of the economists, integration may be either horizontal or vertical. A combination of companies whose business is the refining of petroleum would be a horizontal integration or a union of a line or series of similar units. To bring under unified control not only refineries but by-product factories, oil wells, pipe lines, oil transports, gasoline service stations and other marketing facilities, and perhaps even factories for making such basic commodities as drilling equipment—this would tend toward vertical integration or the union of the various complementary units in a given industry.

But whatever the method, the essential function of industrial combination—the function which gives to the movement a predominantly social rather than anti-social character—has been to serve as an antidote for industrial chaos always threatening and often engulfing the business world. There has been a modern cycle of alternating order and chaos extending back to the medieval origins of modern business. The cycle has been associated with alternating control of markets, including the money market. Before the age of European expansion, when industry was local and when the craft gilds were in their heyday, business was stabilized; the capitalist was a laborer, and the laborer was a capitalist in being or in the making; monopoly prevailed, not for exploitation but for the sake of regulation and security; and markets were controlled by the producers.

Then came the era of expansion when the gilds, accustomed as they were to order and stability, became too rigid to bear the strain of readjustment to rapid change. Distant markets were beyond their ken. Merchants and bankers intervened for handling distant trade. Presently the gilds lost power even in local markets, and producers found themselves to be master craftsmen but masters in no other sense, being subordinated to the merchants as organizers of industry, especially of manufacturing for swelling the exportable surplus. In many industries there was no longer even the master craftsman with his shop, for manufacturing was dispersed among the people of the villages and the countryside with merchant princes furnishing raw materials and even tools and paying a pittance to supplement the income of the workers from the land. Into the confusion of the era of expansion the merchant princes introduced a measure of order and control by means of regulated monopolies held by the great trading companies and associations, and by means of customs and laws applicable especially to interregional and intermunicipal relations. These customs and laws were known collectively as the law merchant, and the name itself is an indication of the fact that neither producers nor consumers but middlemen prevailed in early modern business.

Out of the era of geographical and mercantile expansion emerged the era of invention—the age of the industrial revolution. The old system of regulated monopoly, appropriately known as mercantilism, broke down with the coming of the machine and the factory, as the gild system had broken down under the impact of mercantilism. Seeing the inadequacy of old regulations under new conditions, and being eager to take personal advantage of the new conditions, "Why have monopolies? Why have regulations?"—men were asking each other. Self-interest, it was held, if guided alone by the natural forces of competition and not buttressed by the artificial powers and monopolies of government, is beneficent socially as well as gratifying to the individual. Each part of industry is dependent on other parts. Failure to keep one's place in the ever-moving sequence of the social economy involves its own penalty. Coordination becomes automatic. The mechanism of the exchanges, by registering in price fluctuations not only present demands for goods or for credit but as well the judgment of experts as to future demands, enables producers to coordinate their output with the demands of consumers. Let the economic mechanisms function without governmental interference, and all will be well.

The theory was never given a thorough trial, because *laissez-faire* was adopted by governments in a one-sided manner, giving advantages to the already rich and powerful by removing restraints from them and by retaining restraints on the working classes. In America, the disadvantages of *laissez-faire* were long obscured by the prodigality of nature and the opportunities of the frontier. But before the end of the nineteenth century, even the most ardent of libertarians were wondering why there were recurring panics, increasing bankruptcies, and growing social discontent.

By the latter part of the nineteenth century the manufacturer was usurping the power which the merchant had held since the commercial revolution. When, therefore, renewed attempts at coordination were undertaken, they were mainly under the direction of the captain of industry rather than of the merchant prince. There was thus a tendency toward reversion to control by producers long since lost by the master craftsmen to the middlemen. The popularizing of stock ownership and the rise of the holding company gave bankers and mere stock jobbers advantages which further complicated a confused situation. Coordination whenever consciously attempted in America has generally been by men of the ruthless, domineering type, seeking unification by the subordination (or if need be the destruction) of competitors. Such has been the spirit of a large part of the formal combination movement associated with pools, trusts, and holding companies, and particularly with trusts. The ruthless nature of such combinations was often deemed necessary because of the prevailing political theory of maintaining unrestricted competition, which tended to make confusion worse confounded. On the other hand, "trust busting'' became all the more popular because of the ruthlessness of trust builders.

The legal obstacles in the way of formal combinations made coordination by such methods difficult. At the same time they promoted what has been called the ''Hooverizing'' of industry—a process of informal, voluntary coördination of independent but associated units of business. Encouragement of such activities by the government was begun as a war measure and was continued as one of the outstanding features of Mr. Hoover's headship of the Department of Commerce. The chief agency was an old institution revived, revised, and raised in little more than a decade to a position of nation-wide and even world-wide prominence—the trade association.

TRADE ASSOCIATIONS

Associations of the modern type are traceable to the early days of the industrial revolution in England. During the last quarter of the eighteenth century, the manufacturers of cotton, iron, ironwares, and pottery formed effective local associations and went so far as to organize, in 1785, the General Chamber of Manufacturers of Great Britain. These organizations were the first instances of associations formed by industrialists of the modern type. Despite the difficulties of association in an era of rapid expansion and growing individualism, they survived in one form or another, and were ultimately copied in America.

A few local chambers of commerce, consisting largely of merchants, were formed during the closing decades of the eighteenth century. By 1801, New York, New Haven, Charleston, and Philadelphia had chambers of commerce. But the trade association in the narrower sense had a later origin. In 1854 the Hampden County Cotton Spinners' Association was formed, and in 1865 it became the nucleus of the New England Cotton Spinners' Association. In 1861, the Writing Paper Manufacturers' Association was formed; in 1862, the United States Brewers' Association; and in 1864, the National Association of Wool Manufacturers. Several associations were formed during the quarter of a century following the Civil War. During the closing decade of the century, the movement gained impetus, and after the mobilization of industry in connection with the World War, nearly all of the more important branches of business not already organized formed associations. Any estimate of the number of trade associations depends on the manner of distinguishing trade associations from related organizations. An estimate of the National Industrial Conference Board in 1925 included only such associations as were composed of "persons or firms engaged in a particular trade or industry," that is, "the producers, or distributors, or both, of a particular product or generic class of products." A detailed study of such associations resulted in the conclusion that "it is fairly safe to assume the existence of between 800 and 1,000 trade associations of national or interstate character."

The earlier trade associations were largely concerned with price fixing, limitation of output, and control of employees. The antagonism of the public as expressed in state and federal legislation, notably the Sherman Anti-Trust Act of 1890, led to the development of lobbying. They also served as clearing houses of information. After 1910 a device known as the "open-price" plan was extensively adopted. It was assumed that the proper functioning of competition depended on the fullest possible knowledge of market conditions. If all competitors in a given industry had complete knowledge, the prices demanded would be approximately the same, because they would theoretically be determined by uniform knowledge of the prevailing conditions. The trade association therefore collected information and furnished it to members as a basis for their "voluntary" action in the regulation of prices and output. With the outlawing of this "open-price" plan by the Supreme Court in 1921 and 1923, earlier tendencies toward emphasis on activities generally regarded as legitimate were given renewed impetus.

As a substitute for the maintenance of profits by price fixing, trade associations began to look for methods of reducing costs and increasing sales. With these ends in view, it became necessary not only to collect from associates the routine data on which the "open-price" policy had been based but as well to engage in technological and economic researches. There was a quest for improvements, and an effort to extend the use of improvements among the associates. In cooperation with governmental agencies, there was an extensive standardization and simplification of sizes, dimensions, types, models and patterns, of business forms, and of methods of accounting. It was found that eighty per cent of profits usually came from twenty per cent of the varieties of goods produced. A reduction of the number of varieties resulted in extensive savings.

Many of the common needs of business units were met by associational activity. Traffic bureaus made studies of shipping methods and facilitated arrangements for meeting the transportation needs of associates. In some cases there was a pooling and interchange of patents. Credit information was interchanged and collection agencies were sometimes provided. Other activities included cooperative insurance, joint purchasing arrangements, and group advertising.

Relations with the public, with the government, and with employees came increasingly under the influence of the associations. Disputes between members of an association and even between members and outsiders came extensively under the jurisdiction of arbitration tribunals. In 1927, 415 such tribunals were in operation, and many others were in process of formation. For promoting the movement, the American Arbitration Association was formed. Such extra-legal adjustments have many advantages. Law lags notoriously behind economic changes, and for many cases there is no satisfactory legal precedent. Court procedure entails expensive delays. Litigation impairs good will, while voluntary arbitration is a sign of wholesome self-government and mutual accommodation. Not the least important of the activities of the associations has been the attempted elimination of abuses by the formulation and enforcement of ethical standards. A significant illustration was the agreement of the publishers of periodicals to eliminate fraudulent advertising, an agreement voluntarily adopted at a trade association conference presided over by a member of the Federal Trade Commission.

Probably the most important factor in the rise of trade associations was the World War. The sudden impact of wartime forces threatened industry with chaos at a most critical moment. A sudden shift from its traditional rôle of arbiter to direct participation in economic activities was beyond the capacity of the government. Uncoordinated private business units were even less responsive to the demand for an intelligent and efficient handling of the emergency. Rationing of food, raw materials, labor, and transportation facilities, and the making of technical readjustments for the production of essential goods and for curtailing the output of nonessentials—these and other intricate problems demanded immediate solution. As a practical expediency, the government undertook to deal with entire industries on a national scale by means of existing or newly formed national associations. After the war there was for a time a conflict of opinion in official circles as to the encouragement of associations, but the generally favorable views of President Hoover when Secretary of Commerce prevailed. Referring in a speech at St. Louis on November 2, 1928, to the "enormous growth of associational activities," he asserted that one of the three main functions of government should be the co-operation of the government with voluntary associations "in the promotion of constructive projects of public interest" and "in the cure of abuses by the voluntary establishment of a higher code of ethics and a stricter standard in the conduct of business." It was in accord with this conception that President Hoover, after the stock-market collapse of November, 1929, boldly called upon the industrial leaders of the country, who were loud in their professions of optimism, for "deeds, which speak louder than words," and proposed the formation, on the basis of existing chambers and associations, of a continuing economic council, quasi-official in character, for the coordination and stabilization of business.

BY WAY OF ILLUSTRATION: THE PETROLEUM INDUSTRY

There is no single industry that is consistently typical of tendencies toward the mobilization and integration of capital, but most of the outstanding changes are observable in the petroleum industry. It may therefore be viewed as a concrete embodiment of the forces previously analyzed.

The early history of the industry has already been discussed.[1] With the discovery of methods of drilling for oil and of new ways of using it, many individuals and companies undertook drilling and refining operations. The flow of capital into the industry was one of the early instances of the recent unprecedented mobility of industrial capital.

One of the pioneers was John D. Rockefeller. In 1855, at the age of sixteen, recently arrived from the country, he walked the streets of Cleveland in quest of work. The job he

[1] See above, pp. 270–272.

finally obtained paid him, from September to January, the sum of fifty dollars. Out of this, he boasted in later years, he paid his landlady and washerwoman and "saved a little money to put away." Ten years later, in 1865, he entered the refining business at Cleveland. In 1867 occurred the beginnings of combination with the origin of the firm of Rockefeller, Andrews and Flagler. There soon took shape in the mind of the young Rockefeller a daring plan of dominating the industry by means of a combination of resources, railway rebates, and monopolistic control of essential features of the business.

In 1870 his firm was reorganized as the Standard Oil Company of Ohio, with a capitalization of $1,000,000. Within ten years his company's control of the refining business had grown from about four per cent to about ninety per cent. His earliest plan of domination was by means of a pool controlled by the Standard Oil Company and operated by the South Improvement Company. In this way he was able to secure railroad rebates and thereby to force twenty-one of the twenty-six independent refineries of Cleveland to sell out to the Standard Oil Company.

By 1879 the company had acquired control of about thirty rival companies. In that year its assets, with its extensive interests in subsidiary companies, were transferred by a trust agreement to three trustees. The trustees were "to hold, control, and manage the said stocks and interests for the exclusive use and benefit" of the original owners John D. Rockefeller having the largest interest, namely 8984/35000 of the whole. In 1882 another trust was formed including the capital of additional companies. The interests of the various parties were surrendered to nine trustees, the parties receiving in return trust certificates of equal value. The trustees were given extensive powers for the control of the various companies.

The Standard Oil Company continued to operate under the trust agreement and to extend its operations and consolidate its control of the industry till 1892. In that year its dissolution was ordered by the Supreme Court of Ohio. The new organization was a nominal dissolution only. Twenty constituent companies were formed, and the trust certificates were replaced by a *pro rata* distribution of shares in the twenty companies. The trustees in making this transfer simply placed the shares in the new form in the hands of attorneys, authorizing the attorneys to rearrange the company's business. The men who had been trustees continued to hold a controlling interest in the several companies and to maintain unity of action substantially as before. The company itself was benefitted by the action as a legal occasion for disposing of some of the subsidiary companies no longer serving a useful purpose.

The company's next metamorphosis was in 1899. The New Jersey branch of the company was made a holding company for all stock issues. Its capitalization was increased from $10,000,000 to $110,000,000. Each shareholder in the twenty constituent companies now had the privilege of becoming a shareholder in the New Jersey company.

The company continued to operate as a holding company till 1911, when a Supreme Court decision ordered a dissolution. The basis of the decree was not so much the form of organization as the exercise of monopolistic powers by the company in violation of the laws and especially of the provisions against conspiracy in restraint of trade. The decree was followed by a redistribution of stocks to the stockholders. Shares of stock in the holding company were broken up into shares of stock in the constituent companies in proportion to their capitalization. Those who had controlled the subsidiary companies through the holding company now controlled them directly. Small stockholders were in many cases disturbed by the litigation and were dissatisfied with fractional holdings in the subsidiary companies, which had come to number thirty-three. With the consequent sale of small holdings, even greater concentration of ownership was made possible. Fears of the small stockholders proved to be groundless, for the value of shares rose rapidly soon after the dissolution. The ultimate effect of the decree on control of the industry by the Standard group was to make control more difficult. But the declining proportion of refining controlled by the company was probably due more largely to other factors. These were chiefly the development of new producing fields in the southwest and the far west, and the sudden expansion of demand for gasoline for use in automobiles.

The degree of coordination and integration attained in the oil industry resulted from a policy which was metaphorically described by John D. Rockefeller, Jr., in an address on trusts to the students of Brown University. "The American beauty rose," he said, "can be produced in its splendor and fragrance only by sacrificing the early buds which grow up around it." Even this kind of integration was confined to the refining branch of the industry, and was achieved at the cost not only of the pruning away of rivals but of ruthless disregard of law and of the frequent sacrifice of public honesty. As for the production of crude oil, the cost of industrial disorder included enormous waste of an irreplacable basic natural resource; frenzied speculation; demoralization of oil-producing areas; and dangerous extremes of losses and gains and of expansion and depression. The marketing of petroleum products was accompanied by violent fluctuations in prices. The variations in prices on the same date in different regions were usually unrelated to cost and were caused by efforts to secure or maintain monopolistic control of markets.

The obvious need of coordination for the elimination of ıbuses and for the rational utilization of petroleum led at ength, as in other industries, to the trade association. The ·arly struggles of producers of crude oil and of the inde-)endent refiners with the Standard group gave rise to sev- ·ral ephemeral efforts at associated action, resulting at ength in the National Petroleum Association of 1902. It ıltimately gained the support of such powerful organiza- ions as the Pennzoil, Roxana, Sinclair, Gulf, and Sun Companies. It claimed in 1922 to represent about fifteen per ent of the refining industry. The National Petroleum Mar- ‹eters' Association, its offshoot, the Independent Oil Men of America, and several regional associations, were largely or- anized for promoting the interests of independent pro- ucers, refiners or marketers. The power of the Standard roup was shown by the fact that such associations com- ıonly served their members by informing them of price hanges made by the Standard group so that they might onform. Various other functions characteristic of asso- iations in other industries were exercised by the oil as- ociations, and especially by the National Petroleum ssociation.

As in many other industries, the first comprehensive or- anization resulted from the World War. Out of the Na- onal Petroleum War Service Committee there emerged in 919 the American Petroleum Institute. The difficulties of ıtercorporate action were avoided by confining membership) individuals. The nature of its activities is indicated by its ıain divisions: Accounting and Taxation, Standardization, evelopment and Production Engineering, Technology, tatistics, and Public Relations. Extensive research was ıade possible by special gifts. Its functions are advisory, ut its influence in the correction of abuses, the elimination f waste, and the voluntary coordination of certain phases of the industry has been considerable. The basic problems of competitive drilling and marketing, to say nothing of the questions of public title to subsoil resources, offered seemingly unyielding obstacles to "rationalization" of the industry. But there were repeated efforts to overcome the obstacles. Early in 1929 the international nature of the problems of overproduction and waste was recognized by the American Petroleum Institute in the formation of a Committee on World Production and Consumption of Petroleum and Its Products, the committee consisting of about eighty executives of Standard Oil and independent firms. "It is well known," announced the president of the Institute, "that most of the important oil fields throughout the world are producing an amount of crude in excess of the consumption in markets geographically tributary thereto. This overproduction has developed such an acutely serious situation that the most complete cooperation lawfully possible is essential to prevent its further development and attendant waste." The Institute had previously announced a policy of working in concert with government officials in an effort to devise what were described as cooperative methods of handling rationally the problems of the entire industry as they arise. There resulted a restriction of output—and also a suspicion among motorists not possessing shares of stock that coordination was mainly for maintaining monopoly prices of gasoline.

In the field of associational and governmental cooperation in the business world as a whole, said President Hoover in a campaign speech in 1928, "lie potentialities which have been barely touched." The ultimate outcome of a movement with promising beginnings and with the highest official sanction is a matter of utmost importance. The movement is based on a conception of self-government in business. But what is meant by self-government? A defect in th conception as apparently held by many promoters of trade associations is the limitation of responsibility to the owners of business enterprises. In prosperous eras when profits are assured by means of expanding markets with low prices and high wages, and even in times of slight recession when dangerous unemployment can be avoided by abnormally stimulating the construction of public works, the sense of responsibility of business executives to consumers and workers may perhaps be maintained without undue violence to their conception of self-interest. But comprehensive and abiding self-government must be able to stand severer tests. It must include a mode of compulsion for those who defy the common judgment; and it must be based on the sharing of power and responsibility by all concerned—by consumers and by workers as well as by business executives. Power and responsibility in turn involve the decisive factor of ownership. Even assuming an approximate harmony of interests between consumers and workers on the one hand and the owners of the controlling stocks in business enterprises on the other hand: is the maintenance of such a harmony of interests possible in the inevitably recurring testing times of adversity? Self-government in business is a more far-reaching conception than many of its advocates appear to realize.

CHAPTER XXIII

LABOR

STAGES IN THE EVOLUTION OF AMERICAN LABOR

Laborers as distinguished from capitalists have played a much disputed part in economic life. John Stuart Mill, Nestor of the classical economists, postulated a competitive society. The value of goods competitively produced is determined, he held, by cost of production; and of the elements of the cost of production, "so much the principal as to be nearly the sole" element, directly or indirectly, is labor. David Ricardo, too, made labor "the real foundation of exchangeable value." Karl Marx, who followed in this matter the classical economists, evolved his famous labor theory of value and its corollary of surplus value produced by labor but withheld from labor by the capitalist, and to be expropriated and socialized by the impending social revolution. Later economists, including socialistic followers of Marx, became skeptical of such theories and gave much greater place to monopoly, to scarcity values, to the gifts of nature, and to socially created values like the unearned increment resulting from the growth or the shifting of population.

Who shall utilize the fruits of labor, the monopoly and scarcity values, the unearned increment, and the free gifts of nature? The social importance attaching to individuals and groups is determined largely by the answer to this question, not by a theoretical solution of the problem of value

Labor's attempt to answer the question has been responsible for the emergence of labor as a self-conscious group or as a group impinging on the consciousness of other classes.

The history of American labor may be divided into three main stages. The first is an undifferentiated stage of practical identity of labor and capital, in agriculture and the earlier simple handicraft industries. The second stage is marked by the emergence of a distinct working class, not so much in the consciousness of the workers or in class organization but rather in natural status and external regimentation. The third stage is marked by the emergence of self-consciousness and by internal organization for increasing labor's portion of the social income. There is a possible fourth stage, already attained in some countries but not in general recognized by American labor even as an ideal. This is the stage of political organization of workers by brain as well as by hand, with a comprehensive program for socializing the ownership and management of industry.

For industry as a whole and for the country as a whole, there are no exact boundary lines of dates between the stages. In agriculture, there is still in many cases an identity of capital and labor. On the other hand, in some branches of craftsmanship the third stage (group consciousness, internal organization and deliberate group action) was reached locally by the end of the eighteenth century. The Journeymen Cordwainers of Philadelphia, for instance, after a lockout in 1799, forced upon their employers a compromise agreement by collective bargaining through joint representation. By the last quarter of the nineteenth century, internal organization on a national basis had extended so far as to carry the labor movement nationally into the third stage. At the same time, the external regimentation of labor by subjection to machine technique and to the discipline of large, impersonal business organizations accentuated the separation of labor alike from ownership and from management.

FORMATIVE FORCES

It is because of the failure of American labor until recent decades to reach the stage of group consciousness and effective organization for concerted action that labor as such has heretofore played no major rôle in this recital of American industrial history. The long delay was due to several retarding influences. The ideal of the craftsman's life was an integrated process extending from apprenticeship to possession of a shop. For a long time it was relatively easy for apprentices and journeymen to become master craftsmen. For a much longer time the ideal survived, and the hope of becoming masters gave to apprentices and journeymen an influential if illusory individualism and sense of kinship with the master craftsmen.

More important in promoting individualism and in retarding the integration of the working classes in this country were the influences of the sea and the frontier. Writers of history and fiction have made much of the frontier as a formative factor in American life, somewhat to the neglect of the sea. During colonial days, the fisheries and the various forms of illicit trade as well as legitimate commerce by sea afforded an outlet for discontented elements, an opportunity for adventure, and a source of countless fortunes. Before the War of 1812, and later during the decades preceding the Civil War, in the days of glory of the Yankee clipper ship, American trade and fisheries expanded to such proportions as to make the sea a rival of the frontier in drawing away the restless and ambitious workers who might otherwise have taken part in an effective working-class movement. Trade by sea and the demands of frontier communities reacted in turn upon the older areas by increasing the opportunities of those who remained at home. After the Civil War, pioneering under the Homestead act continued for many years to maintain a spirit of individualism inimical to a general working-class movement.

Closely connected with frontier individualism was the reaction against autocratic government and the diversion of working-class activities into political channels. Substantial changes resulted. The franchise was extended. Public education was advanced. Judicial decisions were somewhat liberalized, as in the case of Commonwealth *vs.* Hunt in the Massachusetts Supreme Judicial Court in 1842, recognizing the legality of trade unions. Working-class hostility to monopolies and corporations contributed to the triumph of Jackson and the overthrow of the second Bank of the United States. President Van Buren was induced in 1840 to issue an executive order establishing the ten-hour day on government works. About the middle of the century, several state legislatures were induced to pass laws limiting the number of hours of labor. Working men were influential in securing the enactment of the Homestead law.

But whatever the gains, the political activities of the workers repeatedly disrupted promising organizations and made concerted economic measures difficult. There were alternating waves of political agitation, humanitarianism, cooperation, socialism, and simple trade unionism. The gains of prosperous periods were usually wiped out by recurring panics, and by the floods of immigration which disturbed the homogeneity and reduced the bargaining power of labor.

Because of the various retarding influences, national group consciousness and effective national organization for concerted action are not discernible before the last quarter of the nineteenth century. By that time, the retarding influences were being effectively counteracted by three main factors tending to promote working-class integration. One of these was the nationalizing of the markets by the development of transportation facilities with an accompanying tendency toward national uniformity of economic conditions. Goods produced under different wage scales and labor conditions and competing in the same market tended to drive wages to the level of the lowest competing unit, and national organization therefore became necessary as a measure of self-defense. A second factor was the subjection of the workers to machine technique, with automatic discipline, with loss of economic independence, and with "green hands" bidding against skilled workers. The third factor was the regimentation of workers by their employment in large plants or large groups by big, impersonal business organizations. These three factors converged during the decades following the Civil War, at a time when maritime interests were negligible and when frontier opportunity was declining.

LOCAL FOUNDATIONS

During the second quarter of the nineteenth century, local groups of workers participated in varied political, humanitarian, educational, and cooperative activities. But beginning about the middle of the century, there was a decided tendency on the part of the skilled workers to withdraw from the earlier heterogeneous organizations and to form local unions confined in membership to themselves and limited in purpose to such purely economic motives as getting higher wages. By 1854, such local skilled unions existed in nearly all of the cities. The depression beginning in that year wiped most of the unions out of existence. A later revival of business was followed by a revival of unionism, but again in 1857 the panic ended the life of most of the unions. Only the strongest unions, like the iron molders', survived, and these became the nuclei of the first national federations. But the federations of the 'fifties were merely advisory committees, with the New York locals playing the leading rôles.

For half a decade after the panic of 1857, even local unionism was generally defunct. With the wartime rise in prices and increasing demand for labor, a revival on a more permanent basis became possible. It is estimated that during the year 1864 the number of local unions increased from less than a hundred to nearly three hundred. A conservative estimate of 1869 put the total number at 1,093. During the next few years there was a rapid increase.

The first effective type of federation was local. The various unions of a given town formed a trades assembly or council. Beginning in 1863 with Rochester, the movement spread rapidly, and by the end of the war every city of importance had an assembly of representatives of the local unions. These in turn promoted the unionizing of additional trades, and thus by thorough local organization the way was prepared for national federations.

NATIONAL FEDERATIONS OF LOCAL UNIONS

The year of the revival of local trade unionism (1864) witnessed the formation of four national federations. Six national unions had already been formed, three before the Civil War and three during the earlier years of the war. Between 1864 and the panic of 1873, twenty-six federations came into being, making a total of thirty-two by 1873.

Among the more prominent federations were the Iron Molders' International Union (including some Canadian locals); the union of machinists and blacksmiths; printers; locomotive engineers; plasterers; cigar makers; coopers; and shoemakers. The stove molders, says Professor Andrews in his notable contribution to Commons' *History of Labor in the United States,* "have epitomized the American trade union movement not only throughout the 'sixties but even to the present day.'' The national federation was formed as a result of competitive conditions growing out of the nationalizing of the market. Its formation was soon followed by the organization of employers' associations to combat its influence. These in turn led to long-drawn-out conflicts and finally in 1890 to pioneering in the field of national trade agreements. But before this occurred, the molders' union went through the typical phases of cooperative production, general social reform, and political agitation—a temporary reversion to the tendencies of the 'thirties and 'forties.

ABORTIVE LABOR COMBINATIONS

With local unions extensively organized and with these in turn united in local trades assemblies and in national federations of particular trades, the next step was logically a national union of all trades in a comprehensive organization. There was an unfortunate rivalry for leadership between the local trades assemblies and the national federations. At a labor union congress held in Baltimore in 1866, the problem of a national organization was met by a somewhat vague agreement that there should be a National Labor Union. The union was to function mainly by means of an annual congress. Representation was a cumbersome compromise between the rival claims of the national federations and the local trades assemblies. The outstanding issue at the moment was the eight-hour day, and ''eight-hour leagues'' were also given representation. The pressing problems of trade union organization and methods were relegated to a secondary place in favor of political agitation connected with the eight-hour day, land reform, currency, and taxation. Some effort was made to extend and coordinate trade-union activities in the narrow sense, but the powers of the national officials were slight and the difficulties were insuperable. After 1870 most of the influential trade unions withdrew their support, and the National Labor Union merged with the National Labor and Reform Party.

The next attempt at comprehensive national organization was in 1873. At the call of the presidents of several of the leading national federations, a congress met in July of 1873 at Cleveland. This congress attempted a trades union organization resembling the later American Federation of Labor. Its failure was undoubtedly due in the main to the panic of 1873. Then followed an era of floundering in the cross currents of politics, cooperation, and trade unionism. Many of the local unions were forced to dissolve. The trades assemblies and the national federations were virtually without reserve funds, were little more than advisory bodies, were dependent for support on the degree of success attained in securing favorable terms from employers, and were constantly losing their ablest leaders because of the lure of politics or of business. A decline of trade unionism during the industrial depression of the 'seventies was therefore inevitable. The number of national federations, such as the Molders' Union, declined from more than thirty to less than ten, and most of the survivors were temporarily helpless. When the movement reached its nadir, shortly after the centennial of independence, there were probably not more than 50,000 active, dues-paying unionists in the entire country.

Declining wages; widespread unemployment; hostility of employers' associations; extensive lockouts, blacklistings, and legal prosecutions; disastrous strikes; riots, disorders, and crimes associated with secret societies such as the Molly Maguires but popularly attributed to labor unions; floods of immigration further weakening the workers' competitive power and lowering the standard of living—such were the conditions accounting for the disintegration of the labor movement. Coming at the time of the centennial of independence, and within a few years after a war for the liberation of labor in the south, they were not without ironical significance.

It was the extreme hostility of employers to trade unions during the era of industrial depression of the 'seventies that accounts for the next phase of the national working-class movement—a secret organization known as the Noble Order of the Knights of Labor. It was organized locally by Uriah Smith Stephens in Philadelphia in 1869. Secrecy, which was at first a source of strength, was later abandoned because of criticism. During the early 'eighties the growth of the Order was phenomenal; its decline was equally rapid. Its ideal strength, and at the same time its practical weakness, was its assumption of a non-existent solidarity of labor. Its history is more picturesque than important. It is an episode in the interlude between the disruption of the movement toward nationalization during the 'sixties and the rise of the American Federation of Labor.

THE AMERICAN FEDERATION OF LABOR

While the Knights of Labor were momentarily monopolizing the labor stage, socialism, syndicalism, and greenbackism were contending for the spotlight. But in the meantime, with returning prosperity and increasing demand for labor, there was a revival of the trade unionism of the 'sixties. New leaders, among them Samuel Gompers, were coming to the front. They were insisting on economic aims and methods in place of political tactics; on satisfactory agreements with employers rather than on producers' cooperation; on militancy but not on revolution; and on a practical if somewhat selfish and shortsighted utilization of the superior bargaining power of skilled workers for promoting the immediate interests of the skilled workers without much concern for the unorganized and unskilled masses. In this way they were able to attract those working-class elements which had given strength to the Knights of Labor, and that organization, which had aimed at the solidarity of all the workers, was left with little besides its magnificent ideal. The new leaders, meeting at Pittsburgh in 1881, formed the Federation of Organized Trades and Labor Unions of the United States and Canada. In 1886 the name was changed to the American Federation of Labor.

The growth of the new organization was not rapid. The membership of the constituent unions at the end of the first decade was only about 200,000. This was the period of conflict between the Order of the Knights of Labor, with its ideal of solidarity, and the Federation with its appeal to the skilled workers to go their own way and feather their own nests. The issue came to a head in 1886, at a trades union conference at Philadelphia and a General Assembly of the Knights of Labor at Cleveland. At Philadelphia, war was virtually declared on the Knights of Labor. "Nevertheless, we recognize the solidarity of all labor interests," affirmed the chieftains of the unions—a recognition which was to find virtually no place in union policy. At Cleveland, the General Assembly of the Knights took up the challenge. While recognizing the services rendered to humanity and to labor by trades unions, they "believe that the time has come, or is fast approaching, when all who earn their bread by the sweat of their brow shall be enrolled under one general head." In an address to the iron and steel workers' union, it was urged that "unskilled labor must receive attention, or in the hour of difficulty the employer will not hesitate to use it to depress the compensation you now receive. That skilled or unskilled labor may no longer be found unorganized, we ask of you to annex your grand and powerful corps to the main army that we may fight the battle under one flag." Further negotiations for amity between the Knights and the Federationists proved futile. There followed the rapid decline of the Knights, the thorough entrenchment of the Federation in the skilled trades, and the decay of organization among the unskilled workers.

Even the skilled workers found it hard to hold their own during the economic depression of the last decade of the century, but with industrial revival in 1898 there was a rapid growth in Federation membership till in 1904 its numbers had grown to 1,676,000. The strength of the Federation is shown by the fact that it successfully weathered the industrial storms of 1907. After 1910 there was again a rapid expansion, continuing with slight interruptions till 1920, when the membership exceeded 4,000,000. There was a subsequent decline. Changes in membership resulted not only from the general ebb and flow of unionism but as well from the adhesion of new trades to the Federation, as when in 1916 the International Union of Bricklayers, Masons, and Plasterers with 80,000 members joined the Federation. Some organizations of skilled workers, notably the railway brotherhoods, refrained from formal affiliation, but cooperated, especially in regard to questions of public policy. Because of the nature of their occupations, the railway brotherhoods emphasized insurance and fraternal functions.

The old fight between local trades assemblies or councils embracing the various trades and the national or international unions confined to single trades was won by the latter. The Federation's principle of organization was based not on the local assembly of trades but on the national trade union. At the convention of 1881, when the Federation was organized, only eight national trade unions were represented. Year after year the number increased till it passed beyond the hundred mark. The ideal was constantly one of autonomy for the constituent trades, with federated action only in cases of clearly defined common interest or conflicting interest. The number of delegates to a convention was determined by the number of dues-paying members of the constituent unions. An overwhelming majority of representatives were delegates of the national and international unions. The convention chose a president, a secretary, a treasurer, and eight vice-presidents. These officials formed an executive committee in charge of the Federation's work. The income was derived from a small percentage of the dues of members of the constituent unions. The Federation was concerned in part with the immediate problems of relations between employers and employees, but for the most part indirectly, through the particular constituent union involved in a given controversy with employers. It was concerned with harmonizing and coordinating the often conflicting elements within the Federation; with extending unionization into new fields; and with promoting favorable public opinion and public policy.

Although the American Federation of Labor and the railway brotherhoods were founded on the specialized craft or trade, they found it necessary to yield, here a little and there a little, to industrial unionism, which calls for joint organization of skilled and unskilled in a particular industry. The rapid changes in technology and in the integration of business units made the old craft distinctions in many cases obsolete. Such organizations as the United Mine Workers of America at length took their places in the Federation by the side of the older craft unions. During the opening years of the new century, the Federation was forced to recognize the internal amalgamation of related crafts into "departments," as the Building Trades Department, for solving problems of jurisdiction among the crafts and for maintaining a united front in dealing with employers. After the World War, this basic problem of craft unionism *versus* industrial unionism became so critical and so provocative as to impair seriously the strategic strength of the working classes. Before pursuing this phase of the subject further it is necessary to consider the strategy and tactics of labor and capital in what already seems to be the somewhat remote era preceding the World War.

STRATEGY AND TACTICS OF LABOR AND CAPITAL BEFORE THE WORLD WAR

The so-called revolutionary labor movement aimed, by cooperation, by socialism, or by syndicalism, to substitute for the prevailing relationship of wage-paying private employer and wage-receiving private employee a relationship between men and managers as joint owners or as joint agents of the community in enterprises for satisfying wants rather than for making profits. The so-called "business" unions (the American Federation of Labor, the railway brotherhoods, and similar groups) had the primary object of merely influencing the terms of employment within the existing economic system, mainly in regard to wages and more or less incidentally in regard to such matters as hours, working rules, comfort, and healthfulness. As to numbers and immediate influence, revolutionary unionism was negligible. Its main immediate effect was to arouse a bitter and oftentimes unreasoning hostility and to give rise to absurd popular exaggerations concerning the Industrial Workers of the World as being interested only in sabotage, *ca' canny* or "soldiering on the job," and terrorism, and as threatening seriously the overthrow of existing institutions. A study of the American mind would include its views of revolutionary labor. But a study of American labor is mainly concerned with the more conservative or "business" unions.

Oftentimes no consistent, orderly course was followed, but back of labor strategy was in general the idea of an agreement entered into between the employers and agents of the workers. In the older, simpler conditions of labor, when the employer had at least semi-personal relations with each of his workmen, the idea of such collective agreements naturally occurred to no one. But with increasing size of plants and numbers of workers, impersonal and group relations became necessary; men were tagged and numbered and tied as it were to machines. Furthermore, with the bewilderingly rapid changes of transition to modern industry, there came an increasing sense of insecurity, which inevitably turned men's minds toward the need of common action.

On the other hand, the workers were not owners, but had come to be identified intimately, almost inseparably, with the machines and materials and buildings owned by the employer. The men were so many "hands." The employer, as owner of the mill if not of the mill "hands," had power by sanction of law to do as he pleased with his property. Those who were not themselves owners but were responsible, as managers, for profits as the price of their jobs, were even less inclined to surrender any share of their authority to the workers in determining wages and working conditions or to yield to demands which seemed to encroach on the profits of the owners. However reasonable to outsiders might appear the idea of conferences with union representatives for adjusting the terms of employment, to insiders the suggestion almost invariably appeared to be preposterous.

The thought occurred to labor leaders (notably among early leaders to Terence V. Powderly of the Knights of Labor) that if a joint conference was insufferably repugnant to employers, complaints might be adjusted by a board of arbitration to which both sides could present their cases. But boards of arbitration as well as joint conferences were long regarded by employers as inconsistent with their proprietary rights and interests. Wrote George F. Baer, spokesman of the anthracite coal operators, to a correspondent who suggested a conciliatory policy in the great strike of 1902,—"You are evidently biased in favor of the right of the working man to control a business in which he has no other interest than to secure fair wages for the work he does. I beg of you not to be discouraged. The rights and interests of the laboring man will be protected and cared for —not by the labor agitators, but by the Christian men to whom God in his infinite wisdom has given the control of the property interests of the country, and upon the successful management of which so much depends."

Grievances of individual workers in connection with accidents and certain other matters could be aired in the courts; and in some states, administrative boards were at length established for dealing with such matters as accidents and factory conditions. But there was little administrative authority and less of public sentiment in favor of such authority, even for dealing with incidental matters. For adjudicating basic industrial disputes, there was no public authority. As for action in the courts, the unions were helpless because incorporation necessary to give them standing in the courts would have subjected them to a fatally unequal struggle with wealthy and influential employers; and because the law and the bench, by virtue of historical origins, natural conservatism, and economic affiliation, were guardians primarily of property and the propertied classes.

No matter in what direction the leaders of the unions turned in quest of peaceful and publicly sanctioned methods of participation in shaping the terms of the employment contract, they found the way was barred. It is hardly too much to say that the inevitable result was resort to the strike. Before the rise of the strong and permanent unions, and since then in poorly organized industries, strikes sometimes occurred sporadically and spontaneously with little conscious thought of their being necessary substitutes for joint conferences and trade agreements. Furthermore, there were occasionally minor labor uprisings of a revolutionary nature with the idea not of forcing a more favorable wage contract from employers but rather of harassing the capitalist and preparing the way for a revolutionary transition to a different economic system. But these were exceptional. The strike was essentially a method of forcing employers into joint conferences or before boards of arbitration for the purpose of joint determination of the employment contract.

As early as 1872, during an era of industrial expansion, there was a strike of about a hundred thousand workers, mainly in the building trades of the New York area, for the eight-hour day. The strike was successful. Soon thereafter, from 1874 to 1877, when internal quarrels among the unions and industrial depression combined to give strategic advantages to employers, there was a general tendency to lower wages and to throw off such restraints as the unionism of the 'sixties had been able to impose. Strikes of unprecedented extent and seriousness resulted in textiles, cigar making, coal mining, and railroading. Workers became desperate, often disregarded the prudent counsels of leaders, and in one important case (in coal mining in the Ohio region) repudiated an adverse arbitration award which they had pledged themselves to accept. There was widespread unemployment. Innumerable hopeless vagabonds tramped from town to town. Lawless elements survived from the wartime demoralization. Masses of crude immigrants, thrust into the raw industrial centers that had sprung up since the Civil War, were often without employment and ignorant of the laws and customs of the country. Employers were ruthless in their determination to crush the unions as well as to reduce wages. Lockouts, blacklistings, spying, riots, murders, and the breakup of unionism accompanied the strikes.

With the return of prosperity in the 'eighties, conditions favored an attitude of assertiveness by labor. Offensive rather than defensive strikes began to occur. The strikes among unions connected with the Knights of Labor were often unsuccessful, and this fact contributed to the shift from the Knights to the Federation. It was during the 'eighties that the boycott by unions of goods made by offending employers came into prominence to supplement the strike as a method of influencing employers—a method used with varying success until the Supreme Court in the Danbury Hatters' case, in 1908, declared it illegal and even went so far as to affirm the liability of individual members of the union for the payment of triple damages under the Sherman anti-trust law. About the same time, a decision virtually recognized the legality of the "blacklist" used by employers. These and similar decisions, combined with the conservative attitude of the Senate in blocking legislation desired by unionists, forced the American Federation of Labor finally to abandon its aloofness from politics. But its main weapons remained economic. Recognizing the need of solidarity within a given trade if effective trade agreements were to be maintained, the unions began about 1885 a vigorous campaign for the union "closed shop." Employers countered with a demand for the "open shop"—in theory the right to employ either union or non-union men, but a right which was naturally used by those opposing trade agreements to maintain non-union closed shops.

The principal objective of unionism remained the trade agreement. In the attainment of this objective, the early 'nineties were marked alike by losses and gains. Iron and steel workers had been strongly organized and had secured agreements virtually national in character. But in 1892, on the expiration of a three-year agreement with the Amalgamated Iron and Steel Workers, the powerful Carnegie Company, under the influence of H. C. Frick, a bitter opponent of unionism, offered a virtually impossible contract. An ultimatum offered as alternatives the acceptance of this contract or the abandonment of collective bargaining. The disastrous Homestead strike resulted. The non-union policy then adopted was inherited later by the United States Steel Corporation.

About the same time the stove molders won a victory which assumed in a sense the importance of a precedent. Their trade agreement was preceded by bitter conflicts, including both strikes and lockouts. The national solidarity of each side was demonstrated in 1887 when a local strike at St. Louis led to sending of patterns to the plants of other companies, and this in turn led to refusal of workers at other plants to make use of the patterns. The agreement finally concluded became not only a precedent but in a measure a model. Committees chosen by the molders' union and the National Association of Stove Manufacturers were to confer jointly each year for amending the general agreement. Each association was to enforce the terms of the agreement on its members. Local disputes were to be adjusted by joint representatives. Responsibility for the government of the industry, in regard to industrial relations, passed from employers to joint representatives of employers and employees.

It is a significant fact that the next outstanding agreement was not in a narrow field of labor represented by the older craft unions, but in the soft-coal industry, representing the newer industrial unionism. This agreement, made in 1898, covered the central competitive bituminous coal district, and followed a general strike in that area. During the next few years, many such agreements were made, some national, many more regional, and a large number local in character. The adoption of an agreement in the anthracite coal industry as a result of arbitration following a strike in 1902, gave tremendous impetus to the movement by demonstrating the self-restraint of the workers and the moderation of their leaders and by focusing public attention favorably on the demands of the unions for orderly participation in the government of industry. The work of the National Civic Federation, founded in 1901 and composed in part of prominent business men, was devoted largely to promoting trade agreements. The movement was checked by intensive propaganda for the "open shop" and by the powerful hostility of the United States Steel Corporation, but by the outbreak of the World War the general principle of the trade agreement had been accepted very widely as being of almost axiomatic validity. While labor's part in the government of industry and its share of responsibility for the proper conduct of industry were severely limited even by the trade agreement, its development was generally heralded as a desirable step toward industrial order and "constitutionalism."

In the meantime, the change of policy of the American Federation of Labor toward politics had begun to show results. Due largely to its influence, important changes were made in the legal status of workers. In many states laws were passed for the regulation of hours, factory conditions, and even wages (as in the case of minimum wage laws for women). There was widespread recognition of the principle of employer's liability for industrial accidents. Numerous popular changes in educational systems were introduced. By such measures there was an extension in many directions of the functions of government supposedly in the interest of the laboring classes and at the expense of the older *laissez-faire* conception. But judicial decisions such as the Danbury Hatters' verdict, the growing use of injunctions in labor disputes, and the control by employers of local administrative and police agencies in the industrial centers demonstrated in the first place that the conflict between capital and labor had not abated; and in the second place that seeming legislative gains of labor were often rendered ineffectual by the less conspicuous but more powerful forces connected with the interpretation and the enforcement of law.

WAR AND NEW TACTICS

The World War diverted European labor from production into military channels and at the same time increased the demand for consumption goods. The result was a frantic demand for American commodities. This not only opened up vast markets abroad to American producers but by adding to American prosperity it stimulated consumption in America. Exports of merchandise before 1914 had hardly attained two and a half billion dollars in value. By 1920 they had reached a total of more than eight billion dollars. Expressed in the form of indexes for eliminating the effects of price changes, and with the year 1913 as a base of 100, by 1920 the quantity of domestic exports had risen to 137; the price, to 241; and the total value, to 330.

Upon America's entry into the war, the favorable position of labor was temporarily enhanced by two special circumstances previously non-existent. One of these was the desire of the government to conciliate the workers and to mobilize them effectively for industrial as well as military purposes. Samuel Gompers and his colleagues were suddenly invested with eminent respectability and semi-official power comparable to the position of the business men who occupied newly created positions at Washington at a dollar a year. Labor organizations were taken into partnership with the government in a manner analogous to the status of trade associations of employers. Recognition of the union, long demanded by union leaders, became an accomplished fact on a grand scale. The second circumstance which temporarily favored labor was the unprecedented willingness of employers to raise wages. This in turn was due in part to the cost-plus arrangement for awarding contracts. Since in many cases the contractor's profit or commission was a percentage of the cost, any increase in the cost augmented the profit. The usual resistance to wage increases was therefore broken down by automatic additions to profits. There was also an abnormal competition among industrial plants for the skilled labor that was insufficient to meet the sudden demand for a large increase in output.

Union wage rates per hour rose gradually from a base of 100 in 1913 to 114 in 1917, and rapidly thereafter till they soon more than doubled the 1913 rates. In the meantime hours had been reduced, but the rates of wages per full-time week trailed only a little way behind the hourly rates. Non-union wages followed in general the same trend, but were affected more readily by such factors as casual and irregular employments. Statistics of wages are usually extremely inadequate from the point of view of showing the real status of working-class income because of the difficulty of correlating price changes with changes in wages and of discovering the total number of days or hours of employment per year in the cases of those who work for daily or hourly wages. A daily or hourly wage scale is the scale made available by the employer's records, but the effective wage of the worker is not his hourly or daily wage but rather his yearly income expressed in terms of buying power. Nevertheless, in spite of rapidly rising prices, the employment conditions prevailing before the industrial depression of 1921 gave to the working classes up to that time an unprecedentedly favorable position.

With the beginning of deflation in 1920 there was a scrimmage for new positions of strategy and a quest for new tactics in the relations of employers and employees. Farmers were confronted with a vastly extended acreage to meet war needs no longer existent. They were poorly organized, were in no position to profit by tariffs because of a surplus of their principal crops calling for export, and were unable to shift any of the burdens of deflation to other groups. In other branches of industry, powerful organizations with vast reserves of wartime profits enabled business men to retreat to new positions with relatively slight losses. In order to hold their losses in check, there was not unnaturally a general effort to reduce wages as well as personnel, and a widespread movement toward the abandonment of trade agreements in the older industries and their exclusion from newer industries, as the making of automobiles.

Organized labor was equally determined to retain its advanced positions occupied during the war, and if possible to win new territory. The great offensive of labor was in the steel industry, which had successfully resisted all efforts of union organizers. The workers included large numbers of the "new immigration" from eastern and southeastern Europe—Jugo-Slavs, Czecho-Slovaks, Rumanians, Greeks, Italians, Poles, and several other nationalities. The twelve-hour day, the seven-day week, long shifts, the extensive use by employers of blacklisting and of spies or "under-cover" men, and the control by the corporations of the community life of the workers—these were the outstanding conditions which led to the great steel strike of 1919.

The American Federation of Labor took the lead in organizing the workers. The Federation officials had been outspoken in supporting the war and in opposing revolutionary economic ideas. But the Federation adopted the principle of industrial unionism for the steel industry, and one of its officials, W. Z. Foster, had given expression several years earlier to "one-big-union" ideas in a pamphlet on syndicalism. There was a division among labor leaders as to the ultimate aims of the labor movement. There was a recurrence in a new form of the older feuds over craft unionism *versus* industrial unionism, over independent skilled unionism *versus* working-class solidarity, and over "business" unionism *versus* idealistic and revolutionary unionism.

Although there was little difference of opinion as to the immediate aims of the strike, employers were able to exploit effectively the existence of radical views among the workers and their leaders. This was a time of intense nervousness and high tension following the war. The anti-German propaganda was followed by an even more intense and bitter anti-Russian propaganda. Foreigners who had the audacity to strike in "God's country," which had just succeeded in making the world safe for democracy, must surely be either pro-German or else in sympathy with the Bolsheviks. To call a person a pro-German or a "Bolshi" was an answer to all arguments. In the emotional orgy of the post-war period, there was little rational thought and little effective demand for logical evidence. Mr. Gary, an ex-judge, and chairman of the Board of Directors of the United States Steel Corporation, rebuffed a committee of the Interchurch World Movement offering mediation with the repeated statement that the only outcome of a victory for unionism would be Sovietism in the United States and the forcible division of property!

Civil rights of the "hunkies," as the foreign-born workers were commonly called, were virtually non-existent. Newspapers with remarkable unanimity refused to state the strikers' case or even to print such obviously non-partisan facts as the number of workers on strike. An investigating committee of the Interchurch World Movement reported that "despite the fact that the demands for better working conditions, a six-day week, eight instead of ten, twelve or fourteen hours a day, and for recognition of labor's right to organize, etc., the newspapers before and during the strike asserted and reasserted in various direct forms and in various ways of implication that the objects of the strike were 'revolutionary' and 'Bolshevik' and that the strikers were 'disloyal' and 'un-American.' Approximately 300,000 strikers were out during the first fortnight of the strike, but instead of this fact and the conditions and causes which had produced the strike, the Pittsburgh newspapers as well as most of the press of the whole country found space for extracts from the reprint of Foster's 'Syndicalism.'" Foster's book had long been out of print and was now reprinted as anti-union propaganda. The result of it all was the failure of the strike.

The steel strike may be taken as an illustration of the tactics of employers generally in capitalizing the internal feuds of organized labor and the irrational wartime hatred of Germans, Bolsheviks, foreigners, and radicals then dominating public opinion.

But while organized labor failed to make advances, it generally held its trenches. There was for a time widespread unemployment, there was a decline in union membership, and ultimately there was a recession in territory covered by trade agreements, notably in soft-coal mining and railway shop crafts. But during the early post-war offensive of capital against unionism, labor held its main lines of defense. Union rates per hour (counting 100 for 1913 as a base) fell from 205 in 1921 to 195 in 1922, but thereafter advanced, and hours per week were somewhat shortened. If the early post-war offensive of labor in unorganized industries was unsuccessful, so was the onset of capital against labor in the organized plants.

In the meantime there was a flank attack on unionism in the form of the "company union." This was not unknown before the war, but was mainly a post-war product. It has been estimated that by 1919 145 companies had organized 200 councils for about 400,000 men. By 1926, the number of companies had grown to 430, the number of councils to 915, and the number of workers affected to 1,400,000.

There were many variations but certain traits were common to the several forms. Most of them granted to the workers only an advisory power or the right of consultation, decision being left to the management. A few included the privilege of submitting an ultimate issue to arbitration. A few extended the right of minority representation on the board of trustees. In general, the officials of a company union were required to be employees of the company, which thereby automatically had power of life or death, economically speaking, over the representatives of the employees. Significant, too, was the fact that since employees only could ordinarily serve as officials, the company union was deprived of the services of specialists devoting their entire time to the technical problems of the employment contract and its administration. Ordinarily, there was no arrangement for enabling one shop council to maintain contacts with other councils of the same company. Still more rarely was it possible for the councils of one company to maintain organic relations with the councils of another company in the same industry. Powers of the company union were generally of an advisory nature only, and even the advisory powers were limited to such problems as hours, working conditions, shop rules, and in a few instances the readjustment of wage scales. The wider field of responsibility for formulating and carrying out general business policies was usually ignored alike by trade unions and by company unions. And yet a rational handling of the labor problem even in its narrower aspects requires an understanding of the general problems of business policy. This larger aspect of industrial responsibility involves in turn the ownership of industry, the legal powers of owners, and the limitations imposed on proprietary powers by public policy.

Slight as was the authority or responsibility of the trade union in connection with joint conferences and trade agreements, there was obviously a recession, in the company union, from working-class responsibility. Some company unions were formed in unorganized industries to overcome the apathy of the workers and perhaps even to arouse the workers to a sense of responsibility as a prelude to the exercise of responsibility. But unquestionably the company union movement was in large measure a flank attack on independent unionism for undermining the power of organized labor.

Nor was the flank attack on the older unionism confined to the use of the company union. Employers learned in wartime and during the post-war efforts to cut down wages that relatively high wages were not always incompatible with large dividends. There emerged the idea of granting relatively high wages and short hours on a non-union basis as a part of a system of "prosperity" in which the workers would consider unionism a useless pother. Methods of maintaining or increasing profits other than by reducing wages were emphasized. Mass production was developed, especially in the automobile industry, and extended to various industries. The detailed study of the technique of production, beginning with F. W. Taylor's system of "scientific management" in 1895, and extended in actual use by such men as Henry Ford, led to the more efficient use of man power and machinery. The elimination of waste in labor, in materials, in marketing, in the various processes of production, became almost a cult. Higher wages and shorter hours were justified not only as methods of promoting efficiency and reducing labor turnover but as well on the ground that workers would spend their money in buying and their leisure in using additional consumption goods. Men began to think in terms of an endless cycle of expansion—more wages, more demand for goods, more output, more profits. Supplementary methods were devised for keeping the workers contented: propaganda; welfare work; the company union for airing grievances and serving as a sort of safety valve; sale of shares of stock, resulting in the workers thinking of themselves as capitalists. Tied up with the idea of "organizing prosperity" was the exclusion of foreign competition in the labor market by limiting immigration and in the commodity markets by keeping out foreign goods.

There was little attempt to rationalize the new tactics; but by implication if not in the form of explicit statements, there were certain underlying assumptions. It was commonly held, by employers, that the ordinary worker was not interested in taking on himself any of the burdens of responsibility for industrial policy, or in working out any socially equitable sharing of the product of industry beyond the necessary costs of production, but that his interest extended only to holding a "good job" and having a "good time." It was assumed, in the second place, that the employer's interest included the maintenance of good wages and short hours in order to have contented and prosperous and therefore efficient workers. On the basis of these two assumptions, it was further held that there is a fundamental harmony of interests between employers as autocratic but benevolent rulers of business and employees as efficient and obedient workers.

Whether or not the assumptions were valid, the new tactics resulted in a remarkable degree of acquiescence and complacency on the part alike of employees and of those who were not directly concerned with the labor problem. But there were critics of the new tactics and of the assumptions underlying them. Even granting the validity of the assumptions in times of prosperity and expansion, is it possible even for "organized prosperity" to escape occasional periods of recession and adversity? It was held that ultimately the European nations would recover from their post-war depression, and that the backward oriental and Latin-American peoples would emerge from their apprenticeship in modern technology and business organization. Competition, it was believed, would become increasingly keen. Restrictive immigration laws and protective tariffs were viewed as likely in the long run to defeat their own ends by causing retaliation abroad and higher prices at home, demoralizing international relations and domestic politics, and diverting enterprise into uneconomic channels. The savings accompanying mass production, elimination of waste, etc., could hardly be expected to make possible an indefinitely continued simultaneous expansion of profits and wages, especially after the general adoption of such methods in competing countries. Conventional forms of finance were stabilized by the Federal Reserve System; but installment buying and stock-market speculation might at any moment get out of hand. In a word, it was held that from various causes even "organized prosperity" would sooner or later meet with reverses.

In a time of adversity, can autocratic employers reasonably be expected to reconcile their ideas of high wages and contented workmen with "good business"? They will naturally try to hold their losses in check by lowering wages or at least by reducing the number of their employees in preference to allowing profits and dividends to suffer. In other words, the pressure of adversity will follow the line of least resistance—employment and wages must bear the brunt of adversity unless the workers retain their power through organized effort to withstand reductions.

During the ensuing period of conflict between employers and workers, what may be expected of the workers? Individually irresponsible, and without organizations or with organizations having no authority, they may be expected to do one of two things. It is conceivable that they will yield with docility and bear as best they can the chief burdens of hard times in the form of lowered wages or unemployment. But accustomed as they have been to some of the amenities of life, this is hardly likely, and certainly from their own point of view hardly a desirable sequel to irresponsibility, however prosperous. The thing that they are most likely to do, after the manner of irresponsible people when subjected to stress and strain, is to strike out wildly and become riotous if not revolutionary—a sequel to autocratic prosperity hardly desirable from the employer's point of view. In hard times, employee stock ownership and bonuses will sharpen instead of dull the edge of discontent, for supplementary income, then most needed, will be cut off.

But even during the high tide of the so-called "Coolidge and Hoover" prosperity, workers were confronted with many problems calling for responsible concerted action impossible on the part of company unions. One of the gravest of these was the insurance problem. Efficiency, it is said, is bringing prosperity. But efficient machinery often means fewer workers. The younger man is supposedly more efficient than the older, and so in the name of efficiency the older men are more likely to be supplanted by machines. In the name of the same efficiency, the older man is more likely to be denied employment elsewhere. Even the corporate insurance plans for accident and sickness benefits and old-age pensions aggravate the problem they are supposed to solve. Premiums on group insurance policies, covering in 1929 about six million workers, were paid by the employers. The younger the employee, the lower is the premium. The tendency is toward the hiring of younger men when more men are needed and toward the firing of older men when fewer men are needed. Thus it comes about that after forty it is increasingly dangerous for a worker to lose his job or to hazard a change of jobs. Even if there is no threat of unemployment, a change of jobs means loss of insurance rights, and thus insurance administered by the employer becomes an instrument for the control of the employee. Here are some of the gravest of social problems, which the policy of employers aggravates and which the view of politicians hardly comprehends—until the workers by concerted action force the issue.

Autocratic control of business by employers and irresponsible acquiescence by employees entails present costs and future dangers which rational students of industry can hardly view with complacency. Possibly the cure for the ills of irresponsibility in industry as well as in politics is more responsibility. Possibly certain bold labor leaders may after all be on the side of social wisdom in looking even beyond the trade agreement and viewing labor organizations as "the germs of the future organization of industry as a whole."

PART VIII

THE NATION AND THE WORLD

CHAPTER XXIV

NATIONAL ECONOMY

MERGING OF SECTIONS AND SHIFTING OF CLASSES

The Civil War joined the sections and classes of America into a more or less artificial unity. But with the nationalizing of technology, capital, and labor, there was a fusion of sections and a flux of classes which resulted in a national consolidation far more effective than the forcible union of the victors and the vanquished.

The main features of latter-day technology are mechanized industry and mass production. The technological changes already discussed [1] were rapidly extended over the country. New mechanized industries, as automobile making, came into being. Old industries not much affected by the early industrial revolution, as agriculture, began their metamorphoses. Wherever mass production was carried on, it transformed the immediate vicinity by its concentration of capital and labor and its control of the inflow of materials and outflow of goods. Remoter regions became tributary to the centers of mass production by furnishing supplies and labor and affording markets for the vending of the output of mass-production technique, whether Chicago packing-house meats or Detroit automobiles or New York periodicals or Hollywood moving pictures.

Mass production called for a national market. The larger the output and the more rapid the turnover, the smaller

[1] See above, ch. 21.

need be the margin of profit. In machinery of all kinds, the producer's propaganda for a national market was readily effective because of the advantages of standardized and interchangeable parts and service facilities connected with replacements and repairs. By means of radio broadcasting chains and of periodicals with national circulation, the establishment of a national market became possible not only for meeting existing wants but for gratifying wants created by the advertiser. On a scale of numbers and territorial extent unprecedented in history, people throughout America began to experience the same economic wants and to gratify them by using the same standardized commodities.

Mass production with a national market was made possible by business organizations on a national scale. Corporations were formed with shares bought and sold by brokers everywhere, and with factories, distributing centers, and marketing facilities in the leading cities, north, south, east, and west.

Labor organizations became national in membership, and labor became so mobile as to shift with ease from region to region. With the mechanizing of labor and the standardizing of jobs, there was a shifting of workers from industry to industry as well as from region to region. The mobility of labor; the interchange of ideas as to the management of labor; and the standardizing and regimentation of labor under machine technique, mass production, and national markets: such influences resulted in an equalizing of wages and labor conditions in the several sections. Finally, there was a diffusion of capitalistic psychology among employees as well as consumers by the direct extension of stock ownership and its indirect extension by insurance companies, savings banks, and other agencies.

The natural differences between Mississippi, Massachusetts, Kentucky, and Montana are obviously the same as during the earlier history of the country. These differences mean a permanent sectionalizing of important activities. Modern man works wonders, but an interchange of the shipping and fisheries of Massachusetts and the cotton plantations of Mississippi, or of the blue-grass industries of Kentucky and the wheat plantations and cattle ranges of Montana, is obviously beyond his power. At the same time, the natural traits which differentiate the sections are now but trivial obstructions in the way of economic and cultural consolidation, whereas formerly they were almost insurmountable obstacles. Reverting to the figure of the crucible, the sectional economies are being fused in the crucible of industry into a politico-economic amalgam.

Alabama and Pennsylvania have been differentiated by nature. But there is a wider cleavage between the owners of factories and foundries and the "hands" who work in them, whether in Pittsburgh or in Birmingham, than between the two states. In the crucible of industry, the sections fuse more readily than the classes. But comparative national solidarity has been effected without a fusion of classes. This has been largely due to the remarkable fluidity of classes, and to the almost universal hope of getting out of one's own class into a more prosperous one—by the route of education and the professions, or of advancement in business, or of stock market speculations, or of a lucky break.

When the frontier no longer lured men westward, and when large business units under management of corporations were rising rapidly on every hand in the closing decades of the nineteenth century, it was thought that class lines would at last be sharply drawn. But invention, new resources, rise of towns, and growth of service industries (as those created by the automobile) opened up new opportunities for wealth and power far outrivaling the frontier. The restrictions on immigration eased the tension of working-class fears of unemployment. Mass production lowered prices and enabled the workers, in imitation of millionaires, to ride in automobiles, to wear what passed for silks and furs and diamonds, to see (in the "movies") and hear (in the "talkies") the stars of the stage, and to read in the national periodicals the same edifying stories of the heart throbs of the rich heroine and the poor hero (or *vice versa*), of poor boys who made good, and of the beneficence of big business. The sale of stocks and bonds in small denominations to employees and consumers, whatever may have been its results in adding to the income of the working classes, was not without considerable effect in making every man psychologically a capitalist.

Classes and sections remain. But in the crucible of industry they have not prevented the creation of a new national amalgam.

GEOGRAPHICAL DISPERSION OF CAPITALISTIC INDUSTRY

National fusion in the crucible of industry, while not dependent on the nation-wide dispersion of the actual plants of capitalistic industry, was undoubtedly promoted thereby. One of the most obvious instances of the dispersion of capitalistic enterprise in remoter regions is lumbering. In 1889 the output of board feet in the United States was 23,842,000,000; in 1925, 38,339,000,000. In the areas extending from Maine to Minnesota and from Kentucky to Missouri, there was a rapid decline amounting in many states to virtual extinction. The net gain resulted from the rapid expansion of lumbering in the southern states and the far northwest.

From equally obvious causes, the petroleum industry shifted from Pennsylvania to western areas of the Appalachian field and extended to successively discovered pools till seven distinct major fields were simultaneously being exploited, from Pennsylvania to California and from Louisiana to Montana. By virtue of the remarkable deposits of iron in the Lake Superior region, and of the perfecting of transportation facilities, the iron of that region formed an increasing proportion of the country's total. By 1913, about 50,000,000 tons, out of a total of less than 62,000,000, came from the Lake Superior deposits, and the proportion was later increased. This meant a remarkable localization of iron mining, but in a remote area not adapted, as were older mining regions, to smelting and the fabrication of iron. In consequence the iron ores, with some pig iron, were shipped from the mining region and dispersed over widely scattered areas for the various later stages of manufacture. Of the 392,250 tons of bauxite (from which aluminum is made) mined in the United States in 1926, 371,570 tons were produced in the state of Arkansas. As in the case of the Lake Superior iron ores, the processes of reduction and manufacture were dispersed.

These and similar instances of capitalistic industry in remoter regions have obvious explanations in the character and location of natural resources. In the case of manufacturing industries the dispersion is less pronounced, and there has been a tendency for raw materials, as of mines and oil wells, to find their way to the older manufacturing centers. The continued concentration of manufacturing on or near the northeastern seaboard is illustrated by the fact that in 1925 the New England states and New York, New Jersey, and Pennsylvania utilized almost two-fifths of the primary horsepower of the entire country devoted to manufacturing, while their population was hardly two-sevenths of the total. But the rate of increase in these states was much less rapid during recent decades than in some other sections of the country, notably the automobile-producing states, the textile centers of the south, and the states of the

Pacific coast. By 1890, Illinois had taken third place among the states in gross value of manufactures.

Although many influences operated in favor of the older eastern manufacturing centers, the economic advantages of newer regions became so apparent as to attract a large proportion of the newer industries (as the making of motor cars) and of the newer establishments of the older industries (as cotton spinning). The principal factors affecting the location of industrial establishments are connected with the quality and costs of labor, of power, and of raw materials; taxes and other features of public policy; and accessibility to consumers' markets. The basic problem of the manufacturer is to reduce to a minimum the various costs extending from the construction of his plant to the vending of the consumption goods.

Efforts to solve this problem have accounted largely for the geographical dispersion of manufacturing. The automobile industry was established strategically between supplies of iron and of coal and in a region not far distant from the center of the consumers' market. Cotton spinning has tended to migrate to the source of the raw material and at the same time to seek the supposed advantages of low taxes, cheap labor, and abundant power. In 1890, New England had 10,934,000 active cotton spindles and the southern states had 1,570,000. In 1926, New England had 15,526,000 and the south had 17,574,000. Petroleum refineries have tended to follow the course of the drillers. Meat packing and by-product factories have followed the ranges and the stock yards from Cincinnati to St. Louis, Chicago, Omaha, and Fort Worth. Paper making has shifted, with the use of wood pulp in place of rags, from the textile centers and the great cities to the evergreen forests of Maine, New York, Wisconsin, and remoter regions. Portland cement, which was long confined in the main to the Lehigh valley, responded at length to the consumers' markets and the supplies of cheap fuel and materials in the south and west. The Lehigh valley mills, which, in 1887, had produced three-fourths of the country's total output, accounted for hardly more than a fourth in 1914, and there was a later decline in the proportionate output of the Lehigh valley region.

The discovery of rich coal veins remote from older manufacturing centers, and the invention of devices for transforming both water power and coal into electric energy, have led to innumerable industrial shifts in quest of cheaper power. The use of electric power in textile mills began in the 'nineties, and during the following decade it became a prominent factor in the dispersion of textile manufacturing, especially in the south. The generating of electric power has itself given an industrial tone to regions which would otherwise have remained agricultural if not in a state of nature. But far more important is the rise of power-using industries in the vicinity of generating plants. With the enlarging radius of economical transmission, the area of industrialization has rapidly expanded. These effects have been particularly noteworthy in the south and the middle west. Between 1907 and 1922 there was nearly a seven-fold increase in the number of kilowatt hours generated in the country as a whole. But in such widely separated areas as Ohio, Michigan, Wisconsin, Iowa, Virginia, Texas, Idaho, and most of the southern states, this rate of increase was far exceeded.

In the unifying and nationalizing of the country, politically and economically, there has probably been no factor more influential than the almost universal possession, actual or anticipated, of factories, mines, oil wells, power plants, or other forms of capitalistic business. Even in remoter villages there has existed a credulous faith in the prosperity-inducing magic of a shoe factory or a pickling plant even when lured within the village bounds by a burdensome bonus raised by local subscriptions. This faith has been a powerful solvent, psychologically speaking, of differences between north and south, city and country, capitalist and wage worker, Wall Street and Main Street.

OLDER INDIVIDUALISTIC INDUSTRIES IN THE CRUCIBLE

In farming, the most widely diffused, the most fundamental and the most conservative of all industries, there have been conflicting tendencies which are at the heart of the modern "farm problem." The early colonial New England village and the fateful plantation of the south each involved cooperative and communal features. But the ideal generally and persistently upheld in America has been the independent farmstead owned and operated by an extremely individualistic farmer, aided by his family, with possibly a hired "hand" or two. This ideal was responsible for the transformation of the older land policy into the homestead system. It was responsible for the development of a system of governmental financial aid to farmers. From 1916 to 1926, the Federal Land Banks made loans to about 400,000 persons on farms averaging about 180 acres in size, the loans averaging about $3,000. There has arisen and flourished in America, especially in the cities, a veritable cult—the cult of "the independent farmer."

But the farmer who fails to shake off a conception that fittingly attended the bygone self-sufficing economy of the frontier is finding that his individualism is an increasingly costly luxury and that his independence is largely confined to an obsolescent or a spurious literature which feeds the fancies of discontented city dwellers.

With the passing of the frontier and its free land, with the rise of cities and the capitalizing of the unearned increment, and especially with the abnormal demand for farm products combined with monetary inflation during the World War, the prices of farm land rose so high as to make farming a capitalistic and often a speculative enterprise. In 1900 the value of farm land was about $13,000,000,000. During the decade from 1900 to 1910, its value more than doubled, and during the two decades from 1900 to 1920, more than quadrupled. But during the succeeding five years —the years of monetary and market deflation—the values declined from $54,800,000,000 to $37,700,000,000.

It is true that when prices of farm land are correlated with general price changes, it is found that after 1925 there was a slight gain in the average price of farm land per acre. But there is no interpretation of changes in the values of farm lands that enables one to escape the conclusion that farming is expensive and hazardous, and that its rewards, other than a precarious existence, are going increasingly to those who make it not "a way of living" but a capitalistic business articulated intelligently with other phases of modern economy. This conclusion is the more inevitable when one considers the development of scientific agricultural technology. The farmer's utilization of the new technique requires an increasingly long and costly training and an ever greater outlay for machinery, fertilizers, better breeds of plants and animals, and similar essentials of improved farming. In a word, the individualistic ideology and habits of a large proportion of the farming population are in conflict with the agricultural revolution, which is the latest phase of the industrial revolution.

The older ideology and habits go back to the time of subsistence farming. The main aim of the farmer was to extract the essentials of a living from his farm, buying few goods and selling any surpluses incidental to the supplying of his own requirements. The first breaches in subsistence farming were made by the extension of transportation facilities to the farming regions, giving access to markets. Then came the invention of farm machinery and the revolution in its manufacture by means of the technological changes in the making of iron and steel and in the processes of mass production. The average value per farm of farm implements and machinery in 1890 was $108; in 1925 (after price deflation and increases in the number of market gardens classed as farms but using little machinery), $422. During the second decade of the present century the number of horses and mules on the farms remained virtually constant at about 25,000,000 in spite of the rapid increase of farm population and of land in cultivation. Since 1920 the number declined till in 1927 it approximated the number in 1890—about 17,500,000. It has been estimated that during the decade following the World War, the number of tractors increased almost tenfold, from 80,000 to 767,000. A chart prepared by Mr. Arthur Huntington of the American Society of Agricultural Engineers reveals the fact that the primary power used in agriculture per agricultural worker rose from a base of 100 in 1850 to 200 in 1890 and to 225 in 1910. During the single decade from 1910 to 1920, with the rapid introduction of the tractor, of electricity, and of other forms of power, Mr. Huntington's chart line of primary power rises with dizzy abruptness from 225 to 330. As might be expected, a statistical study reveals the fact that in general the variations in the horse-power per agricultural worker are approximately the same as the variations in value of crops per agricultural worker.

The advantages of mechanized and large-scale farming are apparent from some typical agricultural contrasts. On adjacent farms in Iowa, with approximately the same quality of soil, the cost of producing a bushel of corn in 1923 was in one case fifteen cents and in the other, seventy-five cents. In the corn belt corn planters are used which plant four rows at a time and cover forty acres in a day. Power-drawn cultivators are used. One of these "rotary hoes" is described as having "twenty-nine revolving wheels, each of which carries sixteen points, which make 464 ground punctures per six feet of travel. Those that carry seven-foot sections, tractor drawn, cover fifty to sixty acres per day." Later stages are also mechanized, as by harvesters for cutting and binding the corn, and by the power devices used in connection with putting the corn into silos. By such methods there has been, in places, a reduction from sixty man-hours to five man-hours per year per acre.

From 1910 to 1925 the number of apple trees is estimated to have declined 36 per cent, but the output increased. The farm orchard gave place to the large commercial orchard, with a large initial outlay and requiring expert supervision and costly equipment for spraying, pruning, etc., and for marketing the fruit.

In Iowa, which is a relatively progressive farm state, the production of eggs per hen is about fifty as compared with 140 to 200 on the commercialized farms of the regions which specialize in poultry. In these regions, it has been shown that with mechanical feeding and watering arrangements and power devices, one man can handle flocks of 10,000, as compared with a maximum of 1,500 without the specialized equipment.

After the Civil War, there was a tendency in the south toward the breakup of plantations into small farms. The new revolution in the cotton country means, among other things, a renaissance of large-scale farming but under conditions radically different from those prevailing in the time of slavery. There are tractor-drawn machines for planting and cultivating cotton, for dusting or spraying it against boll weevils and other pests, and for harvesting it. Even the aeroplane has been used for dusting cotton. There is new machinery for removing burs and cleaning the lint in the ginning process, thereby making practicable the use of mechanical pickers or harvesters. In a portion of Texas where hand-picking was reported as costing $15 per bale, mechanical harvesting, still in an experimental stage, reduced the cost to $2.78 per bale.

Compare the hand scythe or cradle for cutting and the hand flail for threshing wheat with the power-operated combined header, thresher, and cleaner, by which an acre of standing wheat can be prepared for market in fifteen minutes. The industrial revolution in urban business affords few contrasts more remarkable.

The use of silos, dairy equipment, fertilizers, and innumerable other costly scientific improvements, as well as expensive machinery, has tended to make farming a large-scale, capitalistic business. Specialized branches of rural business, as dairy products, poultry, sugar cane and sugar beets, rice, and fruits (not only tropical and semi-tropical fruits, as oranges, but the more widely grown fruits, as apples, grapes and peaches) have been particularly susceptible to revolutionary changes. The extension of the farming area to marginal lands requiring irrigation or the draining of swamps has commonly been on a capitalistic basis. Still another factor in making farming a business rather than a "way of living" has been the enlargement of the market. This resulted from transportation facilities, the rapid growth of cities, refrigeration, the perfecting of canning and preserving processes, and the building of food factories.

The market problem illustrates, in fact, a most important phase of the transition from traditional farming to farming as a business. How can the farmer reduce the fluctuations in output and in prices? How can he avoid having to sell his crops at the time of harvesting when prices are depressed by a glutted market? How can he reduce the inequality between agriculture and manufacturing resulting from the manufacturer's market being protected and his own market being controlled by world competition? What is the remedy, if any? Individually he is helpless. Again, there is economic pressure against the traditional system of small-scale, individualistic farming.

All these changes have already had some effect on land tenure and the size of farms. The tendency was long in the direction of independent ownership and operation of small farms. This was accentuated by frontier opportunity, the Homestead Act, the breakup of many southern plantations, and opportunities for market gardening near growing eastern cities. From 1860 to 1880, the average size of farms decreased from 199 to 134 acres. Later the tendency was reversed. The percentage of improved farm land operated by the owners declined from 62.5% in 1910 to 53.7% in 1925. In the regions that are primarily agricultural, the percentage of farmers owning their farms generally declined. In Iowa, the decline was from 65.1% in 1900 to 55.3% in 1925; in South Dakota, from 78.2% to 58.5%; in Arkansas, from 54.6% to 43.3%; in Texas, from 50.3% to 39.6%. In some states, particularly those with large cities, where city dwellers in large numbers have bought a few acres of land and become "amphibians," the figures superficially indicate a tendency toward increased ownership of farms. Owners' equities have declined because of mortgages. In 1920, 29.1% of the total value of mortgaged farms was covered by mortgages. In 1925, 41.9% of the total value of such farms was reported under mortgage. Nor should one overlook the fact that in the meantime foreclosures had put extensive farm properties into the hands of holders of mortgages.

The farmer, in the midst of the agricultural revolution, is

confused and restless. The present small-farm unit is uneconomical for the utilization of machinery and scientific technology and the application of business methods. But there are obvious economic advantages of machinery and scientific technology and business methods in the reduction of labor and other costs, in the increase of output alike in quantity and quality, and in the solution of marketing problems. There are certain tendencies that appear to be inescapable. The production and marketing of agricultural goods is increasingly controlled by those who use the new technique. The use of the new technique is increasingly beyond the reach of the individualistic, small-scale farmer. The individualistic, small-scale farmer is necessarily giving place either to the cooperative small-scale farmer or to the large-scale individual farmer, or to the agricultural corporation controlling either plantations or "chain" farms after the manner of the "chain-store" corporations.

Socially, the advantages are overwhelmingly with small-scale cooperative farming. Can individualistic farmers overcome their aversion to cooperation? Or will they struggle against the rising tide till presently they drift afield as farm "hands" just as the earlier craftsmen became mill "hands"? In any case there is not room in the new system for all of the agricultural population. The surplus farm labor constitutes a social problem which the farmer alone can do little to solve, and which, if rationally handled, must be considered a part of the national, indeed world-wide, problem of stabilizing employment.

NEW INDUSTRIES IN THE CRUCIBLE

The creative power of science in application to business and the unifying force of modern industry find expression nowhere more strikingly than in the establishment of new industries on the basis of newly discovered resources or of newly invented processes for using natural resources. Particularly prominent among these are the food-making, automobile, chemical, and electrical industries.

Packing, milling, brewing, and distilling were early instances of capitalistic industry. But packing was formerly limited to such processes as salting and smoking of meat, especially pork. With the introduction during the 'eighties of ice refrigerators in the packing houses and of refrigerator cars and ships, the packing and long-distance shipment of fresh meats became practicable. Later improvements included the "endless chain" or overhead conveyor, mechanical scrapers, and innumerable devices for mechanizing most of the processes from slaughtering the animal to the shipment of the meat and the by-products of the industry. By-products have become increasingly important since the rise of applied chemistry, as is evidenced by the fact that about fifty pharmaceutical products are supplied by packing houses.

Associated with packing but more significantly with other phases of food preparation, was the evolution of canning processes. Mechanical heating and sterilizing devices, mechanical preparation of fruits and vegetables, mechanical sealers, scientific control of the various processes, and can-making machinery—these were the principal changes which led to a rapid expansion in the output of canned fruits, vegetables, and soups till in 1925 the value of the output of factories with products worth $5,000 or more totaled more than $600,000,000.

Other instances of new industries are to be found in the rapidly developing chemical and electrical fields. Electrical machinery, apparatus and supplies, which, at the end of the last century, hardly equalled in value a hundred million dollars, mounted in value during the first quarter of the present century till in 1925 they totaled $1,653,550,000. The

Federal Radio Commission estimated that in 1928 there were 12,000,000 radio receiving sets in use.

New chemical processes have given rise to thousands of new commodities. A characteristic instance is rayon, earlier known as artificial silk. Rayon became commercially important after the World War, with an output increasing from less than 22,000,000 pounds in 1921 to about 110,000,000 pounds in 1928. Rayon, like innumerable other synthetic products of modern chemistry, is derived from cellulose. The main sources of cellulose are wood and cotton. The making of rayon gave rise to a new spinning process, by which the cellulose solution is driven through a nozzle with tiny holes and solidified as thread by contact with acidulated water.

Among the notable indirect creations of chemistry is the aluminum industry. Before 1852, the cost of reducing aluminum ores was so great that a pound of aluminum was valued at $500. In that year the cost was so greatly reduced by the chemical researches of Deville that the price of aluminum fell to $11 per pound. Further studies led to a reduction in price in 1888 to $4 per pound. Later still an electro-metallurgical process put the reduction of aluminum ores on a commercial basis. Aluminum first appears in official statistics for the year 1883, when the output was 83 pounds. In 1925 the domestic output of bauxite, the basic ore, and imports of bauxite for consumption, totaled 670,000 long tons.

The control of the aluminum industry early passed into the hands of a single organization, the Aluminum Company of America. Its position was fortified by its control of outstanding deposits, by tariffs, by technological knowledge and experience, and by numerous subsidiary companies at home and abroad for controlling deposits, power sites, reduction plants, and market relations throughout the world.

The aluminum industry is interesting because it typifies

the rapid rise of new industries of the modern type. It is also an instance of the interdependence of modern economy. Its ramifications are not merely nation-wide; they are world-wide. Its connection with other industries is illustrated by the fact that changes in the output of aluminum have maintained a remarkable correlation with changes in the automobile industry. From forty to fifty per cent of aluminum has been used in the construction of automobiles, with aircraft also using large quantities.

Even more intimately connected with the automobile industry are the rubber and the petroleum industries. During the first quarter of the century the value of rubber goods increased from about $100,000,000 to about $1,250,000,000, and of this gigantic output, approximately three-fourths consisted, in value, of automobile tires, tubes, and accessories.

Before the rise of the automobile industry, petroleum was chiefly valuable in the form of kerosene for light and fuel. Gasoline was then regarded as a virtually useless by-product in the making of kerosene. In 1926 the refineries of the country produced 12,588,828,000 gallons of gasoline, mainly for consumption in automobiles. The production of kerosene amounted to only 2,594,256,000 gallons—less than a fourteenth of oil consumed, as compared with more than a third in the case of gasoline. Lubricants made from petroleum and used largely in automobiles amounted in the same year (1926) to 1,356,306,000 gallons.

The automobile industry, on which so many other industries depend for their phenomenal expansion if not for their existence, is itself the most spectacular and important of all the newer industries. The four automobiles in the United States in 1895 had increased within three decades to nearly 20,000,000; three years later, in 1928, the number of passenger cars and motor trucks registered in the

United States was 24,592,370; and in the following year production reached a new high level. The remarkable rise of the automotive industries has already been discussed.[1] The automobile is probably the most important single factor in the merging of sections, the shifting of classes, and the creation of a unified economic nationalism.

THE REVOLUTION IN SERVICE INDUSTRIES AND MERCHANDIZING

A generation ago, a person who travelled in the horse-drawn vehicles of that age and was unfortunate enough to have a breakdown was not likely to find it so serious as the fatal ending of the wonderful one-hoss shay, but he had need of both patience and ingenuity. If the accident too greatly taxed his skill and the resources available at the moment, a blacksmith, a woodworker, or other skilled craftsman was called upon to repair the damage by making a new part or perhaps by sending to the factory in a distant city. The coming of the automobile and of other standardized machinery wrought a revolution in the service industries. The old-fashioned skilled mechanics, with forges, lathes, and other devices, and with an age-old heritage of mechanical lore and manual dexterity, were supplanted by garage keepers and dealers in interchangeable parts.

As early as 1920 there were more than 42,000 garage keepers and managers. Filling stations, their ungainly shapes vieing with their gaudy colors for the attention of the motorist, were to be found at every crossroad as well as on the city streets. To be able to buy the same brand of gasoline or tire or battery and to replace a broken or worn-out part with an exact duplicate of the original, whether one is in Baltimore or Seattle; in Turtle Creek, Pennsylvania; Ranger, Texas; Red Wing, Minnesota; or Modesto,

[1] See above, pp. 332, 333, 336.

California,—this fact is a symbol of a truly revolutionary change in American economy and American society.

The service stations for motorists were originally owned for the most part by the individuals who operated them. The larger oil producing and refining companies later established stations of their own. By 1925 they sold about one-fifth of their output of gasoline direct to consumers by means of their own stations. In 1926 the larger companies reported ownership of 13,644 stations.

This tendency is symptomatic of a general revolution in merchandizing. In market and fair, producers and consumers met and made direct interchange. Long prominent in the distributive system were the pedlar; the cross-roads country storekeeper; the tailor, the cobbler, and other craftsmen with their shops; agents of manufacturers, who took retail orders (as for lightning rods); and shopkeepers who handled the residue of goods produced in factories and often acted as agents for the sale of country produce. With the rapid shift to factory-made goods after the Civil War, larger shops with many varieties of goods (department stores as they came to be called) came into increasing prominence. Pioneers were A. T. Stewart and R. H. Macy in New York, John Wanamaker in Philadelphia, and Marshall Field in Chicago.

In the field of specialized shops, as grocery stores, the small shopkeeper, owning and managing the shop, long withstood the encroachments of big business. But in the early years of the present century the small independent shopkeeper began to retreat before the onslaughts of the chain-store owners. One of the earliest successes of the chain-store idea was not in the field of the specialized commodity shop but of the specialized price shop—the 5-and-10-cent stores with their later variations. In the small towns, department stores often came under the control of large companies operating chains of stores. The specialized commodity stores that formed most successful chain systems were those that handle groceries, drugs, men's apparel, shoes, candy, and tobacco. In spite of falling prices, the sales by grocery, candy, and 5-and-10-cent chains more than doubled in value between 1920 and 1926; and other chains made rapid gains. Chain-store sales in 1928 increased in value, in the different groups, from 1.6 per cent to 18.2 per cent over sales in 1927.

Nearly all of the distinctive features of the postoffice—postal money orders, free delivery, special delivery, rural delivery, sorting of mail in transit, cheap standardized postal rates, and parcel post—came into existence since the closing years of the Civil War. The most important innovations, from the point of view of the country's merchandising system, were probably rural free delivery, inaugurated in 1897, and the parcel-post system, which was effectively organized during President Wilson's first administration. With these changes, the mail-order houses were enabled to take a major part in the retail distributive system. The great mail-order houses, notably Sears, Roebuck and Company and Montgomery Ward and Company, became the most widely and familiarly known of all business institutions. Before the days of the parcel-post system they had developed an extensive business by means of freight and express shipments, but their later expansion resulted largely from rural free delivery and parcel post.

Department stores, chain stores, and mail order houses compete in a measure with each other. But there are certain large areas of the retail distributive field which can most economically be occupied by each. Moreover, the nature of the competition is affected by the overlapping of interests, by mergers of various kinds of enterprises under the same general management, and by interlocking directorates.

Far more important than the competition between the different types of large-scale enterprises is the retreat of the small shopkeeper and independent retailer before the advance of big business in the distributive industries. Whatever may be the advantages of the old system, the fact remains that consumers were attracted not only to nationally advertised goods of standardized appearance and quality but to stores of more than merely local reputation and patronage. It is held by some that local responsibility, patriotism, taste, and initiative suffer. But whatever may be the controverted results, good or bad, it is apparent that the revolution in merchandising is a part of the process by which America has been put through the unifying crucible of industry.

HOUSEHOLD INDUSTRY IN THE CRUCIBLE

After the spinning wheel and the hand loom had passed even from the attics of the older homesteads, the typical home continued to retain important economic functions. These functions were exercised in the primitive manner of the older household industry that centered around the wheel and the loom. But at last the industrial revolution not only deprived the home of most of its economic functions but transformed the technique of its few remaining economic activities.

For various phases of household work, substitutes outside of the home were found, as restaurant and hotel service and the foods prepared in canning, preserving, packing, and delicatessen establishments. The worries of blue Monday, the traditional wash day, were dissolved in commercial laundries. Tailoring duties were relieved by factory-made apparel. The work of supplying light, water, and sometimes even heat was taken over by public utilities corporations operating central plants.

The remnant of work required in the home was mechanized in large degree. Automatic gas and electric appliances range all the way in action from making coffee by switching on the electric coffee percolator on rising in the morning to tuning in the bedtime slumber music on the radio. Even home amusements are no longer homemade but machine-made and standardized. The dance tunes of the national radio advertising "hookups" (to which dance in standardized "makeups" and costumes the inhabitants of New York and Seattle and of points between) have a sameness which reminds one of the indistinguishable qualities of the products advertised.

CULTURE, INC.

The triumphant advance of modern industrialism brought successively under its régime the various phases of transportation, mining and other basic industries, the principal secondary manufactures, the more successful farming operations, merchandising and service industries, household work, and finally, the realm of culture.

Modern schools are factories. Room after room alike. Rows of desks fastened to the floor in geometrical precision. Standardized text books. Rigid methods in application to all students of a given grade or class. Regimentation of students by teachers; regimentation of teachers by principal and superintendent; regimentation of supervisors by the community; regimentation of the community by the routine of the machine and by the ideas and patterns of behavior fixed by the masters or would-be masters of machine-made wealth and power. Such is the picture, with many notable exceptions, of mass education in America. Boards of trustees and superintendents and presidents of public institutions are primarily business men (unless politicians). Private educational institutions are big business enterprises, holding stocks and bonds and real estate and spending in many cases many millions of dollars annually.

Closely associated with education is the world of sport. But whether academic or extramural, it has been rapidly transformed, within a few decades, from friendly individualistic games to gigantic competitive conflicts, involving business arrangements and financial operations comparable to other great industries. An early indication of the trend was the development of the Cincinnati Red "Stockings" into a successfully managed professional baseball club in the decade following the Civil War. Professional baseball was organized on a national basis in 1876, when the National League was formed. It is to the 'seventies and 'eighties that various other national sporting activities and organizations are traceable, as the National Association of Amateur Athletes, the Intercollegiate Athletic Association, the Rowing Association of American Colleges, the Kentucky Derby, the Intercollegiate Football Association, the United States Lawn Tennis Association, and the League of American Wheelmen.

How odd to a later generation is the Harvard announcement in 1874 of a football game with McGill University with a fifty-cent admission for the purpose of helping to entertain the visiting team. Even more curious is the statement of policy of a religious institution in 1872 as quoted by Stuart Chase in his notable chapter on play in Professor Beard's *Whither Mankind:* "We prohibit play in the strongest terms. . . . Let this rule be observed with the strictest necessity; for those who play when they are young will play when they are old." Those who are inclined to be ironical concerning the former religious inhibitions may be reminded that the development of sports into big business enterprises has also been effective in restraining the spirit of play. A few participants, "nerve tensed stalwarts," are fighting for money or for the fame of victory; a multitude of spectators are in quest of a thrill or of easy money by betting on the winning horse or man or team; and a business corporation is making handsome profits or an academic corporation is earning money for a bigger and better stadium.

Passing from schools and sport to other phases of contemporary culture, the observer notes the conspicuous places held by the literary products of the east and the artistic output of the west. Printing was one of the earliest of the mechanized industries, but the determination of what the printer should print and of what the reader should read long remained largely an individualistic matter. But syndicated news and feature articles, standardized types of literary entertainment, and mass production of national periodicals with circulation running into the millions,—such tendencies reduced the personal and genuinely creative element of popular literature to a minimum.

Tradition, the glamour of the metropolis, the relatively populous character of the east—such circumstances enabled New York to secure and maintain its primacy in the mass production of standardized literature. But in the field of art described sarcastically by the devotees of the "legitimate" stage as canned art, the west with its climatic advantages built its factories (called studios) and formed its corporations with such surpassing skill as to furnish not merely America but a large part of the world with moving picture reels. It has been estimated that for moving pictures the American public has paid in a single year the sum of $1,500,000,000.

The coming of the radio gave the east with its great electrical establishments an opportunity to weight the scales of mass-production culture in its favor. The making of radio apparatus, as well as of the earlier phonographic devices, has been largely in the east, where also the principal recording is done and whence the principal chain radio programs are broadcast. Both east and west have prospered. East, west, north, and south are edified and entertained by the same syndicated news, the same great national periodicals, the same diverting dance tunes snatched from the air by a turn of the radio dial.

CHAPTER XXV

EMPIRE

WHAT IS IMPERALISM?

In the technical view of the political scientist, the imperial relation is primarily the relation between a governing people and groups that are governed. But imperialism has far transcended political forms and relations. Political equality and national sovereignty may exist in form while at the same time there is economically or in other ways a subordination and therefore in essense an imperial rather than an international relation. Those who are concerned with realities back of appearances will hardly object to classifying the kingdom of Egypt as a part of the British empire or the republics of Cuba and Liberia as parts of the American empire.

THE NEW IMPERALISM

Out of the maritime revolution of the age of discovery arose the succession of empires beginning with the Portuguese in the early sixteenth century, continuing with the Spanish and the Dutch, and finding culmination in the triumph of the English over the French in the Second Hundred Years' War (1689–1815).

During most of the nineteenth century, other peoples were in no position to challenge England's imperial ascendancy. England had the unequaled advantages of the new industrial technique and business organization. The remnants of the Portuguese and Spanish empires which had survived the onslaughts of Holland, France and England were dismembered by the Latin-American revolts and the expansion of the United States. France was humiliated and weakened by the Napoleonic wars and the later revolutions and the disastrous military adventures of Napoleon III. Russia was expanding over the Great Plain of northern Asia, but was backward industrially and politically, and her imperial ambitions to open up windows on the southern seas were readily thwarted by England in alliance with the Turks and others. Germany and Italy were "geographical expressions," not empires, not even national states. America was in possession of vast unsettled areas, was disturbed by uncoordinated economic groups, and was mainly concerned with internal development and unification.

Even Englishmen, though by no means voluntarily giving up any part of their place in the sun, were nevertheless inclined to discredit and even to abandon the older imperialism. With the acquisition of imperial territories there had been formulated the system of mercantilism [1] for regulating and monopolizing the economic enterprises of the empire and for coercing the territories into economic as well as political subordination. Then came the three-fold assault on mercantilism—the rebellion of the American colonies, the rise of the *laissez-faire* economists beginning with the publishing in 1776 of Adam Smith's *Wealth of Nations,* and the demands of the newly risen great industrialists of the machine age for the leveling of economic barriers as obstacles in the way of trade expansion. Englishmen commonly came to hold the view that the all-important objective of public policy was command of markets—of markets for buying food and raw materials

[1] See above, ch. VIII.

and for selling manufactures. Furthermore, it was widely believed that this objective could best be attained not by subordinating foreign territories to British rule but by promoting throughout the world a policy of unrestricted freedom of trade.

Under these circumstances the early modern imperialism with its mercantilistic system of regulation and monopoly was discredited and became decadent. The abandonment of mercantilism, the extension of colonial self-government, and the encouragement of world-wide unrestricted trade relations were policies which apparently were vindicated by an era of unparalleled prosperity.

But the rise of the new imperialism, in which America shared, was not long delayed. France revived and reentered the ring. After a series of revolutions and disastrous military adventures, political stability under control of the bourgeoisie was attained after 1870 in the Third Republic. Already there had been expansion in Africa, and business men increasingly demanded imperial opportunities. By 1870 Germany and Italy had become national states. The economic basis of German unification was laid as early as 1834 in the Zollverein or customs union. The formation of the empire was immediately preceded and followed by the rapid industrializing of Germany. This caused an increasing need for markets and gave point to the Kaiser's demand for a place in the sun and for the fulfillment of Germany's destiny on the sea. Italian unification was attained by the flaming nationalism of Mazzini and Garibaldi and by the astute diplomacy of Cavour. In 1870 Victor Emmanuel captured his own capital from the pope. Then came dreams of ancient imperial glory. The Russian bear came out of hibernation. Pan-Slavism promoted Russian ascendancy over all the Slavs, and over any other peoples whom destiny had placed athwart the Balkan pathway of the Russians in heir quest of warm-water ports. Industrialism, stimulated ›y French capital, was stirring even the sluggish Russians nto abnormal activity and intensifying their age-old desire o break through the barriers between them and the great naritime channels of trade. The Turk, long a sick man, took o bed, and raised acutely the question of disposing of his ›ossessions in the strategic region of the eastern Mediter-anean. The Orient awakened. America came of age; politi-al unity was attained, and infant industries grew to lusty naturity.

Most important of all the factors in the new imperialism vas the loss by England of her monopoly of machine tech-ique and business efficiency. The world was divided into ndustrialized and unindustrialized regions, with the former ountries competing for the control of the latter. Particu-arly important were the tropics. By means of tropical ygiene, modern transportation and communication, and cientific processes (as the vulcanizing of rubber), white nen conquered the tropics and acquired new incentives for he seizure and exploitation of such areas.

In a word, the new imperialism was brought about by wo main factors. Nationalism gave political unity, power, nd ambition. Industrialism directed national energy into mperial channels. In America as in Europe, the fusion of ationalism and industrialism in the latter part of the ineteenth century created the new imperialism.

CONTINENTAL CONSOLIDATION

The expansion of the territory of the United States to ontinental dimensions was at the expense of the Indians nd the Spanish-Americans. By the people of the United tates, this has commonly been viewed as merely a process taking possession of their natural heritage. From the point f view of Indians and of Spanish-Americans, it would probably be described as a form of imperialism, which, in the case of the Indians, was particularly ruthless and destructive.

By the middle of the last century, the control of the continent westward to the Pacific had passed conclusively to the United States. Soon thereafter (in 1867) Alaska was acquired from Russia. Canada remained politically a part of the British empire. But the people, the land, and the economic life north and south of the boundary offered contrasts less extreme than did the people, the land, and the economic life of the northern and southern portions of the United States. A prominent American scholar, noting these conditions, once exclaimed, "Whom God hath joined together, let no man keep asunder." He overlooked a subtle psychological factor (a feeling of unity), which is as essential to the happy political union of peoples as it is to marital felicity. At the same time, Canadian trade was largely with the United States. American branch factories were built in Canada. At the beginning of 1924, American investments in Canada amounted to $2,425,000,000, British investments totaling only $1,890,000,000. Americans owned a controlling interest in a large proportion of the leading manufacturing industries. By 1929, American private investments in Canada are estimated to have grown to $4,120,000,000. American emigrants as well as American capital flowed extensively northward. Much to the discomfiture of Mars, the long stretches of boundary by land, by river, and by lake, were left without defenses. In an economic sense Canada came to be perhaps more significantly a part of the American than of the British empire.

After the mid-century extension of American control to the Pacific, there followed the struggle for political centralization, the building of telegraphs and railroads, the extension of the frontiers westward and eastward till the met and ceased to be, and the merging of sections and classes in the crucible of industry. These developments extended the American horizon to the Caribbean and prepared the way for the first phase of overseas expansion.

THE SOUTHWARD COURSE OF EMPIRE

Long before Americans even reached the region formerly known as the Great American Desert, there was a demand for overseas expansion southward. The first phase was initiated by the settlers beyond the Appalachians in the valleys of the Ohio, Cumberland, and Tennessee rivers. With them, the outstanding question was the free navigation of the Mississippi, which meant in effect the annexation of the lower valley. After the acquisition of Louisiana in 1803, the people of the Great Valley generally faced southward until the railroads bound them to the east. But the undisputed control of the river itself was not thought to be enough. The navigation of the Mississippi was held by many to demand the annexation of Cuba. Its control by America was forecast by John Quincy Adams as early as 1823. Its strategic location in relation to the trade of the Mississippi and the Mexican Gulf, and its charms as the Pearl of the Antilles, continually attracted southward the covetous eyes of Americans.

In the meantime, in 1823, the Monroe Doctrine had been formulated. It was originally designed as a protective measure to check the intervention of European absolutist governments in the new world. It later was developed into a theory justifying American occupation to checkmate Europeans, and into a policy of intervention by the United States in Latin-American countries in connection with loosely defined contingencies supposedly involving a menace to American interests. Since the American government opposed European intervention, and since disturbed conditions often existed, the idea was adopted of the American government assuming an ill-defined measure of responsibility for European as well as American interests in disturbed areas of the western hemisphere.

With the rise of the slavery issue and the struggle for territories for the rival extension of slave labor and free labor, there were many proposals for territorial expansion in various tropical or subtropical areas adapted to slavery. But the Civil War and the abolition of slavery of course put an end to this agitation.

With the acquisition of California and Oregon and their rapid mid-century settlement, interest in an isthmian canal for making possible an all-water route to the west became for a time intense. In the Caribbean region, English interests then predominated. But England condescended, in 1850, in the Clayton-Bulwer treaty, to bind herself not to control or fortify the proposed canal, in return for a similar agreement by the United States and for American recognition of British claims in Honduras. American interest in the canal was soon thereafter diverted by the Civil War, and later by the construction of transcontinental railways, which were long adequate for connecting east and west.

The question of the canal was revived from time to time but the Clayton-Bulwer treaty was an effective obstacle to independent American action. Toward the end of the century a combination of circumstances induced England to consent to a modification of the Clayton-Bulwer treaty in favor of the United States. England's controversy with Venezuela led in 1895 to a remarkable outburst of war spirit in the United States because of England's alleged violation of the Monroe Doctrine. Soon thereafter England was involved in the Fashoda incident with France over control of the Egyptian Sudan. The Boer War further emphasized in the minds of Englishmen their country's diplomatic isolation. The result was a policy of conciliating America by means of the Hay-Pauncefote treaty of 1901, abrogating the Clayton-Bulwer treaty. Specifically, the treaty recognized the primacy of American interests in the isthmian canal. But the larger significance of the treaty was its implied acknowledgment of the results of the Spanish-American War in substituting American for British ascendancy in the Caribbean region.

TERRITORIAL FRUITS OF MANIFEST DESTINY

"It is beyond question the destiny of our race to spread themselves over the continent of North America. . . . The tide of emigrants will flow to the south, and nothing can eventually arrest its progress." Thus wrote President Buchanan as early as 1858. Such views were held by many throughout the nineteenth century, and were commonly associated with ideas of racial superiority and of the duty to "confer the blessings and benefits" (again quoting Buchanan) of superior civilization on benighted regions. Such naïve egotism found expression first in the virtual extermination of the natives of the continent, and later in the fratricidal conflict for supremacy between rival groups of the "superior" race. But after the Civil War and the fusion of discrete elements in the crucible of industry, there was a revival and an extension of the doctrine of manifest destiny.

Cuba had been the first objective of overseas expansionists in the early years of the century. It was Cuba that precipitated America's formal entry into the arena of the new imperialism.

American intervention in 1898 in the Cuban revolt against Spain was caused by a curious combination of forces. A powerful factor was the blatant journalism of a new type now first capitalizing in a large way the emotional and instinctive responses of the newly discovered general reader. One publisher claimed the doubtful honor of having spent a million dollars for war propaganda. Tales of terror in Cuba fed the minds of millions of readers, and caused proponents of intervention to think of themselves as high-minded deliverers of the oppressed. Joined with altruism and humanitarianism were other motives. War with the Spanish tyrant, in addition to freeing the Cubans (exclaimed a western senator), "would increase the business and the earnings of every American railroad; it would increase the output of every American factory; it would stimulate every branch of American commerce; it would greatly increase the demand for American labor; and in the end, every certificate that represented a share in an American business enterprise would be worth more money than it is today."

There were intimate economic relations between Cuba and the United States before the war. The American secretary of state estimated American investments in Cuba in 1896 at $50,000,000. The Cuban trade engaged at times as much as twenty-five per cent of American shipping devoted to foreign trade. American capital controlled important mining industries, as chromium and manganese, essential to the steel industry, and not found in the United States in readily workable deposits.

The most important of America's economic relations with Cuba were connected with sugar. During the two decades preceding the war, Cuban prosperity had come to be dependent on the American market for sugar. The increasing consumption of sugar in the latter part of the nineteenth century made sugar the principal Cuban industry and led to its capitalistic transformation, with American capital and skill as well as the American market for sugar playing important parts. In 1890 the Spanish government imposed additional restrictions on non-Spanish trade with Cuba. This was followed by an amendment to the McKinley tariff of 1890, threatening the loss by Cubans of their American market for sugar as well as the curtailment of the tobacco market. Spain yielded and reciprocity in trade was arranged. An era of expansion and prosperity ensued in Cuba. But in 1894 the Wilson tariff ended reciprocity, curtailed the American market for Cuban exports, and encouraged Spain to increase the duties on imports into Cuba. The output of Cuban sugar fell from more than a million long tons in 1894 to 225,000 tons in 1896. Thus the economic stage was set for the Cuban revolution, with an acute realization by Cubans of their economic dependence on the United States.

The war of 1898 was begun almost entirely without premeditated purpose of territorial additions by the United States. It resulted, nevertheless, in the founding of an overseas empire. As in the case of the Civil War, which was not directly caused but was none the less effectively utilized by eastern capitalists, so in the case of the Spanish-American War, the business interests were not immediately responsible for precipitating the war but were quick to make use of the imperial opportunities it afforded them.

Cuba itself became a republic. But it was subject not only to the ever-broadening interpretation of the Monroe Doctrine but to specific limitations of sovereignty in its constitution. Before the American army of occupation withdrew, the Cuban constitutional convention was required, as a condition of the withdrawal of the army, to incorporate as a part of the constitution the provisions of the so-called Platt Amendment to the military appropriations bill of 1901–2. The Cubans were required to bind themselves not to allow any other foreign power "any lodgment or control over the said island" for any purpose whatever. The

United States, on the other hand, was to reserve the Isle of Pines and the privilege of buying or leasing naval or coaling stations (a right later exercised, as in the leasing of Guantanamo), and was to have the right of intervening and redirecting the course of Cuban policy. Thus America reserved the potential privileges of sovereignty, political and military, without assuming the direct responsibilities of governmental administration. Thus was fulfilled, somewhat ironically for Cubans, the prophecy of President McKinley in 1899, when he said that Cuba in the future would be "bound to us by ties of peculiar intimacy and strength."

Other portions of the Spanish empire, not involved at all in the disputes which caused the war, were seized and retained as American territories. These were Porto Rico, the Philippine Islands, and naval stations in the Pacific. The fact that the new imperialism was not wholly a result of the Spanish-American War is indicated by the earlier political as well as economic ascendancy of the United States in the Hawaiian Islands, but formal annexation was postponed till 1898. American influence was earlier evident also in the Samoan Islands. In 1900 the Tutuila group in the Samoan Islands was definitely annexed; in 1904, the Panama Canal Zone, important out of all proportion to its area, was acquired in the Rooseveltian big-stick manner from Panama; and in 1917, after prolonged negotiations, the Virgin Islands in the West Indies were purchased from Denmark.

POLITICAL SOVEREIGNTY *versus* ECONOMIC SUZERAINTY

The reservation of potential political sovereignty in Cuba was of course an important guarantee of continued control. But mainly significant was the increasing ascendancy of American business men and the virtually complete economic dependence of the island on American trade and investments. These tendencies gave to the renunciation of active sovereignty by the American government a quality obviously factitious.

During the military occupation of Cuba, the American government announced a policy of refraining from the granting of concessions and franchises of an economic nature, as for mining or building railroads. But "revocable permits" were granted, certain old franchises were subject to cancellation, and native authorities were "encouraged" to open the way for American economic penetration. The Cuban authorities granted innumerable concessions and franchises, not exclusively but largely to Americans. By 1927, according to an estimate in the Havana *Bulletin* of the American Chamber of Commerce in Cuba, American investments totaled nearly a billion and a half dollars. The largest investment, $800,000,000, was naturally in sugar. Railroads and public utilities accounted for $230,000,000. In government bonds, the holdings amounted to $100,000,000.

Potential Cuban wealth, as in mineral resources, came largely under American control. American investments in mines were estimated in 1927 as amounting only to $35,-000,000. This trivial investment covers one of the world's most valuable iron deposits, the reserves controlled by American companies having even been compared with those of the Mesabi range in the Lake Superior region. On account of the possession of ample present sources of ore supply at home, the Cuban deposits remain virtually untouched.

As for trade, the Cubans have at times sent to the United States more than eighty per cent of their exports, and have bought from the United States about two-thirds of their imports. In spite of the small size and population of the island, in 1926 it ranked fifth in value of exports to the United States, its exports being exceeded only by those of Canada, Japan, British Malaya, and the United Kingdom. In imports from the United States it ranked seventh, trailing the United Kingdom, Canada, Germany, France, Japan, and Australia.

It is often assumed that the watch and ward maintained by the American government over the Cuban government has been responsible for the economic ascendancy of Americans in Cuba. But other factors of decisive importance are geographical proximity; the complementary nature of the economic life of the island and the mainland; and the advantageous economic position of Americans resulting from the World War. At the time of the Spanish-American War, American foreign investments totaled about $500,000,000, and Cuban investments amounted to about $50,000,000. The American occupation and political influence in Cuba led to no immediate marked expansion of Cuban investments. Up to 1913, they had hardly more than doubled, while total foreign investments increased far more rapidly till they were five-fold greater than before the Spanish-American War. Since the World War, on the other hand, American investments in Cuba expanded startlingly. From 1913 to 1927 there was probably a fifteen-fold increase, as contrasted with approximately a four-fold increase in all foreign investments.

By way of contrast, it is particularly significant to observe that Great Britain, in spite of the drain on her financial resources during the World War, maintained a strong lead in corporate investments in the Philippine Islands. A recent estimate put such British investments at almost double the similar American investments. Political rule by America in the Philippine Islands no more prevented British financial ascendancy in the Philippine Islands than the political connection of Canada with England prevented American economic ascendancy in Canada.

In the development and maintenance of American economic suzerainty in Cuba, the peculiar political position of the American government in the island has been a contributory but hardly a paramount factor.

Imperialism in the form of economic suzerainty is by no means confined to Cuba. In degree and manner varying with location and local circumstances, Americans are the arbiters of the destinies of many peoples beyond the recognized boundaries of the American territorial empire. The economic penetration of Canada was mentioned earlier. Canada is vitally dependent on American trade and capital, but its relation to the United States is of course not at all comparable to that of many of the Latin-American countries. Panama, Colombia, Nicaragua, Bolivia, Santo Domingo, Haiti,—these countries are in a state of such obvious economic vassalage to American business men that there is little distinction between them and Cuba or even Porto Rico as parts of the American empire.

Economic suzerainty is not necessarily dependent on political sovereignty, but Americans, in promoting their economic interests abroad, are not unnaturally inclined to utilize the political influence of their government. Investors in oil or minerals, railways, factories, or public securities are likely to think in terms of the laws and jurisdiction of their own country. They are easily put into a state of nervous apprehension as to the safety of their investments, due either to the alleged instability of governments in "backward" countries or to the competition of rival business men of other countries. There is therefore a temptation to wrap their national flag about themselves (and their investments). If anyone then dares to strike them, the national emblem is insulted, the national honor is in jeopardy. Diplomatic support, intervention (by arms or by "peaceful penetration"), political control—these are the objectives, in many cases, of those who are interested financially in "backward" regions.

Thus the economic imperialist weaves a variegated network of concessions, loans, extra-territorial rights, industrial investments, tariffs, diplomatic intrigues and influences, interventions, and (when conditions favor) annexations. The pattern, if cleverly wrought, conceals from the casual observer the ruthless conflicts of world-encircling corporations for control of oil, rubber, iron, sugar, water power, loans, and other basic elements of power. In the meantime to the peoples of the nations the texture of empire presents in its outward appearance a pattern of national greatness, of racial superiority, and perhaps of Christian service in civilizing the benighted.

CHAPTER XXVI

WORLD ECONOMY

THE VAIN IDEAL OF SELF-SUFFICIENCY

Few peoples have had such varied and abundant natural resources as Americans, and such extensive complementary forms of economic enterprise. The agricultural regions were themselves complementary in character, interchanging, for example, the wheat of the plains and the fruit and dairy products of the valleys. The rural sections furnished food and raw materials and afforded markets for the manufacturing centers. Within the continental boundaries there were abundant opportunities for all forms of business and for the energy and capital of the people. Successive frontiers were conquered. Continental railways were built. The productive plant (railways, factories, agricultural improvements, lumber mills, mining equipment, etc.) was constantly expanded. A vast protected home market was exploited. These various circumstances gave Americans a position unique among the civilized peoples, making possible a remarkable degree of self-sufficiency.

After the Civil War, Americans depended largely on foreign shipping to convey their surplus goods to markets and to bring them the finer manufactured goods not made at home; and for the rapid development of industry they required vast quantities of foreign capital, so that before the World War America was continuously a debtor nation. But these circumstances tended to promote a feeling of need for even greater self-sufficiency. Americans did little to reach out into the world and identify themselves with the world economy which was made inevitable by the industrial revolution.

But the transformation of business by the industrial revolution brought to Americans as well as to other peoples a realization of the impossibility of continued national self-sufficiency. Then followed the era of the new imperialism with its impossible ideal of self-sufficing imperial economy and its debacle in the World War. In the dear school of experience during and after the war, men learned that in the new age of space-conquering technology and world-embracing business enterprise, imperial as well as national economy is yielding place to world-wide interdependence and integration. What is the history of America's connection with this tremendously significant development?

TRADE AND SHIPPING

America's trade with other countries has fluctuated with the important changes in American economic history. Colonization was in the first instance largely a phase of commercial expansion. The mercantile system presupposed a set of complementary economic relations, the colonies importing manufactures and exporting their cruder products. The American Revolution in its economic phase was an attempt to throw off the restraints of mercantilism and attain self-sufficiency. The legal restraints Americans threw aside; but the basic economic conditions denied them self-sufficiency. They continued to find it more profitable to devote themselves to basic industries and to import large quantities of manufactures in exchange for their cruder products. The Napoleonic era, however, brought a further reaction against European connections and promoted the absorption of energy and capital during the succeeding era in westward expansion, internal improvements, and domestic trade and manufacturing.

But the growth of the cotton industry furnished a basis for the revival of trade. Exports of cotton increased in value from less than $30,000,000 in 1830 to almost $200,000,000 in 1860. The total value of exports of both domestic and foreign merchandise in 1830 was about $71,700,000, and in 1860, about $333,600,000. Imports increased in value from about $62,700,000 in 1830 to about $353,600,000 in 1860.

This rapid expansion of exports and imports was a part of the so-called triangular ante-bellum system. The southern cotton industry was the base of the triangle. The west supplied the south with provisions and some of the cruder manufactures. The east supplied both west and south with manufactures, in part domestic but in large degree imported. The east also provided a large proportion of the shipping facilities alike for the export of cotton and for the import of manufactures. Before the Civil War, more than two-thirds of exports and imports by sea were carried in American vessels, which also busily plied the oceans in successful rivalry for the carrying trade of other countries.

The Civil War disrupted the triangular trade. The war coincided approximately with the time when steam and iron supplanted sails and wood in ocean transportation. These revolutionary changes renewed the maritime ascendancy of England. In America, the policy of high protection, coinciding with various other forces, led to the rapid development of manufacturing, the value of the products of manufacturing industries increasing from about $1,886,000,000 in 1860 to almost $10,000,000,000 thirty years later.

The total foreign trade increased, but not so rapidly as during the heyday of the cotton kingdom. With the exception of the year 1892, exports were less than a billion dollars in value till 1897. Imports failed to reach a billion dollars in value till 1903, and fell below that sum the following year. The more rapid tempo of industry as well as the increasing participation of America in world trade since the end of the nineteenth century found expression in the rapidly mounting figures of both exports and imports. Exports in 1925 were valued at almost five billion dollars, and imports at about four and a quarter billions. The significance of these figures, particularly of imports, will become more apparent in connection with the discussion of the interchange of raw materials and manufactures.

Since the Civil War and the substitution of steam and iron for sails and wood, America has remained continuously dependent on foreigners for marine transportation facilities. The proportion of American imports and exports conveyed in American vessels declined slowly before the Civil War and rapidly thereafter. In the case of imports the decline was from 94.2% in 1830 to 10% in 1910; and in the case of exports, from 86.5% in 1830 to 7.5% in 1910. Thereafter the tendency was in the opposite direction.

But America has remained dependent on foreign bottoms in spite of herculean efforts (at least in expenditures) during the World War to build an independent mercantile marine. For a time the vessels built at public expense during the emergency of war enabled Americans to carry more than half of American imports and exports in American vessels. But in 1926 only one-fourth of exports and less than one-half of imports were in American ships, including the public vessels of the Shipping Board. American efficiency, unequaled in many fields, was unable in maritime transportation to stand the gaff of competition.

INTERCHANGE OF RAW MATERIALS AND MANUFACTURES

The economic theory prevailing during the colonial era of American history assigned to the colonies the rôle of furnishing cheap raw materials in return for dear manufactures. Americans later attempted to reverse the rôle. Particularly prominent in these attempts was the policy of protective tariffs. While there is commonly a grossly exaggerated view of the effects of tariffs, such laws have undoubtedly helped to determine the direction of investment of available capital and employment of available labor. Whether or not the direction thus taken was most advantageous depends, of course, upon the point of view.

The Republicans, true to their pre-election promises of 1860, enacted a tariff moderately protective in nature—the Morrill bill of 1861. Additional duties were levied from time to time till by the end of the war the average rate of import duties was 47 per cent as compared with 19 per cent preceding the war. The high duties were justified as a matter of practical expediency in getting money for the war, and as a temporary defense of manufacturers from abnormal foreign competition due to the high internal revenue duties. But once having secured such protection, the protected interests, freed from the troublesome opposition of the planters to tariffs, refused to yield, and indeed secured additional protection in some cases after the war. It was not till the second administration of President Cleveland that the tariff of 1894 reduced the general level from about 50 to about 40 per cent. This was soon followed by another upward trend in rates, which continued till the first Wilson administration, when the Underwood tariff of 1913 brought downward revision. The Underwood tariff was in operation for less than a decade, when the upward trend was resumed.

The protective principle may apply to the protection of any conceivable commodity in which there is competition. But tariff making since the Civil War has been controlled in the main by the manufacturing interests. Tariffs have therefore been mainly important in discouraging the importation of manufactured goods and in encouraging, if not by absence of duties, then at least by relatively low duties, the importation of raw materials and other goods demanded by the manufacturers. The proportion of crude materials imported duty free has been consistently high, ranging from one-fourth at the end of the Civil War to nine-tenths in 1897 and four-fifths in 1925. During the same period, the percentage of duty-free finished manufactures imported was generally very small, the largest percentage being about fifty per cent in 1918.

The increasing dependence on imported raw materials is indicated by the general figures of imports. Before the Civil War, the proportion of crude materials was rarely as large as a tenth of the total imported merchandise. Recent importations range from one-third to two-fifths of the whole. It was not till after 1880 that the value of imported raw materials equaled a hundred million dollars. Thereafter the increase was so rapid that by the end of the century such imports had risen in value to about $282,000,000, and by 1925 to about $1,750,000,000. There was a strikingly parallel increase in the exports of finished manufactures. The annual average from 1876 to 1880 was less than a hundred million dollars in value, but by 1900 the value of such exports had risen to about $332,000,000, and by 1925 to almost $2,000,000,000.

In other official categories of exports and imports (crude foodstuffs, manufactured foodstuffs, and semi-manufactures) similar changes have occurred. But the remarkable reversal of conditions in regard to the classes known as crude materials and finished manufactures is particularly significant in revealing the new position occupied by the United States in world economy—a position of two-fold dependence on markets for manufactures and on sources of raw materials.

All civilized peoples are interdependent. Their interdependence is indicated in a general way by such figures of imports and exports as have just been given. But evidence of a more conclusive nature is found in even a brief and fragmentary analysis of the nature of the crude materials imported by America. Fortunately for the general student, there is an authentic as well as intensely interesting survey of the subject. This is *Dependent America,* a book by W. C. Redfield, former Secretary of Commerce.

In the basic manufacturing industry, the making of steel, there are abundant supplies of iron and coal at home. But many essential materials are imported. Steel making is an elaborate chemical process requiring various constituent and auxiliary elements, the exact constituents as well as their proportions depending on the type of steel desired. The president of a great steel corporation stated in 1921 that forty commodities, imported from fifty-seven countries, were involved in the making of steel by his company. Chromium, for example, is essential to the steel of many important articles of peace and war, as armor plate, projectiles, high-speed cutting tools, and parts of internal combustion engines. American ores, if used exclusively, would be exhausted, according to an official report, in five years. Other elements wholly or partly imported and vitally important in the steel industry are manganese, tin, tungsten, nickel, and vanadium.

Why is it that American imports from British Malaya in 1926 exceeded in value the combined imports from England, Scotland, and Wales? The answer is rubber. The value of crude rubber imported in 1860 was $1,427,000; in 1926, the value was more than half a billion dollars. To cut off imports from foreign countries would mean the virtual elimination of rubber from American industry. Synthetic rubber or other substitutes for the imported article might ultimately be produced commercially. In the meantime, imagine the condition of industry, particularly the automobile industry, without rubber.

"A pair of boots," says Mr. Redfield, "is a league of nations." The hides for the tanneries and the tanning materials come from all parts of the world. In July, 1925, hides (pelts weighing more than twenty-five pounds) came from twenty-seven countries; "calf skins from twenty-two countries; sheep and lamb skins from twenty-nine; goat and kid skins from thirty-one; and other hides and skins from twenty-four. In all, sixty countries sent us some kinds of animal pelts that one month." The proportion of imports to native products varies, but "in general, it is correct to say that we get from abroad half of our calf skins, over one-third of our hides, all our goat skins, and nearly two-thirds of our sheep skins." As for tanning materials, the best sources of vegetable tannin are exotic trees, as quebracho (deriving its name, "axe-breaker," from its hardness) of Argentina and Paraguay; wattle, a kind of acacia, a native Australian tree produced on wattle plantations in Natal; and the mangrove of Madagascar and east Africa. For some forms of tanning, a mineral instead of a vegetable material is used; but for this mineral (chromium salts) America is even more dependent on outside supplies than for vegetable tannin.

In connection with warfare, Mr. Redfield lists thirty articles which the experience of the World War revealed as essentials in methods of fighting then in vogue, for which America is wholly or partly dependent on other countries.

Industrial processes, warfare, the home, recreation,—all phases of life depend on contributions from other countries.

Wool, silk, linens, furs for hats, jute, bristles and brushes, wood pulp for paper, innumerable essential oils, gutta percha, coffee, tea, chocolate—but to add to the list is a work of supererogation, or an unprofitable elaboration of the obvious. "Kipling, in his 'Letting in the Jungle,' has drawn a vivid picture of results like those which would inevitably follow a continued attempt at full self-dependence on the part of any modern nation." By the interchange of raw materials and manufactures America has definitely entered the complex and interdependent and civilized sphere of world economy.

FINANCIAL INTERDEPENDENCE

One of the principal motives for the investment of American capital beyond the American boundaries has been to develop or control the sources of raw materials for American industries. American investments in Canada in 1924 included, for example, $560,000,000 in mineral and forest products, particularly paper from wood pulp. About the same time, American investments in Mexican petroleum, mining and smelting, plantations and timber totaled almost a billion dollars. Investments in Bolivia were mainly in oil and tin; in Chile, copper, nitrate and iron; in Peru, copper, oil and vanadium (Americans controlling the world's richest vanadium deposits, of utmost importance in the making of steel). Honduras affords an illustration of American investments in tropical fruits. A single company's investments in that country increased from $45,628 in 1900 to about $25,000,000 in 1923. Not only banana plantations were controlled by the company, but railways, roads, docks, and other facilities. American capital also controlled chicle plantations, silver mines, and concessions for petroleum. In the rubber country of Malaya extensive plantations have been secured by American rubber companies. In Liberia a concession has been secured for a million acres with projects for the expenditure of a hundred million dollars for the development of rubber plantations.

These are characteristic illustrations of the outflow of American capital in a world-wide quest of natural resources and raw materials. There have been various other causes of foreign investments; and the investments, for whatever purpose, have assumed three main forms. An elementary classification is the one adopted by Robert W. Dunn in his admirable book on *American Foreign Investments:* (1) public securities issued by foreign governments, national, provincial, and municipal; (2) securities issued by foreign corporations or business concerns; and (3) direct investments in enterprises owned, controlled, or operated by Americans.

The most important investments in foreign business enterprises assume the third form. They cover not only the exploitation of natural resources and production of raw materials but the carrying on of manufacturing enterprises, construction work, and the building and operation of railroads and public utilities. Studies made in 1925 revealed American petroleum interests in at least a score of countries; manufacturing enterprises owned by Americans in twenty-five countries; public works under construction by American firms in sixteen countries; public utilities other than railroads under American control in twenty-five countries; and extensive American investments in railroads in fourteen countries.

The total private investments of Americans abroad in 1924 were probably between nine and ten billion dollars. Estimates for the early part of 1929 placed the total beyond fifteen billion dollars. As late as 1913, American investments abroad amounted to only about $2,600,000,000; and foreign investors owned at least twice that amount in America. The suddenness of the transition from debtor nation to rivalry with Great Britain for the place of world's chief creditor nation was due to the World War.

American business organizations have undergone a transformation which corresponds to the new place occupied by Americans in world finance. Early small-scale houses gave place to a large number of gigantic banking firms with branches and correspondents throughout the world. The handling of the innumerable issues of securities of unparalleled size during and since the World War gave such firms unprecedented wealth and power. A mere list of securities issued by foreign public authorities in terms of dollars, offered by American firms or syndicates of firms, and outstanding October 1, 1925, filled fourteen pages of Dunn's *American Foreign Investments,* and included forty-one countries (for example, an issue of $150,000,000 by Japan, the bonds being handled by Morgan & Company, Kuhn, Loeb & Company, and other firms). Leading industrial securities outstanding in 1925 and offered by American firms included twenty-eight countries.

Not only the older houses with traditional connections abroad, as Drexel in Philadelphia and Morgan in New York, but also the larger national banks, became associated more closely after 1913 with international finance. The Federal Reserve act of 1913 authorized Federal Reserve banks with capital and surplus of not less than a million dollars to maintain foreign agencies. Most active in this connection was the National City Bank, which opened a foreign office in 1915 and within a decade had branches and subsidiary or affiliated organizations throughout the world.

International bankers, in addition to handling securities, have often made formal contracts with various governments, particularly in the Caribbean region. These contracts involve loans by the bankers and various guarantees and concessions to the bankers. Some of the lesser countries have given up a large degree of their sovereignty by granting concessions and liens on customs revenues, railways and other property, and by surrendering the administration of customs or other revenues. A significant collection of such contracts for loans and concessions is readily accessible in Dunn's *American Foreign Investments.*

A characteristic illustration of the recent development of world-encircling activities of American corporations is found in the case of the General Motors Corporation. This company, like the United States Steel Corporation and various other combinations, was formed in connection with the so-called trust movement for the coordination and control of competing business units. In actual form, it combined various features of modern corporate organization. Certain companies were merged into an integral operating unit. Various other companies became associated by means of the holding company device. According to announcement made by the corporation in 1927, its constituent and affiliated companies numbered seventy-six—thirty-one manufacturing units, seventeen domestic and Canadian sales companies, six real estate companies, two financing and insurance companies, and twenty companies in the "export and overseas group."

In 1911 was formed the General Motors Export Company. By 1928, in Europe, eight subsidiary companies had been formed; in Asia and Australasia, eight; in South America, three; and in Africa, two. After 1924, assembly plants as well as sales offices were maintained abroad. It was announced in 1929 that the finished products were handled by six thousand dealers in more than a hundred foreign countries. The export organizations employed more than eighteen thousand persons. Net sales, wholesale, of cars and trucks by the overseas sales organizations increased from less than twenty million dollars in 1922 to more than a quarter of a billion dollars in 1928.

In 1929 a new policy was announced. By the purchase, for $30,000,000, of an interest in the Adam Opel Company, leading motor car manufacturers of Germany, the General Motors Corporation became an international manufacturing as well as distributing organization. Various other companies announced a policy of establishing factories as well as sales agencies abroad.

A significent tendency toward the internationalizing of business is in connection with international cartels. These have been defined as "associations or combinations of producers or traders from two or more countries which aim at some degree of market control and regulation of competition." The number known to have existed in 1914 was 114. The World War disrupted many of them but there was later a revival and extension of the movement, as in the formation in 1927 of an international rayon cartel which, in the course of two years, controlled more than eighty per cent of the world's output of rayon. In their formative stages international cartels have remained in most cases mainly European.

What has so far been said about financial interdependence has directly concerned not the governments but private investors. Not more important, perhaps, but more familiar is the position of the American government as a creditor of the allied nations since the World War.

Great Britain had extensively financed her dominions and allies before America entered the war, partly, however, by borrowing through banks from private investors in the United States—American investments in allied victory. After America entered the war, the governments opposed to the Central Powers were granted loans by the American government, totaling in various forms the gigantic sum of about ten and one-third billion dollars. Upon the refusal of the United States to cancel the obligations or to pool the war debts (which would have meant extensive cancellations by the United States), Great Britain's main concern was to secure from Germany and from her allied debtors sufficient funds to meet her obligations to the United States. The other victorious powers were interested in securing from Germany as large an indemnity as possible, and in reducing their obligations to the United States to the lowest figures possible. The American government proceeded on the assumption of the technical validity of the securities granted by its debtors. It offered concessions as to terms of payment and interest and as to its claims against German reparations, but refused to concede what many economists held was necessary if extensive debt payments were to be possible, namely, a reduction of tariffs to enable the debtor peoples to restore their markets for goods.

The repeated readjustments of the intricate financial relations of the various governments led to a further expansion of American private investments. The collapse of the German monetary and commercial systems after the treaty of peace led to the Dawes Plan and the international supervision of reparations, and in 1929 to the Young Plan. The first requisite for payment of reparations was the economic restoration of Germany. This in turn necessitated outside capital. The revival of German business and the payment of reparations were made possible by means of loans marketed largely in the United States.

The post-war period was marked by the struggles of the peoples with the problems of exhausted energies, inflation, deflation, disorganized foreign exchanges, reparations, war debts, tariffs, and stabilization. Out of it all there emerged, in the consciousness of economists and business men and in a measure even in the minds of politicians, the conviction that the destiny of all the peoples is bound up with the fate of each. America's continent-embracing dominions and wealth of resources and relative geographical remoteness from the other more powerful national groups gave to Americans a feeling of self-sufficiency. But this inevitably yields to the pressure of the realities of America's new position as outstanding participant in world economy.

THE ECONOMIC FOUNDATIONS OF WORLD POLITICS

Slowly after the commercial revolution of the sixteenth century and rapidly after the industrial revolution of the nineteenth century, the peoples of the world have been moving toward an integrated world economy. Outstanding economic activities transcend the boundaries not merely of nations but of empires and are world-embracing in their scope. Raw materials are color blind, remarks Professor Moon in his *Imperialism and World Politics;* they recognize no national flag. "There is now a power [observes the editor of a conservative metropolitan daily] virtually independent of politics—a power that owes only the most shadowy allegiance to any government. It is American finance."

National and imperial boundaries are transcended by world-encircling technological facilities—motor cars and air ships, telegraphs and telephones, cables, wireless telegraphs, radio broadcasting, and moving pictures, with commercial television awaiting merely the perfecting of technical details. World economy is reenforced by the world-wide interchange of cultural elements. Science knows no boundaries. Libraries, art galleries, concert halls, like raw materials, are color blind in the presence of national flags. The great religions and religious organizations of the world transcend the frontiers of nations, empires, and races, and preach (though they sometimes fail to practice) the principles of toleration, brotherhood, and unity.

In politics the rate of change has been much slower. Politicians are likely to be laggards. The line of least resistance is in utilizing the traditional phrases and the group taboos, making the eagle scream, beating the drum, waving the flag, wearing a halo of patriotic devotion. But economic and cultural integration bring new times. New times breed new men, even in politics, with visions beyond their provincial valleys. In an age of automobiles and airplanes the politician may for awhile remain pedestrian and suffer from anchylosis, but sooner or later even the laggard makes an effort to catch up with the procession.

The old American nationalism, self-sufficing and pretending unrestricted sovereignty, is already dead. It expired with the nineteenth century. Its passing was marked by such events as the Spanish-American war, the invention of the wireless telegraph, and the formation of such world-embracing groups as the house of Morgan and the General Motors Corporation. The mask of nationalism survived as a disguise for the new imperialism.

But economic integration already makes imperialism antiquated. The greatest of empires depend on markets and raw materials beyond their frontiers and on the intertwining of financial interests throughout the world. The real character of imperialism, when it wears the mask of nationalism and is unrestricted by international control, was inscribed in blood during the World War. It means conflict. It means not only bitter rivalries between the imperialistic nations for control of subordinate peoples, but it also brings recurring struggles of the subordinated peoples for freedom from imperial domination. War in the past has been destructive—the path of history is littered with the wrecks of warring empires. But the destructiveness of the next imperial conflict—if there is one—overwhelms the imagination and can hardly mean less than the destruction of western civilization, or at least its transition to other peoples. Nor is it particularly reassuring to remember that in the forseeable future the chief imperial rivals are the British and the Americans.

But there is evidence that in the costly school of experience men are learning the necessity of political integration to conform to the facts of economic and cultural interdependence. They are even discovering that the preservation of nationality itself in any comprehensive and democratic sense depends on the international coordination (not the imperialistic subordination) of national groups in a system of world politics in accord with the realities of world economy. Internationalism is being recognized not as the negation of nationality but as its fulfillment, its guarantee of protection against the encroachments of imperialism.

PART IX

INDUSTRY AND THE NEW SOCIAL CONSCIOUSNESS

CHAPTER XXVII

ICONOCLASM AND IDOLATRY

MODES OF APPROACH TO ECONOMIC PROBLEMS

Social consciousness is of course a figure of speech. Consciousness with the individual is an awareness accompanying the functioning of the brain. Since there is literally no social organism, no social brain, there is literally no social consciousness. But when the individuals of a group are subjected to similar stimuli and are led to respond in a similar manner, there emerges not literally a group mind but certainly a group mentality, a group attitude, a collective way of viewing things, which for lack of a better term is called a social consciousness.

Such a phenomenon is as old as human society. But there are distinctive traits about the social consciousness of recent generations that justify the term "the new social consciousness." Historically there have been two main attitudes toward the ideas and the institutions existing at any particular time. There is now a third, and it is this third point of view which gives peculiar significance to the present age.

The earliest attitude, prevailing among primitive peoples and surviving in some quarters among the most advanced, is an attitude of irrational or tempermental acquiescence in the existing order. Among savages, such an attitude results from fear of the unknown. The forces of nature are deified. Departure from accustomed ways, if unsuccessful, is believed to be a penalty imposed by the angry gods. Primitive life becomes a life of taboos and restraints and conformities. In more advanced societies, the innovator may not be adjudged guilty of offending the gods, but there is nevertheless among many, particularly the heirs of wealth and power and social privilege, a worshiping of "whatever gods may be," a wreaking of earthly if not of divine vengeance on the innovator, in a word, an idolizing of the existing order.

In contrast with the attitude of the idolators is that of the idol-breakers, the iconoclasts. Their attitude involves a varying degree of dissatisfaction, maladjustment, pessimism concerning the existing order of society, due possibly to inherited personal traits but more generally to birth outside the privileged classes with their hereditary wealth and social status. The iconoclast would destroy the existing order not for the purpose of making possible a new system but with the idea of going back to a better way of life, real or imaginary, of an earlier time. The iconoclast would break the idols of his age in order to facilitate a return to what he believes to be the true faith of an earlier age.

In contrast alike with idolatry and iconoclasm, which are basically tempermental attitudes, there has lately emerged the rational idea of a science of society. In all the history of mankind it is likely that there is no development quite equaling in importance and in possibilities this new point of view. Its origins and significance can best be appreciated when viewed in contrast with contemporaneous expressions of iconoclasm and idolatry in relation to industry.

THE "MUCKRAKERS"

Both Roosevelt and Wilson owed their power in large degree to "the literature of protest." Those who had "saved the Union" in the 'sixties had peculiar advantages when, in the following decades, they undertook to "open up the country.'' Patriotism became, if not a refuge of scoundrels, at least an aid for business men whose rule of action was

> "The good old rule, the simple plan,
> That they shall take who have the power,
> And they shall keep who can."

Brutal competition was followed by pitiless, coercive combination. The prevailing attitude of the industrial chieftains (or ''barons'' as they were often called) was summed up in a famous saying attributed to one of them—''the public be damned''—a saying which symbolizes an era.

But with the close of the century that era came to an end. The public passed from an attitude of acquiescence to a mood of fierce criticism and defiance. There were many symptoms of the change. It was in 1896 that Bryan's ''Cross of Gold'' speech not only set the Democratic convention ablaze but spread like a prairie fire across the country. In the same year an obscure country editor, William Allen White, with his editorial on ''What's the matter with Kansas?'', attained an enduring national fame. A California farm boy, turned teacher and poet, published a poem in 1899, ''The Man with the Hoe,'' which was reprinted in virtually every newspaper in the country and which caused its author, Edwin Markham, to be hailed seriously as ''at once the despised prophet'' and ''the accepted high priest'' of the bloodless revolution impending in America. There was a remarkable vogue of cartoons picturing the ''common people'' as a mild-mannered, long-suffering individual maltreated in various ways by a bloated, brutal, domineering person symbolizing the trusts.

There soon followed ''the literature of exposure,'' particularly popular during the early years of the century. There were innumerable books and articles on the trusts and a nineteen-volume governmental report by the Federal Industrial Commission on the same subject. Outstanding among the publicists were Lincoln Steffens, who exposed the corrupt relations between politicians and business men in the cities; Ida M. Tarbell, author of a *History of the Standard Oil Company;* Upton Sinclair, author of *The Jungle*, a carefully documented novel describing the misdoings of "Packingtown"—a novel which was rejected by five publishers but which, when published, brought the author immediate world fame; and Dr. Harvey W. Wiley, who, as a chemist and a public official, exposed the dangers of food adulteration in the early stages of the transition of food preparation from the home to the factory.

The author of a novel could hardly be held legally accountable for libel. But most of "the literature of exposure" was by writers who could take refuge under no such defenses. Authors and publishers were therefore careful to verify every statement and to make sure of being in possession of legally valid evidence in support of their charges.

President Roosevelt himself used Sinclair's *The Jungle* in his fight for federal food control. But later, in characteristic fashion, he sought to profit by the reaction against some of the extremes of exposure, and denounced such literary tendencies as "muckraking." The term was fixed alike upon the just and the unjust, and the early years of the century came to be dubbed the era of the "muckrakers." In their ranks were representatives of "yellow" journalism. In their work there was much journalistic posing. They were likely to be superficial, with virtually no questioning of basic assumptions. Their success was largely a result of their ministering to the popular mood of hostility to big business. They were iconoclastic in the sense that by exposing the abuses of big business they gave impetus to the anti-trust movement, the aim of which was a return to small-scale, individualistic business. This movement was unsuccessful in its primary aim, but it profoundly affected the course of American politics and led to the most pretentious recent formulation of iconoclastic social philosophy—namely, Wilsonian liberalism.

LIBERAL ICONOCLASM

The dissatisfaction which gave rise to the "muckrakers," and which they in turn promoted, was the basis of the popularity of Roosevelt. He cleverly utilized it and kept it within bounds, but had no consistent philosophy of his own. It was largely the basis of the unpopularity of President Taft, whose ability as an administrator was counteracted by his ineptitude in recognizing and utilizing the prevailing public sentiment. The spirit of exposure and reform, which Taft was unable either to quell or to utilize, was capitalized by President Wilson in the formulation and attempted application in public policy of liberal iconoclasm, called by him "the new freedom."

It has been the fate of political parties in America to have cross currents making logical and consistent policy difficult. In President Wilson's party, one current had its source in the times when America was a nation of farmers and villagers; a current which flowed out, in Wilson's time, from the southern and western village regions with William Jennings Bryan at its crest. Another current, of later origin, had its source in the springs of industrialism of the east and middle west. Similar cross currents existed in the Republican party. There were the regular or "standpat" Republicans, with whom the newer, large-scale business interests were associated; and there were the insurgent or progressive Republicans, with views approximating those of Wilson.

Wilson's great political achievement was the converging of the two main Democratic currents into a single channel on which he could maneuver the ship of state. He was able to win power partly by the diversion of progressive Republican elements into Democratic channels, and partly by a clever capitalization of widespread discontent with monopolistic big business.

"I take my stand absolutely," he asserted, "on the proposition that private monopoly is indefensible and intolerable." Monopoly, he held, had gained control of the economic processes of the country, not as a result of economic laws or natural forces but because of the partnership of government with big business in granting or tolerating tariff favors, discriminations in freight rates, control of credit, etc. Monopoly is a perverted, artificial arrangement; competition is the natural or ideal economic state. He looked forward to a day of economic opportunity for independent, small-scale enterprise as opposed to the day when free-born Americans must be "employees or nothing." He proposed to lead his people out of the wilderness of monopoly into the promised land of competitive freedom and equal opportunity.

In his devout faith in the beneficence of competition there was something suggestive of the metaphysical preconceptions of the classical economists, which Professor Veblen delighted to talk about in words of learned length if not of thundering sound. But at least in one respect President Wilson was unlike the classical economists (as well as some others more recent), for they assumed the existence of a competitive state and afterwards (in the words of John A. Hobson) made some allowance for conditions not being in accord with the assumption. Competition, according to President Wilson, was not an actually existing state determined by natural economic laws; it was a condition which did not exist but which ought to exist and which might be brought into existence by a process of governmental and social readjustment.

The first step was to be a breakup of the stronghold of monopoly—the partnership of government and big business. The government having thus been freed, it was in turn to be used to free the people from the thralldom of monopoly. But what is freedom? According to the classical economists, the natural complement of the competitive concept was political *laissez-faire.* But the let-alone doctrine was rejected. Its rejection resulted from Wilson's conception of the "new freedom." "What is liberty? You say of the locomotive that it runs free. What do you mean? You mean that its parts are so assembled and adjusted that friction is reduced to a minimum, and that it has perfect adjustment. We say of a boat skimming the water with light foot, 'How free she runs!' when we mean, how perfectly she is adjusted to the force of the wind, how perfectly she obeys the great breath out of the heavens that fills her sails. Throw her head up into the wind and see how she will halt and stagger, . . . how instantly she is 'in irons,' in the expressive phrase of the sea. She is free only when you have let her fall off again and have recovered once more her nice adjustment to the forces she must obey and cannot defy." Modern industrial society has come to be a machine, a ship, demanding nice adjustment of the parts to each other and of the whole to its environment. "A new economic society has sprung up, and we must effect a new set of adjustments."

Thus President Wilson found a basis for his policy of enlarged governmental functions. But it was not entirely consistent with his competitive ideal. The parts of a machine are not made to compete; they are intended to cooperate and secure mutual adjustment and efficiency. One is forced, after all, to reject either his competitive ideal or his ideal of liberty maintained by cooperative social adjustment.

Of course a presidential candidate must be allowed a popular appeal, or as the English used to say, a "cry."

Readers of Disraeli's *Coningsby* will recall how Tadpole and Taper were discussing the necessity of a "cry" during the election attending the accession of Queen Victoria. Taper at length produced a slip of paper and said, "I think, Mr. Tadpole, that will do!" Tadpole took the paper and read, "Our young Queen and our old institutions!" Perhaps Wilson found it necessary to compromise by adopting the cry, "Our young industrialism and our old liberties!"

In any case, his exaltation of the functions of government in the cooperative adjustment of the parts of the economic machine was hardly consistent with his exaltation of the competitive state. He failed to recognize the necessity of making the functions of government conform to economic forces, no less than it is necessary for the boatman to make his functions conform to the forces of wind and wave. An understanding of economic forces compels a recognition of the impossibility of harmonious social adjustment in a competitive régime. Unlimited competition tends toward the operation of business units at a loss. Continued operation at a loss means self-destruction. This in many cases is the outcome, as witness the bankruptcy figures. But in general the result is acceptance of the only alternative to self-destruction, namely, a coming together, either through the law or else in defiance of it, either tacitly or formally, to put an end to unlimited competition.

Since the establishment of modern individualistic business, the different nations have made varying degrees of progress away from the competitive state. In the international field, unlimited competition brought on the suicidal World War, and it threatens self-destruction in other forms.

President Wilson's "new freedom," as well as the general movement of which it was the most conspicuous expression, was iconoclastic because it postulated the destruction of "monopoly" in order to maintain a system of "free competition.'' It was essentially futile because ''free competition'' was the negation of the cooperative social adjustment which he himself desired. The liberal iconoclasts rowed hard but the economic tide was against them. The overwhelming of Wilsonian liberalism was the end of an era.

THE NEW IDOLATRY

''We Thought He was a Burglar'' is the title of a cartoon by Orr. ''Public Opinion'' in 1908 was pictured in a night shirt, with a gun (the ''Anti-trust Law''), peering fearfully into the darkness beyond his door at the approaching shadowy figure of a burglar (''Big Business''). In 1928 the same ''Public Opinion'' had dropped his gun, and his face was wreathed in grateful smiles as he welcomed the same ''Big Business,'' who, instead of being a burglar, turned out to be Santa Claus loaded down with packages labeled ''High wages and steady employment,'' ''Mass production, lower prices,'' and ''Foreign trade.''

This cartoon cleverly pictures one of the most remarkable transformations of public opinion in American history. The cloud had lifted from big business. America's banks and stock exchanges had become her principal temples. Her most influential prophets and priests were her leaders of mass production and world finance.

Why the new idolatry? Not without significance was the reaction against Wilsonian liberalism. The ''new freedom'' of a restored competition was submerged by an unprecedented growth of big business and by the integration of business units under governmental direction as a necessary measure of wartime efficiency. Wilsonian liberalism, having unleashed the dogs of war and propaganda, was by them devoured. After the Russian revolution, the anti-German rage became anti-Russian and counter-revolutionary in nature, and thus the earlier mild reaction against liberalism became an almost insane hostility to socialism. European and particularly Russian socialism came to be viewed as embodying the forces of evil; and conversely, American private capitalism was idealized and idolized.

Another factor in the change of attitude was the new position of business as a result of the war. The war put America on top of the world in wealth and economic power; and it put big business on top in America. The wartime needs resulted in a compulsory regimentation of business men and integration of business units and in a new relation between business and government. In the coordination of economic life for war objectives even the exponent of the competitive "new freedom" found that small, competitive, independent business units were mere obstructions. If integration in war was necessary, why was it not desirable in time of peace? As a result of the war, big business was in a remarkably strategic position.

But a final and vitally essential factor in causing Mr. Public Opinion to look upon Big Business as a Santa Claus instead of a burglar was the seepage of profits through to consumers and workers. During the war, this resulted largely from the "cost plus" arrangement with the government—the higher the wages, the greater the cost, and therefore the larger the profits. The relatively advantageous economic position of the United States after the war tended to promote a general sharing of prosperity. Perhaps even more significant was a change in policy by which leaders in mass production reduced their prices and increased the wages of their workers in order to promote efficient workmanship and to expand the market for their goods among the workers and the masses of the people. Profits, real or hoped-for, from the diffusion of stock ownership also played a part. In an age when nearly everybody owned at least a share of stock, the old cries of "monopoly," "Wall Street," and "predatory wealth" lost their popular appeal.

DISILLUSION

There remained a few to denounce the new idolatry. They consisted in part of survivors of the liberal debacle. Insurgency and progressivism in the Republican party and the Wilsonian "new freedom" gave rise to exaggerated hopes. The war, the propaganda that accompanied and followed it, and the new popular attitude toward economic questions brought to the older liberal a feeling of frustration and disillusion. Popular approval of the war, of a vindictive peace, and of the sway of the captains of industry after the war, was viewed as a product of propaganda—a regimentation of men's minds by the control of the agencies for the diffusion of knowledge. Disillusioned liberals were re-enforced by literary and economic "realists." The depressing mediocrity of the average community was pictured in *Main Street*, and of the average middle-class person, in *Babbitt*. H. L. Mencken laughed sardonically at the "boobocracy." The age was denounced as an era of vulgar indulgence among the rich and of the unthinking regimentation, economic, social, intellectual, moral, of the masses of the people. Naïve survivals of the liberal mythology, as for example the view that the war was fought to make the world safe for democracy, were overwhelmed with ironical laughter, as were the equally naïve assumptions of the new idolatry—as for example, the view that big business was the Santa Claus of the common man.

The spokesmen of disillusion had their place, however superficial and transitory. They were hopelessly negative and iconoclastic. But their sharp arrows of irony punctured many an inflated idea. Their fresh winds of realism cleared away much of the fog alike of decadent liberal opposition to "monopoly" and of the new unthinking acquiescence in the supposed beneficence of big business. By such methods the exponents of disillusion, although themselves iconoclastic, did much to free the popular mind of iconoclastic as well as of idolatrous conceptions, thus clearing the way in some degree for a more general recognition of the scientific point of view and mode of procedure in dealing with social problems.

CHAPTER XXVIII

SCIENCE IN INDUSTRY [1]

TECHNOLOGICAL RESEARCHES

"Acceleration rather than structural change is the key to an understanding of our recent economic developments." Thus reported the President's Committee on Recent Economic Changes in the United States. Why the acceleration? Probably the principal cause is the conscious effort, of which the work of the Committee on Recent Economic Changes is an illustration, to subject industrial processes to scientific analysis and rational control. In this effort the outstanding successes have been in technological researches.

Henry Adams, "pondering on the needs of the twentieth century," observed in the light of his own educational experiences that "the American boy of 1854 stood nearer the year 1 than the year 1900." At least in respect to scientific and technological subjects, the succeeding half century wrought a remarkable change. It was in 1862 that the Morrill Act inaugurated the policy of federal aid to technological education. Two years later the National Academy of Sciences was founded. In 1865, instruction began in the Massachusetts Institute of Technology, a pioneer institution of its kind. By the early years of the twentieth

[1] Parts of this chapter are based on the author's article, "Are Social Studies Sciences?", in *Social Forces*, March, 1929.

century, scientific and technological education had advanced from small beginnings to a position of preeminence.

In the colleges, universities, and schools of technology, training in the principles of the several sciences is acquired. From the students and the faculties of these institutions are secured most of the members of the technical staffs of corporations, governmental agencies, and research foundations.

Governmental bureaus undertake investigations in geology, mining, weather conditions and weather forecasting, innovations and improvements in plants and animals, control of pests, standardization, and innumerable other subjects vital to industry. It was recently estimated that of a total of more than $200,000,000 expended in a single year in the United States for industrial research, mainly technological in character, the agencies of government expended about a third.

In recent years virtually all of the larger industrial corporations have established extensive laboratories. The staff of the General Electric Company, once described as "the most notable group of industrial researchers in the world," has included Steinmetz, Langmuir, Coolidge, and Whitney. It was reported in 1928 that the budget of the American Telephone and Telegraph Company called for about $15,000,000 for the company's laboratories, which were engaging the services of about four thousand persons. Trade associations and other joint agencies carry on extensive researches.

The National Research Council, organized in 1916, representing varied public and private agencies of research in the natural sciences, and magnificently equipped and endowed, functions chiefly in the coordination and integration of research.

RESEARCHES IN BUSINESS ADMINISTRATION

In 1927 a noted engineer, John Hays Hammond, addressed a meeting commemorating the origin in 1881 of the first collegiate institution of business administration in the United States—the Wharton School of Finance and Commerce of the University of Pennsylvania. Mining fifty years ago, he said, was in the pick and shovel stage but today is directed by scientifically trained geologists. In dealing with the problems of business and political and social life we are still, he asserted, in the pick and shovel stage.

In 1921 was published the report of a committee representing various engineering societies for studying elimination of waste in industry. This report estimated that for the six representative industries surveyed, fifty to eighty per cent of responsibility for waste lay with faulty management. The committee's recommendations included improvement of organization and of executive control, and the utilization of research to that end.

The new attitude of mind illustrated by this report on the elimination of waste found varied expression. Organizations devoted to industrial statistics and researches in business economics originated with few exceptions after the World War. A pioneer organization was the Brookmire Economic Service, founded in 1904. As early as 1910 the Bureau of Railway Economics was organized. In the following year a Bureau of Business Research was established at Harvard University. In 1916 leading business executives undertook an ambitious program of research by means of the National Industrial Conference Board. Corporations, chambers of commerce, trade associations, schools of business, and research foundations, to some extent before the World War but mainly afterwards, inaugurated general policies and specific programs of research and evidenced an increasing respect for facts.

An illustration is afforded by the retail trades. It was reported that in 1928 there were ninety trade associations of retailers engaged in researches for 130,000 constituent retail organizations. There was a Retail Research Association serving retailers throughout the country. Standardized accounting systems were provided for the exact determination of costs. The experiences of all the member stores were made available for each member. Experts were provided for the solution of the specific problems encountered by any member. Researches were undertaken in connection with various problems, particularly the elimination of waste.

Studies of business conditions by agencies of government multiplied. The Department of Commerce, which was not established as an independent department till 1913, became the principal governmental center of the new research activities. The department furnishes general data concerning business conditions, undertakes on request the investigation of innumerable specific problems, and acts within certain limits as a coordinating agency.

Coordination of efforts and assimilation of data are also effected in a measure by private agencies, particularly by the National Bureau of Economic Research, organized in 1920, with directors from corporations, associations, and universities, and with a research staff of its own. Significant, too, as a research organization and particularly as a clearing house of information and a stimulus to cooperation is the American Management Association.

In a word, a revolutionary change of attitude is apparent in the widespread effort to place business management as well as industrial technology on a scientific basis.

THE SCIENTIFIC BASIS OF RESEARCH

The transformation of technology within his own memory, said John Hays Hammond, had resulted from researches in physics, chemistry, and geology. "In view of the number and magnitude of problems and the number and complexity of facts, we need to equip ourselves as definitely for research in these fields as in the last fifty years we have in the physical sciences. We need great research laboratories for the organized and continuous study of problems of business and political and social life."

It is a curious fact that ages ago men attained a scientific attitude and applied a scientific method in the study of the remotest parts of their environment, the stars, but approached their immediate environment, and especially themselves, in a scientific manner only in recent generations. To be sure, the basic science, mathematics, necessarily came first, and it continues as a tool of all the rest. But after mathematics, the first of the sciences was astronomy. Between the founding of mathematics by the Greeks and the establishment of astronomy by Copernicus, Galileo, Kepler, and Newton, there lies a gap of more than a thousand years. The basic facts in the work of these astronomers were the formulation of natural laws concerning the planetary system, and the acceptance of the general idea of law in respect to nature as a whole. The extension of this conception of law beyond astronomy occurred first in physics and later in chemistry.

Astronomy, physics and chemistry came into conflict with traditional views and vested interests at many points. But these sciences dealt not with man, not even with life in its lower forms primarily, but rather with planets and atoms and impersonal forces. Readjustments of older views to these sciences were therefore effected with relative ease (though science had its martyrs). But in the nineteenth century men turned their attention increasingly to data concerning the age and history of the earth, and the origin and development of living forms, including man. Thus was begun a new era in the history of the conception of natural law. The new science of geology literally unearthed the secrets of the earth. Biologists, using the evidence of fossils and other data, formulated the great generalizations which are the foundation stones of the modern science of biology, and chiefly the cell theory and the doctrines of evolution.

Thus the scientist extended the conception of natural law not only to planets and the activities of so-called inanimate nature but as well to the realm of life, including man himself. With the general acceptance of evolutionary doctrines, many adherents of older views were seized with consternation. But after all, Darwinian evolution was basically organic, not mental, evolution. It was believed that the profane hands of the scientist could reach no farther than the physical organism. The mind was to be a last secure stronghold of the egocentric view, which puts man apart from nature and considers him to be a law unto himself.

Now comes the psychologist to contest even that realm. Psychologists are still at work with the débris of older views in an effort to establish the foundations of a science. Not till 1874 was the world's first laboratory of psychology founded. This was in Germany (by Wilhelm Wundt) and its influence was not effective elsewhere for several years. It was not till 1896 that scientific clinical psychology was initiated, its origins being in the Psychological Laboratory and Clinic founded by Professor Lightner Witmer at the University of Pennsylvania.

Society is not an independent entity, but is composed of

individuals. The social studies, as sciences, necessarily awaited the establishment of biology and psychology on a scientific basis, because these are the basic sciences concerned with the individual units of society. The social studies, therefore, are only in process of becoming sciences.

BEGINNINGS OF ECONOMIC SCIENCE

Forerunners of modern astronomers were the astrologers. They studied the heavens with diligence and acquired a vast amount of information. Why were they not scientists? Their method was inadequate, but mainly their preconceptions were unscientific. One still hears such phrases as to be born under a lucky star. The astrologers read the heavens because they believed that in so doing they could read the destinies of men—or in any case impose such a belief on the credulous. Forerunners of modern chemists were the alchemists. In their attics and cellars, with their awe-inspiring paraphernalia, they learned much about matter and its chemical transformations. But they, like the astrologers, had their preconceptions; and their purposes were hardly scientific, as when they sought a magic philosopher's stone or an elixir of life essentially supernatural in character.

Astronomy had its astrologers; chemistry had its alchemists; and economics had its mercantilists. The mercantilists had their preconceptions. The chief of these was the paramount importance of gold and silver in national economy. Based on this preconception was the view that public policy should primarily aim to maintain and increase the supply of money, particularly by means of a "favorable" balance of trade. Their zenith was in the seventeenth century.

The mercantilists were followed by the "classical" economists. They came in with the industrial revolution. Their great perconception was competition. They assumed the natural existence of a competitive state and considered any attempted interference by governments with the "laws" of competition to be the height of folly. Beginning, so far as England was concerned, with Adam Smith's *Wealth of Nations,* published in 1776, and continuing with Malthus, Ricardo, Mill, and various others in England and their disciples in other countries, the classical economy dominated the field of economic thought until there arose a lusty rival centering around the greatest of nineteenth-century economic treatises—Karl Marx's *Capital,* the first volume of which was published in German in 1867, the second and third volumes in 1885 and 1894.

This epochal work was not without its preconceptions hardly deemed by some to be of scientific character. But it was the basis of what was commonly called scientific as opposed to Utopian socialism. It was an elaborate analysis of economic conditions and forces viewed historically and contemporaneously. The analysis involved a conclusion concerning the trends of economic evolution in the machine age. Machine technique, said Marx, means socialized and integrated processes of production by large groups of individuals working together. But since ownership of machines by individual workers is impossible, there is a progressive concentration of the ownership of capital in the hands of a few. These tendencies toward socialized processes on the one hand and individual or private ownership and control on the other hand are in conflict. Ownership involves the power of appropriating (or "expropriating") the surplus product of labor. Laborers cannot individually but can collectively prevent this. The result is the inevitable rise of "collectivism" among the laboring classes, for the purpose of socializing not only the processes but also the ownership and control of industry, thereby utilizing for themselves the surplus product of their labor, which, under private capitalism, is "expropriated" and used by the owner.

All this was set down not as propaganda for or against a set of policies but as scientific analysis of the actual processes of economic evolution. It was accepted by many as having a validity comparable to the doctrines of organic evolution as set forth by Charles Darwin somewhat earlier. On the other hand, just as Darwin was assailed as a pseudo-biologist and a rebel against revelation, so Marx was denounced as a propagandist and a subverter of social order. The fires of controversy failed to consume either the Darwinian or the Marxian doctrines. Marx in economics, like Darwin in biology, emerged as one of the giant figures in the formative era of economic science.

But the science is even now without adequate data or method for the scientific verification of such large generalizations as were attempted alike by the classical economists and by Marx. Later economists have rarely had objects so ambitious but have been more interested in improving the technique of their subject as a more effective instrument of scientific analysis.

TOWARD A SCIENCE OF SOCIETY

It is recognized that economics and other humanistic studies have never attained a scientific status comparable to that of the so-called natural sciences. Furthermore, the facts are more complicated and more likely to be bound up with conflicting interests and points of view. If the humanistic studies are to furnish a scientific technique and a scientific attitude for the handling of industrial and other social problems, these studies must themselves become more truly scientific.

Economics can no more successfully be isolated from history and the other social studies and from the basic sciences of biology and psychology than can physics or geology be isolated from chemistry. Successful progress in the direction of a scientific status depends on abāndonment of the method of alluvial diggings and placer washings by individual sourdoughs and the adoption of cooperative, coordinated methods of exploiting the veins of gold in the humanistic sciences.

Recent tendencies of scholars have been in the direction of coordination and integration such as brought success in the natural sciences. Early organized activities are traceable to the 'eighties. The American Academy of Political and Social Science was instituted at Philadelphia in 1880; the American Historical Association was founded in 1884; and the American Economic Association, in 1885. But most of the organizations were formed much later.

In 1919 was founded the American Council of Learned Societies, with its fifteen constituent groups in the humanities and the social studies. Its first purpose was mainly to represent American scholarship in the International Union of Academies. But it soon became interested in the encouragement of research and sponsored many enterprises, including a survey of research activities, the awarding of grants in aid of scholarship, and the preparation of a *Dictionary of American Biography.*

More limited in its field of activity, and more intimately connected with research, is the Social Science Research Council. It was organized in 1923 to represent the seven national associations connected with history, economics, political science, sociology, statistics, psychology, and anthropology. In the fields of study which it represents, it approximates the functions of the National Research Council in the natural sciences. One of its undertakings looking toward the coordination of efforts and the integration of results was the establishment of a monthly journal, *Social*

Science Abstracts, covering the periodical literature of the world in the social studies.

Complete and definitive knowledge in any field is not attainable. But the remarkable increase of interest in the social studies and the expansion of facilities for research in these fields indicate a distinct possibility of the establishment of the social studies on a scientific basis.

It is one thing for scholars to establish a science, and it is quite another thing for those who are wrestling with personal and social problems to make scientific use of the principles and data resulting from scientific research. Is it possible to subject our economic behavior, individual and collective, not only to scientific analysis but to rational control for the attainment of scientifically determined aims?

A counsel of perfection is vain. But a survey of the past reveals with striking clearness a progressive advance of the scientific spirit over enlarging areas of action as well as of thought. Men as mere apprentices in science have shown themselves to be capable of what seemed but yesterday to be such miracles as learning the secrets of the planets and harnessing the energy that moves among the stars. It may be that a longer apprenticeship will enable them to make effective use of science as a guide to human understanding and the rational control of their own economic behavior. In any case, the tendencies in that direction lend peculiar interest to the latest age of industrial history.

NOTES ON BOOKS

The suggestions here given are offered because the books named are relatively dependable and at the same time in most cases so non-technical and well written as to appeal to those who are not professional historians or economists. Those who may wish to make intensive studies in any particular phase of the subject will naturally consult such readily available bibliographies as Channing, Hart and Turner's *Guide to the Study of American History* and the lists in such specialized and scholarly works as V. S. Clark's *History of Manufactures in the United States.*

The recent fashion in historical writing calls for works planned comprehensively and carried out in detail by cooperating specialists. Among such enterprises, one of the earliest and most successful was *The American Nation,* edited by A. B. Hart. The economic emphasis varies with the different volumes. More attractive to the student who is not a specialist is the series called the *Chronicles of America,* edited by Allen Johnson and published by the Yale Press. Particularly worth while for those whose main interest is industrial history are A. B. Hulburt's *Paths of Inland Commerce,* W. E. Dodd's *Cotton Kingdom,* H. Thompson's *Age of Invention,* W. L. Fleming's *Sequel of Appomattox,* S. J. Buck's *Agrarian Crusade,* J. Moody's *Railroad Builders,* B. J. Hendrick's *Age of Big Business,* and S. P. Orth's *Armies of Labor.* The Yale Press has also attempted a popularization of American history in a series called *The Pageant of America,* consisting of illustrations with descriptive and connective data. The volumes dealing with economic history are those by M. Keir (*March of Commerce,* and *Epic of Industry*), and R. H. Gabriel (*Toilers of Land and Sea*). A series of outstanding distinction and importance for industrial history is *A History of American Life,* edited by A. M. Schlesinger and D. R. Fox.

Among the more comprehensive productions of individual historians, the work of the great pioneer in history with a social emphasis, J. B. McMaster's *History of the People of the United States,* is still valid and in many passages intensely interesting. Other outstanding general works are J. F. Rhodes' *History of the United States Since the Compromise of 1850*, E. Channing's *History of the United States*, E. P. Oberholtzer's *History of the United States Since the Civil War*, Mark Sullivan's journalistic but important *Our Times*, and Charles A. and Mary R. Beard's *Rise of American Civilization*. In these works, all periods and nearly all phases of American history are presented, and there is generally apparent the rare union of literary distinction, scholarly care, and regard for the social and economic aspects of history.

It is often a great convenience to be able to refer to outstanding documents and other contemporary sources without having to go to voluminous or not readily accessible collections in libraries. Following is a selected list of books containing extracts from original sources:

Bogart, E. L., and C. M. Thompson, *Readings in the Economic History of the United States*. N. Y., 1916.

Bullock, C. J., *Selected Readings in Economics*. Boston, 1907.

Callender, G. S., *Selections from the Economic History of the United States, 1765–1860*. Boston, 1909.

Flugel, F., and H. U. Faulkner, *Readings in the Economic and Social History of the United States*. N. Y., 1929.

Hart, A. B., *American History Told by Contemporaries*. 4 vols. N. Y., 1897–1901. Vol. V, 1929.

MacDonald, W., *Select Charters and Other Documents Illustrative of American History, 1606–1775*. N. Y., 1889. (Two additional volumes of similar character by the same editor deal with later history).

Porter, K. H., *National Party Platforms*. N. Y., 1924.

Ripley, W. Z., *Trusts, Pools, and Corporations*. Rev. ed., Boston, 1916.

Statistical Abstract of the United States. A cumulative annual publication of great value issued by the government; "a digest of data collected by all statistical agencies of the national government, as well as those of a considerable number of private agencies and one or two of the states."

Stevens, W. S., *Industrial Combinations and Trusts*. N. Y., 1913.

There follows a brief list of books on special topics, particularly those relating specifically to the contemporary industrial scene:

Adams, J. T., *Our Business Civilization*. N. Y., 1929.

Beard, C. A., *Economic Interpretation of the Constitution*. N. Y., 1913. This noted work was followed by *Economic Foundations of Jeffersonian Democracy*.

Bowers, C. G., *The Tragic Era*. Boston, 1929. Reconstruction.

Caldwell, O. W., and E. E. Slosson (eds.), *Science Remaking the World*. N. Y., 1923.

Chase, S., *Men and Machines*. N. Y., 1929.

Clark, V. S., *History of Manufactures in the United States*. 2 vols. Washington, 1916, 1928. Revised 3-volume edition, N. Y. 1929.

Commons, J. R., and Associates, *History of Labor in the United States*. 2 vols. N. Y., 1918.

Dewey, D. R., *Financial History of the United States*. N. Y., 1903, and various revised editions.

Dunn, R. W., *American Foreign Investments*. N. Y., 1926.

Dunn, R. W., *Company Unions*. N. Y., 1927.

Edie, L. W. (ed.), *The Stabilization of Business*. Introduction by Herbert Hoover. N. Y., 1923.

Foerster, R. F., and E. H. Dietel, *Employee Stock Ownership in the United States*. Princeton, 1926.

Holland, M., *Industrial Explorers*. N. Y., 1929. Sketches of leaders in the new field of industrial research.

Johnson, E. R., and others, *History of Domestic and Foreign Commerce of the United States*. 2 vols. Washington, 1915.

Kirsh, B. S., *Trade Associations*. N. Y., 1928.

Lynd, R. S. and H. M., *Middletown*. N. Y., 1928. An inductive sociological study of great value.

Mayer, J., *The Seven Seals of Science*. N. Y., 1927. A history of science correlating the social studies with the natural sciences.

Moon, P. T., *Imperialism and World Politics*. N. Y., 1927.

Odum, F., and C. Jocher, *Social Science Research*. N. Y., 1929.

Ogg, F. A., *Research in the Humanistic and Social Sciences*. Report of a survey conducted for the American Council of Learned Societies. N. Y., 1928.

Paxson, F. L., *History of the American Frontier*. Boston, 1924.

Phillips, U. B., *Life and Labor in the Old South*. Boston, 1929.

"Popular Ownership of Property: Its Newer Forms and Social Consequences," in *Proceedings*, Acad. of Pol. Sci., Vol. XI, No. 3 (Apr., 1925).

Recent Economic Changes in the United States. Reports by the Hoover Committee of the President's Conference on Unemployment and by the Special Staff of the National Bureau of Economic Research. 2 vols. N. Y., 1929.

Redfield, W. C., *Dependent America*. Boston, 1926.

Roe, J. W., *English and American Tool Builders.* N. Y., 1916. New edition, 1926.

Steinmetz, C. P., *America and the New Epoch.* N. Y., 1916. An interesting view of "cooperative industrial production," by one of the greatest of engineers, in striking contrast with the ideal of competitive individualism ably set forth about the same time in Woodrow Wilson's *New Freedom.*

Stocking, G. W., *The Oil Industry and the Competitive System. A Study in Waste.* Boston, 1925.

Tugwell, R. G., T. Munro, and R. E. Stryker, *American Economic Life and the Means of Its Improvement.* N. Y., 1925.

Van Hise, C. R., *Concentration and Control: A Solution of the Trust Problem in the United States.* N. Y., 1912.

Warshow, H. T. (Ed.), *Representative Industries in the United States.* N. Y., 1928.

Waste in Industry. A Report by a Committee of the Federated Engineering Societies. N. Y., 1921.

INDEX

INDEX

DATE DUE

GAYLORD

PRINTED IN U.S.A.